D0291197

SHADOWLAND

★★★★★ *"AN EXPLOSIVE EXPOSE ON THE INSIDIOUS OCCULTISM*
OPERATING BEHIND THE DEEP STATE SHADOW GOVERNMENT!"
— JOEL RICHARDSON, NYT BESTSELLING AUTHOR

BEST-SELLING AUTHOR OF *SABOTEURS*

INTERNATIONALLY ACCLAIMED EXPERT ON THE OCCULT

SHADOWLAND

FROM JEFFREY EPSTEIN TO THE CLINTONS,
FROM OBAMA AND BIDEN TO THE OCCULT ELITE,
EXPOSING THE DEEP-STATE ACTORS AT WAR WITH CHRISTIANITY,
DONALD TRUMP, AND AMERICA'S DESTINY

THOMAS R. HORN

FOREWORD BY ROBERT L. MAGINNIS

SENIOR PENTAGON ANALYST, LIEUTENANT COLONEL, U.S. ARMY RET.

DEFENDER

CRANE, MO

SHADOWLAND

From Jeffrey Epstein to the Clintons, from Obama and Biden to the Occult Elite: Exposing the Deep-State Actors at War with Christianity, Donald Trump, and America's Destiny

Defender Crane, MO 65633 ©2019 by Thomas Horn.
All rights reserved. Published 2019. Printed in the United States of America.

ISBN: 9781732547803

A CIP catalog record of this book is available from the Library of Congress.

Cover illustration and design by Jeffrey Mardis.

All Scripture quotations from the King James Version unless otherwise noted.

CONTENTS

Foreword

By Robert L. Maginnis
Senior Pentagon Analyst
Lieutenant Colonel, US Army Ret.

We are living in exciting and frightening times! It seems that not a day passes without a new national cultural or political scandal bubbling up from Washington's evil swamp, which gives most of us that queasy feeling that the world is upside down. This is especially true because the Deep State and its progressive political cadre incessantly attack President Donald Trump while starry-eyed 2020 progressive presidential candidates promise nirvana and free everything to a post-Christian and trusting public that should know fully well those are utterly empty promises.

Yes, many Americans—even some Christians—are gullible to the siren call of progressives and vulnerable to the lies of the Deep-State cabal and their liberal media companions, the essence of what Tom Horn exposes in *Shadowland*. Tom helps open your eyes to the fact that many Americans have succumbed to a national pathos—taken captive by a host of occult connections, true evil influencers that could well destroy this country and make her irrelevant for the end times.

Shadowland exposes those occult influences hidden especially within Washington's Deep State, and our morally lost culture as well—thanks to the "leadership" of the progressive political movement that is determined to seize the reins of America through their nefarious, evil ways. It is with this background that Tom Horn delves into high-profile lives and issues most writers genuinely fear to tread by calling out the rank evil that pervades many among our ruling elite and their nefarious, corrupt, and morally debased shenanigans.

That's why I'm both excited but also sobered about Tom's new work. Frankly, I'm frightened, because if the current direction of America isn't quickly reversed, all hope is lost. *Shadowland* addresses true, although shocking, accounts of real elites and actual tragic events we've all heard about in the nightly news that reflect just how far America has fallen, especially in the last couple of decades. Tom provides a new perspective on how this rampant evil could lead to America's demise, a pleasing outcome for the world's dark forces.

I trust Tom's judgment on such critically important issues because I've come to know him. I met Tom in 2014, first telephonically and then in person as he agreed to publish my second book, *Never Submit*. I could tell from our initial meeting that Tom is a special, insightful, spiritually aware, and wise man. I value his counsel and have learned much about his inspiring life story by sharing time with him over many meals and long car rides, and by just sitting around the kitchen table conversing with him about so many issues challenging America and, especially, the contemporary Christian.

Tom asked me to write the foreword to *Shadowland* because I've vicariously experienced much of what he so clearly addresses in these pages. *Shadowland* is about the evil within our culture, especially inside the bubble of our nation's capital city, Washington, DC. America's capital city, on the surface (at least around the National Mall, with its beautiful monuments), is captivating to the naked eye. But beneath the charming surface, it hides deep darkness and wickedness. *Shadowland* addresses many of the issues directly associated with that ever-present dark cloud of spiritual warfare covering Washington, the place that has been my home for most of the past half century. For numerous years, I've seen firsthand some of the things Tom writes about, starting when I was a cadet at the United States Military Academy in West Point, New York, when on breaks I would visit my mother, who worked in the White House in the 1970s as the personal secretary to world-famous psychic Jeanne Dixon before she married a wealthy Washington businessman. Through her tangled, insider web of Washington-establishment friendships, I met some true movers and shakers and saw the ugly underbelly of Washington's evil, the elite, and experienced the true Deep State long before it became a household term.

Thirty years ago, I returned to work full time in Washington's wasteland of political and cultural intrigue, thanks to the US Army, which assigned me to the Pentagon, where I served as a member of the government's largest bureaucracy. I ended that career as a member of the Pentagon's work group that wrote President Bill Clinton's homosexual policy, Don't Ask, Don't Tell, which for me was a baptism under fire inside the rank evil of the Deep State.

After retiring my Army uniform, I joined the Family Research Council to work on contentious cultural and spiritually charged issues. I lobbied on Capitol Hill for Christian value-related legislation such as abortion and human rights, worked with many federal government agencies on issues like drug abuse and HIV/AIDS, and spent considerable time engaged with the media as a broadcast analyst for Fox News and a columnist for *Human Events*. Today and for the past seventeen years, I'm back at the Pentagon very much embedded in the Washington scene, and I experience the Deep State every day inside the capital's bubble.

Those many years and experiences compelled me to write two books Tom published: *The Deeper State* and *Progressive Evil*. Both expose aspects of the unsavory reality of this modern era, America's Sodom and Gomorrah-like culture, and the pervasive spiritual warfare sparking the skies across this formerly great nation. Tom picks up where I left off with *Shadowland* to reveal some of the worst of that evil for our country and the head-on attacks on our nation's rich Christian foundation.

Shadowland takes the reader on a wild ride, a trip that only a few years ago would have been considered pure mythology. Unfortunately, now, in 2020, Tom's writing exposes the stark truth about the deep corruption across America among some of the ruling elite and explains how we've been duped by occult influencers, rank demonic forces. Yes, America has tumbled far from where our founders started this formerly great nation to a place from which we may never recover.

Much as Tom did in his past works like *Saboteurs* and *Belly of the Beast*, in *Shadowland* he unmasks the true nature and reason for America's fall. He guides the reader through the deep crevasses of the now-infamous Russia hoax, the evil influence of fake news, progressives' advancement of radical socialism, and the dark legacy of some high-profile narcissist elites. *Shadowland* will both intrigue you and keep you turning the pages wanting more.

Tom reminds us of how we are momentarily enjoying a respite from the full impact of corruption perhaps just before the final downfall of America. He reviews recent history to recall that President Trump, perhaps a modern Cyrus-like figure, came to the Oval Office promising much—and his first term delivered on that promise. He campaigned for the presidency with promises to return the power to the people by robbing the Deep State of its ill-conceived influence while exasperating progressives and their seen and unseen allies and exposing cancerous corruption, such as that of former Director James Comey at the Federal Bureau of Investigation and John Brennan, the former head of the Central Intelligence Agency. Mr. Trump fought hard and successfully against the liberal media, which spewed little more than lies via its incessant fake news. In spite of these challenges, the president rebuilt America's economy and returned to our country's heartland many jobs robbed by the likes of the communist Chinese. President Trump deserves our applause and another term in office, but not if the shadowland agents of doom and gloom have their way.

Mr. Trump's non-reelection in 2020 could well explode the progressive agenda on America, unleashing all manner of evil for our country and the world. That's a real danger, and one every American voter must consider, even if he or she disagrees with some of the president's idiosyncrasies.

You won't regret investing your time in reading *Shadowland*. It will open your eyes to the pervasive, occult-like influences corrupting our federal government, Congress, the intelligence community, our media, and—more broadly—our culture. These radical influences are evident across this country, from the police-attacking thugs in New York City to the progressive-ruled, needle- and feces-infested streets of the once-beautiful streets of cities like San Francisco. Tom exposes the evil cabal's tricks, frightening manipulations, and failed ideologies like socialism.

Shadowland comes onto the scene just as Americans voters begin to focus on the critical 2020 presidential election to decide which road to take into the future. It's an open-eyed primer to help spiritually aware Christians understand just what's at stake, and it lifts the veil on the future to reveal America's possible demise, shedding light on whether this once-great nation can reverse course and be relevant in the not-too-distant prophetic end time.

chapter one

Shadowland's Egregores

In January 2018, in my book *Saboteurs* and subsequent documentary *Belly of the Beast*, I worked with Beltway intelligence insiders to unmask an occult underbelly operating behind many "Deep-State" Washington, DC, power brokers and establishment career politicians. I began by pointing out how, on January 20, 2017, with four of his predecessors listening—George H. W. Bush, Bill Clinton, George W. Bush, and Barack Obama—newly elected US President Donald J. Trump "spoke straightforwardly to establishment, bureaucratic, deep state, shadow-government elites in a way nobody had seen or heard before. He made it clear that his agenda had not ended on the campaign trail and that he had gathered on the West front of the Capitol to announce more than the orderly and peaceful transition of power from the Obama administration to his."[1]

Trump went on to explain to his massive American audience and former executive branch leaders that he did not plan to merely transfer power from one administration to another, but rather intended to strip authority from Washington, DC, and return it to the American people.

"For too long," he stated boldly, "a small group in our nation's Capital has reaped the rewards of government while the people have borne the cost. Washington flourished—but the people did not share in its wealth.

Politicians prospered—but the jobs left, and the factories closed. The establishment protected itself, but not the citizens of our country. Their victories have not been your victories; their triumphs have not been your triumphs; and while they celebrated in our nation's capital, there was little to celebrate for struggling families all across our land. That all changes— starting right here, and right now, because this moment is your moment: it belongs to you. It belongs to everyone gathered here today and everyone watching all across America. This is your day. This is your celebration. And this, the United States of America, is your country."[2]

With that declaration of war introduced against powerful antagonists (both ancient and contemporary, visible and invisible), Donald Trump found himself immediately demonized by a Soros-funded, Obama-era swamp machine (numerous sources, including criminal attorney Robert Barnes, concluded early on that the shadow man directly responsible for the Deep-State de facto coup attempt that America endured the first three years of Trump's administration was none other than Barack Obama,[3] and in September 2019 this was confirmed by the Department of Justice [DOJ] inspector general's report[4]), whose ruling elites energized their brainwashing mechanisms against the great disruptor of the American empire, the SHADOWLAND permanent governing class, pushing the "Russia Collusion" narrative through incessant deceit, demagoguery, and mass hysteria aimed at insinuating that the newly elected president had colluded with Russians to influence the 2016 election. Ironically, evidence eventually surfaced to confirm that there really was massive Russian meddling, and that it was not Trump, but Obama and Hillary, who had been hard at work behind the scenes with these enemies of the state treasonously weaponizing our intelligence agencies to subvert the US electoral process.

This is not hearsay. Hundreds of documents showing that the Obama Justice Department worked directly with Fusion GPS, the opposition research firm hired by the Clinton campaign to frame President Trump, were uncovered and released by government watchdog group Judicial Watch in 2019.[5]

As Andrew McCarthy for *National Review* put it:

There really was a collusion plot. It really did target our election system. It absolutely sought to usurp our capacity for self-determination. It was just not the collusion you've been told about for nearly three years. It was not "Donald Trump's collusion with Russia."

Here is the real collusion scheme: In 2016, the incumbent Democratic administration of President Barack Obama put the awesome powers of the United States government's law-enforcement and intelligence apparatus in the service of the Hillary Rodham Clinton presidential campaign, the Democratic party, and the progressive Beltway establishment....

Plan A was to get Mrs. Clinton elected president of the United States. This required exonerating her, at least ostensibly, from well-founded allegations of her felonious and politically disqualifying actions.

Plan B was the insurance policy: an investigation that Donald Trump, in the highly unlikely event he was elected, would be powerless to shut down. An investigation that would simultaneously monitor and taint him. An investigation that internalized Clinton-campaign-generated opposition research, limning Trump and his campaign as complicit in Russian espionage. An investigation that would hunt for a crime under the guise of counterintelligence, build an impeachment case under the guise of hunting for a crime, and seek to make Trump un-reelectable under the guise of building an impeachment case.[6]

Donald Trump himself has allegedly said Obama committed treason "by engineering a plot to spy on his presidential campaign, a move that led to the lengthy and politically explosive Russia probe."[7]

What Leftist Enemies of America Have Been Up To

During the 2016 elections, the Deep State sought to thwart all likelihood of Donald Trump being elected to one of the most powerful positions in the world—president of the United States of America. The narrative created and reported through the mainstream media was that the Trump campaign colluded with Russian officials to defeat Clinton. The storyline told to the American people solely focused on the fabricated connections of the future president with Russia, while ignoring and even making blatant efforts to cover up the actions of the Democratic party, the Deep State, and Clinton.

Polls reported that the Republican candidate would lose terribly in his plight to defeat Democratic candidate Clinton in one of the most intriguing elections in the nation's history. Though the former reality television star had a household name from shows such as *The Apprentice,* and with whom many were familiar as a real estate tycoon, his emergence into the political realm was a surprise to many, as his field of expertise seemed to be in the business realm rather than at 100 Pennsylvania Avenue. However, his quest for justice and truth was matched with resistance and force from the underlying Deep State as it sought to eliminate the threat he posed of exposing evil and corruption.

It is widely understood that Trump's style of delivery with his words in speeches and on Twitter is not always conducted with the greatest amount of tact and poise. But it is this recklessness that also ignites a drive to not be overcome by a narrative fed to the mainstream media and delivered to the American people. "Fake news" has become a laughing point for some, but to those asking questions beyond what is given in their daily news update, the term holds water, as they understand that Trump does not seek to eliminate the First Amendment. Rather, he seeks to hold those responsible who have a duty and allegiance to the American people to protect the Constitution.

What is reported and shaping the opinion and knowledge provided for the American public should be facts, not a fictitious narrative to appease the agenda and coverup of the Deep-State elites' ties to power and economical control. The Society of Professional Journalists Code of Ethics is to "seek truth and report it, minimize harm, act independently, be accountable and transparent."[8] Yet the media of today's America has lost its alliance to such credibility.

The 2020 presidential elections are fresh grounds for battle and the attempted removal of the president. It is an opportunity to recreate the elections of 2016 and frustrate his chances of securing a second term.

Viewed in chronological order, the Russia-Trump Hoax was not just an elaborate plan to disrupt the success of the forty-fifth president, it was also a running narrative to cover up the evil actions of those in power in the swamp of Washington, DC—most notably, those of Clinton.

The Clinton Investigation

Hillary Clinton was confirmed to the role of Secretary of State under the presidency of Barack Obama in January of 2009. It was during her time at the State Department that the United States consulate in Benghazi, Libya, was attacked. The event took place on September 11, 2012, the eleven-year anniversary of the collapse of the World Trade Centers in New York. Four US government personnel were killed in Benghazi: US Ambassador Chris Stevens, Sean Smith, Glen Doherty, and Tyrone Woods.

In her initial response to the public and to the victims' families, Clinton blamed the incident in Benghazi on an anti-Islam YouTube video in a speech she delivered at the return of the four Americans killed. However, she told her daughter, Chelsea, that it was from an Al-Qaeda group.[9] A later review would show that the video was not a major focal point of the administration or military.[10]

In May of 2014, the House of Representatives Select Committee on Benghazi was established to evaluate the actions of the government agencies involved in the events leading up to, during, and after the night of the September 11, as well as the State Department's Accountability Review Board. The investigation looked much deeper into the deaths of the four

Americans as well as the circumstances surrounding the attack and decisions made by the White House and State Department before, as well as what was told to the public.

The Select Committee on Benghazi released a report on their findings.[11] Representatives said that the government is expected to save the lives of American citizens serving in harm's way, but that it did not try in Benghazi, and that the administration told one story in private but another to the public.[12]

The Accountability Review Board (ARB), which was established by the State Department, was intended to produce recommendations of preventative measures in the event of a future situation. The report shows that four of the five board members were picked by Clinton herself.[13] However, the board never even interviewed Clinton or examined her or Ambassador Stevens' emails. To seal the incredulous lack of attention by the board, the final report from the ARB was reviewed and changes were recommended by senior staff of the State Department before it was finalized.[14]

The Obama administration also lacked efforts to support the House's requests and consistently delayed in providing timely responses that would have enhanced the investigation and assisted in finding the truth behind the cause and details surrounding Benghazi. Their final report would address the withholding of information for Congress on the part of the White House.[15]

The Obama administration, as well as the State Department under Clinton, was extremely delayed and troublesome in producing information. Clinton did not testify before the Senate Foreign Relations and House Foreign Affairs Committees until January of 2013—which was four months later. It was at this testimonial that Clinton was questioned for a possible motive, to which she responded, "What difference, at this point, does it make?"[16] She would leave the State Department the following month.

Three months after the formation of the committee, the State Department turned in fifteen thousand pages of documents.[17] Of these pages,

eight had either been sent or received by Clinton. It was in these documents that her use of "hdr22@clintonemail.com" and "H," rather than a
state-issued .gov address, to send and receive government information was
used, which allowed her to maintain control of her correspondence and
government information—a direct violation of the Freedom of Information Act.[18]

Clinton knew the use of a .gov address was proper procedure. However, she knowingly used "hdr22@clintonemail.com" and "H," and supported her actions by pointing to former Secretary of State Colin Powell's
use of nongovernment-issued accounts. Communication between Powell
and Clinton shows their discussion of the use of personal devices such as
her Blackberry.[19] The National Security Agency also disagreed with the
use of the Blackberry based on its lack of security, and they offered to provide a more secure phone, similar to the one used by Obama.[20] Yet Clinton continued to use the Blackberry, rather than the more secure device,
claiming it convenient to use just one gadget.[21]

As the House Benghazi Committee sent numerous letters asking for
documents pertaining to Clinton's time as secretary, the State Department
continued to respond in an untimely manner.[22] And in March of 2015,
the secretary's attorney reported that requested documents from 2011–
2012 had been deleted—a direct violation of an order to maintain relevant documents.[23] Trey Gowdy would address that Clinton maintained
control of information relating to Benghazi and Libya for nearly two years
after leaving her position with the State Department.[24] Clinton's lawyer,
David Kendall, said all records were given to the State Department.[25]

In March of 2015, Gowdy subpoenaed all documents relevant to
Libya, Libyan weapons programs, Benghazi, and post 2011–2012 statements.[26] Even into the summertime of 2015, new paperwork related to
Benghazi was submitted that was not turned in when Clinton supposedly
gave everything to the State Department that pertained to work that was
not personal, such as topics relating to yoga and Chelsea's wedding.[27]

In April 2015, amidst the analysis and scrutiny, Clinton announced
that she would be running for president.

Throughout the timeline, she made several contradicting statements regarding whether she was sending or receiving classified information. She initially stated that no classified information was sent.[28] Later, she changed her statements that she did not send or receive any information that was marked as classified.[29] She would later say that using the private server was not the best decision and that she took responsibility.[30]

The research continued deep into the 2016 presidential election, but closed in July. Clinton was exonerated. FBI Director James Comey made the recommendation to Attorney General Loretta Lynch that no reasonable prosecutor would pursue charges, because, though her actions were extremely careless, there was no criminal intent.[31] Lynch had previously asked Comey to refer to the entire situation as a "matter" rather than an investigation.[32] Just one month prior to the close of the analysis, Lynch and Bill Clinton met on a tarmac in Phoenix, Arizona.[33] The notes report that the AG claimed the meeting was purely social, but it happened just days prior to Clinton being interviewed by the FBI.

The FBI probe into the matter was reopened when discoveries were found on the laptop of the husband of one of Clinton's top aides, Huma Abedin.[34] The laptop was one shared by Abedin and her husband, Congressman Anthony Weiner. Weiner was under investigation for having an online relationship with a minor when his laptop was seized by the FBI.[35] It was during this search that more details pertinent to the Clinton case were stumbled upon.[36] Comey told Congress that documents from Weiner's computer were examined and that the previous recommendation not to prosecute remained.[37] A 2018 report by the Inspector General showed the discovery on the laptop was quickly passed through in an effort to close the investigation in light of the approaching election in November.[38]

Under Comey, the FBI investigation came to a close and provided the impression to the public that the situation surrounding the presidential candidate was thoroughly scrutinized, but later inquiries brought an interesting discovery. The Senate Finance Committee's examination of the former secretary's mishandling of classified information revealed that, of some thirty thousand emails sent or received by Clinton, only four were not also sent to carterheavyindustries@gmail.com.[39] Upon a quick Google search of "carter heavy industries," members realized it was similar to the name of Chinese company Shandong Carter Heavy Industry Ltd.,[40] thus raising concern that someone else had gained access to Clinton's communications.

The Carter Heavy Industries Gmail was set up by Paul Combetta, who worked for Platte River Networks. In an interview Combetta had before the 2016 elections, he referred to it as the "dummy" drop box and as an archive for all of Clinton's correspondence.[41] The deeper look into this occurrence revealed that the FBI was aware of Combetta's actions, yet chose to continuously refer to it as the "dummy account" rather than name it in their report on the Clinton probe released just prior to the 2016 elections. But it was not just this explanation that raised concerns over Combetta's decisions.

In March of 2015, Combetta used BleachBit, a computer disk cleaner, claiming an intention to clear up space and memory.[42] He also alleged that he was aware of the order to maintain Clinton's email data, but not data on the server, which housed thousands of archived documents. The catch in the situation was that the DOJ granted him immunity, thus protecting him from testifying and being accountable for his actions.[43] Though the possible connection to a Chinese company raised concern, they concluded in the report that they could not locate ties to the foreign company.[44]

Information and oversights such as these into the actions of Combetta were extensive and numerous on the part of the FBI, and evaluations in hindsight of the decisions made by the Justice and State departments and the FBI were still underway and making new findings even into 2019.

The former secretary's lack of transparency and honesty, even as far back as Benghazi in 2012, continued to be scrutinized as more details of agencies mishandling investigations and inquiries into her actions continued to be revealed. Reports from the House Benghazi and Senate Finance Committees showed vital facts necessary for truth were extensively covered up and overlooked by the State Department, ARB, and FBI. And it was at this time that the mainstream media's attention and coverage shifted to Trump and his alleged ties to Russia, Putin, and the Kremlin.

Russia-Trump Hoax

When the intended focus began to shift towards Trump, the underlying connections among those who were against the incoming president began to take root, and the mishandling of information and facts proliferated. It began when Fusion GPS, a private investigation firm in Washington, DC, was paid by the law firm that represented the Democratic National Convention and Clinton for President to investigate the Trump campaign on supposed ties to Russia.

Fusion GPS also had links with the Department of Justice through a recent hire brought on just prior to the onset of the probe into Trump.[45] Nellie Ohr, an employee of the firm, was married to Bruce Ohr, the assistant deputy attorney general at the Department of Justice, allowing the DOJ to be in a position to receive information on the Republican candidate through Nellie Ohr. Bruce Ohr would then take what he had received and connect it with Christopher Steele. The Steele dossier would soon emerge, along with the onset of the official investigation into the Trump campaign, both of which were highly controversial and based on fabricated claims.

Fusion GPS hired the former MI-6 spy to write the Steele dossier, which was comprised of sixteen memos and was intended to investigate Trump and possible ties to Russia. The dossier opens with the header, "US Presidential Election: Republican Candidate Donald Trump's Activities in Russia and Compromising Relationship with the Kremlin."[46] The dossier claimed certain members of the team had close ties to the Kremlin, even as close as Putin. It was written from June–December 2016, and was the evidence cited to support the application to the Foreign Intelligence Surveillance Court to spy on Trump.

Though the report was used as evidence to confirm claims to the court under the Foreign Intelligence Surveillance Act, the document was never verified before being thrust into the public domain on BuzzFeed and used to support the narrative of Trump colluding with Russia.[47] The popular website even pointed out that the assertions in the report were not verified. Amidst the attention-building around the dossier, Trump tweeted that these records were "fake news."[48]

In his memos, Steele claimed Carter Page was working as a secret Russian agent embedded within the campaign and mentioned that he served as "intermediary" for Trump to the Kremlin.[49] The memos asserted that he had met with an ally of Putin and the president of Rosneft Oil, which is mostly owned by Russia. The campaign advisor had a history of connections with Russia through his time working for Merrill Lynch and as an investment banker, focusing on emerging energy. In one of the meetings Page allegedly had with Russians with ties to Putin, it was brought up that they had access to Clinton messages and information that could bring down her campaign.[50]

Controversy did arise when Kellyanne Conway, the campaign's manager, told CNN that Page was not a part of their team,[51] even though Trump had previously told the *Washington Post* in an interview that Page was one of his advisors.[52] Page left the campaign in September 2016, and the Foreign Intelligence Surveillance Act (FISA) application was submitted the following month.

There were numerous claims of ties to Russia on the upcoming president's team. One was the connection of General Michael Flynn, who was the selection for national security advisor. Flynn's alleged connections to Russia came from a conversation he had with former Russian ambassador to the United States, Sergey Kislyak, in December 2016, just prior to the new administration coming into the White House.[53] Flynn was interviewed by FBI agents Peter Strzok and Joe Pientka regarding Russian interference into presidential elections. Even Strzok, who was heavily laced in anti-Trump actions,[54] said Flynn seemed truthful in his interview regarding what was said in the phone call.[55] However, Flynn's honesty regarding the legal phone call was not enough to maintain his freedom. Though Flynn did nothing wrong in his conversation with Kislyak, he did plead guilty to charges of lying during his interview with the FBI.[56] Transcripts of Flynn's conversation with Kislyak have yet to be released.

FBI Deputy Director Andrew McCabe prosecuted Flynn for making false statements to the FBI in an interview.[57] The director and future national security advisor had an unpleasant history, and it seemed the issue was not past. In a letter to the judge assigned to Flynn's case, FBI agent Robyn Gritz addressed the character contrast between Flynn and McCabe, describing Flynn as a kind friend and McCabe as an intimidator, void of dedication to truth.[58] Flynn had been outspoken in support of Gritz's sexual discrimination case against McCabe. Flynn worked closely with the female agent and even spoke to the media regarding her favorable conduct and work ethic for the country.[59] So when Trump asked Flynn to be his national security advisor, there is reason McCabe would have personal desire to remove him from such a position. Much like Trump, the general was weary of the Deep State and their conduct, as well as the potential risk for being bold and adhering to do what is right. Flynn had also been outspoken against Obama and Clinton regarding Benghazi in his speech at the Republican National Convention.[60]

From this whirlwind of connections, the investigation from the FBI of Crossfire Hurricane was born. Interestingly, the investigation began just days after the Clinton probe ended. Even more, Strzok and Page were having an affair and were both, as shown in texts between the two, anti-Trump.[61] The president would later tell the media to look at the investigators, referring to the inappropriate relations and connections all too common between the agencies and those leading them.[62] Crossfire Hurricane would later morph into the Mueller Investigation in May 2017 under former FBI director, Robert Mueller. It would continue until March 2019 when the *Mueller Report* was finished.

The report would find its way to the desk of US Attorney General William Barr in March 2019. Barr concluded that neither Trump nor any American colluded or conspired with Russia to hijack or influence the 2016 elections,[63] and that Trump did not obstruct justice in the process of the investigations.

These findings were not satisfactory to the Deep State, and the narrative continued on through his first term, even into the Ukraine phone call regarding former Vice President Joe Biden and the cry to impeach the president—all of this in spite of the actions taken against Trump during his campaign when there were no foundations for collusion, which Republican Sen. Lindsey Graham pointed out following the Justice Department Inspector General Michael Horowitz's report that focused on the FBI's wiretap of former Trump campaign foreign policy adviser Carter Page and authorization to investigate the Trump campaign's so-called ties to Russia.

Horowitz found seventeen "significant inaccuracies and omissions" in the FISA application and renewals process for the Russia probe into the Trump campaign (and actually fifty-plus irregularities in the report's endnotes) that led Graham to conclude in opening statements before the Senate Judiciary Committee that a "massive criminal conspiracy" had been perpetrated "to defraud the FISA court, to illegally surveil an American citizen and keep an operation open against a sitting president of the United States—violating every norm known to the rule of law."

Graham went on to describe what the Horowitz investigation discovered as "an abuse of power I never believed could actually exist in 2019."[64]

Meanwhile, when, following the illegal Russia hoax arrangement and conclusions by the Inspector General it became clear that neither the IG nor the *Mueller Report* was not going to support incriminating evidence that "the Donald" was complicit with foreign actors (and that we might finally get a reprieve from the incessant "Trump is a racist, sexist, cheating xenophobe" stratagem), many on the right were tempted to sigh with relief and hold out hope that the hysterical attacks on and typecasting of every breath Trump made would finally give way to our elected officials returning to the jobs for which "we the people" had actually put them in office.

Unfortunately, that hasn't and isn't going to happen anytime soon. The Deep-State cabal of formidable, unrepentant, and unelected bureaucrats working behind the scenes with career Trump-hating operatives in the intelligence community and at the State Department are hell-bent on sabotaging the people's president at every turn. Thus, when the Russian narrative failed, they simply turned to "obstruction of justice," then pivoted toward "Ukraine-gate" and any other "high crimes" they could hallucinate to insinuate impropriety justifying impeachment.

Why? Because Donald Trump never has been (and now never will be) a member of the DC Insiders Club. And, as Derrick Wilburn wrote recently for Townhall, "The Club has been effectively insulating itself from the American people, enriching itself and its family members [i.e., Joe Biden, his son, the Clintons, and others like them] by burying self-pay schemes in the largess of government, and Trump is a threat. There are dark corners inside the Club's clubhouse, lots of them, and Trump is wandering around with a flashlight."[65]

Wilburn is right, and there are significant reasons I contend that the Club empire striking back will continue with staged melodrama and media-collusion hysteria fueling the "Trump Derangement Syndrome" that is not about to fade, the deep dark details of which I will disclose later in this work. Fact is, things are about to get much worse—supernaturally and in the physical domain. What you will learn should chill you to the bone.

As *New York Times* bestselling author David Horowitz, a conservative who once considered himself a '60s radical and Marxist, recently warned: "The Democratic Party is now in the hands of the Bernie Sanders... Barack Obama radical left"[66] and "liberals fantasize about 'exterminating' people who do not agree with them."[67]

Lest some think Horowitz is exaggerating the risks, liberal news sites like the Daily Beast and MSNBC are now openly advocating for leftists taking to the streets in organized viciousness to overthrow the government Americans put into place[68] and, if necessary, literally destroy the majority of people in this country who supported the outcome of 2016.[69] MSNBC spokespersons actually called for "mobs with pitchforks" to throng Trump supporters' homes, while the liberal Shock Theater group posted "Death Camps for Trump Supporters Now" across Patchogue, Long Island, New York, not long ago.[70] Even Supreme Court justices were recently warned by liberals that they had better "heal" themselves (reach decisions favoring progressives) or face being "restructured."[71] Recent polls show that a majority of Americans believe the threats from liberals are substantive and that the country is on the "edge of a civil war."[72]

It therefore might be prudent to brace yourself for what is brewing if such extremists have their way. The corrupt media, collusive press, rancid witch-hunting, race-baiting, impeachment-hungry goons behind the "RUSSIA! RUSSIA! RUSSIA!" "IMPEACH! IMPEACH! IMPEACH!" phantasmagoric psychodrama are not about to give up their hunger for power. Even now, they plan increasing chaos for repealing the will of the grassroots (you and me), which, I fear, will endure until at last a collision of biblical proportions between conservative Christians, freedom-loving Americans, and Marxist infiltrators spills over into the streets of this once great nation. That's because this rabbit hole goes far deeper into the bowels of the underworld than most can start to comprehend.

In the next chapter, we will analyze why this is all happening and why, starting with the elements most easily discernable, even predicted, by celebrated visionary George Orwell.

chapter two

How Celebrated Visionary George Orwell Imagined Progressives' Final World Order

In George Orwell's dystopian novel *1984*, the fictional setting of Oceania was depicted as having four "Ministries" under the figurehead of Big Brother: Love, Peace, Plenty, and Truth.

The Ministry of Peace actually perpetuated unending wars; the Ministry of Love oversaw suffering and torture against those who would not adhere to the Party line; the Ministry of Plenty weaponized starvation through socialism; and then there was the Ministry of Truth, the propaganda arm of the government media that employed "doublethink" and "newspeak" as the official dialectic of the state.

"Newspeak" is the term Orwell invented for controlled language: restricted grammar and limited vocabulary as "a linguistic design meant to limit the freedom of thought—personal identity, self-expression, free will—that ideologically threatens the régime" of Big Brother and the Party, who thus criminalized such concepts as "thoughtcrime" contradictions of the English Socialist Party orthodoxy (INGSOC).

Today, in America, the nonfiction version of the Ministry of Truth has materialized and is fully operational through the Orwellian tools of modern Marxists and social media manipulators, including Google and

Facebook blacklisting Christian and conservative commentary by burying search results and exhibiting bias in their artificial-intelligence, shadow-banning algorithms.

This activity has contributed to moral decline across the United States. As US Attorney General William Barr told a University of Notre Dame Law School audience late in 2019, attacks on freedom of expression and on religious liberty have resulted in the moral decline that has contributed in part to increases in polarization and suicides, mental illness, and drug addiction. Worse, Barr said the attack on religious liberty and freedom of unapproved speech is not random, but "organized destruction" by "secularists and their allies [who] have marshaled all the forces of mass communication, popular culture, the entertainment industry, and academia in an unremitting assault on religion and traditional values."[73]

At the nineteenth annual Barbara K. Olson Memorial Lecture at the Federalist Society's 2019 National Lawyers Convention, Barr added:

> In any age, the so-called progressives treat politics as their religion. Their holy mission is to use the coercive power of the State to remake man and society in their own image, according to an abstract ideal of perfection. Whatever means they use are therefore justified because, by definition, they are a virtuous people pursuing a deific end. They are willing to use any means necessary to gain momentary advantage in achieving their end, regardless of collateral consequences and the systemic implications. They never ask whether the actions they take could be justified as a general rule of conduct, equally applicable to all sides.
>
> Conservatives, on the other hand, do not seek an earthly paradise. We are interested in preserving over the long run the proper balance of freedom and order necessary for healthy development of natural civil society and individual human flourishing. This means that we naturally test the propriety and wisdom of action under a "rule of law" standard. The essence of this standard is to ask what the overall impact on society over the long run if the

action we are taking, or principle we are applying, in a given circumstance was universalized — that is, would it be good for society over the long haul if this was done in all like circumstances?

For these reasons, conservatives tend to have more scruple over their political tactics and rarely feel that the ends justify the means. And this is as it should be, but there is no getting around the fact that this puts conservatives at a disadvantage when facing progressive holy war, especially when doing so under the weight of a hyper-partisan media.[74]

But declining values and loss of hope among citizens as defined by Barr are largely collateral damage. The end game is actually the overthrow of the Trump administration and anybody who supports him, according to Google insider-turned-whistleblower Zachary Vorhies.

"I saw something dark and nefarious going on with the company and I realized that they were going to not only tamper with the elections, but use that tampering with the elections to essentially overthrow the United States," Vorhies stated in a recent public interview.[75]

Google has warned Vorhies to stop talking,[76] and we pray for his safety. Meanwhile, the monster monopoly and social-media conglomerate continues thumbing its nose at antitrust laws by helping Deep-State subversives and "state-owned" media bullhorns such as CNN and MSNBC to actively engage in political vendettas in hopes of overturning the non-establishment's president and the people's 2016 election choices.

But don't take my word for it.

Rich Higgins, former staff member of the White House National Security Council, confirms: "The Trump administration is suffering under withering information campaigns designed to first undermine, then delegitimize and ultimately remove the president."

While these studious observations by Higgins are correct, it didn't stop Gen. H. R. McMaster (Obama Shadowland enforcer?) from firing Higgins for unveiling what is going on.[77]

As an Army veteran and former Pentagon specialist in Irregular Warfare

(IW)[78] at the Department of Defense, Higgins knows what he is talking about when he warns (in a seven-page memorandum, the "Memo That Rocked Washington" that wound up on Donald Trump's desk) that both Democrats and fake Republicans are currently using Orwell's imagined tactics in a real-life effort to bring down the forty-fifth president: "This is not politics as usual but rather political warfare at an unprecedented level that is openly engaged in the direct targeting of a seated president through manipulation of the news cycle," Higgins went on to say.

Among the IW instruments employed by Big Brother's modern Ministry of Truth reflected in Higgins' memo is the kind of brainwashing devices (doublethink and newspeak) that the book *1984* portrayed as are also producing the type of cognitive dissonance among citizens that Obama's community-agitation wing Organizing for Action (OFA)—with its 250 offices nationwide and liberal billionaire George Soros' new $80 million anti-Trump network (which I detail in the book *Saboteurs*)—is producing in US neighborhoods today.

Regarding the OFA's current efforts, I warned in *Saboteurs*:

> Young liberal activists, like Manchurian candidates, have been activated to oppose the new administration at every turn—immigration reform, Obamacare replacement, border security, and more. They are also aided in that effort by the Obama Foundation, whose IRS-approved mission is supposed to be for funding and operating a library to house the former president's official papers for posterity, much like other presidents have done.

But Obama is taking his foundation down "the same controversial—and, by some accounts, illegal—post-presidency path of his predecessor Bill Clinton," according to documents reviewed by the Daily Caller News Foundation's investigative group.[79] The foundation's language that caught the eye of Caller's investigators involves not just building and maintaining a library, but diverting funds for "activities reflecting President Obama's values and priorities throughout his career in public service."

In other words, the nonprofit foundation serves whatever Obama needs to shadow, obstruct, resist, and subvert the policies and directives of the Trump administration.

And make no mistake, Obama has made this personal. He himself is overseeing the *blitzkrieg*. The former president has swiftly returned to his early station as a radical Saul Alinsky-style agitation organizer.

Alinsky, the 1960s radical who wrote *Rules for Radicals,* and by whom Obama and Hillary Clinton were guided, once said, "In the beginning, the organizers first job is to create the issues or problems. Creating the problems allows people to feel so frustrated, so defeated, so lost, so future-less in the prevailing system that they are willing to let go of the past and chance the future."[80] This is the playbook the Obama team is using today to create the appearance of "issues and problems" and a general sense of desperation among Millennials so that people will "feel so frustrated, so defeated, so lost, so futureless" that they turn to them for solutions.

According to Alinsky biographer Sanford Horwitt, Obama and his presidential campaign and polity were so guided by this kind of Alinsky-based radicalism that Obama chose to follow in his footsteps as a Chicago-based community organizer. For three years during the 1980s, "Obama worked for the Developing Communities Project, which was influenced by Alinsky's work, and he [Obama] wrote an essay that was collected in a book memorializing Alinsky."[81] (Of course, Alinsky dedicated his work to Lucifer, the original radical and inspiration for those who follow his example.)[82]

This is why, at Organizing for Action, it is Obama himself who "is intimately involved in OFA operations and even tweets from the group's account," writes Paul Sperry for the *New York Post*.

> In fact, he gave marching orders to OFA foot soldiers following Trump's upset victory [and is] overseeing it all from a shadow White House located within two miles of Trump. It features a mansion, which he's fortifying with construction of a tall brick perimeter, and a nearby taxpayer-funded office with his own chief

of staff and press secretary. Michelle Obama will also open an office there, along with the Obama Foundation.[83]

Valerie Jarrett, former senior advisor and close confidante of Obama, has also moved into the 8,200-square-foot, $5.3-million nerve-center mansion to assist Obama in organizing the mounting insurgency against Trump's stated objectives regarding Reagan—like economic policies, government deregulation, and middle-class jobs programs. According to Washington insiders, Obama's goal in this is straightforward—to fuel the "resistance" that will force Trump's resignation or see him impeached. Investigative reporter Matthew Vadum said it this way:

> Former President Obama is waging war against the Trump administration through his generously funded agitation outfit, Organizing for Action, to defend his monumentally destructive record of failure and violent polarization. It is a chilling reminder that the increasingly aggressive, in-your-face Left in this country is on the march.[84]

In 2019, the Obamas worked with Netflix to continue efforts at rehabilitating their failed policies and to further denigrate Trump in the public mind by releasing a propaganda film titled *American Factory*, which attempts to downplay the return of manufacturing jobs (hundreds of thousands of them) generated the first three years of Trump's administration. These jobs are the ones president Obama famously said in June 2016 "are just not going to come back." Now that they (and much more) have, Obama is faced with the need for a new tactic, and the hope is the Netflix film—intentionally released ahead of the 2020 election—is but one of many efforts that can diminish Trump policy successes by insinuating in this film's case that Chinese investors will use these jobs to enslave American workers.

Good luck with that.

Thus, like Orwell's *1984* masterpiece, Shadowland funding of doublethink and the media's newspeak have been especially deployed to create "chaos memes" among the public so that peer pressure and people's natural desire to "fit in" can be used against them to generate group-think talking points, attitudes, and hive-mind conformities Big Brother requires.

Undeniably, this echoes what psychologists call the "illusion of truth" phenomenon (verified through clinical studies as highly effective), which basically means if you repeat a lie enough times people will eventually believe it. "Repeat a lie often enough and it becomes the truth," is a principle of indoctrination attributed to Nazi politician and Reich Minister of Propaganda under Adolf Hitler, Joseph Goebbels. CNN and the "impeach Trump" crowd understand the effectiveness of this dark practice and have deployed it unrelentingly since 2016.

There is an occult aspect to all this, too (whether or not the propagandists realize they are thus functioning as fleshy gloves of invisible supernaturalism), involving misinformation memes and chaos magic, which we will detail as we move through this work.

Even some "Christians" are buying into the lies, with churches organizing summer camps to teach grade-school kids how to become Antifa activists,[85] and with even the largest Protestant denomination in North America, the Southern Baptist Convention (SBC), officially adopting racial-identity politics that strike at Christianity itself.[86] Along the way, if a free-thinking individual or company of citizens recognizes or mentions any weakness in the philosophy or contradictions in the party's line, it is "akin to blasphemy" and subjects those persons "to disciplinary action and to the instant social disapproval of fellow Party Members."[87]

In other words, Orwell foresaw exactly the kind of political rhetoric we hear on nightly news and in the contagious attempts at castigating opinion and free speech being generated today throughout the government's left, across college campuses, and in major cities of the United States.

Will "Deepfake" Technology Bring Oceana's Doublethink and Newspeak Efforts to a Whole New Level?

The young man stood before President Kennedy. His body bounced as he rocked his weight across his feet, creating an up-and-down motion with his stance.

One may have surmised that the reason for the young man's bodily movement was his uncontainable excitement at being present at the White House with the College Football All-America Team for the privilege of meeting the president, or possibly it was the thrill of being on live television with his comrades. Standing in the Oval Office amongst the bustling media and his teammates, perhaps he was giddy with an overwhelming sense of accomplishment.

However, the surprising answer for the man's unusual body language would come momentarily when he approached the president to shake his hand.

"Congratulations, how do you feel?" President Kennedy asked.

Still bouncing, the man replied, "I gotta pee."

The president turned to his colleagues, giving off a good-natured chuckle despite the awkwardness of the moment, "I believe he said he has to go pee."

What a minute, what?!

When, in the history of our great nation, did our *president* appear on *national TV* and announce that another man needed to "pee?"

The concept seems ludicrous, yet anyone who has seen the 1994 movie *Forrest Gump* has witnessed such footage.[88]

How is this possible?

What Is a Deepfake?

Deepfakes are computer-manufactured videos, often featuring famous people such as celebrities or politicians, that are produced by mapping neural networks within the face and then using those points of imagery to "swap" faces between two people, bringing an individual who was never actually there into the final product.[89] (Coming next is "full body" deep-fakes…but that's for another book.)

The technology used in *Forrest Gump* was some of the earliest of its kind, developed to generate scenes such as the one referenced above. When the film was made, this type of trickery was available only to the best in Hollywood with the equipment and software only filmmakers had access to. However, this type of movie-making mastery, thanks to new strides in software development, is now easily available across the Internet to anybody via numerous downloadable apps. Furthermore, the digital realism attainable with this type of software is more convincing and simpler to use than ever, meaning the type of training and expertise (not to mention time and money) it once took to produce such high-end results can now be obtained by anyone with an Internet connection.[90]

While the newest deepfakes often involve an actual "swapping" of faces between an actor and a "target" (the unsuspecting person who, unbeknownst to them, is about to star in a production without their own knowledge or consent), tampering with imagery to skew people's concepts of an individual is not necessarily new, and has not always involved trading actual faces. It can be as simple as lightly tampering with lighting or speed—as illustrated by a recently doctored video of House Speaker Nancy Pelosi, wherein the speed was slowed just enough to make it appear that she was under the influence of some type of substance, slurring her words as her eyes dragged dully across the screen.[91] During the weeks following the release of this altered video, headlines and social media assertions regarding her mental capacities during the address raised questions about her competence in general.[92]

The untampered video, played at regular speed, showed the speaker giving a simple address.[93] Other pranksters have used the same technology to superimpose Nicholas Cage's face into movies he didn't star in, such as *The Disaster Artist, The Sound of Music*, and an entire scene of *Friends*[94] wherein each of the six comrades' faces were mutated into his.

Other efforts went so far as to plug Cage's face into the role of Lois Lane in the Superman movie *Man of Steel.*[95]

Reddit is a social website where users post material, usually via hyperlink, that others can view and rate based on their own opinions. The term "deepfakes" originally showed up on this site, where a user by the same name began to create and publish pornographic videos in which the faces of certain celebrities were imposed over those of the actors in Reddit's films.[96] Before long, the notion caught on, and many freelance software writers began to create similar versions of the programs. Soon, these were introduced on the Internet, many of them free. Despite early attempts to contain and eliminate the production of such films, the means had been released, and the trend gained momentum. Now, new, often harmless or silly versions of such deepfake creations emerge almost daily—usually targeting celebrities or politicians—and the technology is here to stay.[97]

How Does Deepfake Work?

Many are familiar with whimsical websites like JibJab that allow users to upload and paste an image of someone's face into an animation—typically a dance routine. This (now outdated) software often misses the mark when it comes to authenticity; the result is typically silly-looking, with a visible disconnect between the head and body of the image, creating a caricature-like effect. But the technology available today to produce a high-quality deepfake has progressed far beyond this simple cut-and-paste technique.

To understand how a computer program can *convincingly* interchange the images of human faces, it helps to have a basic understanding of how the technology in this area has evolved over recent years. The software that generates deepfakes is widely available; whether you realize it or not, you've probably had your own interactions with it. For example, you or someone you know may have taken a selfie that morphs one's face into, say, a puppy's, or that makes one look much older or younger. Or, you may have experimented with filters that add such features as horns, haloes, or beautiful, glowing flowers to the top of a person's head. If you've done this, then you've tinkered with the very technology that makes these sometimes-deviant, deepfake videos possible.[98]

Recall the first time you saw this type of app, likely on your smartphone or a social media account: It's likely that the interface as a first step in the setup said it needed to create a "mask," or digital image, of your face. This springs from technologies that have been in operation since the end of the 1990s in a variety of applications.[99] Since its initial development, however, the technology's effectiveness has greatly improved, with much more accurate depictions of superimposed faces.[100] Essentially, this new and improved software not only reads the whole face like its predecessors, but it's now able to detect key, pinpointed locations on the face from which expressions are generated, such as the borders of the lips, the areas around the eyes and nose, the borders of the jaw, and the continuous line that indicates the shape across both brows.[101] Then, using the textures, colors, and measurements of the facial structure, the system creates a "point-mask,"[102] similar to a digital, three-dimensional map of the face. By tracking these interconnections across motions, the user is able to

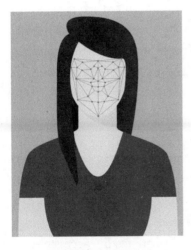

Digital points of contact allow the image of one face to be seamlessly fused into another.

move his or her facial image on camera while the program traces the movements of the face and keeps the point-mask in place.[103] This causes the digital "add-ons" (such as the flowers, etc.), to appear to remain attached to the image, even when the person is in motion.

Understanding this, it becomes more apparent how a computer can effectively superimpose one face over another. All it takes is for both faces to have a point-mask created (which can effectively be done via multiple still-frame images if live video is not available), and then to fuse one person's key point locations to correlating spots on the other person's image. This is why the result doesn't look like a dated, cut-and-paste process, but rather, one's face appears to literally *become* the other's. Similarly, this is why, when meshing together the facial images of two people whose bone structures are very different, the result undeniably looks like the target's face, but with something appearing "off."

Many deepfakes currently circulated are produced good-naturedly, like the collection of laughable Nicholas Cage movies. However, someone wanting to create a convincing deepfake for malevolent purposes would begin by making a live-action video of the desired content, then fusing the target's face into place by simply uploading a variety of images of the unsuspecting person into the desired software. This is why celebrities and politicians can be particularly vulnerable to this type of forgery: Their pictures are easily accessible, and the more images of a person one is able to upload, the more convincing the swap will be, due to the point-mask having plenty of facial angles to map. Because the software maps the features during movement, it follows the points of motion during speech, causing the incoming face to follow the expressions of the originally filmed individual. Once the face swap has been made, the computer then checks and rechecks itself, correcting signs of counterfeiting until it no longer detects flaws in the video.[104] All it really takes is a simple app and an actor/actress "of similar build [and body language] and most of the work is done for you by the algorithms."[105]

Furthermore, the target's voice can be copied with software that uses an adaptive algorithm to analyze the fluctuations and pitch of a person's voice, along with vocal tones. Once this analysis is completed, all one needs do is type a desired phrase into a computer and the audio will "speak" the words, digitally matching the voice of the man or woman analyzed.[106] Again, this is one reason celebrities and politicians are easy targets for deepfake efforts; abundant audio clips are readily accessible.

Modern software, unlike the older, cut-and-paste technology—is the digital equivalent of attaching one person's skin and soft tissue to another's skeleton. This said, it is understandable that some deepfakes are more easily identified than others. As mentioned earlier, if the two facial images being fused don't have similar bone structure, the result is the image of a face that is almost identical to the target, but that still appears slightly off.

Take, for example, the deepfake that morphed James Franco's face into that of Nicholas Cage, making Cage the "replacement" star of the counterfeit version of *The Disaster Artist*. Because Franco's face has a wider bone structure than Cage's, it's fairly easy to see that, despite the fact that it's Cage's *face*, something isn't quite right about it: The cheekbones of the image are wider set, and the jaw is broader than Cage's.[107] However, the image of Keanu Reeves' face after it is placed over that of Tom Hanks' *Forrest Gump* is an absolutely convincing replacement.[108] On the other hand, in another example, it's easy to see that President Trump's face has been superimposed over Alec Baldwin's in a creative revamp of a *Saturday Night Live* impersonation.[109]

Another way to spot a deepfake is body language and structure. Since the images are acted first by an impersonator, mistakes in mimicking the target's body language or even differences in build at times give away the switch. However, as mentioned previously, a good impersonator/look-alike can overcome a lot of this variance. Further, artificial intelligence is being used to perform checks and rechecks via a perfection technique called generative adversarial networks (GAN), which will soon make it nearly impossible *even for a computer* to distinguish the real from the fake. Using GAN, computer software "compete[s] with itself,"[110] essentially checking the fake for telltale flaws, then correcting them until the software itself is fooled.[111] This "image-generating software" is said to "keep improving until it finds a way to beat the network that is spotting fakes, producing images that are statistically precise, pure computational hallucinations."[112]

Who Can or Would Make a Deepfake?

Remember back in the late 1990s, photo production went beyond developing rolls of film and became digital? Perhaps you recall those early days of mainstream digital photography, when Photoshop had recently become available to the general public, and it was an exciting new way to edit your own pictures. Women could easily "shed" pictorial pounds, men's hair could become suspiciously fuller, and whimsical projects—such as pasting Aunt Sally's face over that of the Statue of Liberty—became a satisfying pastime for those looking to add some innocent spice to their vacation images. Such alterations are easily spotted by the naked eye and are now dubbed "shallowfakes."[113]

It certainly seemed like harmless fun as long as three elements could be counted upon: (1) the alterations were easily spotted due to rudimentary software, (2) augmentations were harmless or complimentary (such as trimming a few inches off the hips), or (3) the changes were imposed over a still-frame pic. Why is this? The answer is simple: People see no harm in making innocent adjustments to pictures, and even if an alteration *does* seem malicious or questionable, people like to believe that they can always go to the moving footage for a true, *trustworthy* documentation of *actual events*. But with deepfake, the public no longer has any such certainty.

In the 1990s TV series *Babylon 5*, Captain Sheridan of the space station the series was named for had, in a political altercation, been betrayed by a friend and turned over to adversarial forces. These captors tortured, starved, intimidated, and attempted to bribe the steadfast captain to get him to confess to false charges, but he held his ground. In the face of impending execution, Sheridan's captor explained that even if he refused to meet their requests of confession *unto the death*, he would still confess, but posthumously:

> The best way out for everyone is for you to confess…whether… [the confession is] true or not, it doesn't matter. Truth is immaterial, they can sell it, and [if you cooperate] they will let you live. Note: I said, it [confession] was the *best* way; I didn't say it was the *only* way. The other way, Captain, is a *posthumous* confession. Your signature is not a problem. They have your image on file—they

can *create* you reading the confession.... I'm told that, as of this morning…[posthumous confession] is an acceptable option.[114]

When this scene was produced and aired in 1997, the average viewer never would have dreamed that software already in place would rapidly morph into the elements necessary to make such a threat possible. This scene, a portrayal of futuristic sci-fi at its finest, caused gripping suspense because the implications of the interrogator's suggestion were a complete violation of a person's code of ethics, conduct, and rights to make his or her own choice about what (or what not) to engage in. There remained a certain sense of safety, however, because of the (at that time) knowledge that one would never *really* be subjected to such a violation. One could not just *create* footage of other people doing something they had not—or *would never have*—done…right?

However, advancements in technologies (such as Photoshop), which as noted, in earlier days were easily identifiable and largely used for innocent fun, have taken a malevolent and potentially disastrous turn. As these digital capabilities improve for both still-frame and video technology, it is quickly becoming simpler for fraudulent images and videos to be made that are nearly—or completely—impossible for the naked eye to spot. "Before deepfakes, a powerful computer and a good chunk of a university degree were needed to produce a realistic fake video of someone. Now some photos and an internet connection are all that is required."[115] Software now exists to literally decode the movement of a person's lips in relation to his or her words, and then generate an image that makes it believable that the inserted words actually come from the subject's face.[116] This new face can then be seamlessly fixed over another person's to appear to be a part of the con-man's moving body.[117] The extraordinarily frightening element of this technology is that a person can be (and many already have been) depicted as taking part in activities that are, at the very least, intensely personal, and at worst, depraved and even heinous—and worst of all, without consent.

Will Deepfakes Impact the 2020 Election?

US government officials are increasingly concerned that this trend could impact the election of 2020 as well as those in subsequent years. Since deepfakes can be so convincing, the worry remains that even those who carefully scrutinize news sources will be unable to spot fakes—and this says nothing of those who are unaware of the many types of deception that permeate the media, thus may carelessly cast misinformed votes. The pressing query on the part of all who look ahead to the next election is what would happen if a damaging deepfake were to be released just in time to sway the election's outcome, but is not brought to light as fraudulent until after the votes are counted.

Deepfake videos could even "cause worldwide chaos and pull society apart," according to experts.[118]

> EU tech policy analyst at the Centre for Data Innovation Eline Cheviot warned that there is a growing imbalance between technologies for detecting and producing deepfakes and that this means there is a lack of tools needed to efficiently tackle the problem.
>
> And she warned humans are no longer able to spot the difference between deepfakes and the real thing, and so are unable to stop weaponised fake news from spreading.[119]

In a recent article discussing such a possibility, Karl Stephan of Texas State University stated: "It takes time and expertise to determine whether a video or audio record has been faked...by the time a video that influences an election has been revealed as a fake, the election could be over."[120] Surely, even as efforts are made to perfect software that could identify fakes, the fakers are upping their own game, counteractions that result in and feed a strange game of cat and mouse that many authorities remain unsure they can win. Even as it stands, a recent fake featuring Obama was perceived to be real, even by those who know him personally.[121]

On the other hand, some have expressed concern that deepfakes will only fortify the beliefs of those who have already made up their minds, whether right or wrong. To explain further, some people hear or see what they want, and anything that reinforces their position is welcome—fake or not.[122] And, unfortunately, once a video has been viewed and accepted by the public, experts say many are resistant to newly emerging truths regarding the fake: "Once the doubt has been sowed...[about details later revealed to be misinformed] a non-trivial portion of viewers will never forget that detail and suspect it might be true."[123]

Particularly vulnerable to such fakery are voters who remain on the fence during the final days preceding an election. For some voters, simply knowing that fraudulent videos indeed circulate will keep their votes headed in the right direction. They will investigate before changing their decisions (however, this *still* doesn't alleviate the issue of a deepfake being nearly impossible to verify). Those who watch the pre-election fiascos casually, however, and who aren't wholeheartedly invested in *any* one candidate, will be easier targets for a late-timed, incriminating deepfake to persuade them with deceit,[124] essentially stealing their vote.

The threat to our nation by these deviant productions goes farther than the possibility of unjustly swaying the outcome of an election. Republican senator of Florida, Marco Rubio, has explained that, whereas previously, national security would likely only be threatened by a physical attack, modern technology has left us vulnerable to a strike against our "internet system...banking systems...electrical grid and infrastructure, and increasingly...the ability to produce a very realistic fake video"[125] adds to this problem. For example, imagine the crisis that would ensue if someone were to create a fake alerting the public to a national emergency, declaration of war, announcement of a pandemic, or worse.[126]

For these reasons, the US government is currently working with artificial intelligence (AI) experts across the country to tighten security regarding these fakeries and ramp up the software for detecting fraudulent releases. The House Intelligence Committee has been holding hearings with AI experts to strategize what can be done to stop the situation, while

Congress has been deliberating how to design legislation that could likewise regulate the creation and spread of such productions—a phenomenon taking place in such volumes that those attempting to stop them are overwhelmingly outnumbered. In response to the enormity of the task, computer-science professor Henry Farid of the University of California flatly stated: "We are outgunned."[127] Creating legislation against deepfakes is more complicated than it may seem at first glance: Government officials face obstacles barring "governmental overreach and the perceived threat to the First Ammendment."[128]

Involved in the prevention of electoral disturbance due to fakery is DARPA (Defense Advanced Research Projects Agency), which recently announced that it will be working to create resources for identifying and containing harmful deepfakes. The agency is currently building new tools for verifying videos, as older ones "are quickly becoming insufficient."[129] Precautions now being taken to safeguard the upcoming election from fraudulent videos that may mislead voters include banking gratuitous amounts of footage of key personalities expected to be involved in the 2020 election to encrypt a clear digital study on how their faces and bodies move while they talk, a signature set of unique movements involving distinct body language and facial expression that they call "fingerprinting."[130] Essentially, DARPA and the government are working together, utilizing these personalized characteristic databanks to produce a website where new videos involving these people can be uploaded and verified as true or false before they're released to the mainstream media. The goal was, by the end of 2019, to have all key 2020 election players effectively fingerprinted for safeguarding against fakes.[131]

However, this doesn't alleviate the concern that a good impersonator will mimic the facial expressions and body language of a targeted person. Furthermore, experts state that "detection techniques that rely on statistical fingerprints can often be fooled with limited additional resources."[132] Once uploaded, a video in question would be sorted by AI first for what DARPA calls "semantic errors,"[133] such as potential flaws that point to errors in editing, including "mismatched earrings."[134] Then, they would be arranged by category: whether the production was made for a malevolent reason or otherwise. Based on these results, a video would be flagged for "human review."[135]

The hope behind DARPA's endeavor is that those in the media will upload videos to verify authenticity before running stories based on them. However, one has to wonder if this approach will be successful. First of all, should a video be flagged for "human review," what would be the time frame for such scrutiny? Surely, those within the media who have come across a story will want to be the first to release it. It is difficult to imagine members of the press being willing to wait for verification of video submission before running a story. Certainly, for at least some, the fear will be too pressing that another news agency might get the jump on the breaking news while they are awaiting additional review. And, unfortunately, the success of such an undertaking will require the cooperation of *everyone*. As it stands, stories are often released in the media before agencies or individuals have taken the time to verify all of the facts. And, this only accounts for reports from news agencies, with no involvement from individuals on public outlets who share articles and information without considering accountability of any kind. A person who really wants to hurt a candidate's reputation could simply post a deepfake on social media, bypassing news agencies completely. All it takes is one well-timed, convincing fake and an entire election has the potential to spiral into a direction it may not otherwise have taken. Furthermore, software often takes time to perfect. Can we indeed trust that what is "verified"—even by agencies such as DARPA—is authentic? What if a deepfake video was mistakenly (or not so mistakenly…) affirmed as real? How many careers would be ruined? Just as frightening, how many wrongdoers could be protected by false videos that somehow act as "prove" their nobility? As experts work furiously to build a verification system using AI, the aforementioned GAN technique (generative adversarial networks) could just as quickly sabotage these efforts to determine what is authentic. Without a surefire way of digitally validating videos, the 2020 election holds the undertone of "Buyer, beware."

To appreciate how damaging deepfakes can be to modern society, it helps to understand a concept known as gaslighting. Gaslighting is a manipulation technique wherein one person makes others doubt their own reality until they are easily controlled because they've lost trust of their senses. The term originated from the 1944 movie *Gaslight*, in which a husband, in an effort to make his wife doubt her own sanity, continues to change the light level in their home, pretending he doesn't notice any difference. This makes the wife doubt her own senses, until the man's true intentions come under scrutiny. In modern arenas, this tactic is said by *Psychology Today* to be employed commonly by "abusers, dictators, narcissists, and cult leaders."[136]

The issue, in relation to deepfakes (especially considering the upcoming 2020 election), is that, as people lose trust in their own perception, they often become less determined to closely follow the actions of those around them. This lack of willingness to hold others accountable is a byproduct of underlying suspicion that they are only about to—once again—find that they've been duped. A certain danger is attached to the demoralization of a public that no longer knows what is real and what is not, which sources to believe and which cannot be trusted. By and large, people begin to succumb to a certain fatigue from the mental rollercoaster of the continual extension and removal of hope. It is demoralizing enough, without deepfakes, for a population to trust political figures who fail to follow through on campaign promises. Consider how much worse it would be if candidates began to adamantly deny the very content of videos on which individuals based their voting decisions. Not only would this hold devastating ramifications for the 2020 elections, but such activity would likely severely damage future voter interest and turnout.

Deepfakes could easily be used to sabotage the elections of 2020 and subsequent years, not only by discouraging voter involvement, but (obviously) by the false information they could spread that would likely be received by a trusting public as true. Good candidates could easily be portrayed in pornographic or otherwise compromising settings, and unfortunately, even if such videos were eventually confirmed to be fakes, the damage to the candidate's reputation would have been done. Very few people would see their campaign revitalize after such a blow.

Not only can deepfakes be used to destroy good reputations of innocent people, but they likewise can be an excuse for someone who *has* done wrong. In other words, someone caught—with videographic evidence—committing a legally or morally incriminating act could attempt to escape censure by claiming that the evidence is a deepfake. And, since deepfakes are so difficult to verify, a claim of fraudulence could soon be as difficult to confirm as an assertion of validity. This loss of confidence in what people see and hear is equivalent to the ultimate "gaslighting" of a populace. With such doubt placed on what we experience via our own senses, how can we trust the results of our own elections or know how to vote? Many media reporters and political observers agree that this is a concern. Claire Wardle, an expert in online manipulation, social media, and tracking of mis- and disinformation, as well as cofounder of First Draft,[137] stated: "As public trust in institutions like the media, education, and elections dwindles, then democracy itself becomes unsustainable."[138]

What's Really Scary about Deepfakes

Particularly concerning about deepfakes is that they override a person's consent. It has been mentioned already that countless videos have been made portraying certain celebrities in pornographic situations. Vengeful exes sometimes create damaging images to accomplish satisfying revenge. Those who may want to undermine high-profile CEOs or individuals whose jobs would be placed in jeopardy should they be found in a compromising situation—such as ministers, coaches, or teachers—may take such actions against these unsuspecting individuals.

When people choose not to engage in certain activities and then they're portrayed as participating in those activities, the effect can be highly destructive. For example, someone depicted, publicly, in a sexually compromising situation without consent would be similar to the violation felt if one's own body was subjected to this override of consent. Furthermore, reputations that stand to be destroyed by a video that goes viral may not be easily repaired once the truth about a deepfake is revealed, should its fakery *ever* be verified and made public.

Additionally, this technology's potential for undermining the innocence in culture as a whole is alarming. Consider the beautiful, wholesome works of times gone by that could be corrupted. It has been mentioned previously that Nicholas Cage's face has been swapped out for many leading actors and actresses in a variety of movies—not the least whimsical is that of Julie Andrews in *The Sound of Music.* That's a great example of this technology being used for harmless and silly fun. But consider other types of face swaps. What kind of corruption could be injected into an old movie starring Doris Day with Rock Hudson, Vivien Leigh with Clark Gable, or Audrey Hepburn with Gregory Peck? The technology's threat to previously innocent works adds to the negative impact these fakeries could have upon modern society.

In addition to the need for new legislature and image-verification systems to counter the emerging menace presented by deepfake technology, some agencies—such as the Social Science Research Center—along with other authorities are suggesting a new type of precaution: "immutable life logs."[139] What are such things? They are a digital trail of a person's moves, locations, and actions, making it "possible for a victim of a deepfake to produce a certified alibi, credibly proving that he or she did not do or say the thing depicted."[140]

Let's get this straight. To prevent a predatory, digital violation, we must allow the 24/7 tracking of a digital counter-bully to act as a guardian over our *real* circumstances. Does this sound like a prelude to the mark of the beast? Even for minds less conspiratorial than what is required to jump to such conclusions, the invasion of privacy is ominous. Furthermore, once we relinquish our solitude and consent to the invasion of having each moment of our lives recorded digitally, we have no guarantee of where the data will be stored, who will have access to it, how it could be used against us, or to what outside agencies this data could be sold.[141] Further, there is speculation that coupling such material with geo-location technology would likely be highly accurate at predictive tracking. This means that not only will anyone with access to such personal information know where we *have been,* but would likely analyze algorithms within the data that would also reveal where we *are going.*[142] In other words, we will never be alone or have privacy again.

How do we keep ourselves from being duped?

Data & Society researcher Britt Paris explains that, while legislation and image-verification software are a good start, the battle against deepfakes needs to take place in the public forum; platforms that propagate or tolerate the spread of deepfakes must be held accountable.[143] These entities must be exposed and victims vindicated—publicly. Furthermore, Paris recommends that information outlets that hide behind the excuse that the volume of such fakery is too numerous to address should dial back their volume and hire more employees until they can effectively manage their content.[144] Certainly, many companies will balk at such a solution, but Paris argues that this is part of the due diligence that should be required of any organization.

Claire Wardle, mentioned previously, has in mind another method of countering deepfakes, one that, if put to use, would be the best solution: Check facts before you act, vote, or post a video on social media.[145] She states that the responsibility rests equally upon outlets and individuals. Social media and press hubs, Wardle says, need to be held responsible for their content, but the general public has a duty to verify what they are sharing: "The way we respond to this serious issue is critical," she says. "If you don't know 100%...don't share, because it's not worth the risk."[146]

Oceania's "Deepfake" Year-Zero End Game

To achieve its goals, Orwell's Oceania obscures details of the nation's past and the rise of Big Brother's totalitarianism through chronological muddying. Whether through deepfake storytelling or historical revisionism, monuments of previous wars and administrations are smashed, histories are reimagined, and insults to the government's status quo are demonized to diminish any lasting resistance to authoritarian rule.

In political theory, this also relates to the term "Year Zero" reflected in such historical events as the 1975 takeover of Cambodia by the Khmer Rouge and to the "Year One" of the French Revolutionary calendar.[147]

> During the French Revolution, after the abolition of the French monarchy (Sept. 20, 1792), the National Convention instituted a new calendar and declared the beginning of the Year I. The Khmer Rouge takeover of Phnom Penh was rapidly followed by a series of drastic revolutionary de-industrialization policies resulting in a death toll that vastly exceeded that of the French Reign of Terror.

The main idea behind Year Zero "is that all culture and traditions within a society must be completely destroyed or discarded and a new revolutionary culture must replace it, starting from scratch. All history of a nation or people before Year Zero is deemed largely irrelevant, as it will ideally be purged and replaced from the ground up."

This kind of history purge is happening across America today, from rewriting the role of religion in this nation and removing paintings of George Washington at San Francisco's George Washington High School[148] to eliminating Confederate statues and monuments nationwide.[149]

Also like Orwell's dystopian vision, along with their Year Zero stratagem, the hypocrisy by the left is suffocating.

Remember when Democrat "bastions of liberty" bemoaned ISIS turning the Syrian city of Aleppo into rubble by bulldozing the antiquities of the ancient city of Palmyra? Or how the social radicals cursed the incivility and loss of historical artifacts? Indeed, when a new simulacrum of the pagan Archway of Baal (that was destroyed at Palmyra) was recreated, it was immediately sent globe-trotting to be erected wherever the world's liberal elites gather. This in-your-face reconstruction was widely celebrated by so-called champions of freedom, who conveniently failed to mention how children in olden times were carried through such archways and sacrificed to the Baals of the ancient world—something far worse than any confederate soldiers did.

Yet now, the same liberals who cried to high heaven over the destruction of Baal's bloodstained gateway have done an about face and pulled out their Oceania playbook. Suddenly, like Isis before them, they, too, want historical monuments that offend their sensitivities and contradict their political posturing crushed, including Civil War markers and statues from public grounds that are connected to the slave-owning side of our past. It's immaterial how contradictory such doublethink and newspeak is; the end game is all that matters. The maintenance of power and the uninterrupted establishment of cross-party monopolies require whatever deflection and tortured logic is needed to be manufactured until citizens accept as substantive those "viewpoints" that Big Brother wants maintained on the streets and in the echo chambers of fake news outlets, especially if such can be used to infer wrongdoing or failure to act on the part of the Trump administration.

Thus, a new French Revolution Year One mindset is on the march to erase America's politically incorrect antiquity despite the fact it was the Revolutionary War and then the Civil War on this continent that ultimately led to the abolition of slavery here and eventually around the world.

Students of history have often looked with interest at the French Revolution and what dynamics caused it to result in the Year One horror of death and torture under Robespierre compared to the Revolutionary War in America that resulted in unprecedented freedoms and monetary success. While citizens in this country were rejoicing in newfound liberty, in Paris, more than twenty thousand people were beheaded in the guillotines. The years following in France were marked by a reign of terror leading up to Orwellian totalitarianism and Napoleon (whose name actually means Apollo incarnate, the same spirit that will inhabit Antichrist, according to the book of Revelation). Why were the American and French Revolutions followed by such contrasting conclusions? The difference was that the American Revolution was fought on Christian principles of liberty, while the French Revolution—like many of the statue-smashing leftists and neofascist agitators reflect currently—was anti-God. The forces behind the French Revolution were out to eliminate people of faith as the enemies of France and to shut the mouths of God-fearing dissenters. They even placed a nude statue of a woman on the altar in the church at Notre Dame and proclaimed the God of Christianity dead. Soon thereafter, the French government collapsed (by the way, this is why I placed a so-called "Easter egg" reference on the cover of my book *Blood on the Altar*—a book about the coming genocide of true Christianity—in the form of a gargoyle from the Church of Notre Dame, a silent gesture nobody seemed to catch).

And make no mistake about this, either: Many of the people involved in such revolutions as the French one—like those occultists in Washington, DC, briefly mentioned at the start of this chapter—are aware that their politics can be assisted or "energized" by powerful supernaturalism, which they seek to make covenants with and that, under the right circumstances, can take on social vivacity of its own (see Ephesians 6:12).

For instance, concerning the French Revolution specifically, some scholars note how practitioners of occultism comingled with evil non-human energies that emanated from their actions, symbols, and incantations and that, once summoned, were released upon a gullible society to encourage a destructive collective group mind. As people passed these "thoughtforms" or memes from one to another and the ideas became viral, the power and reach of "the entity" spread with it until it became an unimaginably destructive force. Writing about the Masonic involvement in the French Revolution, Gary Lachman makes an extraordinary and important observation about such immaterial destructive forces—which had unseen plans of their own—released as a result of occult politics:

> Cazotte himself was aware of the dangerous energies unleashed by the Revolution.... Although Cazotte didn't use the term, he would no doubt have agreed that, whatever started it, the Revolution soon took on a life of its own, coming under the power of an

egregore, Greek for "watcher," a kind of immaterial entity that is created by and presides over a human activity or collective. According to the anonymous author of the fascinating *Meditations on the Tarot*, there are no "good" *egregores*, only "negative" ones.… True or not, *egregores* can nevertheless be "engendered by the collective will and imagination of nations." As Joscelyn Godwin points out, "an *egregore* is augmented by human belief, ritual and especially by sacrifice. If it is sufficiently nourished by such energies, the *egregore* can take on a life of its own and appear to be an independent, personal divinity, with a limited power on behalf of its devotees and an unlimited appetite for their future devotion." If, as some esotericists believe, human conflicts are the result of spiritual forces for spiritual ends, and these forces are not all "good," then collective catastrophes like the French Revolution take on a different significance.[150]

Fast forward to today, and anyone who thinks the eradication of public knowledge about the role God played in American history and even our Civil War is divorced from supernaturalism or will stop with a few monuments being pulled down is in for a history lesson of their own. Behind the chaos-magic and/or meme-magic nonstop deployment by fake news outlets and sufferers of Trump-Derangement Syndrome are deceiving spirits called *egregore* above and "archons" and "kosmokrators" in the Book of Ephesians. These are rulers of darkness who work in and through human political counterparts, commanding spirits of lesser rank until every level of earthly government can be touched by their influence. Their currency includes propaganda (or "deception" and "lies," as the New Testament describes), and as surely as Orwell's protagonist Winston Smith spent his time at the Ministry of Truth modifying the past by correcting "errors" in old newspapers that embarrassed the party, today's revisionists empowered by deceptive spirits will not be satisfied until their versions of doublethink and newspeak control everything the masses, *especially Bible-believing Christians,* can know, think and say. This is why, by the way, California lawmakers recently proposed Resolution 99 to govern what church leaders and religious counselors will be allowed to preach or say in the future.[151]

In this regard, America and the world could be entering a prophetic, ruthless form of censorship that will undergird a time when all, both small and great, will bow before "a king of fierce countenance" (Daniel 8:23). With imperious decree, this Man of Sin will facilitate an Orwellian one-world government, universal religion, and global socialism. Those who refuse his Oceaniac empire will inevitably be imprisoned or destroyed until at last he exalts himself "above all that is called God, or that is worshiped, so that he, as God, sitteth in the temple of God, showing himself that he is God" (2 Thessalonians 2:4).

Before we get to that and the supernatural forces operating within the Deep State toward a luciferian end game, in the next chapter we connect the material truths behind the Obama birth certificate investigation to the forces backing the Russia Hoax, further drawing the curtain aside on those Orwellian forces plagued with Trump Derangement Syndrome and hatred of American Christians and conservatives. Chapter 3 is the only "guest" chapter in *Shadowland*. It is by my friend and a man deputized by Sheriff Joe Arpaio as an official media liaison for the birth certificate inquiry (and thus more qualified than I am on this subject), investigative writer Carl Gallups.

chapter three

The Deep-State Connection to the Obama Birth-Certificate Scandal

By Carl Gallups

The only people who don't want to disclose the truth
are people with something to hide.
—BARACK OBAMA (2010)[152]

P lease believe me when I tell you this…

America has probably never had a president with so much to hide as does Barack Obama. Nor, has it ever had a president who has worked so hard at hiding it.

The vast majority of America's citizens have never laid their eyes on the information you will see over the next few minutes of reading. Furthermore, every major claim made in this chapter is backed by contextually referenced material, largely gleaned from the mainstream leftist media itself. They often convict themselves with their own words, without even realizing it.

Prepare yourself. If you love America's constitutional republic, what follows will not be easy for you…

Barack Obama, during both his first bid for the White House and in the ensuing years after gaining office, eventually put the United States through what seemed to be a never-ending gyration of legal battles, obfuscation, doublespeak, and misdirection campaigns. Most of it was orchestrated to effectively muddy the waters concerning his genuine *birth narrative*.

Oh, I know. You've probably been convinced that Obama's birth story was "officially" determined to be a "settled issue" long ago. However, as you will soon discover for yourself, nothing could be farther from the truth. You've been duped by the fake news industry.

The Birth-Certificate Narrative

The most tangible part of that overall narrative revolved around the legitimacy of Obama's purported birth certificate. The attempted forensic verification of that document ultimately became the laser focus of a well-known, five-year-long criminal investigation of the now-infamous long-form Certificate of Birth of Barack Obama. That investigation was initiated by former Sheriff Joe Arpaio of the Maricopa County Sheriff's Office (MCSO) in Phoenix, Arizona.

Barack Obama's own administration placed that document on the White House website in April 2011 in the form of a digital PDF photocopy—of *something*.[153] We now believe that the specific document the PDF reproduction claims to represent does not exist in any official and legal format anywhere. It *can't* exist, because the PDF is a proven fraudulent and completely fabricated document, from the ground up.[154]

That 2011 PDF certificate was made public by Obama's administration in a harried attempt to squelch the ever-continuing birth narrative firestorm. The melee had been sparked off during Obama's *first run* for office in 2007–2008. By late 2008, his administration had displayed on the Internet a Hawaii *short-form* Certificate of Birth as the only evidence "proving" he had truly been born in Hawaii. But that document only fired up the growing controversy. The "certificate" was riddled with issues.

As former CNN commentator Lou Dobbs phrased the matter on his nationally syndicated radio program just after Obama took office in his first term, "This peculiar little document [has] some issues. We have a certification of live birth that doesn't have a signature, or an attestation of *any kind,* attached to it."[155]

Dobbs was merely echoing the obvious as well as the mounting national angst concerning the matter. And, he was eventually fired from CNN for daring to doing so.[156] However, much to the consternation of the left, as time went on, Obama's true birth narrative became an issue that simply refused to die. Even retired generals and a major university law professor were weighing in on the subject—for very good reasons, as you will soon discover.

It was for these widely publicized concerns that, by late 2010, a billionaire real-estate mogul named Donald Trump had also joined the fray. Using the mainstream media as his sounding board, Trump ramped up the ever-growing pressure for then president Barack Obama to produce a legitimate long-form birth certificate. He challenged Obama to produce something that authoritatively identified his hospital of birth, the doctor's name, and the parents' names.[157]

And so it was that Donald Trump could eventually take credit for pressuring a sitting US president to "put up or shut up" regarding his highly controversial birth narrative.[158] And Obama had finally acquiesced. Furthermore, certain Deep-State[159] players were determined to eventually make Trump pay for his deed. But that would come later.

The Big Lie

For a long time now, there's been too much secrecy in this city. This administration stands on the side not of those who seek to withhold information but with those who seek it to be known.
—Barack Obama (2009)[160]

It wasn't long after the Obama long-form PDF birth certificate was finally posted that growing national scrutiny was calling attention to numerous "problems" within that new photocopy file as well. Very early on, it appeared to a number of creditable people that the document had been manipulated, and maybe even fabricated—from scratch. The Internet burst ablaze with renewed and invigorated conspiracy theories. Oddly, the match had been lit by the Obama administration itself and was gladly egged on by Donald Trump.

The thought of something this reprehensibly immense involving America's brand-new and first African-American president was so surreal that it could not even be imagined by most of the country's populace.

Precisely because of that pervasive and powerful psychological influence, the Obama birth-certificate scandal would soon become America's *Big Lie.*[161] A large swath of the American public was being effectively brainwashed, largely through the vehicle of *fake news.*[162] Adolf would have been proud.

Enter Sheriff Joe Arpaio

A striking consequence of this strange new national psychosis would soon become embarrassingly apparent. Not a single bona fide law enforcement agency on the planet dared to formally examine the PDF from a purely investigative and forensic perspective—that is, until Sheriff Joe Arpaio— *America's Toughest Sheriff*[163]—got involved in August 2011.

I became personally involved in this case sometime around the first of 2012 by serving as a media outlet for Sheriff Arpaio's investigation. I had been the host of a popular talk-radio program on a twenty-five-thousand- watt Gulf Coast AM news/talk station for more than a decade. During that time, I had the sheriff and his lead investigator in the case on my show a number of times.

In January 2016, I flew to Phoenix, Arizona, to meet with the sheriff, who deputized me as a special deputy, as we all knew the official MCSO investigation would later that year be concluding. Sheriff Arpaio wanted to establish an official chain of information exchange with me so that there might be accountability among us all as the case was wrapping up.

Not only had I been a reliable media outlet during the investigation, but I also had been, in the 1970s and '80s, a decorated deputy in two Florida sheriff's offices, with criminal investigative experience as well. My Arpaio-linked deputation did not involve direct investigative input in the Obama fraud case, nor have I represented myself in that way. However, my law-enforcement experience enabled Sheriff Arpaio to trust me with a high level of information exchange in the case.

And so it was that on December 15, 2016, in Phoenix, Arizona, at their third[164] and final press conference on the Obama PDF issue, after five long years of investigating, Sheriff Arpaio revealed the culmination of the investigation's stunning findings.[165] The evidence they presented was overwhelming. I was present at that news conference. We'll examine those findings a little later on in this chapter.

Didn't Fit the Narrative

The discoveries of the obvious birth-certificate fraud that were revealed that day simply didn't fit the agreed-upon narrative of the left. That narrative was a brazenly deceitful tale they had been crafting, like a giant, corporate science-fair project, for eight long Obama-term years. In truth, the media didn't quite know how to "spin" the unarguable hard evidence they had just witnessed.[166] However, a few of the reporters in the mainstream media who saw it live appeared to have been absolutely stunned.[167]

Nevertheless, instead of faithfully reporting what they had been shown, the bulk of the national media simply ignored the forensic details of that report altogether—regardless of the fact that it was the most explosive allegation leveled against a sitting president in America's history. *Someone had committed a series of serious federal crimes in order to digitally fabricate a major identifying document for America's commander-in-chief.*

Before we get to those brutally condemning forensic discoveries, let's first consider the backdrop to the buildup of this entire scenario. Once you are aware of the foundational elements in the matter, the context of the criminal investigation and its findings will dramatically add to your understanding of what is happening in today's political realm in America. It will also shed light on the level of the Deep State's involvement in the entire affair. *Trust me.*

To keep this narrative moving in a straight and coherent line, I have arranged the information around twelve strategic fact points.

Fact #1: It All Started with the Clinton Democrats

I know. I know. Many argue that it has already been proven that Hillary Clinton had "nothing to do with the birther narrative." However, as you will soon see, that mantra simply is not true. It is yet another fabrication of a deceitful storyline, skillfully constructed by the fake news. Now, let's forensically deconstruct that politically expedient fairytale.

The Plan

The phenomenon of the Obama eligibility question took shape during the 2008 Democratic primary—a truth that makes perfect political sense. It was initially moved along by the Hillary Clinton campaign and some of her top operatives, along with many of her most loyal supporters across the nation.

The Clinton scheme had been to totally discredit the quickly rising new star, Barack Obama, and to thus secure Hillary as the Democrat frontrunner in the 2008 election. This ploy eventually became such a well-known fact that, by 2015, even the wildly left-wing *Politifact* had to bluntly admit the fact.

> It's an **interesting** *bit of history* that the **birther movement** appears to have *begun with Democrats supporting Clinton* and *opposing Obama.*[168] (Emphasis added)

CNN admitted the same thing concerning the question of Hillary's 2007 involvement in pushing the Obama identity narrative:

Bottom line: [Hillary] Clinton *stoked questions* about Obama's identity.[169] (Emphasis and brackets added)

Clinton Panic Breeds the Narrative

The truth was that in the face of Obama's quickly growing popularity, Hillary could feel her presidential "entitlement coronation" rapidly slipping from her grips. And, of all things, it was happening at the hands of a mere one-term, relatively unknown, African-American senator from Illinois—the newest *dream candidate*. Even then Senator Joe Biden, later to become Obama's vice president, weighed in on the storybook status of Obama's rise in the polls:

> "I mean, you got the first mainstream African-American who is articulate and bright and clean and a nice-looking guy," Biden said. "I mean, that's a storybook, man."[170]

To top it all off, Barack Obama's own publicist, Acton & Dystel,[171] for a full seventeen years (1991–2007) had ubiquitously distributed Obama's bio narrative through various national media outlets and publicist networks. They categorically claimed that Obama had been born in…wait for it…*Kenya*!

> *Barack Obama*, the first African-American president of the Harvard Law Review, *was born in Kenya* and raised in Indonesia and Hawaii.[172] (emphasis added)

Coincidently, the only time Acton & Dystel even considered removing the unabashed claim of Obama's "Kenyan birth" from their literature was when he commenced his run for the office of president. This was right about the same time Hillary was making certain that Obama's own life's story was becoming a question of constitutional eligibility. At that important juncture, as soon as the narrative made national headlines, Acton and Dystel declared the Kenyan-birth declaration to be a mere (*seventeen-year*) editor's mistake. But the question was still out there, sweeping the national political scene. And apparently Hillary was just fine with that. By that time, the public was sufficiently confused in the matter. And, that's just what she was counting on.[173]

So…Hillary Clinton, in fact, began to publicly question Obama's "American roots," just as she had been advised to do by her top campaign officials.[174] Dutifully, Hillary pounced on the narrative like a Serengeti lion stalking a wildebeest in the tall grass of the African plains.

Hillary's Top Advisors Lead the Way

It is now a profusely documented fact that the very crux of the birther narrative, and the campaign agenda surrounding that account, was originally *introduced to the masses* by Hillary's own top campaign advisors, Sidney Blumenthal[175] and Mark Penn.[176] This fact is one that the media is still loathe to repeat.

In fact, Mark Penn even wrote a *campaign-strategy memo* urging Hillary to persistently question Obama's "lack of American roots" because it "could hold him back." That document still exists in official archives.[177]

Furthermore, it was the second-largest newspaper corporation in the nation—the liberally biased *McClatchy Company*[178]—that was unequivocally involved in helping spread that Clinton-campaign-planned birther message:

James Asher,[179] [Pulitzer Prize winning investigative journalist] the former Washington bureau chief of McClatchy, [and current DC bureau chief of the Associated Press] has publicly claimed that **Clinton aide and confidant [Sidney Blumenthal]** *was spreading the rumor* that **Barack Obama was** *born in Kenya* and *therefore not eligible* to be president.

Blumenthal [Hillary's chief campaign advisor] actually admits he was pressuring McClatchy to investigate rumors related to Obama's family in Kenya but *claims he never went so far as to push the dreaded birther rumor.*

A second McClatchy reporter in Kenya, however, confirms he *was* asked to look into *the birther issue,* and *everyone concedes* Asher and Blumenthal were in contact.[180] (Emphasis and brackets added)

MSNBC Goes Birther

Even MSNBC's own Chris Matthews reported on Hillary's stoking of the original birther movement. All the way back in December of 2007, during Obama's first White House run, Matthews had expressed his unease with the increasingly public and incendiary Hillary-speak. He voiced his concern on a live episode of *Hardball with Chris Matthews:*

> MATTHEWS: So, what is [Hillary] up to here? Is she pushing how great [Obama] is for *having been born in Indonesia,* or what, or simply *reminding everybody about his background, his Islamic background?*[181] (Emphasis and brackets added)

Matthews' outrage serves as documented evidence that Hillary was in fact spreading, or unquestionably perceived to be spreading, the birther narrative in late 2007. This is a fact that, even today, the Hillary camp tries to cover up and deny.

MSNBC—Still Going Strong in 2016

However, the adamant claim that Hillary was the one who started "the whole thing" was *still* being promoted by MSNBC representatives during her run against Republican candidate Donald Trump in 2016.

In a scandalous live MSNBC morning show Joe Scarborough, Mika Brzezinski, and John Heilemann dared to spill the beans once again. The three of them became emotionally vocal about their perception of the matter on an episode of *Morning Joe* led by Joe Scarborough himself.

> SCARBOROUGH: I guess we have to get our digs in on Hillary Clinton here, because…[the birther narrative] all started with her and her campaign—passing things around in the Democratic Party.… *It started with Hillary Clinton,* and it was spread by the Clinton Team.… *That is the truth.*

> BRZEZINSKI: [She did it] on 60 Minutes…. We're just telling the truth. Sorry.

> HEILEMANN: It *was* the case. I'm *affirming* the Scarborough-Brzezinski assertion.[182] (Brackets and emphasis added)

60 Minutes Catches Hillary in Doublespeak

That is not to mention Hillary's own dubious comments that she made on that Brzezinski-referenced CBS *60 Minutes* interview, when, asked if she really thought Obama was a Muslim, Hillary first appeared to sincerely insist that she *did not think* Obama was a Muslim. But then she quickly qualified her statement with the words "as far as I know." Then, she further tempered her answer by smugly proclaiming, "He is whatever he says he is."

Leftist Media Reacts to Hillary

The media was incensed with Hillary's coyness and what they considered to be her oh-so-obvious doublespeak—a political maneuver for which she had become quite renowned. They even characterized her interview responses as "the sleaziest moment of the campaign."[183]

Media Matters reported the fracas:

Journalists at NBC, MSNBC, *The New York Times*, *Chicago Sun-Times*, *Time*, *The New Yorker*, and *The Washington Post*, among others, declared her response had been wholly deficient. Worse, ***Clinton's answer simply confirmed that she was running a "slimy," "nasty" contest.*** It was a "galling" comment; ***"the sleaziest moment of the campaign."***[184] (Emphasis added)

The only fairly frontline media voice that immediately came to Hillary's defense regarding that interview—desperately trying to spin her answers into a more positive meaning—was *Media Matters*. That often-dubious publication is an unquestionably hard-left media site, one that just happened to have been founded by a longtime Hillary and Bill Clinton family friend David Brock,[185] and liberally funded by the far-left billionaire George Soros.[186] Gee. How convenient for Hillary.

Think of it. What we have documented thus far is that Hillary, Blumenthal, Penn, and a number of other hardcore Hillary supporters, as well as the MSNBC network representatives Chris Matthews, Scarborough, Brzezinski, Heilemann, and other bona fide leftist, mainstream sources (the McClatchy Company—at least) either fueled the original birther movement or unquestionably perceived that Hillary herself was responsible for it. And it was all predicated on the coattails of Obama's own publicity literature, a narrative that had been internationally distributed for almost two decades previously—clearly making Obama himself the very first "birther." This is a very inconvenient truth for the left—but, it is documented truth nonetheless.

Believe it or not, there's still more. Much more…

A Democrat Hawaii Governor

In 2011, just two years into Obama's first term as president, newly elected Democrat governor of Hawaii, Neil Abercrombie, made an unbelievably bold inaugural promise. He claimed that he would end the birther narrative "once and for all."

In yet another stunning *birther move* by a well-known Democrat, Abercrombie vowed to personally and publicly produce the Obama Hawaii birth certificate. Certainly, Obama had to have cringed when he heard the news.[187]

Shortly after making his claim, Abercrombie realized he had embarrassed himself. He was flatly unable to make good on his pugnacious promise. To make matters even worse, Abercrombie had been a longtime friend of the Obama family, and later admitted he *had not* first contacted the White House about his campaign vow before attempting to produce the highly disputed records.[188]

Politifact described the disarray:

> The Associated Press reported that Abercrombie's office had ***ended its effort* to make public more information about Obama's birth.... The state's attorney general had told the governor that *he can't disclose* birth documentation *without the person's consent.*"** "There is nothing more that Gov. Abercrombie can do within the law to produce a document," Abercrombie spokeswoman Donalyn Dela Cruz said.[189]

Wait a minute!

So, the American public was being asked to believe that even the Democrat governor of Hawaii was not "allowed" to produce the hardcore evidence he had personally promised the electorate? Were we really to understand that even the duly-elected constitutional and chief executive officer of the state of Hawaii had *no access whatsoever* to the original document? Not even to verify its literal presence within the Hawaiian archives? And, were we being asked to believe that even his personal friend, Barack Obama, whom Abercrombie was trying to exonerate, would not give the governor of Hawaii permission to access the files? How odd. How improbable. How inconceivable. *Yet—how deliciously convenient.* So, dutifully, the mainstream media declared the matter to be "over."

Meanwhile, during the fallout of Abercrombie's faux pas, Politifact reported yet another hugely embarrassing chapter to the relentlessly ongoing saga. Coming from a completely left-field foul hit, the spin control almost got completely out of hand:

> On Minnesota's KQRS-FM radio Jan. 20, 2011 *Hollywood reporter* Mike Evans, claiming to be *a longtime friend of Abercrombie's*, said *the governor had told him* that he had in fact searched "everywhere" at Hawaii hospitals and that "*there is no Barack Obama birth certificate in Hawaii. Absolutely no proof at all that he was born in Hawaii.*"[190] (Emphasis added)

Doubling down—and on that very same day—the inconveniently loose-lipped Mike Evans made his earth-shattering claim yet again on Austin's KLBJ-AM during another live interview. A mere six days later, however, very convenient to the Obama administration, Evans summarily had a "change of heart" and literally walked back on his entire claim. Evans even changed and denied the foundation of his original narrative altogether. The surreal episode appeared as if a Tinseltown movie producer had scripted the narrative especially for this Hollywood reporter—and he had merely "played the part." In that second interview, Evans explained:

> He called Abercrombie's office *after reading online reports* that the governor couldn't find Obama's birth certificate but that Abercrombie did not return his call. "*I haven't talked to Neil since he's been governor,*" Evans said.[191] (Emphasis added)

In light of his initial enthusiastic insistence of the truth of his conversation with Abercrombie, during his first two viral interviews conducted in major radio markets, a number of people believed that Mike Evans was either one of the poorest fibbers the world had ever heard, or worse yet, the Deep State had "gotten to him."[192]

Regardless of the documented evidence you have read thus far, the leftist mainstream publication *Politico,* just before the elections in November 2016, one more time endeavored to defend Hillary against the "she started the birther narrative" allegation. Apparently, it felt it *had* to do so. Because, to its ever-growing consternation, that claim had now been publicly leveled against Hillary Clinton, by Donald Trump himself, in a live presidential debate. Now the entire planet was talking about the issue—again![193]

To get the heat off of Hillary, that *Politico* article attempted to bring the commencement of the birther narrative to the doorsteps of a single person. It desperately needed a "scapegoat."

> In fact, birtherism, as it's been called, *reportedly* began with *innuendo* by *serial Illinois political candidate Andy Martin*, who *painted Obama as a closet Muslim in 2004.* That spiraled into a concerted effort by conspiracy theorists to raise doubts about Obama's birthplace and religion—and essentially *paint him as un-American.*
>
> *Martin,* who briefly launched a little-noticed presidential campaign last year, *has disavowed the movement he's often credited with starting.*[194] (Emphasis added)

I have to interject a very important point here. I find it downright humorous—and shamefully duplicitous—that *Politico* would characterize Martin as one who "painted Obama as a closet Muslim" and as "un-American." It used that particular characterization of Martin in a brazen attempt to impugn his character. In fact, presenting Obama as a "closet Muslim" is *exactly what Hillary Clinton did*…and she got called out by her own leftist peers for doing it! Yet Hillary is declared "innocent" for doing so, while Martin is declared to be an outright villain.

Hillary's campaign even circulated a picture of Obama wearing customary Muslim garb in order to call into question his "traditional American" loyalty, and to promote his perceived "closet Muslim" stature.[195] At the very same time she was doing that, Hillary's own campaign advisor was pushing her to "question [Obama's] American roots" because it "could hurt him." It seems *Politico* just couldn't help itself and slipped right into its own pit of slimy deception.

However, *Politico* did have to ultimately "admit" that the rumors had in fact started within the Clinton circle. Yet, even that nefarious confession, again, obscured the genuine truth of the matter:

> **Some hardcore Clinton backers** circulated the rumors in 2008, but the **campaign itself** steered clear.[196] (Emphasis added)

The "hardcore Clinton backers" were at least, as we've already noted, Sidney Blumenthal, Hillary's chief campaign advisor,[197] and Mark Penn[198]—an important Hillary campaign advisor who documented the strategy in an archived campaign memo. And the campaign did not "steer clear" of it, the truth of which is clearly documented. Furthermore, if Blumenthal and Penn were not *hardcore Clinton backers*, as well as officers of her campaign, what else were they? The *Politico* fake-news spin machine appeared to be at it again. And so, the Big Lie continued to advance—while most of America yawned.

Fact #2—Very Important People Knew

Months before Obama's PDF "birth certificate" was released on the White House website, and long before Sheriff Arpaio's investigation officially commenced, several unexpected bombshell statements were also released to the public arena. This time, they were from prominent, high-ranking US military officers, as well as a renowned Harvard Law professor.

In June 2010, the *Post & Email's* Sharon Rondeau interviewed Ret. Maj. Gen. Paul Vallely who, at the time, was a highly respected national security expert and a popular Fox News contributor. In that interview, Vallely leveled several shocking "insider" accusations:

Mrs. Rondeau: What **about the Joint Chiefs of Staff?** Even aside from the eligibility question, **they must know that something is terribly wrong.**

Gen. Vallely: **Well, they do, but they won't do a thing about it.** They won't address it; they won't even talk about it. **The fix is in. The Obama administration is a bunch of Chicago gangsters,** and **they put the fear of God in all these people** that you're not to say anything about this, and if you do, you might as well retire and move on. But **that's the type of mindset we have now in Washington.**[199]

But there's still more. In September 2010, Lt. Gen. Thomas McInerney had also joined the fray over Obama's true identity. General McInerney, a West Point graduate who ran the Alaskan air command during the Exxon Valdez disaster, and also a Fox News analyst making over 144 appearances on that channel, declared:

> [The president] is *the one single person* in the Chain of Command *that the Constitution demands proof of natural born citizenship.* This determination is fundamental to our Republic, where civilian control over the military is the rule. According to the Constitution, the Commander in Chief must now, in the face of serious—and widely-held—concerns that he is ineligible, either voluntarily *establish his eligibility by authorizing release of his birth records or this court must authorize their discovery.*[200] (Emphasis added)

Next, in December 2010, a respected medical doctor and a lieutenant colonel in the US Army, Dr. Terry Lakin, was court-martialed and sentenced to prison over the Obama birth issue.

Lakin had refused to deploy to Afghanistan because of his growing concerns over President Obama's constitutional eligibility. It was Lakin's plan to insist upon securing a copy of Obama's genuine birth certificate as a part of his court-martial. Lakin had the support of three retired American generals who reportedly possessed the same trepidations concerning Obama's birth narrative.

Just before Lakin finally advanced to the court-martial proceedings, it was determined by the military judge, Col. Denise Lind (a *registered Democrat,* according to voter records[201]) that President Obama's eligibility' and his birth certificate had *no relevance* in the case. Thus, under Lind's authority, that military court never examined Obama's eligibility to be the legitimate commander in chief of America's superpower military machine.[202] Apparently Colonel Lind didn't care where her "boss" was born. How wonderfully advantageous for continuing to cover for Obama's *secret.*

Then, in May 2011, just after the Obama administration had posted the PDF certificate on the White House website, Major General Vallely weighed in once again. This time, his comments were especially stunning and took the Obama birth-certificate saga to an entirely new level.

In a recorded interview, Vallely attested:

[Obama's] *actual birth certificate has never been found in Hawaii nor released from Hawaii hospital there,* Kapiolani hospital there, if it in fact did exist. *We've had three CIA agents,* retired, and some of their analytical associates look at it, and *all came to the same conclusion, that even the long-form was a forged document.*

No members of Congress will take this on. The word I get out of Washington is that they don't want to challenge this *because it would be in fact a felony offense and in some cases may be even treasonous and [they are] afraid of a black backlash from some of the urban areas....*

*I think they're (the FBI) covering for this administratio*n. I think the *corruption within this administration is so proliferated through the agencies of government* now, we're just in a bad situation here. I think the lack of confidence in our government is growing and many feel that *not only all the members of Congress but even our courts are corrupted at this time.*[203] (Emphasis added)

Those are monumental admissions coming from the mouth of a retired major general, especially when one considers how deeply connected a man of his prominence would have been with Washington, DC, insiders. He basically described to a tee what we now call the Deep State.

General Vallely alleged that Obama's FBI (headed by Mueller and followed by Comey), the Obama-era Congress, and the Obama-era courts—all, in one way or the other—were involved in covering up the facts surrounding Obama's birth, facts that three retired CIA agents had discovered early on—namely, *Obama's PDF "birth certificate" was a forged document.*

As mentioned earlier, a distinguished Harvard Law professor weighed in on the Obama identity scandal as well. In early 2011, Dr. Charles E. Rice, professor emeritus with the Law School of Notre Dame University, penned these words:

> [Those whom] the media and political pundits dismiss *as "birthers" have raised legitimate questions.* That legitimacy is *fueled by Obama's curious, even bizarre, refusal to consent to the release of the relevant records....*
>
> This is potentially serious business. *If it turns out that Obama knew he was ineligible when he campaigned and when he took the oath as President, it could be the biggest political fraud in the history of the world.* As long as Obama refuses to disclose the records, speculation will grow and grow without any necessary relation to the truth. *The first step toward resolving the issue is full discovery and disclosure* of the facts.[204] (Emphasis added, brackets added)

Of course, to this day, there has never been a *full discovery and disclosure of the facts* before a federal investigatory body.

Fact #3—It Was Never a Birther Issue to Sheriff Arpaio

Many are surprised to learn that at no time in Sheriff Arpaio's formal criminal investigation was the inquiry ever pointedly concerned with where Obama was born. Yet, the fake news has continued to disseminate this falsehood, regardless of the hard facts that are documented in a number of mainstream media sources.

- "This investigation was never about where President Obama was born," Arpaio said. "We were going to investigate a government possible forged document." (*The Hill*) [205]
- "I don't care where he's from," Arpaio told the crowd of about two hundred. "We are looking at a forged document. Period." (*AZ Central*) [206]
- "Think of it! We were trying to clear the president. But that didn't happen," Arpaio said. (*USA Today*) [207]
- "I started this because of a fake document. I didn't care where the President came from. I didn't care at all." (*CNN*) [208]

It's clear that finding the exact origin of Obama's birth was never the presenting issue for Joe Arpaio. Their investigation was simply not a "birther" matter.

Nor was there ever really a question as to whether a genuine birth certificate existed somewhere within the recesses of the Hawaii Department of Health[209] except for the obvious investigative fact that *if* a legitimate one *did* exist, it would have certainly cleared up the issue. For that very reason, early on, investigators from the MCSO did travel to Hawaii's Department of Health to seek out such a genuine certificate from government officials there.

However, instead of being offered any kind of appropriate assistance, they ran into a bureaucratic brick wall of obfuscation. They were refused any legitimate cooperation and were never allowed to see a birth document for Barack Obama, which only increased their suspicion that something was deeply amiss in this slowly unfolding mystery.

That official MCSO investigation was continually harangued for its efforts by several well-known Obama sycophants and even Fox News commentator Bill O'Reilly.[210]

Those detractors still insist to this day. They say things like: "But there are birth announcements for Obama in Hawaiian newspapers! This settles the matter!"[211]

To which Sheriff Arpaio has responded in this manner: "We are not investigating highly questionable newspaper birth announcements. We are investigating a forged and fabricated fake birth certificate apparently activated on behalf of the president—which is a federal crime. Someone in this case has committed several felonies to forge this document and then display it on a government website."

That truly was *all* that their central investigation was ever focused upon. In fact, that was all that was needed in order to prove that someone tied to the Obama administration had committed a series of very serious federal crimes—perhaps even crimes of treason.[212]

Fact #4—Obama, the Chief Hider of Documents

We were asked "what are you proudest of from your administration?" You know what I said?—"[Obama] said the same thing as I did—[We had] not one single whisper of scandal."
—Joe Biden (2019)[213]

Once Barack Obama won his first presidential election in 2008, his subsequent refusal to release a huge number of his personal records was beginning to offend the sensibilities of millions of concerned Americans on both sides of the aisle. The most questionable of all of those identifying documents was *Obama's Hawaiian birth certificate.*

After all, why in the world would any legitimate, American-born president *not* want the citizens of America to see his original paper-copy birth certificate, backed up by the microfilm copies if necessary—especially if his eligibility to legitimately hold the office was in serious question? There's nothing particularly personal about an innocuous legal document that simply proves the state, date, parents, doctor, and the hospital of one's birth. *Unless*—to use Obama's own words—one "has something to hide."[214]

It appeared mind-boggling that Obama would not open up for inspection his original paper birth certificate and the microfilm files that would accompany it. As Sheriff Arpaio has said on numerous occasions, "If Obama would just do that, this whole issue would be over that very same day!"

> [Arpaio said] "Show. Us. The. Microfilm," he demanded. "I said it awhile back. Show. Us. The. Microfilm. And we'll all go back home and forget this! Where is the microfilm? Where is the microfilm? Is it in Hawaii? The Department of Health? What's the big secret?"[215]

But Barack Obama never did offer the microfilm or the certified hard-copy paper document. To this day, the public has yet to lay eyes upon those items. Instead, the investigation was categorically maligned by the *fake news* media for even suggesting that such a common-sense, drama-ending approach should ever be taken. We were simply supposed to take Obama's word on the matter—backed up by the sycophant fake-news media.

To put this matter in its proper perspective, consider the reaction of the media, Congress, and federal law enforcement agencies if the subject in question was Donald Trump's birth narrative—and his complete lack of transparency in producing his identifying documents.

The Obama Executive Order

The orchestrated withholding of a number of Obama's other personal records appeared to be approaching the epitome of abject hypocrisy as well, especially in light of the executive order that he had signed on *the very first day* of his brand-new presidency.

Believe it not, that executive order was *not* one that allowed Obama to lock down *his own* personal documents, as had been widely reported.[216] Rather, Obama's first-day order rescinded a President Bush-era executive order that actually prevented presidential records from being made public *after* a president left office.

On the day Obama signed Executive Order 13489,[217] he also made a statement for the public record. Given what we now know about Obama's years of obfuscation concerning practically every element of his own past, his words had an ominously phony ring to them:

> For a long time now, there's been too much secrecy in this city. This administration stands on the side not of those who seek to withhold information but with those who seek it to be known. The mere fact that you have the legal power to keep something secret does not mean you should always use it. Transparency and the rule of law will be the touchstones of [my] presidency.[218] (Brackets added)

By the end of Obama's presidency in 2016, his oft-repeated vow of providing *complete transparency* had changed dramatically. In fact, it had practically melted into oblivion. The policy reversal was such a vivid and historically unprecedented event that even normally left-leaning news organizations had become perplexed.

Following is an excerpt of a *CBS News* article summarizing the reversal:

> WASHINGTON—The Obama administration in its final year in office spent **a record $36.2 million** on legal costs **defending its refusal to turn over federal records** under the Freedom of Information Act, according to an Associated Press analysis of new U.S. data that also showed poor performance in other categories measuring transparency in government.
>
> **For a second consecutive year, the Obama administration set a record** for times federal employees told citizens, journalists and others that despite searching they *couldn't find a single page of files that were requested.*[219] (Emphasis added)

National Archives Records Missing

To make matters infinitely worse, as late as June 10, 2018, the nation learned another scandalous fact regarding the Obama administration's "wholesale destruction" of records—potentially *a federal crime.*[220] This time it concerned the records of the National Archives.

Real Clear Politics reported the matter:

> **The accumulation of recent congressional testimony has made it clear that *the Obama administration itself engaged in the wholesale destruction and "loss" of tens of thousands of government records* covered under the act as well as *the intentional evasion of the government records* recording system by engaging in private email exchanges. So far, former President Obama, former Secretary of State Hillary Clinton, former Attorney General Lynch and several EPA officials** have been named as offenders. **The [Obama] IRS suffered record "losses" as well.**[221] (Emphasis and brackets added)

But that's not all. The *Post & Email* reported in June of 2018 that the MCSO Obama birth-certificate investigation ran into the very same problem when attempting to examine the National Archive records. Their investigator wanted to examine certain international travel records that related to the specific years of Obama's supposed birth date. But the National Archives could not produce them.[222]

Earth-shattering

> We've had three CIA agents, retired, and some of their analytical associates look at it, and all came to the same conclusion, that even the long-form was a forged document.
> —US Army Major General Paul Vallely[223]

When the 2011 PDF "birth certificate" had finally been posted, the Obama administration proclaimed that this copy of his "original" Hawaiian birth certificate was meant to prove once and for all that Obama was eligible to hold that office. [224]

Sheriff Arpaio had, on several occasions, insisted that he had originally expressed no interest in the Obama birth-certificate fracas *at all*. However, Arpaio admitted that he became engaged in the case only when he was running for another term as sheriff in the upcoming 2012 election. During that time, he said he was incessantly approached by a large contingency of his supporters. They were asking him to investigate the matter.

Those voters argued that if the Obama birth certificate was truly a fake, then the citizens of Maricopa County could be defrauded during the upcoming 2012 election, and would certainly have already been defrauded in the 2008 election. They insisted upon an investigatory answer to that legal question of election integrity. They finally presented the sheriff with a lengthy petition, imploring him to investigate the Obama 2011 PDF birth certificate. [225]

As a result, Arpaio formally opened the investigation in August 2011, four months after Obama had posted the PDF. Arpaio insisted that he truly wanted to be the sheriff who *would clear the president* in this growing national matter so that the country could move on from it. [226]

However, instead of being able to clear Obama, Sheriff Arpaio's official investigation eventually uncovered the greatest potential political crime America may have ever experienced, one that would prove to be largely ignored by America's supposed *fourth estate* of government—the "ever vigilant" mainstream media. As Major General Vallely had earlier cautioned: *The fix was in.*

Fact #5—The Deep State Was, and Still Is, Involved

The mere fact that you have the legal power to keep something secret does not mean you should always use it. Transparency and the rule of law will be the touchstones of [my] presidency.
—Barack Obama [227]

Of course, one must also take into account that all three Maricopa County Sheriff's Office press conferences and the entire five-year criminal investigation itself were conducted solely during the years of the uber-powerful Obama presidency. Today, it is no secret concerning the virtual lockdown that Obama's administration held over the courts, Congress, practically all of the mainstream media, federal law enforcement agencies, national records archives, and the DOJ—not to mention a slew of state governors and other important state officials across the nation. Again, generals Vallely and McInerney tried to warn America of the reality of that unholy alliance that was steadily congealing right under our noses.

Big Media Names Shut Out the Investigation

The *politically incorrect* atmosphere that overshadowed the official Obama birth-certificate investigation certainly held its sway over several well-known major media personalities. It even reached into a number of top conservative media corners. In a radio interview in 2019, a few of those big names in media were eventually revealed. These were shows that purportedly were scheduled to interview the MCSO birth certificate lead investigator right after the initial sheriff's office press conference. After they heard the findings, as reported by Sheriff Arpaio, they canceled the interviews. The media programs that reneged on the offer were publicly reported to be the *Rush Limbaugh Show*, Sean Hannity's radio show, and Lawrence O'Donnell of MSNBC.[228]

Fact #6—Political Payback

I started my birth certificate investigation around the same time [Donald Trump] did his.—Sheriff Joe Arpaio[229]

Another important but often overlooked connection to this story is the fact that Sheriff Joe Arpaio was also eventually charged with a federal contempt crime. This charge came after he admitted to neglecting to obey an

Obama-era federal judge's order, which would require the sheriff to cease from enforcing certain federal civil immigration laws.[230]

Arpaio was charged in 2015, almost three years after commencing the Obama birth-certificate investigation, and two years after the public airing of his first two press conferences. Many, including Sheriff Arpaio himself,[231] saw the maneuver as a blatantly political one, having been orchestrated by the Obama administration, through Eric Holder's Justice Department, as payback for conducting the Obama birth-certificate investigation.

Trump Pardons Joe Arpaio

However, it would be the newly elected President Donald Trump who would stir the pot again. Trump pardoned Sheriff Arpaio in August of 2017. That act of exoneration wasn't supposed to happen as far as the Deep State had been concerned. But it was something they feared might happen, on the off chance that Trump might actually win the presidency. With that pardon, the leftists and the *Never-Trumpers* on all sides of the aisle were once again enraged. Their worst-nightmare scenario was slowly unfolding before their eyes. Their complicity in the crime of the ages was perhaps one more very important step closer to being revealed.[232]

Arpaio and his lawyer, Mark Goldman, said they did not contact Trump during this period, nor did they ask anyone in the administration for a pardon. "I didn't ask for the pardon," Arpaio said. "[President Trump] wanted to do it because I think he understood what I was going through."[233]

Also, never doubt, Hillary was *supposed* to have *won* the 2016 presidential election, as far as the Deep-State players were concerned. Practically all the "official" polls had promised them that she would win—right up to the day of the election. And the mainstream fake news was proudly proclaiming the assurances.[234]

Undoubtedly, they had planned that when Hillary Clinton finally walked into the White House as America's first female president, this entire "birther" nightmare—and many other similar illegal scenarios—could eventually just "go away." And, as icing on the cake, *if Hillary had won*, then former Sheriff Arpaio would serve time in a federal prison and would be politically discredited forever.

However, yet again, the dominoes didn't fall in the right direction for Hillary Clinton and the Deep State. By November 2016, Trump was firmly entrenched in the White House—many believed, by the hand of God—to the great dismay of the thoroughly traumatized Democrats. And to add unbearable insult to the already massive political injury, Donald Trump just happened to be the man who had effectually antagonized first-term President Barack Obama into finally posting the questionable long-form birth certificate on the White House website in the first place.[235]

Just before Obama had posted that PDF file, Donald Trump had proclaimed to NBC News:

"If he has a birth certificate he should release it," Trump told NBC News. Trump exudes confidence. [*Trump*] *is so sure of himself, he says he may run for president in 2012.*[236] (Emphasis and brackets added)

However, there had been even more Obama-prodding instigated by Donald Trump. The year after the birth certificate was posted, Trump had issued yet another embarrassing challenge to Obama. In October of 2012, Trump offered Obama five million dollars, to a charity of his choice, if Obama would cough up his other sealed identifying documents—namely, his college records and his passport applications.[237]

Trump was hanging on to Obama's "identity issue" like a bulldog with a death-lock on a piece of red meat. While millions of Americans loved him for it, the left deeply resented his relentless efforts to uncover the truth.

As history now records, Trump did not run for president in 2012. However, on January 20, 2017, he was indeed seated in the White House after winning the 2016 election. He now had the authority that could

finally be used to effectively blow the lid off the Deep State's entire cha-
rade in a number of areas, and not just the issue of the Obama birth
certificate.

As the left collectively fell into a political depression, some of them
began to wonder aloud in FBI text messages, as well as in the headlines
of the nation's fake news organizations: *How could this have happened? Are
there, maybe, any political "insurance" policies out there somewhere?*[238] *Can't
this Trump-atrocity be fixed?*

Fact #7—Enter the Mueller Investigation

Then, just in the nick of time for the left, came the over-two-year-long
Mueller investigation.[239]

That DOJ inquest, under the authority of then self-recused Attorney
General Jeff Sessions,[240] was supposedly assembled to ascertain if Donald
Trump or any of his inner circle had criminally colluded with the Russians
in order to sway the 2016 presidential campaign in his direction, thus
securing his win of the White House.

It would later prove that it was actually Hillary Clinton's campaign
that had colluded with several foreign agents, including the Russians, and
for the explicit purpose of manipulating and influencing the outcome of
the 2016 election. Of course, the *Mueller Report* didn't even come close to
reporting the facts of the Hillary/Russia collusion.[241]

In March 2019, *The Federalist* summarized the story like this:

> After a nearly two-year-long investigation that issued 2,800 sub-
> poenas, interviewed 500 witnesses, and used nearly 300 wiretaps
> and pen registers, **Special Counsel Robert Mueller concluded that
> there was no evidence of collusion by Trump or his associates.**
>
> **But that doesn't mean 2016 was free of Russian collusion.**
> To the contrary, **there is clear evidence that a 2016 presiden-
> tial campaign willfully and deliberately colluded with Russians**

in a bid to interfere with American elections. It wasn't Trump's campaign that colluded with shady Russia oligarchs and sketchy Russian sources to subvert American democracy: **it was Hillary Clinton's.**[242] (Emphasis added)

Some, including President Trump himself, were insisting that Mueller might have been the so-called insurance policy that Peter Strzok had earlier referenced.[243] Strzok made that veiled promise in a now infamous text message with his FBI coworker and paramour Lisa Page.[244]

Along those lines, a March 2019 *Forbes*' article offered this insight:

Strzok testified that the mid-August 2016 text [about an insurance policy] was part of a larger conversation about protecting an "extremely sensitive source" as he and Page considered **how far to lean into the counterintelligence investigation into possible links between the Trump campaign and Russia**, as they didn't think Trump had a very good chance of beating Hillary Clinton in the election.[245]

Don't forget that is was the same Robert Mueller who was the Obama FBI director during the first years of Sheriff Arpaio's investigation of Obama's birth certificate. After Robert Mueller came James Comey.[246]

And, of course, we now know of Comey's attempt to flatly separate himself from the fake Christopher Steele dossier, as reported by *The Hill* in January 2019:

Comey claims he didn't know about [Bruce] Ohr's contacts with Steele, even though his top deputy, McCabe, got the first contact. **But none of that absolves his FBI, or the DOJ for that matter, from failing to divulge essential and exculpatory information** from Ohr to the FISA court.[247] (Emphasis added)

Later, after president Trump fired him, James Comey would publicly announce in an ABC News interview that Donald Trump was "morally unfit" to be the president of the United States.[248]

Fact #8—This Stops at Obama's Doorstep

However, the Deep-State, Obama-era connections to the *Mueller Report* *still go deeper…*

According to a striking statement made by the former director of the Obama administration's National Security Agency, James Clapper, the investigation into President Donald Trump started at the top—in the office of President Barack Obama.

> CLAPPER: **If it weren't for President Obama** we might not have done the intelligence community assessment that we did that set up a whole sequence of events which are still unfolding today, *notably Special Counsel Mueller's investigation.*
>
> *President Obama is responsible for that.* **It was *he who tasked us to do*** that intelligence community assessment in the first **place.**[249] (Emphasis added)

Ironically, the original context of Clapper's statement was that he was attempting to make certain that Obama got the "credit" for what Clapper thought, at the time, was President Trump's certain demise under the final outcome of the *Mueller Report.* It appeared that Clapper wanted the world to know Obama was the hero in this story—and that he, James Clapper, had said it first.[250]

Throughout most of the investigation, the Deep-State power players were more than certain that Robert Mueller's findings would prove to be Trump's Sword of Damocles. The sycophant mainstream media breathlessly reported on their confidence that the indictment sword would soon fall not only on Donald Trump, but also on members of President Trump's family.

By December 2018, *USA Today* was already whipping its base into a frenzy of almost certain expectancy:

> If Justice Department guidelines allowed it, ***there's no doubt Mueller would have already indicted Trump***. The ***net is closing in*** now on family and associates…
>
> **There is now no chance that Mueller's investigation will end with a whimper… there is almost certainly an indictment in the works for one of Trump's inner circle, possibly even a member of his family.**[251] (Emphasis added)

Similarly, the *New Yorker* reported:

> ***The criminality*** of the key figures in the President's inner circle ***is now established***, and they have started to ***implicate Trump himself***.[252] (Emphasis added)

The *New York Times*, in its unabashed pomposity, even went so far as to print a plan to actually go ahead and draft "Articles of Impeachment" against President Trump. That piece was also printed on the confident-laden anticipation of Mueller's certain-to-be findings that would ultimately condemn the president.[253]

However, the *Mueller Report* produced no such hoped-for outcome. In fact, the report effectively exonerated President Trump.[254] On top of that, Trump's Department of Justice, within weeks of the release of the *Mueller Report*, opened a probe of the Mueller investigation itself.[255] As of this writing, that probe is still continuing.

The Trump DOJ probe was being conducted under the suspicion that Mueller's inquest might have actually been predicated upon Christopher Steele's illegal fake dossier. That document, it turns out, had been well-known among Deep-State insiders to have been a fabricated fraud.[256]

In short, the "Trump colluded with Russia" narrative appeared to be collapsing right before the eyes of the Deep State. And, of all things, its demise was being ultimately pinned on the existence of a *fake fabricated document* that was engulfed in lies and intrigue. Any of this sound familiar?

But, because of James Clapper's grandiose announcement, what we *now have* is his embarrassing "oops" testimony stating that this whole matter traces directly back to Obama himself. Imagine that—a man who used a fraudulent document to identify his own legitimacy to hold the office of president, would be behind an "investigation plot" on another president that would ultimately involve a bogus document, one developed with the assistance of several foreign operatives. You can't make this stuff up.

Gee, those pesky fake documents produced by Deep-State operatives and pushed along, or ignored, by top government officials, and even outright lying to federal judges, as well as illegally spying on American citizens[257]—with the full support of the sycophant *fake media*—just keep showing up in this story. What are the odds?

Now, let's finally get to that December 2016 birth-certificate press conference.

Fact #9—The Explosive Third Press Conference

And so it was that in Sheriff Arpaio's publicly televised final press conference on December 15, 2016, the investigation demonstrated how the Obama PDF was nothing more than a manufactured digital file purporting to be a copy of "something"—but it certainly wasn't a copy of a legitimate birth document. It was, from the ground up, a forgery.

And here was the video evidence, right in front of the media's collective faces, in living color.[258] That evidence proved to be a massive humiliation to all who were directly or indirectly complicit in the years of orchestrated cover-up. So, obviously, they could never let the detailed results of that conference see the light of day.

The Video

During the hour-long presentation on that 2016 evening, an eight-minute, spell-binding video was aired, which vividly demonstrated how the Obama birth certificate had been digitally contrived. The fake Obama birth document was also shown to have commenced, more than likely, with a completely blank template that was then craftily pieced together by pulling bits, and even "groups," of information—in a digital cut-and-paste method—from legitimate Hawaiian birth certificates.

The video highlighted what was coined by the investigation as "9 points of forgery" on the Obama document. These handful of forgery illustrations that they were willing to publicly release focused on the angles of date stamps, as well as on groups of typed letters and words. [259]

One of the genuine birth certificates used in creating the Obama birth-certificate forgery—and examined in the forensic analysis—was revealed to have belonged to a Hawaiian-born woman named Johanna Ah'Nee.

The people who were gathered at that December 2016 conference witnessed certain portions of information from the Ah'Nee certificate being digitally "lifted" and placed, then perfectly aligned and mathematically juxtaposed atop Obama's document. Gasps of shock could be heard from a number of audience members as the fraud became glaringly obvious.

The upshot of the press conference was that those particular elements of info from Ah'Nee's birth certificate could not have possibly wound up, under normal circumstances, on Obama's PDF copy from an original that was truly on file at the Hawaii Department of Health, especially since those elements possessed such precision alignment, complete with the same ink splatters and overlaps of letters and words in adjoining information boxes, and at the exact same angles.

It would have been impossible that these things happened by "hand," and it could not have happened by digital manipulation back in the 1960s, when Obama's document was purported to have been originally created. The only way this could have happened would have been through a premeditated and carefully orchestrated digital forgery, available only in much more modern times—some thirty-plus years *after* Obama was born. The video presentation was something a third-grader could comprehend.

Two International Forensics Companies

In addition to this highly irrefutable evidence, the investigation also revealed that it had employed the services of two professional document examination entities, each located on different continents, and each using different and highly creditable forensic methods of examination.

These companies had been sought out to further examine the discoveries the MCSO investigation had uncovered, and to render professional, unbiased opinions in the matter. Neither of the two entities—*FORLABS* in Italy and *Reed Hayes Handwriting and Document Examiner* in Hawaii—was aware that the other was involved in the forensic process.[260]

Each of the two companies concluded that the Obama birth certificate PDF posted on the White House website was more than highly suspicious, containing numerous anomalies statistically consistent with a blatant forgery. They also concluded that the Ah'Nee birth document was in fact at least one of the documents used to create the image of Obama's supposed birth document.

A Forensic Bombshell

On the website of Reed Hayes Handwriting and Document Examiner, Hayes attests to these utterly shocking findings:

> In the past I have been **approached numerous times** to review the birth certificate issue. **I always refused,** *given my political leanings* **and the resulting potential for reaching biased opinions about the matter.**
>
> I finally agreed when…the Maricopa County Arizona Sheriff's

Office Cold Case Posse contacted me in November 2012, reminding myself that **as a handwriting and document examiner my duty is to allow whatever documentation I'm examining to speak for itself** and that I am not an advocate for either side or any party.... I have made a concerted effort to lay personal bias aside and work toward **the most objective opinions regarding the Obama birth certificate matter....**

As stated in my report...the COLB [Certificate of Live Birth] that I examined has **so many blatant oddities that it** *makes me wonder if this particular PDF may have been created in an effort to impeach President Obama.*

Surely the creator of the document (if it is in fact manufactured and not just a color scan) would have been sufficiently familiar with image editing programs **so as to not leave such numerous, noticeable discrepancies in the final product, unless it was intended as an impeachment tool.** Familiarity with basic scanning techniques and image editing procedures should have precluded **such obvious "mistakes."...**

My report also makes it clear that I suspect the document released by the White House **may be a fabricated document** *intended to bring down President Obama. ...*

In short, there are indications that the Obama Certificate of Live Birth released by the White House in April 2011 may be *a manufactured document* **or perhaps even** *an outright forgery.*[261] (Emphasis and brackets added)

Think of it. Hayes insists that the document he examined "has so many blatant oddities that it makes me wonder if this particular PDF may have been created in an effort to impeach President Obama."

He even attested that he believed the document might have been intended to be "an impeachment tool" that was fabricated for the purpose of "bringing down" a sitting president. Really? The PDF was that poorly constructed?

And, don't forget who put that document on the White House web-site in the first place. It was Obama's own administration. Sheriff Arpaio didn't post it there. Nor did Donald Trump.

Mr. Hayes' statements are monumental, because the PDF that he examined is in fact the exact document the Obama camp and the leftist media continues to lean on as evidence that a genuine document is on file at the Department of Health in Hawaii. That document can still be downloaded, as of this writing, on the Obama archived site, and can still be examined by any other legitimate examination company on the planet.[262]

The Bottom Line

The matter of a fake birth certificate's presence on the White House website, placed there by the Obama administration, appears to be a proven fact. What we have, in that specific document, is a professionally and forensically proven federal crime that obviously goes all the way to the Obama Oval Office.

This explosive revelation is the very thing that Sheriff Arpaio has been desperately trying to tell the nation for years. And this is what Congress, federal law enforcement officers, and the mainstream media have com-pletely ignored and/or tried to delegitimize. And, mark my words, this is also a huge part of what the Deep-State players so desperately do not want you to know, because so many are complicit in the cover-up, in one way or another. Sheriff Arpaio's investigative efforts were a monumental embarrassment to them.

So much for the leftist, fake-news, incessant claims that the Obama fraudulent birth-certificate conspiracy "has been debunked." That's just another leftist and fake news fairytale.

Fact #10—Perkins-Coie/Judith Corley/Loretta Fuddy

The saga goes even deeper. The PDF document on the White House website was *hand delivered* to the Obama administration by a partner in the law firm of Perkins Coie. Her name is Judith Corley.

Look at the verification of this fact, as documented on a Washington, DC, legal site, dated April 2011:

It fell to a partner from the Washington office of Perkins Coie [263] to obtain a copy of President Barack Obama's original birth certificate.

According to copies of letters released today by White House officials, *partner Judith Corley* **initiated the process** last week and **planned to travel to Hawaii to pick up two copies. Corley represents the president** in his personal matters, a job she assumed last year when Robert Bauer left Perkins Coie to become White House counsel.

Corley wrote to *Loretta Fuddy* **in Hawaii's state health department on April 22. "I am writing on behalf of my client, President Barack Obama,"** the letter begins.

[It was] confirmed in a news conference today **that Corley did travel personally to Honolulu to pick up copies of the birth certificate.**[264] (Emphasis added)

Now, consider Hayes' words again, particularly those that "wonder if" this PDF "may have been created in an effort to impeach President Obama." Let's now ask the obvious question: "Then…*who was it* that created and/or handled this document?"

So far, we know of only three people: Hawaii Department of Health director Loretta Fuddy, senior partner of Perkins Coie Judith Corley, and whoever actually posted the PDF on the White House website.

Furthermore, if that document was falsely created or manipulated, then why did an "innocent" Obama, or any of his attorneys, not quickly spot these "so many anomalies" and track down the forger(s) themselves? In what real-life scenario can you imagine that the administration of a legitimate president would completely ignore, or miss, a criminally explosive situation like that?

So, what was the media's reaction after that final and devastating press conference, and the findings from Reed Hayes Handwriting and Document Examiner and FORLAB? It was a virtual media shutdown—again. Not a snippet of detailed forensic findings revealed at the conference was relayed to American national television news audiences. It was as if the conference had never been held and the independent expert analyses were never conducted.[265]

The Loretta Fuddy Mystery

As we move forward, we certainly must examine the suspicious case of Loretta Fuddy, especially given the fact that she was the official who physically delivered the Hawaiian birth certificate PDF information to the Perkins Coie partner, Judith Corley.

At this point, Loretta Fuddy would be a key witness in the Obama birth saga. *Right?* Especially in light of document examiner Reed Hayes' allegations that the PDF eventually posted was so "filled with mistakes" that it looked to him like it "may be a fabricated document intended to bring down President Obama."

Wouldn't we want to ask Ms. Fuddy: *Is the PDF info on the White House website the very same info you gave Obama's legal representative—or had it been changed from what you originally gave them?*

Well, conveniently, the world will never get to hear from Loretta Fuddy.

That's because on December 13, 2013, she mysteriously died as the result of a Hawaiian commuter plane crash. Out of nine total souls on board, including the pilot, Loretta Fuddy was the only one who died. *Hawaii News Now* reported that "her cause of death was listed as an irregular heartbeat triggered by stress."[266]

Fuddy was appointed to her position by Governor Abercrombie just *three months before* Obama's long-form "birth certificate" finally made its April 2011 debut on the White House website. *You know...* the certificate to which Hawaii Governor Neil Abercrombie had previously claimed to have had absolutely no access.

Think of it. Just a little more than a year and a half after Obama's birth certificate was posted on the White House server, the newly appointed Fuddy, the only one who would know from whence that information would have originated, was dead. Her voice would never be heard concerning what really happened. How utterly convenient for Barack Obama and company.

The intrigue deepened, yet again.

Who Was Loretta Fuddy?

This leaves us with another obvious question: Who was Loretta Fuddy, and what was her connection to Obama?

Prepare for another jaw-dropping revelation.

In January 2014, an *American Thinker* investigative article documented the startling connections like this:

> Ann Soetoro [Dunham, Barack Obama's supposed mother] and Loretta Fuddy appear to have one **very odd thing in common: both have been linked to the Subud cult, which originated in, of all places, Indonesia** and was founded by the Javanese Muslim Muhammed Subuh.
>
> Note also that **the World Subud organization seems to have been based** in, of all cities…wait for it…*Chicago.*
>
> *Indonesia…Chicago…Hawaii…three locales linked to Obama's life.*
>
> **Now to Ann Soetoro. She was linked to Subud** by her biographer (and *New York Times* reporter) Janny Scott (Harvard '77) in the book *A Singular Woman: The Untold Story of Barack Obama's Mother*, reviewed by the *New York Times.*
>
> …**Of all the persons…that could have been installed as Director of the State Department of Health in Hawaii**, Hawaii alighted on Fuddy—**a leader of a small cult with roots in Indonesia and connections to Ann Soetoro—Obama's mother.**

Second, observe that Fuddy **assumed the Director position in Hawaii in January 2011, just a few months before the release of Obama's long form birth certificate.**[267] (Emphasis and brackets added, parentheses in original)

This revelation brings to mind the old adage, *Where there's smoke, there's surely a fire somewhere nearby.* The problem here is that not only can we see the voluminous column of smoke; we can also hear the crackling of the roaring flame that produced the smoke.

Fact #11—The Deep-State River Runs Through It

Thankfully, America now knows so much more about the infamous Steele dossier and the involvement of the Hillary Clinton 2016 presidential campaign[268] in suborning that fabricated document filled with false information. You know, the same Hillary Clinton who actually fueled the initial "birther movement."

We are also now privy to the various levels of involvement of the DNC, the Perkins Coie Law Firm; and the Obama FBI and DOJ in the Steele dossier matter[269] and the subsequent lying to a FISA court judge that took place by certain government law enforcement officials during the investigation on Donald Trump. That document was fabricated for the sole purpose of illegally spying on his associates, campaign, and the Trump administration.[270]

Knowing all of these facts, and seeing the obvious Deep-State connections involved, why would anyone still express any doubt whatsoever that some of the very same Deep-State players might also have constructed a fake birth certificate in order to prop up an ineligible holder of the office of the president of the United States, especially if those same operatives thought they had the mainstream media in their back pockets—and particularly if they knew they themselves were culpable in the matter of buttressing a man who didn't possess proper birth documents? Of course they **would**. And, apparently, they did.

John Brennan's CIA Connection

Then, in yet another stunning revelation, it was reported that under the John Brennan years as the director of the CIA, there may have been nefarious involvement by the agency in the actual birth-certificate saga.[271]

But that wasn't the only publicly voiced suspicion of John Brennan's potential key roles in certain Deep-State matters of highly questionable intrigue. Even *Newsweek* ran a 2019 article with the title: "Republicans Claim John Brennan Was the 'Evil Force' behind the Intel's Use of Steele's Dossier: They tried to bring down a sitting president." [272]

Could it be that our own CIA, assisted by other Deep-State players, would be involved in such atrocities? Was there really an attempted *coup* of Donald Trump's presidency? If so, did it have anything at all to do with Trump's involvement in Obama's birth-certificate fraud and his present ability to expose the truth of the matter, as well as numerous other Deep-State ploys?

A Coup Attempt?

Victor Davis Hanson is a senior fellow in military history at the Hoover Institution at Stanford University and a professor emeritus of classics at California State University, Fresno. He is the author of more than two dozen books, ranging in topics from ancient Greece to modern America, most recently *The Case for Trump*.

In late November 2019, Hanson wrote a piece for Fox News in which he made his case for a genuine attempted coup against President Trump. Following are a few excerpts from that telling article:

> **Trump's critics have also radically changed their spin on "coups."** **To them, "coup" is no longer a dirty word** trafficked in by right-wing conspiracists. Instead, it has been normalized as a possibly legitimate **means of aborting the Trump presidency.**

Mark Zaid, the attorney representing the Ukraine whistle-blower, boasted in two recently discovered tweets of ongoing efforts *to stage a coup to remove Trump.*

"**#coup has started.** First of many steps. **#rebellion. #impeachment will follow,**" Zaid tweeted in January 2017.

Retired Admiral William H. McRaven recently wrote an op-ed for The New York Times all but **calling for Trump's ouster—***"the sooner the better."*

No sooner had Trump been elected than Rosa Brooks, a former Defense Department official during the Obama administration, wrote an essay for Foreign Policy magazine discussing theoretical ways to remove Trump before the 2020 election, among them *a scenario involving a military coup.*

In September 2018, The New York Times published an op-ed from an anonymous White House official who boasted of supposedly **widescale efforts inside** the Trump administration *to nullify its operations and subvert presidential directives.*[273] (Emphasis added)

One must also consider the fact that even after the failure of the *Mueller Report* to "bring down" President Trump, that report was almost immediately followed by the Trump impeachment proceedings. As of this writing, that inquest is still underway.

In the last days of the November 2019 impeachment hearings, Victor Davis Hanson had this to say about the fiasco:

On the first day of the impeachment inquiry, House Intelligence Committee Chairman Adam Schiff, D-Calif., called his initial two witnesses, career State Department diplomats William Taylor Jr. and George Kent. Far from providing damning evidence of criminal presidential behavior, Taylor and Kent mostly confined themselves to three topics: their own sterling résumés, their lack of any firsthand knowledge of incriminating Trump action, and their poorly hidden disgust with the manner and substance of Trump's foreign policy.[274]

Was an impeachment inquiry just one more Deep-State "insurance policy," poised to be enacted in case the Mueller investigation failed to produce the desired result? After reading the preceding pages of this chapter, what would be *your* best guess?

One might call these kinds of conjectures mere "conspiracy theories." I call the process *critical thinking*—and not being afraid to ask the obvious questions, ones that the mainstream media refuses to ask.

Fact #12—This Is Not Over

My, my. How much deeper can this get?

Think of the ramifications of what we have uncovered and documented thus far. Since it now appears, beyond any reasonable doubt, that the birth certificate is a forensically proven forgery—from the ground up—we have to ask the million-dollar question: *Why?*

Why would a sitting US president and/or the people around him feel the need to fabricate a fake document of identification? In reality, there are only a few plausible answers, and none of them are good ones. The most obvious response is that Obama simply doesn't possess a legitimate United States birth certificate. In that case, he and everyone who assisted him in the ruse are complicit in the biggest act of treason ever perpetrated upon this nation. And, in that case, the office of the commander-in-chief of the world's largest nuclear arsenal and the number-one hyperpower on the planet was usurped by an undocumented alien.

The only other genuine options are these. One might be that Barack Obama has a legitimate birth certificate, but there's a piece of information on that certificate that he did not want, and still doesn't want, the American public to see.

The other scenario might be that he *does* have a legitimate birth certificate, with all the correct information on it, none of which he originally
wished to hide from anyone. However, he simply decided he would run
a scam on the American people for the purpose of sheer political obfuscation—and for the goal of giving him and his supporters the opportunity
to make the conservatives who thought otherwise look like a bunch of
fools.

The problem with any of those options, as insidious as any one of
them might sound, is that they still leave Barack Obama and all the culpable ones around him vulnerable to several federal crimes. Those felonies would at least include the production and subsequent presentation
of fabricated and forged identifying documents—no matter what the reason—and then posting them on a government website—*the White House
website.*

Do you see what I mean?

There simply isn't a good reason for this crime to have been committed. Now perhaps you have a better feel for why the Deep-State players
have been so revved up over this issue—for years.

I assure you, within this one chapter, we've only begun to peel back
the numerous onion-skin layers of the entire story. Some elements of
this saga are already public, but were just too detailed to include in this
discussion. And yet other specifics have still never been released to the
nation. Perhaps that information will ultimately be disclosed within the
context of a legitimate legal hearing, at the federal level, and relatively free
of Deep-State sway.

Just a few weeks before I finished writing this chapter, I was talking
on the phone with former Sheriff Joe Arpaio. I was preparing to go on the
radio that very afternoon to host my own program.

Joe Arpaio told me, "Carl, tell your audience, this is not over. Tell
them that I am continually sending important information over to the
United States Attorney General. I assure you Carl, *this is not over.* That's
all I can say right now."

I believe him.

Disclaimer

All the information in this chapter pursuant to the MCSO Obama birth-certificate investigation is a matter of public record and has been widely reported by several public media sources and on the author's own radio programs—as clearly indicated by the references listed in the endnotes. Absolutely no confidential information that has not already been released to the public has been reproduced in this chapter.

chapter four

Egregores and Body Counts

At the close of chapter 2, I introduced the idea that Shadowland's egregores or demons by any other name can play a role in geopolitics and cultural phenomena, including America's current descent into chaos, and this by design.

Years ago, I recall watching when, for the first time in history, Catholic authorities allowed network television to broadcast an exorcism. Permission was given to ABC's *20/20* to cover the event, and on April 5, 1991, the ritual was televised. The extraordinary moment was a first for network programming, yet something about the show caused my thoughts to wander. In the past, I had been involved with cases of exorcism (on two published accounts, I and others actually witnessed "manifestations" outside our understanding of physics), but now I questioned if perhaps we were missing something bigger—a comparison between what leads to individual possession and a wider cultural phenomenon known in fashionable theology as "geographical demonic strongholds."

I soon questioned that if personal conduct was one route to opening doors to diabolical invasion on the individual level, might nations similarly come under siege to a larger "hive" of nefarious powers through collective behavioral or gestured invitation to evil by those having governing authority? Most adults are aware that if people who preside over legislative bodies sense public apathy, they may abandon their responsibility to govern for the good of the people and, in worst-case scenarios, begin using their positions in power for their own elitist or even occultist aspirations. If this is allowed to continue via the public's indifference and/or lawmakers turning a blind eye, the result can be, according to demonology and select case studies, the regional increase of evil supernaturalism.

To some believers, the origins of this phenomenon began in the distant past when "a fire in the minds" of angels caused Lucifer to exalt himself above the good of God's creation. The once-glorified spirit was driven by an unequivocal thirst to rule, conquer, and dominate. His fall spawned similar lust among his followers, which continues today among human agents of dark authority who guard privileged "cause-and-effect" relationships between supernaturalism and the opportunity for lordship over societies.

The objectives of the occult masters and the very real forces they serve are typically unperceived by average citizens, yet, according to sacred texts, such a collaboration exists between unregenerate architects of society and fallen angels. If the electorate becomes bewitched by this truth, humans in league with demons can increase their control of the machine of municipal government through sophisticated networks of both visible and invisible principalities. This happens subconsciously or intentionally among those vulnerable to the sinister activity.

Multitudes may never comprehend this fact, and that is why some cannot see beyond "flesh and blood" or hold as real the hungry ambitions of "principalities…powers…rulers of darkness…and spiritual wickedness in high places" (Ephesians 6:12). Nevertheless, in my opinion, a complete evaluation of recent American history must take into account not only the visible agents of government, but the significant interaction between spiritual and human personalities.

Among the great religions, there is belief that three sources of spiritual power affect nations: 1) divine influence, proceeding from the domain of God; 2) satanic influence, coming from the sphere of Satan; and 3) human influence. This third influence, being neutral, is available as a conduit for good or evil as it submits to divine or satanic control.

Throughout history, there have been governments and leaders who resisted evil and adhered to the statutes of God. These spoiled the strategies of corrupt minions, both visible and invisible, and made possible the blessing of those nations.

Conversely, there have been times in history when bureaucracy turned its back on higher law, opening the door for "evil angels" (Psalm 78:49) to pervade the direction of societies. These were times when darkness and/or Machiavellian trickery took root in the mindset of majorities, and systems of government and philosophy were influenced by fiendish, unseen counterparts.

As an example, to the ancient city of Corinth, a city known for its pride, ostentation, and lasciviousness (which not only was tolerated, but consecrated through the worship of Venus), Paul said to the church, "the god of this world [Satan] hath blinded the minds of them which believe not" (2 Corinthians 4:4).

Supernaturalism ruling from the air above Corinth "blinded" the perception of Corinthians until the latter were incapable of recognizing their moral and social decay.

It's interesting that the apostle would send this warning to the city of Corinth—a Greek prototype of America's wealth, military strength, and great mental activity.[275] Outwardly, one would have thought these educated gnostics were well equipped intellectually to understand the spiritual ramifications and social significance of their actions. Yet, Paul said their minds had been blinded by the god of this world. Their superior human knowledge, though impressive to intelligentsia, had not protected the Corinthians from the subtle influences filling the atmosphere around them.

It is within this unseen arena of malevolent rulers that some men are organized. Under dark influence, they become orchestrated within a great evil system (or empire) described in various passages as a satanic order. In more than thirty important biblical texts, the Greek New Testament employs the term *kosmos*, which describes this invisible organization or "government behind government" where human ego—separated from God—becomes hostile to the service of others while viewing mankind as personal commodities.

Emanating from this *kosmos*, "old ones" master the air in and around willing men's minds. These deceiving spirits and their invisible cronies operate behind and within influential human colleagues, ordering the activities of entities under their command until every stage of earthly administrations can be influenced by their presence.

According to the Bible, it is this dominion that stands at odds with communities of the world. With vivid testimony to this, Satan offered Jesus all the power and glory of the governments of this world, saying, "All this power [control] will I give thee, and the glory of them [earthly cities]: for that is delivered unto me: and to whomsoever I will I give it. If thou therefore wilt worship me, all shall be thine" (Luke 4:6–7).

Jesus declined the offer from the "prince of the powers of the air."

Throughout history, others have not.

This is a picture of a global system average people never comprehend. If most could see through this veil into the invisible world inhabiting our planet, they would find a reality alive with good against evil, a place where the prize is the souls of men and where legions war for control of its cities and people. The end game for the darkest of these powers—together with their human counterparts—is to stand in the place of God, incarnated and ruling the nations with an iron fist.

I believe this is what we see unfolding now, and it ultimately will require human sacrifice to satisfy the personal and political ambitions of such spirits and men.

How do I know this?

I suspect examples of such have been ongoing for at least the past fifty years of American history and intentionally elevated in recent years as we near the time of the end.

Shadowland's Body Counts

It was the year 1994 and I was actively involved as an evangelist and senior pastor in the Assemblies of God organization when the film *The Clinton Chronicles: An Investigation into the Alleged Criminal Activities*

of Bill Clinton (directed by Jeremiah Films CEO Patrick Matrisciana—
a man who would later become an acquaintance when we both served
with Dr. Chuck Missler as Koinonia Institute Gold Medallion recipients
with senior organizational recognition) burst onto the scene. The movie
was shocking in that it purported to offer eyewitness testimony involving
very serious accusations levelled against Bill and Hillary Clinton, including money laundering, criminal conspiracy, and murder. While the film
was directed by Matrisciana, "the production was credited to Citizens for
Honest Government, a project of a Westminster, California, organization
named Creative Ministries Inc. that had connections to Matrisciana."[276] It
was partially funded by Larry Nichols, who served as Bill Clinton's marketing director for the Arkansas Development Finance Authority in 1988
but who was later fired and became a Clinton opponent. The project was
distributed with help from Rev. Jerry Falwell, who also appeared in the
film.[277]

Chronicles was the first of numerous independent investigations since
that have focused on a "Clinton Body Count" list of associates, people
whom the Clintons are alleged to have had murdered to conceal information that could otherwise threaten to expose involvement with criminal
activity, including:

- Bill Clinton using the office of governor and later the office of
  president to facilitate affairs with or harassing numerous women
- Troopergate, using Arkansas State Police officers to facilitate sex-
  ual liaisons and to intimidate accusers
- Misuse of funds with the Arkansas Development Finance Authority
- Using Bank of Credit and Commerce International to launder
  money
- Profiting from drug smuggling at the Mena, Arkansas, Airport
- Protecting Barry Seals' drug-smuggling activities (Seals was a Trans
  World Airlines [TWA] pilot who became a major drug smug-
  gler for the Medellín Cartel. When he was convicted of smug-
  gling charges, he became an informant for the Drug Enforcement

Administration and testified in several major drug trials. He was murdered in 1986 by contract killers believed to have been hired by Pablo Escobar, head of the Medellín Cartel.)[278]

- Murdering several witnesses to the Mena, Arkansas, drug-smuggling operation
- Covering up the circumstances surrounding the deaths of two boys, Kevin Ives and Don Henry, whose bodies were found on railroad tracks and who supposedly had knowledge of the Mena drug-smuggling operation
- Protecting a state medical examiner who was accused of misstating the cause of death in several autopsies
- The Whitewater controversy, including money laundering and bank fraud
- Using contacts at the Rose Law Firm in Little Rock, Arkansas, to shred documents that would have implicated Clinton in other scandals
- Covering up the cause of death of Vince Foster

Was Vince Foster "Suicided"?

Fifteen years after the release of *The Clinton Chronicles*, I published the book *Journalism Is War* by Pulitzer Prize-nominated investigative reporter for the *Washington Times*, George Archibald. In that work, Archibald recounted how he had been assigned to get to the bottom of the death of Vincent Foster, who had been a leading attorney at the Little Rock, Arkansas, Rose Law Firm, "where Hillary Clinton was a partner when Bill Clinton was governor of Arkansas for 12 years. The Clintons and Vince and Lisa Foster were best friends," noted Archibald, before adding:

As governor, Clinton said one of his few social pleasures was frequent visits to the Foster home, where he swam in the pool and partied with a close circle of friends. It was natural for President-elect Clinton to ask lifelong friend Vince Foster to be deputy counsel at the White House when he was elected as president in November 1992.

But what went wrong that led Vince Foster to blow his brains out with a .38-caliber revolver at Fort Marcy Park near McLean, Virginia, off the George Washington Parkway, on July 20, 1993?

When it happened, many conservative opponents of the Clinton administration expressed doubts that it was even a suicide.

Reed Irvine of Accuracy in Media beat the drum for years saying it was not a suicide and suggested all sorts of scenarios from murder to unexplained death elsewhere....

While Bill Clinton, as governor, was having sexual liaisons with Gennifer Flowers and other women in Little Rock and elsewhere, his wife Hillary was having her own romance with law partner Vince Foster, which ultimately became a full-blown affair. Arkansas state troopers who were members of the governor's security detail said Foster often visited Hillary at the governor's mansion when Clinton was out of town, traveling around Arkansas.

My reporting of the Hillary Clinton-Vince Foster affair was confirmed in 1996 by historian and investigative reporter Roger Morris in his book, *Partners in Power: The Clintons and Their America*: "There would be several sources—including a former U.S. attorney, sometime aides, a number of lawyers, social friends, and many of the same [Arkansas state] troopers who testified about the governor's illicit acts—who described the First Lady's affair, dating to the mid-1980s, with Rose partner Vince Foster. A relationship evident in the semiprivate kisses and furtive squeezes at parties and dinners described by the security guards, it was also an intimate professional bond between two attorneys who worked together on some of their firm's most sensitive cases.

Many thought that the governor was well aware of the affair and ultimately accepted it as one more implicit bargain in their marriage. Clinton continued to treat Vince Foster as the close friend he had been since childhood in Hope, even entrusting him with some of the most crucial secrets of the 1992 campaign. 'Bill knew, of course he knew. But what the hell was he supposed to say to anybody about being faithful,'" Morris quoted "a lawyer close to Foster who was familiar with them all."

Morris reported, as we found, that many Clinton friends and associates thought Hillary Clinton's relationship with Vince Foster "was an understandable and natural response to her husband's behavior. Foster was known to treat her with dignity, respect, and abiding love she was missing in her marriage."

Arkansas state troopers told us that Hillary Clinton and Vince Foster frequently spent time together at a cabin retreat of the Rose Law Firm in Heber Springs, Arkansas, in the lake country north of Little Rock.[279]

Archibald's investigation for the *Times* confirmed suspicions that Foster had become increasingly concerned that someone was going to blow the whistle on his affair with Hillary, as well as the fear over big problems with the Clintons' unfiled personal income tax returns over several prior years "because accountants had cooked numbers regarding gains and losses on the Clintons' Whitewater real estate investments [that] various state and federal Whitewater investigations and criminal prosecutions" overshadowed.[280]

These stresses, combined with turmoil surrounding Foster's wife and children (still back in Little Rock), are often cited as causing Foster to fall "into deep mental depression," resulting in his killing himself with a revolver gunshot wound through his mouth. While Archibald ultimately concluded that Foster's death really was suicide and not murder, when his body was found at Fort Marcy Park overlooking the Potomac River, some saw more questions than answers raised, as Cliff Kincaid for Accuracy in Media reported May 26, 2016:

Foster is the man who knew too much. He had knowledge of various Clinton scandals, including Travelgate, the Waco tragedy, and possibly some illegal activities involving national security. His body was found in a Virginia park on July 20, 1993, and the media accepted the verdict of suicide.

But as AIM founder and late chairman Reed Irvine and I reported on the case, there were so many anomalies that the Special Division of the Court of Appeals ordered an appendix added to Independent Counsel Kenneth Starr's report on the death of Vincent Foster. The appendix exposed serious flaws in the report that cast strong doubt on the suicide finding. These anomalies included:

- No bullet was ever found in Fort Marcy Park, even though Foster supposedly shot himself there.
- The gun that was found in his hand has never been positively identified as his.
- Foster's fingerprints were not found on the gun.[281]

Though Archibald disagreed with Kincaid and Irvine's conclusions, he did see evidence of criminal conspiracy otherwise connected with the Clintons, writing:

Hillary Clinton, who had just returned to the United States from an Asian trip, also orchestrated a White House cover-up of documents in Foster's office on the night he died, because they included all the Clintons' tax records for the prior four years and documents relating to their controversial Whitewater real estate investments.

On Hillary Clinton's orders, late at night on July 20, 1993, while Foster's body lay in the George Washington hospital morgue, several of their staff entered the deputy White House counsel's office suite and removed at least three boxes of Vince Foster's documents from file drawers in his personal office.

It was discovered just months later and reported by *The Times'* intrepid investigative reporter Jerry Seper that the removed documents included records of Hillary Clinton's involvement as a lawyer in behalf of Rose Law Firm managing partner Webster Hubbell's father-in-law, Seth Ward, who was an investor in one of the Whitewater real estate developments.

The boxes were stashed in a closet in the Clintons' White House residential quarters. This was obstruction of the ongoing Vince Foster homicide/suicide law enforcement investigation, pure and simple. The work product reflected in the documents related to Foster's death.

Hillary Clinton's staff loyalists, under directions of Craig Livingstone, known as "dirty works czar" for the Clintons, also wiped material off Foster's computer hard-drive in his office, meticulously kept by his able career civil service assistant, Linda Tripp, who immediately noticed the changes when the grieving staff arrived at the White House on the morning following the suicide.

Tripp told FBI agents about the computer tampering and missing documents when they interviewed her as part of the homicide investigation. For her honesty, Tripp was summarily transferred from the White House to another post at the Pentagon to get her out of the way.

Several years later, Clinton loyalists also transferred young White House intern Monica Lewinsky to Tripp's office at the Pentagon in an effort to save Bill Clinton from himself as he carried on his steamy sexual liaison with Lewinsky. Two women scorned got together, had sympathy for each other, and Tripp got the Lewinsky story out to the media. The rest is history.[282]

Fast forward to June 9, 2017, and Texas congressman Pete Olson went on the Houston-based *Sam Malone Show* and shocked many by saying, "President Bill Clinton intimidated the government's lead lawyer into not seeking an indictment of Hillary Clinton [during the infamous June 27, 2016, tarmac meeting with Loretta Lynch that some believe proved Obama's administration was colluding with Hillary Clinton's campaign to get her elected to the presidency and to cover up her 'gross negligence' and mishandling of classified information on her private email server when she was secretary of state] by telling her, "We killed Vince Foster."

"I guarantee you," Olson said, "they had the conversation where he basically said, 'Mrs. Lynch, call your attack dog off. We've killed people. We killed Vince Foster. We destroyed Webb Hubbell. We will destroy you.' And then what happens to things?," Olson continued. "All of a sudden—well, she did it, yeah, it was all terrible, don't know who got the information, very classified. But no indictment."[283]

Donald Trump later weighed in on the death of Foster as well, insinuating that the Clintons had him murdered, pointing to "very serious" questions about the crime scene that indicated foul play and circumstances of Foster's suicide being "very fishy."[284]

Laura Ingraham's LifeZette website also picked up this tome, intimating that the Clintons were somehow involved in orchestrating Foster's "suicide" as well as being "involved in the murders of several political operatives."[285]

Ingraham's news website even produced a video titled *Clinton Body Count*, which featured an anonymous reporter detailing how "the Clintons have a long history of people in their inner circle dying under mysterious circumstances" before adding that: "Since the 2016 election cycle began, at least three more people with connections to Bill and Hillary have joined that list, sparking a renewed interest in the so-called body count of people who allegedly got in the way of the Clinton machine."[286]

Even before Jeffrey Epstein's name was added to that voluminous list of people connected to the Clintons and possibly possessing incriminating information about them, we and others like Ann Coulter were warning authorities to "Move Epstein to a Super Max Prison Before He Is 'Suicided,'"[287] which obviously went unheeded long enough for his death to occur.

We'll discuss the Epstein case and its connections to murder in the next chapter, but for people unfamiliar with the "Clinton Body Count" list (which numbers from dozens of victims to hundreds, depending on which published inventory one reads), this involves insinuations or conspiracy theories surrounding Bill and Hillary as tied to the murders of countless people, a growing directory that has circulated since the early '90s when GOP activist Linda Thompson began circulating the first group of twenty-six names of victims. Subsequently, her report led to former California Representative William Dannemeyer in 1994 calling for a hearing into the matter. In a letter to congressional leaders, Dannemeyer listed two dozen people "with some connection to then-President Clinton who had died 'under other than natural circumstances.'"[288]

"Bill and Hillary's 'friends' fall off buildings, crash planes, die in freak accidents," noted WorldNetDaily in a recent repost of their similar "Clinton Death List: 33 Spine-Tingling Cases."[289]

"How many people do you personally know who have died mysteriously?," the staff at WND asked, and continued:

How about in plane crashes or car wrecks?

Bizarre suicides?

People beaten to death or murdered in a hail of bullets?

And what about violent freak accidents—like separate mountain biking and skiing collisions in Aspen, Colorado? Or barbells crushing a person's throat?

Apparently, if you're Bill or Hillary Clinton, the answer to that question is at least 33—and possibly many more.[290]

Notable names on WND's "Clinton Body Count" lists include:

- DNC staffer Seth Rich, who was found murdered near his affluent neighborhood in Washington, DC. And while some liberal news sources reported Seth was not murdered by "a squad of assassins working for Hillary Clinton,"[291] others weren't so sure the DNC had not ordered the hit. "It was a contract kill, obviously," White House chief strategist Steve Bannon texted to a CBS *60 Minutes* producer at the time.[292] Newt Gingrich added, "We have this very strange story now of this young man who worked for the Democratic National Committee, who apparently was assassinated at 4 in the morning, having given WikiLeaks something like 53,000 e-mails and 17,000 attachments. Nobody's investigating that, and what does that tell you about what's going on? Because it turns out, it wasn't the Russians. It was this young guy who, I suspect, was disgusted by the corruption of the Democratic National Committee."[293] The Wikileaks treasure trove of emails accordingly revealed "the inner workings of the Clinton Crime Family, otherwise known as 'Clinton Inc.,'" as reported by Coreys Digs. "Within the 20,000-page archive of Podesta emails, the pieces came together to form a network of organized criminal activity, which long-time Clinton aide, Doug Band, referred to as 'Bill Clinton, Inc.' Among the…Wikileaks dump, a 12 page memo detailed how the Clinton aide, who played a key role in the formation of the Clinton Global Initiative, Clinton Foundation, and Teneo Holdings, used his position as a gate-keeper for Bill Clinton, intermingling a tangled web of charity vs. for-profit as well as personal business vs. official business."[294]

- Former United Nations General Assembly President John Ashe, who was found with his throat crushed just before he was scheduled to testify with Chinese businessman and codefendant Ng Lap Seng, who was accused of smuggling millions of dollars into the US, hundreds of thousands of which were illegally funneled into the Democratic National Committee during the Clinton administration.
- MI6 spy Gareth Williams, who had allegedly hacked secret data on Bill Clinton and whose dead body "was found naked, padlocked and stuffed in a 32-inch by 19-inch duffel bag that was sitting in his London bathtub."[295]
- James McDougal, the Clintons' former business partner at the Whitewater Development Corporation, who was found dead "of a heart attack" in a federal prison hospital. At the time, the

Baltimore Sun reported that McDougal "had been cooperating with independent counsel Kenneth W. Starr in the Whitewater investigation," and "his death appears to reduce the legal risks to President Clinton and Hillary Rodham Clinton, and was a clear setback to Starr and his prosecutors."[296]

The list above goes on and on and includes numerous Epstein investigators, some of whom also "died" under mysterious circumstances while on the case (for instance, Palm Beach detective Joseph Recarey, who was being followed, and his trash was rifled with while political pressure was being levelled against him as his discoveries of physical evidence mounted),[297] as well as former Clinton confidantes like Eric Butera, a mole with information on murder; former White House intern Mary Caitrin Mahoney; NBC cameraman John Hillyer, who had been working on the Mena drug-smuggling operation tied to the Clintons; Ed Willey, whose wife, Kathleen (a White House volunteer), became suspicious that the former first lady had Ed murdered; Jerry Luther Parks, "who had been head of security for Bill Clinton's headquarters in Little Rock, Arkansas, during the 1992 presidential campaign and gubernatorial years," who was shot through the rear window of his car with a semiautomatic handgun, whom WND reported had been watching a news bulletin on the death of Vincent Foster when he turned from the television and muttered, 'I'm a dead man.'"[298]

Of course, if we wanted, we could extend the body-count lists beyond the Clintons and Epstein. As I write this chapter, people who accused actor Kevin Spacey of sexual assault are also dying mysterious deaths and falling like dominoes.[299]

But, let's move on, and in the next chapter look at additions to body-count lists more germane to this study, ones about which I will offer opinions—based on known occult signatures and symbolism—that suggest far more than pedophilism was going on at Jeffrey Epstein's "Orgy Island."

Brace yourself, as this includes elitist, Deep-State devil worship…and human sacrifice…

chapter five

Jeffrey Epstein and Shadowland's
Deals with the Devil

In the last chapter, we introduced the idea of Deep-State "body count lists" with the promise that in this chapter we would discuss the man on everybody's mind so recently linked to such inventories—well-connected billionaire and convicted sex offender and trafficker Jeffrey Epstein.

That said, how many know Epstein's association with powerful financial, political, foreign, and domestic spy agencies; organized crime and intelligence assets; private research facilities like the Massachusetts Institute of Technology; monster media conglomerates including the *New York Times*; and countless other cultural elites (hundreds of whom he likely was blackmailing. His infamous little black book held the names of over a thousand such individuals he secretly recorded during sordid orgies at his private island and luxury homes using bugging devices, two-way mirrors, and cameras hidden inside walls [and at least one woman's sensational claims say she was forced in these facilities to have sex with Joe Biden and John McCain])[300] was also connected to dark, pedophilic sex magick?

Before I bring that to light, let me state the obvious.

Epstein was a wealthy financier who molested and facilitated the molestation of numerous children:

After an investigation, prosecution, and plea negotiations, Epstein pleaded guilty and was convicted by a Florida state court of "soliciting a prostitute" and of procuring an underage girl for prostitution on June 30, 2008. He served almost 13 months in custody, with work release, as part of a plea deal; federal officials had identified 36 girls, some as young as 14 years old, who had been molested. Epstein was arrested again on July 6, 2019, on federal charges for sex trafficking of minors in Florida and New York. He died on August 10, 2019, in his jail cell.[301]

On July 23, 2019, three weeks prior to his death, Epstein was found unconscious in his jail cell with injuries to his neck. After that incident, he was placed on suicide watch. Six days later, on July 29, he was taken off suicide watch and placed in a special housing unit with another inmate. The jail had informed the Justice Department that Epstein would have a cellmate and that a guard would look into the cell every thirty minutes. These procedures were not followed on the night of his death. On August 9, Epstein's cellmate was transferred out, and no new replacement cellmate was brought in. Later in the evening, in violation of the jail's normal procedure, Epstein was not being checked every thirty minutes. The two guards who were assigned to check his jail unit that night claimed to have fallen asleep and did not check on him for about three hours. The next morning, Epstein was found dead.

Epstein's removal from suicide watch so soon after he had been found with injuries to his neck, and in such a high-security federal facility, left some prison experts "stunned and angry." Attorney General William Barr ordered an investigation by the Department of Justice Inspector General in addition to the investigation by the Federal Bureau of Investigation, saying that he was "appalled" by Epstein's death in federal custody. Two days later, Barr said there had been "serious irregularities" in the prison's handling of Epstein, promising: "We will get to the bottom of what happened, and there will be accountability."

The evening before Epstein died, he had been in good spirits, according to a source familiar with the case. Epstein told one of his lawyers before they left on Friday, the day before his death, "I'll see you Sunday." Throughout his meetings with his lawyers, which occurred seven days a week and lasted up to twelve hours a day, he remained positive. Epstein was confident that he was going to win the double-jeopardy motion in connection with his related 2008 Florida conviction. Epstein also had hope that, on appeal, he would get bail. The appeal was pending before the US Second Circuit Court of Appeals at the time of his death. On July 23, when Epstein was found unconscious in his jail cell with injuries to his neck, he told his lawyers that his cellmate, the cop, had roughed him up.

The circumstances surrounding Epstein's "suicide" quickly spawned questions and doubt, with President Trump tweeting one suggestion that Bill Clinton was involved in his murder[302] (numerous reports state that "Bill Clinton flew on Epstein's private jet [also known as the Lolita Express] four, 11, or 26 times, depending on who's counting").[303]

Of course, as I write this book, I fully expect the Clintons to point out that Donald Trump was at one time a friend of Epstein, too, and perhaps had the pedophile murdered to conceal negative information related to their friendship, something that Trump-abhorring Rep. Maxine Waters (D-CA) has tried to infer.[304] It should also be noted that, at some point, the friendship between Trump and Epstein ended, with the president claiming he banned Epstein from his Mar-a-Lago resort for sexual misconduct toward a masseuse. The *New York Times* claims the falling-out actually occurred "after a failed business arrangement between them"[305] involving rival bids for the same Palm Beach estate, which Trump was awarded.

"I knew him like everybody in Palm Beach knew him," President Trump said recently. "I had a falling out with him a long time ago, I don't think I've spoken to him for 15 years, I wasn't a fan."[306]

Whatever the case, besides Trump weighing in on Epstein's suspicious death, Lynne Patton, the regional administrator at the Department of Housing and Urban Development, posted on Instagram that Epstein had been "Hillary'd!!" She added the hashtag, "#VinceFosterPartTwo,"[307] a reference to the former Clinton aide we wrote about in the last chapter, whose death by suicide has also been questioned.

Republican political consultant and Fox News commentator Harlan Z. Hill added his two cents: "Dead men tell no tales. Just as Jeffrey Epstein starts to name names, he decides to kill himself? Mkay. Totally believable."[308]

US Rep. Al Green agreed: "The suicide of Mr. Epstein is an impossibility. When an impossibility occurs involving powerful people and possible criminality there must be an investigation to end speculation. Because the public has a right to know, I'm calling for a congressional investigation.[309]

And not all doubters of the official Epstein "suicide" narrative were conservatives. Ultraliberal Trump-hater Joe Scarborough even tweeted: "A guy who had information that would have destroyed rich and powerful men's lives ends up dead in his jail cell. How predictably...Russian."[310]

Another Trump despiser and former US senator, Claire McCaskill, let the world know what she thought as well, saying, "Something stinks to high heaven. How does someone on suicide watch hang himself with no intervention? Impossible. Unless..."[311]

If you, too, find yourself not buying the "Epstein killed himself in jail by hanging" storyline, according to a Rasmussen poll, you are soundly among 70 percent of Americans who also question the "suicide" conclusion:

> The latest Rasmussen Reports national telephone and online survey finds that only 29% of American Adults believe Epstein actually committed suicide while in jail. Forty-two percent (42%) think Epstein was murdered to prevent him from testifying against powerful people with whom he associated.[312]

Nevertheless, on Friday, August 16, 2019, the New York City Chief Medical Examiner's office announced the "official cause" of Epstein's death was "suicide by hanging,"[313] a statement immediately renounced by Epstein's attorneys as well as several health experts.

"We are not satisfied with the conclusions of the medical examiner," Epstein's lawyers stated, adding that they fully intended to conduct their "own independent and complete investigation into the circumstances and cause of Mr. Epstein's death."[314]

Fox News medical contributor Dr. Marc Siegel counted himself among qualified health experts who raised doubts about the "suicide" ruling, publicly maintaining that it was "more likely" that Epstein's death was murder, a conclusion he reached following (among other things) an autopsy that indicated broken bones in Epstein's neck.

"The hyoid bone in the neck being fractured and other fractures in the neck, make it…more likely that it was a homicide than a suicide," Siegel said during an interview on America's Newsroom.[315]

Though the hyoid bone is small and has been known to break in hangings (especially in older people), it more often provides a telltale clue that the person was strangled.

In fact, top forensic pathologist, Dr. Cyril Wecht, appeared on FOX Business Network on August 14, 2019, and stated that only 1 percent of the time do hanging deaths result in broken hyoid bones.[316]

Dr. Wecht, who has consulted many high-profile criminal cases (including the Warren Commission's conclusions on the assassination of John F. Kennedy), is a lawyer and doctor. He pointed out during his interview with Lisa Kennedy on Fox that an extensive Montreal study had found only 2 of 239 hanging deaths (less than 1 percent) resulted in a broken hyoid bone.[317]

Following his initial interview on the Epstein death, Dr. Mark Siegel came back on the news discussing additional bombshell and highly suggestive facts from the autopsy that showed "hemorrhaging in the throat when he died," also a sign of strangulation and not hanging, according to experts who increasingly believe Epstein was murdered.[318]

A couple days after Dr. Siegel's commentary, Dr. Jane Orient, the executive director of the Association of American Physicians and Surgeons and president of Doctors for Disaster Preparedness, admitted she, too, was not convinced by the hanging story, adding, "There is a motive for a lot of people to really want him dead. With probably enough money to contrive to bring that about."

In an interview with WND, Orient pointed out how facts about death by hanging "are well known, since it was used as a form of execution for years. It takes about 1,000 foot-pounds of force to break neck bones and end life."

How could that have happened, she continued, "in a cell with an eight-or nine-foot ceiling, with a bunk bed about seven feet high and a six-foot-tall man.

"According to publicly released information," she noted, "some bones in Jeffrey Epstein's neck were fractured, including the hyoid. The other bones of the neck are the cervical vertebrae—not so easily broken."

Orient then said that for a two hundred-pound man, a death by hanging needs a drop of about five feet. "There is no trap door in the cell...nor is there a movable ladder to stand on," she explained.[319]

In October 2019, famous forensic pathologist Michael Baden (New York City's former chief medical examiner) not only agreed with the conclusions above, but went on record saying that Jeffrey Epstein was indeed murdered, in his opinion, and warned that other people with information Epstein had could be at risk of joining the Body Count list.[320] New York City Mayor Bill de Blasio agreed: "Something doesn't fit here,"[321] and Virginia Roberts, one of Epstein's underage victims, claims the FBI has already warned her there is "a credible death threat made against her" following her disclosure involving Prince Andrew's involvement with the elite pedophiles.[322] Virginia wants people to know that she is not suicidal and if she winds up dead, the Orgy Island crew is behind it.[323]

Besides the anomalies mentioned above, further inconsistencies connected to Epstein's death for which some question the official narrative and suggest a cover-up was perpetrated were recently posted by Gateway Pundit. An adapted partial list of its findings include:

- Before he died, Epstein said he was considering cooperating in "naming names" in his international sex ring.

- Two days prior to his death, documents released for the first time implicated several top Democrats in his pedo sex ring.
- Epstein had dirt on numerous other globalist elites as well.
- He was taken off suicide watch after a failed attempt just two weeks earlier.
- His cellmate was removed and he was left in isolation—unusual for a suicidal individual. Perhaps even more telling is that guards told the cellmate there would be a "price to pay" if he talked about circumstances surrounding the alleged suicide.[324]
- The cameras reportedly malfunctioned so that there was no video. (Later video "turned up" allegedly showing nobody entered Epstein's cell on the day he died. But readers should note it would not be difficult for such film to be manufactured as evidence. Hollywood special-effects types or a crime lab could have convincingly created such.)
- Then, in August 2019, it was reported that at least one camera "stationed in the hallway outside billionaire financier and convicted sex offender Jeffrey Epstein's prison cell had footage," but we were told it "was deemed unusable."[325]
- It was later reported that the cameras showed that the guards did not do rounds, causing Gateway Pundit to ask, "Which is it?"
- The prison guards said they "forgot" to check on Epstein and had slept through their shift.
- There were reports of screaming from Epstein's cell the morning he died.
- The Metropolitan Correctional Center (MCC, the prison where Epstein was locked up) had not seen a successful suicide in forty years prior to Epstein's death.
- Epstein had said he had been the victim of an attempted murder three weeks earlier.
- Epstein was not given paper sheets (which would have made hanging more difficult).
- Epstein was not suicidal, according to medical professionals.

- Epstein told his lawyers on Friday, a day before his death, "See you Sunday."[326]

The list above will undoubtedly grow for years to come as new forensic details come to light and motives of whoever might have wanted Epstein dead are evaluated, followed by possible interrogations. But Michael Brenner, professor of international affairs at the University of Pittsburgh, thinks he knows how this all will ultimately end:

> The Department of Justice, led by Trump's lackey Attorney General William Barr, will insist on controlling all aspects of the investigation. If they can turn up a few snippets regarding the Clintons, they will leak them. Then, the entire affair will slip from public view. We have become expert at losing the past in the mists of the present—like the fog rolling through the Golden Gate—that erase all images on a regular 24-hour cycle.
>
> So, a year or two from now, there will be a low-key announcement that the investigation has found nothing that calls into question the conclusion that Epstein indeed committed suicide—alone and of his own volition. His earlier alleged crimes will be said to be excluded by the statute of limitations or the absence of credible evidence due in part to the deaths of certain principals. One negligent guard will be singled out for dereliction of duty; a letter of reprimand will be placed in his personnel file and he will be punished by a denial of coffee breaks for a full two weeks. Maybe, just maybe, the American Psychiatric Association will devise some new guidelines re. Suicide Watches in prison—without specifically mentioning this incident.[327]

Despite what Brenner writes, I believe something deeper will eventually come to light from all the Epstein conflagrations and that, finally, numerous pedophiles will be tracked down and charged—together with that, an occult underbelly exposed.

Why do I say that?

Because there's a lot more to this story than what the "Low Information Voters" and "Drive-by Media" (as Rush Limbaugh likes to call them) are aware of—secrets that may have only been known by Epstein and his circle that I will detail over the next few pages.

QAnon, Pizzagate, Crowley Occultists and Other Friends of the Family

QAnon is reportedly a very senior military official or group of officers with uppermost military clearance—*Q* clearance—who prefer to remain anonymous (thus "QAnon") while detailing a secret scheme by the Deep State against US President Donald Trump and his followers. "The theory began with an October 2017 post on the anonymous imageboard 4chan [and later 8chan] by someone using the tripcode Q, a presumably American individual that may have later grown to include multiple people, claiming to have access to classified information involving the Trump administration and its opponents in the United States." Q has accused various "liberal Hollywood actors, Democratic politicians, and high-ranking officials of engaging in an international child sex trafficking ring and has claimed that Donald Trump [is] exposing the ring and preventing a *coup d'état* by Barack Obama, Hillary Clinton, and George Soros."

According to Travis View, who has written extensively about QAnon for the *Washington Post*, the heart of the message from the mysterious group is that:

> There is a worldwide cabal of Satan-worshiping pedophiles who rule the world, essentially, and they control everything. They control politicians, and they control the media. They control Hollywood, and they cover up their existence, essentially. And they would have continued ruling the world, were it not for the election of President Donald Trump.[328]

Under Trump as its moral crusader, a movement is said to be quietly afoot inside his administration to expose a child-molesting global elite that will eventually result in "The Storm," a predicted event in which a huge cache of incriminating documents will be unsealed naming thousands of members of these Deep-State pedophile circles involving high-level politicians (including Britain's Prince Andrew, Joe Biden, former New Mexico Gov. Bill Richardson, former Sen. George Mitchell,[329] and numerous others that victims have also named[330]), clergy, and Hollywood insiders who will eventually be arrested and prosecuted.

QAnon has numerous well-known believers, including celebrities like Roseanne Barr and apparently Trump himself (Q claims to be a government insider closely affiliated with Trump), and, at least at times, somebody with security knowledge must actually be behind the operation, as Q has often been ahead of the media in releasing important intel. This includes Jeffrey Epstein's arrest and subsequent "suicide." For example, on July 6, 2019, Epstein was arrested, though a couple days before that, over the Independence Day weekend, a QAnon message-board prophecy claimed that "a group within the federal government has been conducting a secret investigation into a network of elite pedophiles" and that an arrest was imminent. Q speculated this would happen on July 4 or 5. He missed it by one day, but the event happened just as predicted, and "the feds handed out an indictment over a global underage sex-trafficking ring implicating U.S. presidents, heads of government, top lawyers, world-famous actors, and a member of the English royal family." The apprehension "of well-connected financier and convicted sex criminal Jeffrey Epstein on one count of sex trafficking and one count of conspiracy to commit sex trafficking went a long way toward fulfilling the QAnon prediction."[331]

Then there was the "suicide" of Epstein. Nearly an hour before any news outlets received information and reported that he was dead, an anonymous user posted then-unverified details on 4chan, the message board often used by QAnon, before ABC News first tweeted his death.

"Dont ask me how I know, but Epstein died an hour ago from hanging, cardiac arrest. Screencap this," read the post, which was published at 8:16 a.m. alongside an image of Pepe, the green frog that has become a mascot for right-wing Internet trolls.

"That message was posted 38 minutes before the first tweet about Epstein's death from Aaron Katersky, an ABC News reporter, at 8:54 a.m. Five minutes later, the main ABC News account tweeted an article about Epstein's death."

These two examples (there are plenty more oracular prognostications from QAnon) do seem to indicate that whoever is actually behind QAnon and its related message boards includes individuals with access to genuine intel who often disseminate classified information—sources of data hinting at persons inside US government agencies that itch to leak confidential material regarding what it is the swamp creatures in DC are desperate to keep hidden.

According to the *Washington Post*[332] and *New York Times*,[333] whoever is pulling QAnon's strings were also behind the now infamous Pizzagate.

I was on the *Hagmann Report* with Steve Quayle a few years ago when for the first time I heard the disturbing allegations involving so-called Pizzagate, which numerous alt-right bloggers and conspiracy sites in 2016–2017 were inferring involved underage children being trafficked for use by powerful political and underworld figures connected to John Podesta (then Hillary Clinton's campaign chairman), his brother Tony, and Bill and Hillary Clinton (and it doesn't help that the Wikileaks emails included one in which John Podesta mentions his close relationship with former Speaker of the House Dennis Hastert, who was sent to prison over sexually abusing boys and whom the judge called "a serial child molester"). Hastert himself, who was released after serving a little over a year of his sentence,[334] may have been linked to the Wikileaks emails in which dozens of references to "pizza" (149 emails), combined with references to other foods, were viewed as a coded system for pedophiles—a system in which words like "hotdog" with "pizza" equaled a little boy, "pasta" with "pizza" meant a girl, cheese indicatd a "little girl," and so on. The reason a conspiracy grew up around this is partly because of Podesta's disturbing, some say occult, pedophilic art collection, together with the pizza parties he often cohosted with his friend James Alefantis, a man considered to be one of the fifty most powerful people in Washington and the owner of the pizza and music restaurant named Comet Ping Pong. This restaurant is mentioned a dozen or so times in the leaked emails and is the dining establishment where Edgar Welch was arrested for taking an AR-15 rifle and handgun in December of 2016. Hee later told police he was there investigating a story about Pizzagate and Hillary Clinton running a child-sex ring out of the eatery.

Some weeks after Welch was detained, CBS46 evening anchor Ben Swann, whose popular Truth in Media website and *Reality Check* program had launched an investigation into the Pizzagate story, also framed the location as possibly connected with a child pornography ring being run out of DC. Swann questioned why authorities had been unwilling to conduct a full investigation into the allegations and pointed to music bands that play at Comet singing songs that joke about pedophilia and depicting artwork that matches known "boy-lover" symbols (numerous Podesta emails also mention "pizza" and "handkerchiefs," which are said to be coded language for pedophiles). Swann went on to note that two doors over from Comet Ping Pong is another parlor named Besta Pizza, where the logo matched what a 2007 FBI report depicted as a unique symbol commonly used by pedophiles to express their particular preferences in children—a winding triangle that stands for "boy love." Following Swann's report, Besta Pizza modified its logo.

A few days after his first broadcast on the subject, Swann's Truth in Media site disappeared, as did his Twitter, Instagram, and Facebook accounts.

Did somebody tell him to back off, or was it simply his bosses ordering him to quit the conspiracy-themed reporting?

On the heels of Swann abruptly abandoning the story, Alex Jones was likewise somehow pressured into publicly apologizing for promoting similar commentary involving Pizzagate. Whether he, too, had been threatened by a defamation suit or something else, he read from a prepared statement that, to his knowledge, "neither Mr. Alefantis, nor his restaurant Comet Ping Pong, were involved in any human trafficking as was part of the theories about Pizzagate that were being written about in many media outlets and which we commented upon."[335]

Then there was Hillary Clinton tweeting about Pizzagate when Michael Flynn was forced to resign, rubbing it in his face and reminding him how his son had once accused her of running a child-sex ring out of Comet Ping Pong. But the 2016 Inspector General's report included notes written down by the former assistant director of the FBI's Counterintelligence Division, Randy Coleman, involving "crimes against children" that do indeed appear to connect Hillary Clinton, her foundation, and dishonored former Congressman Anthony Weiner with unexplained events involving underage kids.

> After obtaining Weiner's devices, the agent processing their contents discovered "within hours" over 300,000 emails, many of them involving communications between Weiner's wife, Huma Abedin, and Hillary Clinton.
>
> The findings were deemed relevant to the FBI's investigation into Hillary Clinton sending classified information using a private email server.
>
> From Coleman's notes, the exact context of the "Crime Against Children" is unclear, as well as the mention of the Clinton Foundation.[336]

So, regardless of denial, there could be some "there" there, and one wonders why this has not been widely reported or investigated other than brief mention by Laura Ingraham and Sean Hannity on their programs.

Regardless of whether everything surrounding this particular conspiracy was overblown and never had any real substance, a series of police raids since on pedophile circles in the US with ties to international child trading illustrates that such crimes are not only alive and well (including among drag queens who've been linked to Satanism and occult practices that are given access to children during Drag Queen Story Hour [DQSH] at libraries and schools around the US)[337] but often include members of the so-called privileged class who frequently are shielded from prosecution.

For example, child-sex-trafficking investigators from the FBI's New York field office had just conducted an interview with a victim who provided chilling details about allegedly being raped as a young boy by Bill Clinton and pimped out at private sex parties attended by other DC elites, when, just as her bombshell report on the story was being prepared, investigative journalist Jen Moore was found dead in a suburban Washington, DC, hotel and the probe was dropped.[338]

Sometimes the truth remains unknown until after the perpetrators are deceased, as reflected in the recently released FBI files containing "over 300 pages relating to decades-old investigations into the 'Finders.' Analysis of the eye-opening documents, which include police reports and correspondence between various agencies, reveals that the group was a satanic cult and suggests deliberate obstruction of justice by feds and the CIA, which is all the more relevant in light of the recent attention to sexual and child abuse scandals connected with the rich and powerful, and the shady history of US Deep State intelligence agencies."[339]

A report at Natural News notes that Finders child abuse included ritual animal and possibly human sacrifices, and disturbingly, it was Robert Mueller of the Russian Collusion fame who shut down the FBI investigation into this group. The news site adds:

> We know from now-declassified documents that some members of The Finders were also CIA agents, including a woman by the name of Isabelle who worked for the CIA between 1951 and 1971. Records show that travel was made to everywhere from Moscow to North Korea to North Vietnam, though The Finders appear to have been based in the US.
>
> Details divulged through search warrants show that The Finders had—and possibly still have—numerous properties through-

out the US, including a farm in Virginia that was found to have cages that were used to "hold children."[340]

You might also recall Deborah Jeane Palfrey, the "DC Madam" (as she was dubbed by the media at the time), who operated a phone-in escort agency in Washington, DC. She insisted that her operation was legal, but nevertheless was convicted in 2008 of racketeering and money laundering. Her clients included dozens of Washington insiders; lobbyists; FBI and IRS employees; White House, State Department, and Defense Department officials; and so on. But like Jeffrey Epstein, she was found hanging in a storage shed outside her mother's mobile home in Tarpon Springs, Florida,[341] ending the investigation and, once again, sparing elitists of being exposed or prosecuted.

Even so, sometimes people do go to prison, especially when they're not rich and connected and/or have been compromised like Epstein.

A while back, president Trump responded to one such arrest by holding a press conference in which he announced his plan to bring the "full force and weight" of the US government against this "epidemic of human trafficking."[342] This caused former Congresswoman Cynthia McKinney—who once challenged the elite on the floor of the House about their participation in sex slavery—to warn Trump that if he really did go after pedophiles, he should plan to make arrests of both Republicans and Democrats reaching all the way to the top in Washington, DC.[343]

Underpinning her allegation was a 2006 Immigration and Customs Enforcement investigation into the purchase of child pornography that "turned up more than 250 civilian and military employees of the Defense Department—including some with the highest available security clearance." Mysteriously, the Pentagon refused to further investigate these culprits.[344]

One has to wonder why.

Indeed. So widespread is this problem that in July 2019, Representatives Mark Meadows (R-NC) and Abigail Spanberger (D-VA) introduced bipartisan legislation titled "End National Defense Network Abuse" to stop pervasive use of Department of Defense (DOD) computers that have been procuring and sharing pornographic images of children by thousands of US government employees,[345] exposure of whom could be especially effective at adding to body-count lists wherever the focus includes the seedy underbelly of the world's powerful elite.

For example, not one, but two, former GOP senators from Arkansas and Oklahoma were investigating child trafficking involving high-profile individuals (including sitting judges) when in 2019 they were found murdered. According to numerous reports, Linda Collins-Smith (AR) was about to go public with her findings when she was shot to death in her home.[346] Just two days, later former Oklahoma Sen. Jonathan Nichols, who purportedly was also investigating pedophiles and sex-slave traffickers, was found dead in his Norman, Oklahoma, residence.[347]

In July 2019, the home of Mexican investigative reporter Lydia Cacho Ribeiro (on whom I believe the female heroine in the new *Rambo: Last Blood* movie is lightly based) was similarly broken into. Unidentified individuals killed her two dogs and stole her laptop, recorders, and hard drives "containing information about sexual abuse cases the reporter was investigating."[348]

"It's remarkable Cacho is still alive," wrote Kurt Nimmo at the time. "In 1999, she was beaten and raped in retaliation for her investigations. Despite this, she continued to report on sex rings and the trafficking and murder of Mexican girls."[349]

According to our friend Jaco Booyens, a tireless proponent of the war on human trafficking, the examples above are just the tip of a much larger iceberg. Criminal "Nests" and "Webs," as some call them, exist internationally. So far as "Webs," these involve "big child trafficking rings… and large networks [from] internet trafficking on Backpage to cults like NXIVM, Jeffrey Epstein's networks to Hollywood pedophiles [where] localized fronts that portray themselves as saviors of children…build a nest in their local community that has all the makings of a child trafficking front [that] typically have a skilled IT person, doctor, dentist, psychologist, court connections, law enforcement, foster and/or social workers, foster care families, domestic violence and/or homeless shelters, churches, and family members" who make up child-abduction rings. Beth Breen, a former employee of Arizona Department of Child Services, recently breached her gag order and confirmed to Northwest Liberty News that children are often taken from parents and thrown into the state foster system, where torturous and sadistic situations unfold, including sex-trafficking, torture, and even murder.[350]

Conversely, Webs, on the other hand, "are an entirely different beast":

These are fronts for several nefarious dealings, such as money laundering, child trafficking, drug trafficking, land resources, and pay-to-play style schemes. Oftentimes a single web consists of several of these actions. These are larger scale networks that often operate across global territories. You cannot research a web without understanding the mind of the elite corrupt players involved, being familiar with their strategies and tactics, and at least having some knowledge of their end game. This is a whole different level of strategy whereby they operate in webs, the planning spans years, and they all have common goals.[351]

With that in mind, while we know *Next Top Model* (an American reality-television series and competition in which aspiring models compete for the title of "America's Next Top Model")[352] scout Jean-Luc Brunel flew impoverished twelve-year-old triplets in from France as a birthday gift for Jeffrey Epstein to sexually abuse,[353] the truth is that in the United States alone, adults purchase children (sometimes as young as two years old—and no, that's not a typo. Jaco discussed this on a recent SkyWatchTV. com episode)[354] to rape at least 2.5 million times per year! Disturbingly, a report by *USA Today* reveals these predators usually appear to be "ordinary" people— meaning, quite frankly, they could include your friendly neighborhood pals.[355]

How can this be true?

Because, as *Eyes Wide Shut* director Stanley Kubrick implied in his disquietingly erotic 1999 psychological thriller, most people are content not knowing what is happening around them; they go through life with their "eyes wide shut," avoiding acknowledgment of immoral accomplices conducting criminal abuse all around them. Or, perhaps they do see or suspect what is happening, but due to their "power" relationships where financial or political gain is involved, they—like numerous Epstein acquaintances undoubtedly did—turn a blind eye.

"There is no apparent heroic resistance against the secret society of the power elite," Norwegian historian Håvard Friis Nilsen's writes in his essay, "Deterioration of Trust: The Political Warning in Kubrick's *Eyes Wide Shut*." "What we see is an acknowledgment of the futility of control: they can neither control superior powers nor each other; loyalty is never guaranteed; they must be thankful for the moments in which they are awake." Andrew Whalen for *Newsweek* thus adds, "How many people in close proximity to Epstein turned away because of this same sensation?"[356]

Beyond the complexities of social and interpersonal agreements between such human beings, if we may call them that, Kubrick's sordid vision suggested something else in his movie, too, and I believe it's connected to the Epstein murder—err, I mean, *suicide*.

Often associated with the sexploitation of children is a dark, occult element, a breeding ground where affluent members of secret sex societies—shielded from culpability—indulge their vilest urges at the expense of vulnerable children for satanic reasons.

On few occasions, frightening facts behind this truth have been whispered. When ABC News correspondent Craig Spence left his job in the '80s and began "pimping out children to the power elite in the nation's capital [including prominent officials in the Reagan and subsequent George H. W. Bush administrations][357] throughout the 1980s in apartments that were bugged with video and audio recording equipment," he, like Jeffrey Epstein, had his home "bugged and had a secret two-way mirror, and…he attempted to ensnare visitors into compromising sexual encounters that he could then use as leverage." But also like Epstein, he wound up "suicided" at the Boston Ritz-Carlton. However, this wasn't before he "hinted to *Washington Times* reporters Michael Hedges and Jerry Seper, who had originally broken the story, that they had merely scratched the surface of something much darker:

> All this stuff you've uncovered [involving call boys, bribery, and the White House tours], to be honest with you, is insignificant compared to other things I've done. But I'm not going to tell you those things, and somehow the world will carry on.[358]

One shudders to think what Spence was alluding to. Could it be that his dark forces took him into the same gloomy corridors as we believe Epstein's did?

Ritual Sacrifice, Symbols, and Occult Architecture

One of the more widely publicized recent cases connecting cult rituals and sex abuse of minors (and adults, which included ties to Hillary Clinton associates, Senator Chuck Schumer, actress Allison Mack, and other notables) was adjudicated early in 2019 during closing arguments in the NXIVM trial involving self-help guru Keith Raniere. Mr. Raniere was not only found guilty of all charges involving sex trafficking of young illegal immigrant girls from Mexico, but "human experiments and Satanism-inspired rituals took place at the cult, according to the mountains of evidence exposed by this historic trial," BigLeaguePolitics reported:

> The NXIVM sex cult's leader Keith Raniere…aimed for his branding of female sex slaves to be "like a sacrifice," referring to the practice of human sacrifice, which is practiced in Satanic rituals.
>
> "Do you think the person who's being branded should be held to the table, almost like a sacrifice?" Raniere said to his onetime co-conspirator Allison Mack in a 2017 conversation that was captured on audiotape. "That's a feeling of submission.… It probably

should be a more vulnerable position. Laying on the back, legs spread straight, held to the table. Hands above the head, probably held, almost like sacrificial."[359]

One has to wonder if this revealing conversation was later followed by the "disappearance" of any of those young Mexican girls that reporter Lydia Cacho Ribeiro had been investigating. We do know that, as a result of what is called "the law of diminishing returns," sex offenders often feel the need to raise their debauchery to increasingly higher levels in order to continue reaching satisfaction. Did Raniere or his associates advance from his "fantasies" about sex and human sacrifice to actually fulfilling his or their dark longings?

Either way, and with all respect to NXIVM victims, what happened with Raniere and company is likely very small potatoes compared to the satanic pedophilism that assuredly played out on Epstein's seventy-two-acre "Orgy Island" and at his private estate (seventy-two is a mystical number connected to the fallen Watchers angels).

And, as all Freemasons know, often telltale signs of such occult devotion and participation are "openly hidden" in the architecture and symbols that mark surrounding properties for the "members" of these types of secretive groups.

Occultists around the world understand the power of symbols and designs, and realize they are not only for conveying psychological concepts, but are actually meant to coerce mysterious and potent supernaturalism that has been invited to take up residence there. This belief is deeply preserved in all of the Babylonian, Egyptian, Greek, and Roman symbolism that is a part of occult and Masonic history—and, according to famous Freemason Foster Bailey, these symbols intentionally hide "a secret… which veils mysterious forces. These energies when released can have a potent effect."[360] Scottish philosopher Thomas Carlyle once famously added: "By symbols, accordingly, is man guided and commanded, made happy, made wretched." Masons in particular, as a result, are under oath never to reveal the true meaning of their symbols, and when somehow they are compelled to offer explanation, they falsify the statement, even to lower-degree Masons, as explained by Sovereign Grand Commander Albert Pike in the Masonic handbook *Morals and Dogma*:

> Masonry, like all the Religions, all the Mysteries, Hermetic, and Alchemy, conceals its secrets from all except the Adepts and Sages, or the Elect, and uses false explanations and misinterpretations of its symbols to mislead those who deserve only to be misled; to conceal the Truth, which it calls Light, from them, and to draw them away from it.[361]

I raise this issue about Masonic imagery in particular at this point because a careful review of Epstein's Orgy Island and his other private properties provide scenery rich with symbols analogous with Masonic, arcane, and modern magic (including the powerful trident—considered of the utmost importance for sorcery and indispensable to the efficacy of infernal rites) as well as other motifs connected with Masonry and Muslim decorum suggestive of sex slavery.

For example, how many are aware that located on Epstein's Little Saint James "Lolita" island (also known by locals as "Pedophile Island" and "Orgy Island"), where an endless supply of minors was transported by a team of child abductors and forced to partake in debauched ceremonies involving Epstein and his wealthy, world-spanning, pedophile friends, is a temple of very telling design, with a fake painted door and a medieval-era lock on a front door *designed to keep people barricaded inside so that they cannot escape*,[362] behind which is a serpent column connected in history to the Greek sacrificial tripod from ancient Delphi and Apollo (Apollyon—the angel-god of destruction and the spirit Scripture says will inhabit Antichrist). This causes one to question whether the worst extremities of orgiastic rituals carried out at the temple against children may have been underground the occult structure (and could this explain why, on November 7, 2018, Epstein had "a $100,000 self-loading cement mixer delivered to his island using an Express Bill of Lading—an unusual and expensive shipping method that does not require the cargo to be 'released'? This shipping method requires the customer to pay for the goods up front, making them responsible if damage occurs during shipment. In short, Epstein needed this machine fast"[363] and leads to questions of what he was perhaps trying to cover up or seal beneath ground as investigators closed in.)

As our friend at Vigilant Citizen notes regarding this structure, everything on the island "appears to be custom-built to cater to the occult elite's extreme brand of depravity," and this includes the mysterious "temple," which, when one "understands the mindset of the occult elite," makes perfect sense. "It is all about symbolism and ritual."[364]

There are obvious reasons to conclude that Epstein's rape sanctuary was actually fashioned after Hammam Yalbugha—a Mamluk-era building located in Syria.

Epstein's temple, complete with what some believe are "Molech owls" (Canaanite god of child sacrifice) and pagan gods to whom child sacrifices were made, bears uncanny resemblance to Hammam Yalbugha.

Hammam architecture from Mamluk (meaning "property," as in sex slaves)

Why did Epstein model his temple after this specific building? Because of the symbolism attached to it. Indeed, the hammam is a classic example of architecture from the Mamluk era. In Arabic, the word *mamluk* literally means "property" and is used to designate slaves.

During the Mamluk era, children were captured by the ruling class to become slaves. Boys were usually trained to become soldiers, while girls were groomed to become the personal concubines of their masters. Considering the fact that Epstein island was used to import child sex slaves for the elite, the symbolism is perfectly fitting.[365]

But as is typical of Masonic practice, Epstein's island complex also mixed occult symbolism with the Islamic architecture, including standing and balance stones (connected in antiquity with secret knowledge as well as megalithic tombs such as Gilgal Rephaim); golden statues of gods (counting the Greek god Poseidon or Roman Neptune); and cockatiels or Bohemian-grove, owl-like birds with other mythical figures, which orthodox Muslims would have considered idolatry (note that these are the Greek and/or Roman gods who preside over realms of the underworld, earth, and heaven for ancient Greeks who were known to permit sex with children, especially among the rich and powerful, kings, and magistrates, with which Epstein must have equated himself. Note how the lined pattern on Epstein's temple is strikingly similar to the design on the Pharaoh Tutankhamun's headdress.)

Elsewhere on Epstein's island, an unidentified goddess greets people at two locations (at least) who appears to perhaps be the Hindu goddess Kali—goddess of sexuality and violence (among other things), Lakshmi, the Hindu goddess of wealth, or possibly a variant of Shiva, god of destruction (displayed at CERN and thoroughly examined in the book *Abaddon Ascending*). Another strong contender for the enigmatic female figure is Inanna, goddess of sex rites and torture porn (as we would call it today), who wore a headdress similar to Epstein's entity, or Hecate, goddess of witchcraft. Hecate (in particular) is an interesting choice, because I note the figure on Orgy Island guards the head and tail or "gateways" of prominent walkways. In this role, Hecate, the Titan earth-mother of the wizards and witches who helped Demeter after Hades abducted and raped her daughter Persephone, illustrates perhaps better than any other goddess the connection between earth entities, gateways, and the realm of evil supernaturalism. As the daughter of Perses and Asteria, Hecate (Hekate) was the only of the Titans to remain free under Zeus. She was the mother of the wizard, Circe, and of the witch, Medea, and was considered to be the underworld sorceress of all that is demonic. This was because Hecate characterized the unknown night-terrors that roamed the abandoned and desolate highways. She was often depicted as a young maiden with three faces, each pointing in a different direction, a role in which she was the earth-spirit that haunted wherever three paths joined. As the "goddess of three forms," she was Luna (the moon) in heaven, Diana (Artemis) on earth, and Hecate in the underworld. At times of evil magic, she appeared with hideous serpents—spreading demons, encouraging criminal activity, and revealing enigmatic secrets to the crones. At other times, she roamed the night with the souls of the dead, visible only to dogs, who howled as she approached. When the moon was covered in darkness and the hell hounds accompanied her to the path-beaten crossways, Hecate came

suddenly upon the food offerings and dead bodies of murders and suicides that had been left for her by fear-stricken commonfolk. Her hounds
bayed, the ghost torches lit the night, and river nymphs shrieked as she
carried away the mangled souls of suicides into the underworld caverns of
Thanatos (Death), where the shrills of such damned ones were known to
occupy her presence.

As the dark goddess of witchcraft, Hecate, like Isis, was worshiped
with impure rites and magical incantations. Her name was probably
derived from the ancient Egyptian word *heka* ("sorcery" or "magical"),
which may explain her association with the Egyptian frog-goddess of the
same name. This may also explain the affiliation of frogs with witchcraft
and the various potions of frogwort and *hecateis* (Hecate's hallucinogenic
plant, also called aconite), which supposedly sprouted from the spittle of
Cerberus (Hade's three-headed guard dog), which fell to the ground when
Hercules forced him up to the surface of the earth.

Because her devotees practiced such magic wherever three paths
joined, Hecate became known to the Romans as Trivia (*tri*: "three," and
via: "roads"). Offerings were also made to her wherever evil or murderous
activity occurred, as such areas were believed to be magnets of malevolent
spirits, something like "haunted houses." If one wanted to get along with
the resident apparitions, they needed to make oblations to the ruler of
their darkness—Hecate. The acceptance of the oblations was announced
by Hecate's familiar (the night owl), and the spooky sound of the creature
was perceived as a good omen by those who gathered on the eve of the full
moon. Statues of the goddess bearing the triple face of a dog, a snake, and
a horse overshadowed the dark rituals when they were performed at the
crossing of three roads. At midnight, Hecate's devotees would leave the
food offerings at the intersection for the goddess ("Hecate's Supper"), and,
once deposited, they would quickly exit without turning around or looking back. Sometimes the offerings consisted of honey cakes and chicken
hearts, while at other times, puppies, honey, and female black lambs were
slaughtered for the goddess and her *strigae*—vicious, owl-like affiliates of
Hecate who flew through the night feeding on the bodies of unattended

babies. During the day, the *strigae* appeared as simple old women, folklore that may account for the history of flying witches. The same *strigae* hid amidst the leaves of the trees during the annual festival of Hecate (held on August 13), when her followers offered the highest praise of the goddess.

Hecate's devotees celebrated such festivals near Lake Averna in Campania, where the sacred willow groves of the goddess stood, and they communed with the nature spirits and summoned the souls of the dead from the mouths of nearby caves. It was here that Hecate was known as Hecate-Chthonia ("Hecate of the earth"), a depiction in which she most clearly embodied the earth-mother spirit that conversed through the cave stones and sacred willow trees. Elsewhere, Hecate was known as Hecate-Propolos, "the one who leads," as in the underworld guide of Persephone and of those who inhabit graveyards, and as Hecate-Phosphoros, "the light bearer," her most sacred title and one that recalls another powerful underworld spirit, Satan, whose original name was Lucifer ("the light bearer"). But it was her role as Hecate-Propylaia, "the one before the gate" where it appears we see her on Epstein Island. In this manifestation, Hecate was believed to not only control entrances at homes and temples to nefarious evils, but she also had charge of spirit-traversing gateways that she could open into the human mind through the use of psychoactive drugs, a practice employed throughout Greek paganism as well as by shamans of other cultures but condemned in the Scriptures (Galatians 5:20; Revelation 9:21, 18:23) as *pharmakeia*—the administering of drugs for sorcery or magical arts in connection with demonic contact.

Another large figurine on Epstein's Island reminds me of the ancient Green Man (a pre-Christian entity and spirit of nature embodied as a man) if the hair of the individual is of vegetative growth. The word "Hoy" on the image's forehead could be a clear reference to Charles "Hoy" Fort, the famous nineteenth-century writer whose psychic research and schemes about contacting immaterial spirits (ghosts, demons) included the *Book of the Damned,* which featured the existence of "mythological" creatures *connected to the disappearances of people.*

Demonic gargoyles holding shields with six-pointed stars likewise are found in numerous locations on Epstein Island. Gargoyles are often representations of "evil forces" that inflame forbidden desires like sin and temptation, and the six-pointed star is used in occult ceremonial magic as a talisman for conjuring demons. In Acts chapter 7:37–43 and in Amos 5:26–27, God condemned Israel's worship of Molech and his six-pointed "star" to whom children were sacrificed.

With all this in mind, like the black-and-white checkerboard pattern that covers floors of Masonic lodges and meeting places—which members of the Craft describe as representing human life as checkered with good and evil—Epstein's Orgy Island also possesses high-degree, vibrant, labyrinthian shapes, including keystone patterns on the temple (exactly like the Muslim *Hammam Yalbugha*), considered of the highest importance in Masonry and other occult practices for dominance over anything (stone arches or vaults gain stability from placement of the keystone).

Famous freemason Albert Mackey, in his *Encyclopedia of Freemasonry*, said of the keystone:

The stone placed in the center of an arch which preserves the others in their places, and secures firmness and stability to the arch. As it was formerly the custom of Operative Masons to place a peculiar mark on each stone of a building to designate the workman by whom it had been adjusted, so the Keystone was most likely to receive the most prominent mark, that of the Superintendent of the structure. Such is related to have occurred to that Keystone which plays so important a part in the legend of the Royal Arch Degree.... In fact, in the Solomonic era, the construction of the arch must have been known to the Dionysian Artificers.[366]

It is telling and important here that Mackey recognizes the keystone design as dating back to Dionysian Artificers or architects, which modern, high-degree masons esteem as the originators of occult structural designs—the three-dimensional language of "form"—derived from these ancient draftsmen and embedded with secret memories of symbolism, ancient myth and beliefs about gods and elements, and the metaphysical doctrines of the Mystery schools (which Freemasons hold they are the keepers of today). As such, the Dionysian Keystone is a "speaking symbol" for occultists and provides powerful reasoning around Epstein's choice of such designs for his dark guests not only to enjoy at Pedophile Island, but to come under the spell of—enchantment tied to the orgiastic human-sacrifices god that Dionysian architects were named after. As I noted in my book *Zenith 2016*:

Dionysus...is superficially depicted as the inventor of wine, abandon, and revelry, a description that seems inadequate in that it refers only to the basic elements of intoxication and enthusiasm, which was used of the *Bacchae* (the female participants of the Dionystic mysteries [those metaphysical 'mysteries' that Freemasons are keepers of today]; also known as Maenads and Bacchantes) in their rituals to experience Dionysus, the intoxicating god of unbridled human desire.

Ancient followers of Dionysus believed he was the *presence* that is otherwise defined as the craving within man that longs to "let itself go" and to "give itself over" to baser, earthly desires [as happened regularly at Epstein's private island]. What a Christian might resist as the lustful wants of the carnal man, the followers of Dionysus embraced as the incarnate power that would, in the next life, liberate the souls of mankind from the constraints of this present world and from the customs that sought to define respectability through a person's obedience to moral law. Until that day arrives, the worshippers of Dionysus attempted to bring themselves into union with the god through a ritual casting off of the bonds of sexual denial and primal constraint by seeking to attain a higher state of ecstasy. The uninhibited rituals of *ecstasy* (Greek for "outside the body") were believed to bring the followers of Dionysus into a supernatural condition that enabled them to escape the temporary limitations of the body and mind and to achieve a state of *enthousiasmos*, or, "outside the body" and "inside the god." In this sense, Dionysus represented a dichotomy within the Greek religion, as the primary maxim of the Greek culture was one of moderation, or "nothing too extreme." But Dionysus embodied the absolute extreme in that he sought to inflame the forbidden passions of human desire. Interestingly, as most students of psychology will understand, this gave Dionysus a stronger allure among the Greeks who otherwise tried in so many ways to suppress and control the wild and secret lusts of the human heart. Dionysus resisted every such effort, and, according to myth, visited a terrible madness upon those who tried to deny him free expression. This Dionystic idea of mental disease resulting from the suppression of secret inner desires, especially aberrant sexual desires, was later reflected in the atheistic teachings of Sigmund Freud. Freudianism might therefore be called the grandchild of the cult of Dionysus. Conversely, the person who gave himself over to the will of Dionysus was rewarded with unlimited psychological and physical delights. These mythical systems of mental punishments and physical rewards based on resistance and/or submission to Dionysus were both symbolically and literally illustrated in the cult rituals of the Bacchae, as the Bacchae women (married and unmarried Greek women had the "right" to participate in the mysteries of Dionysus) migrated in frenzied hillside groups, dressed transvestite in fawn skins and accompanied by screaming, music, dancing, and licentious behavior. When, for instance, a baby animal was too young and lacking in instinct to sense the danger and run away from the revelers, it was picked up and suckled by nursing mothers who participated in the hillside rituals. On the other hand, when older animals sought to escape the marauding Bacchae, they were considered "resistant" to the will of Dionysus and were torn apart and eaten alive as a part of the fevered ritual. Human participants were sometimes subjected to the same orgiastic cruelty, as the rule of the cult was "anything goes," including lesbianism, bestiality, etc. Later versions of the ritual (Bacchanalia) expanded to include pedophilia and male revelers, and perversions of sexual behavior were often worse between men than they were between men and women. Any creature that dared to resist such perversion of Dionysus was subjected to *sparagmos* ("torn apart") and *omophagia* ("consumed raw").

In 410 BC, Euripides wrote of the bloody rituals of the Bacchae in his famous play, *The Bacchantes*:

> The Bacchantes…with hands that bore no weapon of steel, attacked our cattle as they browsed. Then wouldst thou have seen Agave mastering some sleek lowing calf, while others rent the heifers limb from limb. Before thy eyes there would have been hurling of ribs and hoofs this way and that, and strips of flesh, all blood be-dabbled,

dripped as they hung from the pine branches. Wild bulls, that glared but now with rage along their horns, found themselves tripped up, dragged down to earth by countless maidens hands.[367]

Euripedes went on to describe how Pentheus, the King of Thebes, was torn apart and eaten alive by his own mother as, according to the play, she fell under the spell of Dionysus. Tearing apart and eating alive of a sacrificial victim may refer to the earliest history of the cult of Dionysus. An ancient and violent cult ritual existing since the dawn of paganism stipulated that, by eating alive, or by drinking the blood of, an enemy or an animal, a person might somehow capture the essence or "soul-strength" of the victim. The earliest Norwegian huntsmen believed in this idea and drank the blood of bears in an effort to capture their physical strength. East African Masai warriors also practiced omophagia and sought to gain the strength of the wild by drinking the blood of lions. Human victims were treated in this way by Arabs before Mohammed, and headhunters of the East Indies practiced omophagia in an effort to capture the essence of their enemies.

Today, omophagia is practiced by certain voodoo sects as well as by cult Satanists, possibly illustrating an ongoing effort on the part of Satan to distort the *original revelation* of God, as eating human flesh and drinking human blood to "become one" with the devoured is a demonization of the Eucharist or Holy Communion. While the goal of the Satanist is to profane the holy, sparagmos and omophagia, as practiced by the followers of Dionysus, was neither an attempt at sacrilege or of *transubstantiation* (as in the Catholic Eucharist), *consubstantiation* (as in the Lutheran communion), nor yet of a symbolic ordinance (as in evangelical circles), all of which have as a common goal elevating the worshipper into sacramental communion with God. The goal of the Bacchae was the opposite—the frenzied dance, the thunderous song, the licentious behavior, the tearing apart and eating alive: all were efforts on the part of the Bacchae to capture the essence of the god (Dionysus) and bring him down into incarnated rage within man. The idea was not one of Holy Communion, but of possession by the spirit of Dionysus. When one recalls the horrific rituals of the followers of Dionysus, it's easy to believe demonic possession actually occurred.[368]

Earlier, I mentioned that, in occult and Masonic dogma, the deeper meanings of symbols are often obscured so that only true initiates of the order can comprehend the hidden clues and meanings that otherwise remain inscrutable to most. What appears to be a grand-scale example of this esoteric practice also played out at Epstein's New Mexico Zorro Ranch and on his private island in recent years involving a mysterious large, rectangular, earthen barrier or berm fortification of unknown function. The berm reflects uncanny similarity to the ancient Egyptian Shen or Shenu, a hieroglyphic representation of divinity (whether deities, pharaohs, or other influential persons) dating back to Mesopotamia.

The Shenu is often elongated similar to the berm area on Epstein's island so that it might contain numerous objects, which were then considered magically protected by the pictogram charm and/or the gods associated with the Shenu, including Isis, Horus, Mut, Heka ("frog" goddess connected with childbirth and witchcraft), and other Egyptian divinities.

While images of the enigmatic site on Epstein's island were captured in 2013 bearing a detailed design at that time inside the approximately twenty-foot-high walls with four walkways leading to an inner circle around a square, in 2017 as investigators closed in, it appeared that an intentional effort was made to disguise the uses of the area by replacing the perplexing layout with a temporary tennis court followed in 2019 by an empty containment field. However, the same original design of four walkways inside a confined area leading to a circular midsection continues to be reflected at Epstein's New Mexico Zorro Ranch as well, in a sizable "garden" that at first I thought might be a helicopter pad, but that I later ruled out as such due to all the large, woody landscaping a helicopter would not land on—plus the scope of the field (note the scale of this area compared to Epstein's 26,700-square-foot mansion—once the largest home in New Mexico) not counting the fact that Epstein has a private airport very close by.

Shenu-shaped berm area on Epstein's island with twenty-foot high walls with four walkways leading to an inner circle around a square

Similar "garden" design with main points at Zorro Ranch bears four walkways inside a confined area leading to a circular midsection.

The circular patterns on Epstein's properties first reminded me of Gilgal Refaim (Rujm el-Hiri) an ancient-stone, circular site in Israel. Gilgal in Hebrew means "a circle," while Refaim is connected to the "ghosts" of a race of giants that lived in the Bashan (Golan of today).

These areas and their design are practically identical to ancient cultic sites discovered in olden civilizations worldwide that were circular, square, and/or rectangular. Having a long history predating the time of Christ by thousands of years, these ritual locations typically employed three main components—a temple (often domed like the one on Epstein's island), a second area where ceremonials—frequently elaborate—were performed, and a third geometric pattern area (circle, square or rectangle), where the main sacrificial altar was located.

The figure of a square within a circle in particular is one of the most sacred in occult magic, grimoires, and talismanic arts, as it signifies completeness or perfection in the manifestation of the universe.[369] When the Chinese similarly depict a square inside a circle, it represents the union between heaven and earth or an "Earth temple." As part of a "magic circle," it is considered a purified or safe space in which rituals and ceremonies are conducted. It can serve as a boundary that protects sorcerers from dangerous demons and spirits, or conversely as a doorway where the conjurer reaches into and makes contact with supernatural entities. The four pathways approaching the circle around the square represent the four quarters and elements where the guardians or "Lords of the Watchtowers" (as Freemasons call them) are invoked. Each cardinal point of the magic circle is related to a guardian spirit, and when Freemasons employ the square within a circle, the proper name of Jehovah—as well as Adonai—is invoked for controlling unseen intelligence.

> In the tradition of the 1880s Order of the Golden Dawn a watch-tower or guardian in ceremonial and derived neopagan magical tradition is a tutelary spirit of one of the four cardinal points or "quarters" (north, east, south, and west). They are also variously associated in many traditions with each the four classical elements (earth, air, fire, and water) and stars (Fomalhaut, Aldebaran, Regulus, and Antares). The Watchtowers are invoked during the ritual of casting a magic circle.[370]

In *The Secret Destiny of America*, Manly P. Hall noted as well that the seventy-two stones of the pyramid on the Great Seal of the United States correspond to the seventy-two arrangements of the Tetragrammaton, or the four-lettered name of God in Hebrew. "These four letters can be combined in seventy-two combinations, resulting in what is called the Shemhamforesh, which represents, in turn, the laws, powers, and energies of Nature."[371] The idea that the mystical name of God could be invoked to bind or release those supernatural agents ("powers and energies of nature," as Hall called them) is a meaningful creed within many occult tenets, including Kabbalah and Freemasonry. This is why the seventy-two stars are pentagram-shaped around the deified Freemason, George Washington, in the US Capitol dome. Adept Rosicrucians and Freemasons have long used the "Key of Solomon" and the "Lesser Key of Solomon" grimoires (books of spells) to do just that. Peter Goodgame makes an important observation about this in "The Giza Discovery":

One of the co-founders of the occult society known as the Golden Dawn[372] was a Rosicrucian Freemason named S. L. MacGregor Mathers, who was the first to print and publish the Key of Solomon (in 1889) making it readily available to the public. Mathers describes it as a primary occult text: "The fountainhead and storehouse of Qabalistic Magic, and the origin of much of the Ceremonial Magic of mediaeval times, the 'Key' has been ever valued by occult writers as a work of the highest authority." Of the 519 esoteric titles included in the catalogue of the Golden Dawn library, the Key was listed as number one. As far as contents are concerned, the Key included instructions on how to prepare for the summoning of spirits including...demons.... One of the most well-known members of the Golden Dawn was the magician [and 33rd-degree freemason] Aleister Crowley. In 1904 Crowley published the first part of the five-part Lesser Key of Solomon known as the Ars Goetia,[373] which is Latin for "art of sorcery." The Goetia is a grimoire for summoning seventy-two different demons that were allegedly summoned, restrained, and put to work by King Solomon [according to Masonic mysticism] during the construction of the Temple of YHWH.[374]

Such books routinely contain invocations and curses for summoning, binding, and releasing demons in order to force them to do the conjurer's will at places where four paths lead to a circle surrounding a square, and often within a "boundary" or "berm," where concentrated power can be used to generate doorways into the invisible world.

Also noteworthy is how the berm area on Epstein's Orgy Island was, until recently, laid out with the same geometric pattern that not only Freemasons and occultists employed for reasons already stated, but similar to constructs where Peruvian, Mayan, and Aztecs conducted human sacrifices at four points of entry leading to a circular or square center (or sometime both—a circle in a square and visa-versa) frequently surrounded by walls.

Rectangular ritual site with walls in Peru held remains of 140 children who had been sacrificed in a "Heart Removal" ritual similar to that of the Aztecs.

The temple of Kukulkan (the feathered serpent closely related to Quetzalcoatl of Aztec mythology, to whom human sacrifices were made) at the ancient Mayan city of Chichen Itza depicts four walkways to a center square area.

I believe these ancient ritual-sacrifice sites like the Peruvian, Mayan, and Aztec and the symbolism Epstein had crafted, which appears mingled with Masonic designs, is not by chance.

How so?

The story begins long before the Spaniards arrived in Mesoamerica as chronicled in their hieroglyphic characters (and repeated in oral history) of the sacred, indigenous Maya narrative called the Popol Vuh. Sometime between 1701 and 1703, a Dominican priest named Father Francisco Ximénez transcribed and translated the Mayan work into Spanish. Later, his text was taken from Guatemala to Europe by Abbott Brasseur de Bourbough, where it was translated into French. Today the Popol Vuh rests in Chicago's Newberry Library, but what makes the script interesting is its Creation narrative, history, and cosmology, especially as it relates to the worship of the great feathered serpent creator deity known as Q'uq'umatz, a god considered by scholars to be roughly equivalent to the Aztec god Quetzalcoatl and the Yucatec Mayan Kukulkan. According to Freemasons like Manly P. Hall, no other ancient work sets forth so completely the initiatory rituals of the great school of philosophic mystery, which was so central to America's founding and the design of Washington, DC, than the Popol Vuh. What's more, Hall says, it is in this region where we find the true origin of America's name and destiny.

In *The Secret Teachings of All Ages*, Hall writes:

This volume [Popol Vuh] alone is sufficient to establish incontestably the philosophical excellence of the red race....

These Children of the Sun adore the Plumèd Serpent, who is the messenger of the Sun. He was the God Quetzalcoatl in Mexico, Gucumatz in Quiché; and in Peru he was called Amaru. From the latter name comes our word America. Amaruca is, literally translated, 'Land of the Plumèd Serpent.' The priests of this [flying dragon], from their chief centre in the Cordilleras, once ruled both Americas. All the Red men who have remained true to the ancient religion are still under their sway....

The second book of the Popol Vuh is largely devoted to the initiatory rituals of the Quiché nation. These ceremonials are of first importance to students of Masonic symbolism and mystical philosophy, since they establish beyond doubt the existence of ancient and divinely instituted Mystery schools on the American Continent. (Emphasis added)[375]

Thus, from Hall we learn that Freemasons like him believe "ancient and divinely instituted" mystery religion, rituals, and symbolism important to students of Masonry came to America from knowledge that the Red Man received from the dragon himself. And early American freemasons employed these bewitched designs—as did the Vatican—in fertility objects connected with cult magic of the Egyptians, Greeks, Romans, Mayans, and other ancient cultures—namely, enchanted geometric patterns employing squares and circles with typically four distinct pathways leading to a middle. In occult numerology, the number four is the integer that connects the immaterial world—whether supernatural entities or the mystical concept of man's mind (1), body (2), and spirit (3) with the physical world (4). This is perceived by the occultist as the pathway that joins the initiate with the otherworldly.

These magical components in mind, note how the Washington Monument has four distinct walkways leading to a circular area, in the midst of which sits the square base of the Masonic-designed representation of the male organ of Osiris (or Baal's shaft), to whom rituals were (and are) performed. According to Hall, such wisdom-reflecting architecture echoes the teachings of the human-sacrificing, ancient Maya. This pattern is also reproduced in all the major components of the Zorro Ranch and island berm areas on Epstein's properties—four paths leading to a square encased in a circle. This design is likewise prominently featured in St. Peter's Square at the Vatican, where the square base of an ancient obelisk of Osiris sits inside a circle to which four walkways lead (and one should note that the Obelisk in St. Peter's Square in the Vatican City was cut from a single block of red granite during the fifth dynasty of Egypt to stand as Osiris' erect phallus at the Temple of the Sun in ancient Heliopolis (Ἡλιούπολις, meaning "city of the sun" or "principal seat of Atum-Ra sun-worship"), the city of "On" in the Bible, dedicated to Ra, Osiris, and Isis. The Obelisk was moved from Heliopolis to the Julian Forum of Alexandria by Emperor Augustus and later from thence in approximately AD 37 by Caligula to Rome to stand at the spine of the Circus. There, under Nero, its excited presence maintained a countervigil over countless human sacrifices, including the martyrdom of the Apostle Peter, according to some historians. We will look at the connection to sun-worship of solar deities connected to human sacrifice and Freemasonry and Epstein's island a bit later in the chapter).

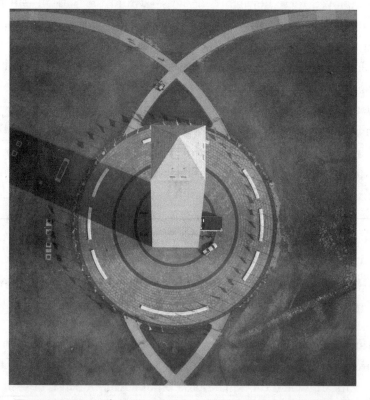

The Washington Monument has four distinct walkways leading to a circular area, in the midst of which sits the square base of the obelisk.

Square base of the Obelisk of Osiris in St. Peter's Square sits inside a
circle to which four walkways lead.

Understanding how identical patterns displayed in Washington DC
and at the Vatican connect with corresponding "living" symbols conveyed
to Freemasons by ancient Mesoamericans, another characteristic of the
mixed modern Masonic symbols and ancient cultic patterns at Epstein's
estates suggests darker possibilities than most of us would care to consider—that the rites of human sacrifice as inspired by those "wisdom"
artifacts from the ancient red man, which Manly P. Hall celebrated, were
performed.

"It is, therefore, a significant fact," famous Freemason John Sebastian Marlow Ward once wrote of the Mesoamerican human sacrifices, "that every year a man was chosen forty days before the date of the festival to represent this god [Quetzalcoatl] and was clothed in his regalia, which included a sceptre shaped like a sickle. He was first bathed in a lake and then robed in the royal and divine robes. At the end of his forty days he was slain by having his heart torn from his body, which latter the worshippers subsequently ate."[376]

Why would ancient and modern worshippers of dark gods mix sex rituals with sacrifice and cannibalization of quite often very young victims? According to another famous Freemason and deeply satanic figure, Aleister Crowley, it is because "for the highest spiritual working one must accordingly choose that victim which contains the greatest and purest force. A…child of perfect innocence and high intelligence is the most satisfactory and suitable victim."[377]

As further elaborated by freemason S. R. Parchment:

The Brothers of the Shadow who are in the flesh are usually very fearful of death and are, therefore, ever in quest of methods for prolonging their physical existence. The biblical statement that man may 'Eat of the Tree of Life and live forever' is not to them a mere statement, and for the purpose of prolonging their lives, they have ferreted out and perpetuated among their clan many nefarious schemes too henious to mention. When these methods fail, as a last resort they sacrifice human beings and feast upon the flesh and blood of their victims.[378]

Did the "Brothers of the Shadow" exert influence at Epstein's gatherings? The ancient brotherhood referenced here were "living men possessed by the earth-bound elementals," according to Russian occultist, philosopher, and cofounder of the Theosophical Society in 1875, Helena Petrovna Blavatsky. These necromancers were élite sorcerers, "devil dancers, and fetish worshippers, whose dreadful and mysterious rites are utterly unknown to the greater part of the population." In general, these mysterious occultists were considered most powerful, cruel, and vindictive, vampire-like enchanters whose capacity to bridge the gap between the material and supernatural worlds was acclaimed by fallen men of the secret societies who likewise sought contact with the four elementals of Blavatsky's Theosophy, which they thought could extend their lifetime.[379]

Knowing what we do now about Epstein's vampiric interest in transhumanism[380] and his bloodlust for immortality, it's perhaps not a stretch to consider whether he participated in such arcane rites inspired by Brothers of the Shadow, including human sacrifice in trade for length of life from these masters of delusion.

For anyone who may think I am stretching the possibilities here, when I asked Dr. Judd H. Burton (an expert on early Christianity and the Greco-Roman World with a PhD in history) what he made of the circular, square, rectangular, and other mysterious objects and facilities on Epstein's island and at his mansion, he responded:

> My initial assessment is that, knowing Epstein, these must have some ceremonial purpose. The square and rectangle have historically been symbols of materiality and the mundane world in the occult. Conversely, circles have represented spiritual and celestial planes. With the placement of a cross in the design, it occurs to me that this may be a location where adepts/participants could perform rites that opened a portal (or whatever appellation you choose), activated likely by the spoiling of innocence and/or bloodshed, in the attempt to communicate with/draw power from the realm of demons/Fallen angels.[381]

Dr. Judd's assessment is based on a long history of occult stone circles or monuments of standing stones arranged in a circle. The size and number of the stones vary, and the shape can be an ellipse or half circle. Some are more complex, with double- and triple-ring designs, often classed separately as concentric stone circles. Stone circles were constructed across the

British Isles from 3300 to 900 BC, with more than a thousand surviving examples, including Avebury, the Ring of Brodgar, and Stonehenge. The oldest is probably the Standing Stones of Stenness, a megalithic stone circle on the mainland of Scotland. It was associated with pagan ceremonies, possibly including human sacrifice and believed to have magical power.[382] Based on radiocarbon dating, it is thought the site was in use as early as 3386 BC.[383]

Before the Israelites possessed the Holy Land, stone circles were similarly erected, including one found underwater at Atlit Yam and another, Gilgal Refaim, found nearby in the Golan Heights. The former is a submerged ancient city where archaeologists discovered a semicircle monument dated to 6000 BC, containing seven 1,320-pound megalithic stones.[384] It has the earmarks of an antediluvian civilization associated with the Nephilim. The latter is linked with the biblical figure Og of Bashan.

Bashan, the land of Rephaim, contains hundreds of megalithic stone tombs called "dolmen" or "portal tombs" dating from the fifth to third millennium BC. In the western part of the Bashan plain of the Golan Heights lie the cobbled stone ruins of the most unusual megalith called *Gilgal Rephaim,* which, in Modern Hebrew, is translated as "Wheel of Spirits" or "Wheel of Ghosts." It reflects an interesting development in the meaning of "Rephaim." In the prophetic books, the term is thought to denote spirits, as it means in Modern Hebrew. But in the writings of Moses, it always meant a race of giants. The early Israelites identified it as "the work of giants (Refa'im, also Anakim, Emim, Zuzim)"[385] but, for now it seems sufficient to say that, in its ancient context, "Circle of the Giants" is a better translation of Gilgal Rephaim. Additionally, if one allows my friend Dr. Michael Heiser's view that *nephilim* is an Aramaic loan word for "giants,"[386] then "Circle of the Nephilim" is also reasonable.

Known as the "Stonehenge of the Levant," legends connect the megalithic ruin to Og of Bashan, the last Nephilim king routed by Moses. Although there has been vigorous debate as to how giants repopulated after the Flood, Jewish tradition holds that Noah allowed a seemingly repentant Og on the ark.[387] We believe a second incursion of promiscuous Watchers "and *also after that*, when the sons of God came in unto the daughters of men" (Genesis 6:4, emphasis added) better explains why the Bible describes Og as "the remnant of the Rephaim" (Deuteronomy 3:11). As a spiritual and genetic "seed of the serpent" occupying the Holy Land, new evidence reveals that Og had inherited the land from an ancient line of aristocratic Nephilim in Bashan.

Oriented so that Mount Hermon aligns due north, some forty-two thousand massive basalt rocks are arranged in four concentric circles—the outermost 520 feet in diameter—and boasting a fifteen-foot high tumulus portal at its center, Gilgal Rephaim is one of the earliest megalithic monuments in the Levant. Based on field work in 2010 by Michael Freikman at the Hebrew University,[388] we suggest it is one of the earliest examples of a necromantic portal, a stone circle design of the Nephilim variety.

Called a portal tomb, portal grave, or quoit, a dolmen is a type of single-chamber megalithic tomb usually consisting of two or more upright stones supporting a large, flat, horizontal capstone (e.g., Stonehenge) that also matches the berm layout of a square inside a circle design on Epstein's island. The fifteen-foot-high tumulus at the center of the Wheel of the Giants is centered on a dolmen. In the past, archaeologists believed the centerpiece was a later addition, but new work by Yosef Garfinkel and Michael Freikman of the Hebrew University discovered more ancient layers beneath those identified by previous archaeologists, as well as a new artifact supporting an earlier origin by an unknown people—we believe the Nephilim.

Israeli journalist Barry Chamish attributed the site to the giants and the immortals from whom they descended. Chamish interviewed Rabbi Yisrael Herczeg, who confirmed "the possibility that giant heavenly beings or their descendants could have constructed the circles."[389] When asked if he meant aliens, Rabbi Herczeg replied, "No, more like fallen angels. Og had children with Noah's daughters and they were hybrid giants called the Anakim or Refaim. They existed in ancient times and the Bible records their presence in the Golan Heights. They could have built Gilgal Refaim."[390]

Geometry and astronomy are also visually connected in the site's design, revealing that it was built, at least in part, as an astronomical observatory or for use in worshiping solar deities. It was laid out as an observatory and stellar calendar capable of calculating solstices and equinoxes by conspicuous alignments.[391] This is further supported by calculations from Yoni Mizrachi, who wrote his doctoral dissertation at Harvard about the site, stating, "the first rays of the sun on the longest day of the year shone through the opening in the northwestern gate…then passed through openings in the inner walls to the geometric center of the complex."[392] These alignments suggest that the ancient giant clans knew something about the periphery of the cosmos and placed a high value on tracking the stars.

Given the megalith's location, extreme antiquity, and Rephaim-giant association, local tradition identifying it as Og's tomb seems quiet plausible. Og's gargantuan carcass is conspicuously absent, but the site was likely looted by successive grave robbers over the centuries. It is safe to say that Og's remains (or merely authentic giant bones) would be priceless museum pieces, but one shudders to imagine the dark utility such rarified relics might attain in the capable hands of a studied dark magus. It hardly seems surprising that, at least as far as the public is told, the dolmen chamber was found empty.

Interestingly, Og achieved status in the afterlife as an underworld enforcer. A reference to Og appears in a Phoenician funerary inscription implying that if one disturbs the bones within, "the mighty Og will avenge me."[393] Apparently, Og's name still carried enough clout for ghoul deterrence many centuries after being dispatched to the afterlife by Moses (Deuteronomy 1:4). Considering the Jewish belief that giants like Og are not eligible for the eschatological resurrection of the dead, the references to Og's afterlife activity are what one might expect—that is, if the tradition preserved in the Book of Enoch is correct.

And now, the giants, who are produced from the spirits and flesh, shall be called evil spirits upon the earth, and on the earth shall be their dwelling. Evil spirits have proceeded from their bodies; because they are born from men, and from the holy Watchers is their beginning and primal origin; they shall be evil spirits on earth, and evil spirits shall they be called. As for the spirits of heaven, in heaven shall be their dwelling, but as for the spirits of the earth which were born upon the earth, on the earth shall be their dwelling. (Enoch 15:8–10)

Taken at face value, Og's burial at Gilgal Rephaim, alongside his afterlife reputation, suggests that the Circle of the Nephilim served as a portal—a site where the evil spirits of Nephilim kings could be summoned. While this idea goes beyond the archaeological evidence, the Hebrew term "Rephaim" offers support. The semantic progression of "Rephaim" from denoting a tribe of giants to meaning ghosts in the underworld suggests an actual change in the entities the term represents. While Moses wrote of giants, by Isaiah's time, the meaning had changed.

Hell from beneath is moved for thee to meet thee at thy coming:
It stirreth up *the dead* for thee, even all the chief ones of the earth;
It hath raised up from their thrones all the kings of the nations.
(Isaiah 14:9, emphasis added)

Where the King James reads "the dead," the Hebrew term is *rapha*, also translated as "shades, ghosts, dead, departed spirits, spirits of the dead."[394] It seems plausible that the semantic range widened as the status of the Rephaim giants crossed over to the underworld. In other words, the definition reflects the actual situation as Og was the last physical specimen in that line. From this, we speculate that the Wheel of the Giants served as a necromantic portal for the deceased Nephilim kings of Bashan, of whom Og was the last of their kind. "For only Og king of Bashan remained of the remnant of giants" (Deuteronomy 3:11a).

Gilgal Rephaim's design as a megalithic stone circle seems suitable for necromantic magic. According to the *Encyclopedia of Occultism and*

Parapsychology, a "magic circle" drawn on the ground is essential to successful necromancy.[395] The circle serves to protect the necromancer as he invokes the underworld spirit. Typically, the dark mage collects personal items and employs a portrait of the deceased being summoned. However, in this case, the very center of the megalithic circle contains the dolmen laid corpse, making the portal all the more powerful. The most powerful forms of necromancy use the actual body, as Francis Barrett explained:

> Necromancy has its name because it works on the bodies of the dead, and gives answers by the ghosts and apparitions of the dead, and subterraneous spirits, alluring them into the carcasses of the dead by certain hellish charms, and infernal invocations, and by deadly sacrifices and wicked oblations.[396]

The Bible confirms the existence of underworld gates, as death has a gate. "Have the gates of death been opened unto thee? Or hast thou seen the doors of the shadow of death?" (Job 38:17). The witch of Endor successfully brought up the spirit of Samuel through the use of a ritual pit and familiar spirit (1 Samuel 28:8–20). The portal to the abyss that opens at the fifth-trumpet judgment could similarly be discussed (Revelation 9:2).

An interesting connection between the Watchers' descent to Mount Hermon and the gates of hell is found in Matthew's Gospel. When Jesus declared of the church that "the gates of hell shall not prevail against it" (Matthew 16:18), He was in Caesarea Philippi at the mouth of the famous cave serving as the Roman "Grotto of Pan" at the southwestern base of Mount Hermon, an underworld portal where, in all likelihood, the Watchers who sinned were delivered "into chains of darkness, to be reserved unto judgment" (2 Peter 2:4). Dr. Judd Burton weighs in on this:

> Jesus may have utilized the actual cave of Pan as a backdrop when referring to the "gates of hell, and that the rock was not Peter, but a large rock in front of the cave." This scenario is possible, given the prophetic meditations of Jesus at Caesarea Philippi,

and a death he felt was imminent, the circumstances necessitated a bolder and more dramatic act of oration than simply spitting in the face of Greco-Roman paganism. Mt. Hermon, with its reputation as ground zero for the tumult of fallen angels, was by far, a more profound image to Jesus' Jewish disciples. Jesus was, in effect, shaking his fist in the face of forces more sinister, more powerful, and more dangerous than those of Rome: the devils and giants who defied Yahweh and who set themselves against Jesus' beloved humanity. He established the church, confirms his messiahship, and did so in the very maw of "the gates of hell."[397]

Sundials, Labyrinths, and Freemasons, Oh My!

Further serious and appropriate connections between the occult symbols and facilities already mentioned on Epstein's properties involving mystical paths, circles, and squares are artifacts that not only beam with "illumination," but that are highly suggestive of human sacrifice similar to those once made to solar deities. This includes the massive sundial on Epstein's island (sundials are believed to have originated in ancient Babylonian astronomy for tracking the movements of solar gods), which bears uncanny resem-

Large sundial on Epstein's Orgy Island with "magic hours" marked by rune sacrifice stones

blance to the face of the "Masonic Man" from classic art and curiously incorporating something like "rune" sacrificial stones (used for incantations and magic spells granting power to subdue and eliminate others) similar to Viking blót spots placed at the open "magic" hours of the clock.

Interestingly, the Old Testament describes the sundial or "dial of Ahaz" in Isaiah 38:8 and 2 Kings 20:9 that likely was of Egyptian or Babylonian design. Ahaz was an evil king of Judah who worshiped such idols and whose abhorrent deeds included sacrificing children, including his own, to pagan gods (2 Kings 16:3; 2 Chronicles 28:3).

Image of the Masonic Man from classic
Masonic literature shows nearly identical face
to the one on Epstein's grandiose sundial.

Around the world, many primal cultures including Egyptian, Mesoamerican, and Indo-European societies developed religious concepts around the worship of the sun, moon, and stars as lords of the heavens and underworld. They associated these respective deities to divine rights of the elite, especially as it pertained to nobility or those having sovereignty over others. These solar gods were credited with beneficial agriculture and demanded human sacrifice to guarantee bountiful crop yields, including entities of pre-Columbian Peru and Mexico that freemason Manly P. Hall cherished.

Anthropology professor John Verano explains why human sacrifice—in this case, to the sun god Huitzilopochtli—held spiritual significance for the Aztecs:

> "It was a deeply serious and important thing for them," says Verano. Large and small human sacrifices would be made throughout the year to coincide with important calendar dates, he explains, to dedicate temples, to reverse drought and famine, and more.
>
> The rationale for Aztec human sacrifice was, first and foremost, a matter of survival. According to Aztec cosmology, the sun god Huitzilopochtli was waging a constant war against darkness, and if the darkness won, the world would end. To keep the sun moving across the sky and preserve their very lives, the Aztecs had to feed Huitzilopochtli with human hearts and blood.[398]

As I've written before, irrefutable evidence exists that early Freemasons and those working with them were aware of these Mesoamerican beliefs, including sundials connected to human sacrifice, and such is actually incorporated directly into the design of the Capitol dome in Washington, DC, as vividly illustrated in the commissioned artwork of Constantino Brumidi. Born July 26, 1805, in Rome, Brumidi was an Italian/Greek painter who made his name restoring sixteenth-century Vatican frescos, as well as artwork in several Roman palaces. Following the French occupation of Rome in 1849, Brumidi immigrated to the United States, where he became a citizen and began work for the Jesuits in New York (viewed at that time as the "hidden power and authority" of the Roman Catholic Church). This work included frescos in the Church of St. Ignatius in Baltimore, Maryland; the Church of St. Aloysius in Washington, DC; and St. Stephen's Church in Philadelphia—namely, the Crucifixion, the Martydom of St. Stephen, and the Assumption of Mary.

Cortez and Montezuma at Mexican Temple, by Brumidi

For reasons that remain somewhat unclear, abruptly in 1854, the Jesuits financed a trip for Brumidi to Mexico, where among other things he engaged in the curious task of making copious notes of the ancient Aztec Calendar Stone (also known as the "Stone of the Sun"), which so famously rolled over in the year 2012.

Immediately upon his return from Mexico, Brumidi took his collection of notes and drawings to Washington, DC, where he met with Quartermaster General Montgomery C. Meigs, supervisor of construction over the wings and dome of the United States Capitol. Brumidi was quickly commissioned to be the "government painter" and began adorning the hallways and Rotunda of the Capitol with pagan frescos sacred to Freemasonry, including the *Apotheosis of George Washington* and the famous *Frieze of American History*. Brumidi died in 1880 and three other artists completed the frieze, but not before Brumidi attached to his historic work—sometime between 1878–1880—a scene called *Cortez and Montezuma at Mexican Temple*, featuring the Aztec Calendar Stone and other important symbolism.

The Stone of the Sun depicted in Brumidi's frieze (the circular object behind the figures on the right) is based on the actual twelve-foot-tall, four-foot-thick, twenty-four-ton, elaborately carved Aztec Calendar Stone, which some scholars believe may have been an ancient sundial[399] connected to the solar deity Tonatiuh. During the pinnacle of Aztec civilization when the Aztec dominated all other tribes of Mexico, this Stone rested atop the Tenochtitlan Temple in the midst of the most powerful and largest city in Mesoamerica. Today, Mexico City's Cathedral, where Brumidi worked, occupies this site. The Spaniards buried the Stone there, and it remained hidden beneath the Cathedral until it was rediscovered in 1790. Then it was raised and embedded into the wall of the Cathedral, where it remained until 1885. Today, the Stone of the Sun is on display in the National Museum of Anthropology in Mexico City's Chapultepec Park.

The inclusion of this symbolism and its accompanying idols in the US Capitol dome is important. The sun god Tonatiuh, whose name is derived from Aztec verbs depicting the sun as lighted or shimmering, is seen at the center of the Sun Stone. He was a solar deity that delivered vital prophecies and demanded human sacrifices. In fact, more than twenty thousand victims per year were offered to him, according to Aztec and Spanish records, and in the single year of 1487, Aztec priests sacrificed eighty thousand people to him at the dedication of the reconstructed temple of the sun god.

Some scholars believe the Stone of the Sun, whose reproduction sits inside the US Capitol dome, was an ancient sundial for tracking the movements of the god that required human sacrifice.

Another connection between Brumidi's Stone of the Sun depiction, Freemasonry, Epstein's island, and the Vatican can be seen in the *Cortez and Montezuma* scene where what looks like a drum sits behind the kneeling Aztec. This image bears the shape of the Maltese cross, a symbol connected in history with the empire of Osiris as starting on the island of Malta. The Maltese cross was adopted by the Knights of Malta (connected with Freemasonry) and the Vatican (where Brumidi first worked and found favor). Readers will immediately note that this shape, once again, involves four paths toward a circular middle, just like the berm image at Epstein's island did before it was obscured.

The Maltese Cross bears uncanny similarity to the four paths leading to a circular middle at Epstein's island, as well as to the Aztec sundial depicting Tonatiuh, the god who demanded human sacrifice.

Connected to all this at the US Capitol building in Washington, DC, is an essential point made by William Henry and Mark Gray in their book, *Freedom's Gate: Lost Symbols in the U.S. Capitol* recognized: "The U.S. Capitol has numerous architectural and other features that unquestionably identify it with ancient [sun] temples."[400] After listing various features to make their case that the US Capitol building is a "religious temple"—including housing the image of a deified being, heavenly beings, gods, symbols, inscriptions, sacred geometry, columns, prayers, and orientation to the sun—they conclude:

> The designers of the city of Washington DC oriented it to the Sun—especially the rising Sun on June 21 and December 21 [the same day and month as the end of the Mayan calendar]. The measurements for this orientation were made from the location of the center of the Dome of the U.S. Capitol, rendering it a "solar temple." Its alignment and encoded numerology point to the Sun as well as the stars. A golden circle on the Rotunda story and a white star in the Crypt marks this spot.... It is clear that the

builders viewed the Capitol as America's sole temple: a solemn…
Solar Temple to be exact.[401]

Are such connections to solar worship, Freemasons, obelisks, and
human sacrifice reflected in the large sundial on Epstein's island? Are the
"rune" sacrificial stones at the open "magic" hours of the clock further
confirmation? There certainly seems to be redundant imagery tied to the
historicity of all these structures and architecture.

For example, as mentioned earlier, the Obelisk in St. Peter's Square at
the Vatican was originally built to stand at the ancient epicenter of Egyptian sun worship at Heliopolis, and some scholars believe the structure
there as well as the one built by Freemasons in America's capital may also
have been designed to serve as the center needle of a giant sundial to follow the movements of the great sun gods, including the Egyptian Ra. Add
to that the fact that ritualized sex (such as I believe occurred with Epstein
and his pals) was central to the worship of solar deities, including those
that demanded human sacrifice. It would be superficial to perceive such
symbolism incorporated in Washington, DC, involving the Capitol dome
(representing the habitually pregnant belly of Isis) and the obelisk (representing the erect phallus of Osiris) as profane or pornographic. These are
in fact ritual fertility objects, the same as those from Heliopolis, which the
ancients believed could produce tangible reactions, properties, or "manifestations" within the material world.

As I've explained before:

The obelisk and dome as imitations of the deities' male and
female reproductive organs could, through government representation, invoke into existence the being or beings symbolized by
them. This alchemy was supported through temple prostitutes
who represented the human manifestation of the goddess (Isis in
this case) who performed ritual sex as a form of imitative magic.
These prostitutes usually began their services to the goddess as

children such as Epstein preferred, and were deflowered at a very young age by a priest or, as Isis was, by a modeled obelisk of Osiris' phallus. Sometimes these prostitutes were chosen on the basis of their beauty, as the sexual mates of sacred temple bulls who were considered the incarnation of Osiris. In other places, such as at Mendes, temple prostitutes were offered in coitus to divine goats. Through such imitative sex, the dome and obelisk became "energy receivers," capable of assimilating Ra's essence from the rays of the sun, which in turn drew forth the "seed" of the underworld Osiris. The seed of the dead deity would, according to the supernaturalism, transmit upward from out of the underworld through the base (testes) of the obelisk and magically emit from the tower's head into the womb (Dome) of Isis where incarnation into the sitting pharaoh/king/president would occur (during what Freemasons also call *the raising [of Osiris] ceremony*). In this way, Osiris could be habitually "born again" or reincarnated as Horus and constantly direct the spiritual destiny of the nation.

This metaphysical phenomenon, which originated with Nimrod/Semiramis and was central to numerous other ancient cultures, was especially developed in Egypt, where Nimrod/Semiramis were known as Osiris/Isis (and in Ezekiel chapter 8 the children of Israel set up the obelisk ["image of jealousy," verse 5] facing the entry of their temple—just as the dome faces the Obelisk in Washington, DC, and in the Vatican City—and were condemned by God for worshipping the Sun [Ra] while weeping for Osiris [Tammuz]). The familiar Masonic figure of the point within a circle is the symbol of this union between Ra, Osiris, and Isis. The "point" represents Osiris' phallus in the center of the circle or womb of Isis, which in turn is enlivened by the sun rays from Ra, just as is represented today at the Vatican, where the Egyptian Obelisk of Osiris sits within a circle, and in Washington, DC, where the obelisk does similarly, situated so as to be the first thing the sun (Ra) strikes as it rises over the capital city and which, when viewed from overhead, forms the magical point within a circle known as a *circumpunct*. The sorcery is further amplified, according to ancient occultic beliefs, by the presence of the Reflecting Pool in DC, which serves as a mirror to heaven and "transferring point" for those spirits and energies.[402]

Although the Hebrew Bible (for example, Deuteronomy 4:19, 17:3) contains strict prohibitions against worshipping the sun, moon, and stars, Ezekiel chapter 8 describes how sun worship was nevertheless observed for a while in the Temple of Jerusalem itself by paganized Hebrews, and even after the Temple was destroyed, the worship of the "queen of heaven" continued (Jeremiah 44:17) during an advent when sacrificing children to gods was widespread.

Around the same time this was happening in the Middle East, across the sea in the West, a trade route of some kind between ancient Mexicans and early American Indians appears to have been established (as thoroughly documented in our books *On the Path of the Immortals* and *Unearthing the Lost World of the Cloudeaters*), which appears to have resulted in the transference of those religious ideas Freemason Manly P. Hall celebrated, including worship of solar deities and human sacrifice.

In fact, I recall when studying the Anasazi (ancient Puebloans of Native American culture that lived in the present-day Four Corners region of the United States—Utah, northeastern Arizona, northwestern New Mexico, and southwestern Colorado) and the question of how these cliff-dwellers disappeared in what seems like overnight, I met up with a native guide at Mesa Verde National Park in southwest Colorado who directed me to the mysterious Sun Temple, an enigmatic structure that overlooks some of the area's most popular attractions, including the Cliff Palace. I wanted to study and measure these ruins because the large and significant site holds much inscrutability in that nobody, including archaeologists and cultural historians, knows what it was for. An eroded

stone basin with three indentations at the southwest corner of the structure suggests that it, too, may have been purposed as a sundial to mark
the changes in the seasons. Two kivas on top of the structure, together
with the lack of windows or doors elsewhere, intimates that it was not
meant for housing, which has led modern Pueblo Indians to propose
that it was some type of ceremonial structure probably planned for ritual
purposes dedicated to the Sun God. The amount of fallen stone that was
removed during its excavation is said to indicate that the original walls
were between eleven and fourteen feet tall. These walls were thick, double-
coursed construction, with a rubble core placed between the panels for
strength and insulation. After studying the Sun Temple and comparing it
to ancient Mesoamerican culture and edifices, it is this author's opinion
(which is as good as anybody else's, since we don't really know) that this
site may have been intended as a place for *human sacrifice* similar to those
of the Aztec and Maya. I say this for a couple reasons. First, Dr. Don Mose
Jr., a third-generation medicine man I met with for a large part of a day
during the *Path of the Immortals* investigation for Defender Publishing
and SkyWatch TV, told us that the oldest legends of the Anasazi, which he
had been told by his great-grandfather (who likewise had been told by *his*
ancestors) included stories of the Anasazi turning to sorcery, sacrifice, and
cannibalism after they "lost their way" and were driven insane by a reptilian creature, which they depict with a halo above his head. (Images of this
being are included in the petroglyphs we filmed inside the canyons, and I
believe they likely attest to the fallen reptile [or reptiles] of biblical fame,
which also misled humanity.) Second, blood sacrifice was a religious activity in most premodern cultures during some stage of their development,
especially as it involved invoking the gods, and the Sun God was typically
chief among them. This included animals and humans or the bloodletting of community members during rituals overseen by their priests. In
fact, the Mayans—who may have influenced the Anasazi, or vice versa—
believed "that the only way for the sun to rise was for them to sacrifice
someone or something every day to the gods."[403]

Labyrinths and Human Sacrifice

Another interesting artifact linked with human sacrifice and reflected at both Epstein's island and at his New Mexico estate are labyrinthian designs, which extend back as far as five thousand years. Strangely, this too may be connected to at least one example of how the Vatican Knights and later Freemasons combined labyrinths with initiatory paths or rituals they connected with Jesus Christ[404] as a "solar deity" (labyrinths were Christianized, especially during the Middle Ages, and placed on floors of cathedrals for use in meditation). This practice continues today; in fact, I witnessed denominational youth camps in Oregon where children were taken into the woods and taught to use tree branches, pebbles, and other "Gaia" products to outline such magic prayer trails, with participants moving through the labyrinths to specific mystical areas where they would then stop and meditate to "connect with the spirit." The occult significance of this symbolism in church youth events is dangerously meaningful, as navigating labyrinths actually began in mythology with the story of Queen Pasiphae and her amorous affair with a sacrificial bull. The union resulted in the birth of the transgenic Minotaur, a creature that lived in at the center of the labyrinth—an elaborate circular maze designed by the architect Daedalus, a craftsman and artist in Greek mythology, and his son Icarus, on the command of King Minos of Crete—*where every year boys and girls were sent to be sacrificed.*

Is this why Epstein's island and his New Mexico estate are littered with labyrinthian imagery and structures? There is no doubt what labyrinths were originally designed for. In mythology, the people of Athens "were at one point compelled by King Minos of Crete to choose 14 young noble citizens (seven young men and seven maidens) to be offered as sacrificial victims to the half-human, half-taurine monster Minotaur to be killed in retribution for the death of Minos' son Androgeos. The victims were drawn by lots, were required to go unarmed, and would end up either being consumed by the Minotaur or getting lost and perishing in the Labyrinth, the maze-like structure where the Minotaur was kept."[405]

Christ in the center of a labyrinth discovered in Alatri, a province of Frosinone in the Italian region of the Lazio

Every year, boys and girls were sent into the labyrinth to be sacrificed to the Minotaur, a creature with the head and tail of a bull and the body of a man.

Very large, labyrinth-like structure seen in aerial photograph of Epstein's Zorro Ranch bears four walkways inside a confined area leading to a circular mid-section.

The Plot Thickens—Jeffrey Epstein, Ghislaine Maxwell, and Crowley Inspired Sex Magick

Some may be aware that Jeffrey Epstein's army of pedophile enablers included the modeling agency MC2—a company financed by Epstein, according to court papers. It was run by his friend Jean-Luc Brunel (who "disappeared like a ghost" in September, 2019),[406] who also served as a scout for the hit television program *Next Top Model* and once flew penniless twelve-year-old kids in from France as a birthday gift for Epstein to rape. Young ladies whom Brunel enlisted as models from all over the world and who were promised careers were also often groomed for erotic exploitation. "Brunel had more than catwalk appearances planned for some of the girls," according to documents unsealed in a defamation case against former Epstein fixer, Ghislaine Maxwell. "He offered up girls as young as 16 for 'massages' with Epstein that often wound up as sexual-abuse sessions, according to documents filed in the lawsuit. In fact, in 2005, 'Brunel called Epstein and left a message that "he is sending him a 16-year-old Russian girl for purposes of sex," the court papers say.'"[407]

In addition to Brunel, other Epstein recruiters included New York City's dance studios[408] and a trove of teen-girl-associated modeling companies with "handlers" like Sarah Kellen (who purportedly kept a long list of underage girls she could call to facilitate Epstein), Deborah Palfrey, Nada Marcinkova, Lesley Groff, Haley Robson, and possibly even Les Wexner, the CEO of L Brands–which owns The Limited, Abercrombie & Fitch, and Victoria's Secret (Maria Farmer blames Wexner for sexual assault by Epstein and his "madam," Ghislaine Maxwell, that she says occurred on his property).[409]

But Epstein's gal pal Ghislaine Maxwell is the one squarely on the radar of investigators, with sex trafficking and conspiracy charges expected to be filed against her as I write this book (notwithstanding she remains hiding out in Brazil apparently evading authorities as I type).[410]

The British socialite, whose father, the fraudulent newspaper proprietor Robert Maxwell, died at sea in 1991, organized the complex logistical operation that fed Epstein's apparently insatiable appetite for erotic encounters with girls as young as 14, according to victims and witness statements from members of his household.[411]

While all that has been sufficiently covered in the news, the rabbit hole between Maxwell, Epstein, the Clintons and sex-magick is more involved than media outlets have yet discovered or disclosed. I say this because, unknown to the public at large, familial (bloodline) networks dating back to the 1930s–'40s involving mystical copulation employed during ritualistic intercourse was conducted by associates of and likely members of these families for the purpose of "seeding" the human race with ancient demonism connected to prophecy and the final days of man.

The story begins in 1936, when three pioneering young men traveled to the Caltech office of prominent aerodynamicist Theodore von Kármán with a request for help in designing a space rocket. Frank Malina, Jack Parsons, and Ed Forman were as serious as they were technically gifted, and their research led to a concatenation of events ultimately establishing the Jet Propulsion Laboratory as well as eventually NASA. But Malina and Parsons are of particular interest in this book's research, as Ghislaine Maxwell's brother-in-law Roger Malina's father was this very man—Frank Malina—one of the original "Rocketmen" from the "Suicide Squad" and a good friend of Jack Parsons, whose own iconoclastic interests in turn involved devotion to the dark teachings of Aleister Crowley.

So as not to confuse the reader, this means there has been a decades-long circle of influence binding the Maxwell family with Jeffrey Epstein, the Clintons, and demonic sexual activity.

And when I say "demonic," I mean that in the most literal sense.

I started becoming aware of just how dark and enduring this history is over a decade ago, following the release of my book *Nephilim Stargates* and a series of televised shows with J. R. Church and Gary Stearman for their *Prophecy in the News* broadcast, in which we discussed the idea of supernatural "portals, doorways, and openings." The concept is actually an ancient one—that gateways between our world and other dimensions exist or can be created, through which entities including what some people call aliens can pass. At one point, the programs with Church and Stearman focused on a theory I had briefly raised involving infamous occultist Aleister Crowley, Jet Propulsion Laboratory founder Jack Parsons, and Church of Scientology founder L. Ron Hubbard and their attempts to create dimensional vortexes that would bridge the gap between the world of the seen and the unseen. In Crowley's case, the ritual was called the Amalantrah Working, and according to him, it became successful when a presence manifested through the rift. He called the being "Lam" and drew a portrait of it. The strange image, detailed ninety years ago, bears powerful similarity with alien greys of later pop culture. Following that, Crowley's devotees Hubbard and Parsons attempted to do the same thing by inviting the spirit of Babylon (their ceremony was called the Babalon Working) through a portal during ritual sex. Their hope was to incarnate the whore of Babylon—a demon child or *gibborim.*

Now, if you're wondering how the Clintons are connected to the sex-magick side of all this, in a segment of my best-selling book *Saboteurs* (Babylon Workings), I explain:

> It was into this pot-smoke-filled, heroin-induced, LSD-taking atmosphere of the 40s that NASA Jet Propulsion Laboratory rocket scientist Jack Parsons and Scientology founder L. Ron Hubbard came up with the infamous "Babalon Working" that allegedly opened a gate that fueled the modern UFO era and maybe played a role in the birth of Hillary Clinton.
>
> I say this with a strong emphasis on *maybe.*
>
> Both Parsons and Hubbard were disciples of Aliester Crowley and practiced his teaching called Thelema as a philosophy defined by the maxim, "Do what thou wilt shall be the whole of the law." It comes from Crowley's *Book of the Law*, which can

be connected to the "Spirit Cooking" ceremonies of the Podestas and Abramovic [revealed in Wikileaks releases], which was channeled by an incorporeal demonic intelligence named Aiwass.[412] Thelema is a narcissistic ideology that undergirds several esoteric magic societies like the AA and the Ordo Templi Orientis that fundamentally oppose God's moral law. Satan targets sexuality because procreation is the human capability that comes closest to the divine. As a result, it's not too surprising that sexual perversion and "sex magick" are essential components of occult rituals. Parsons and Hubbard's "working" entailed all sorts of such aberrant sexual activity....

Parsons and Hubbard's motive was largely self-gratification, but the Working explicitly stated the goal of transforming traditional values. The rituals were aimed at incarnating the archetypal divine feminine and changing culture through her influence. It is a matter of record that feminism and pantheistic monism were sowed into public consciousness from the ivory towers of academia shortly subsequent to Parsons' dark invocation:

The ultimate goal of these operations, carried out during February and March 1946, was to give birth to the magical being, or "moonchild," described in Crowley's works. Using the powerful energy of IX degree Sex Magick, the rites were intended to open a doorway through which the goddess Babalon herself might appear in human form.[413]

Parsons believed that he and Hubbard accomplished this task in a series of rituals culminating in 1946. Parsons' biography preserves a celebratory statement regarding her embodiment in the womb. In a fragment from his writings, Parsons, exhausted and exultant, declared his work a success. He believed that Babalon, in the manner of the Immaculate Conception, was due to be born to a woman somewhere on earth in nine months' time. "Babalon is incarnate upon the earth today, awaiting the proper hour for her manifestation," he wrote.[414]

Accordingly, one would expect a female child was to be born around 1947, and, indeed, such an influential feminist was delivered that year who may offer the most promise for identifying the fruit of Parsons' infamous ritual.[415] That would be none other than *Hillary Rodham Clinton.* Intriguingly, Parsons later referred again to "Babalon the Scarlet Woman" and this time by a particular name in his *Book of the Antichrist.* On October 31, 1948, a full sixty-nine years ago when the female child would have been only around one year of age, Parsons wrote that her spirit contacted him, calling itself "Hilarion," who, he said, would become an international public figure dedicated to bringing the work of the Antichrist to fruition.[416] Why is that important? Because the etymology of Hilarion is the arcane "Hillary."[417]

I asked myself: 1) how many internationally influential feminists were 2) born in 1947 who are 3) named "Hillary" and that 4) have the potential to become the leader of the most powerful nation on earth, which 5) was dedicated from its inception to the enthronement of Osiris-Apollo, who 6) the Bible recognizes as Antichrist and 7) a spirit calling itself "Hillary" made clear to Jack Parsons sixty-nine years ago it is dedicated to helping become king of the earth?

…This came to my mind when reading the Wikileaks email revelations and remembering how Hillary hinted "alien disclosure" would be made if she was elected president[418] and Abramovic, the Podestas and other close Hillary affiliates were manifest believers in the same UFOs and "contiguous aliens"[419] that Parsons and Hubbard sought (the Church of Scientology Hubbard started is based on an alien called "Xenu"),[420] as well as being practitioners of the same Crowley occultism that Parsons and Hubbard were devotees of, and it immediately seemed to me beyond probability of coincidence. Rather, I straightway thought in the days leading up to the presidential election that these modern Thelemists actually believed Hillary is—or could be—the incarnation of the archetype divine feminine, the Whore of Babylon, the "Hilarion" that is set to take the throne of the most powerful nation on earth to assist Antichrist in his bid to rule the entire world.[421]

All of the above is particularly interesting given how, at the writing of this book, former chief executive of the Trump campaign, Steve Bannon, believed the Hilarion at the mystical age "seventy-two" was strongly considering plans for another run at the White House while Mitt Romney likewise was actively trying to influence the 2020 election. Could both of them at mystical "seventy-two" be motivated by supernaturalism stirring a White Horse Prophecy (as outlined in my book *Zenith 2016*?)[422] or in Hillary's case reflect her and Bill's close relationship to the sexually corrupt Epstein and the Parsons-circle alleged paramour-turned-pimp Ghislaine Maxwell's family that could be uncovered if Trump wins a second term?

Time may tell.

Meanwhile, Hillary's obsession with John Podesta's interest in Satanism, Thelemic aliens, and UFOs seems to have also been connected to other Hilarion occultism that started with séances she conducted at the White House with psychic medium Jean Houston, during which she allegedly was visited by the phantom of her political inspiration Eleanor Roosevelt. Former presidential candidate and new ager Marianne Williamson participated in some of these seances with Hillary,[423] and Clinton insider Larry Nichols even claimed Bill Clinton told him that Hillary was a member of a coven in California that regularly met to practice such witchcraft.

> Bill told me that she was going out there, she and a group of women, and she would be a part of a witch's church. Man, when Bill told me that, he could have hit me with a baseball bat. I tried to point out to him, "Do you realize what would happen if that got out?" Of course my job was to make sure it didn't get out.
>
> Now I don't know…if Hillary still partakes in the witch ritual…. But for the better part of many years, Hillary would go

quite often, whether it was regularly once a month, or maybe once every couple of months, she would go out on the weekend simply to be a part of it.[424]

Nichols' allegations are believable, and don't forget it was Bill and Hillary who introduced Wiccan chaplains to the US military. In the leadup to the 2016 election, it also came to light that the UFO interest John Podesta and Hillary were fascinated by "quickly took a dive into the paranormal, which, according to a senior manager, included studying 'bizarre creatures, poltergeist activity, invisible entities.' The reports were subcontracted to a research team led by a psychic espionage researcher."[425] News agencies at the time also uncovered Wikileaks emails tying Hillary and her circle of friends to actual Satanic rituals and other occultist beliefs wherein an unclassified US Department of State letter depicted a ritual partially describing: "with fingers crossed, the old rabbit's foot out of the box in the attic, I will be sacrificing a chicken in the backyard to Moloch."[426]

Moloch (Molech) is of course the ancient Canaanite demon connected with child sacrifice.

Wow.

The idea that some of the world's most powerful people were eagerly worshiping demons and attempting to put themselves into contact with "extraterrestrial intelligence" from a "contiguous universe" that included bizarre creatures, poltergeist activity, and invisible entities indicates the Parsons-Crowley level of ritual supernaturalism was not superficial and was occurring right when Hillary was on the presidential campaign trail promising to release specifics about government information on aliens and UFOs. This illustrates how seriously their fascination with occult forces truly is. Hillary was even "familiar enough with the topic to correct Jimmy Kimmel in a late-night television interview," Derek Gilbert and Josh Peck point out in their book, *The Day the Earth Stands Still.* "When Kimmel asked Hillary Clinton about UFOs, she said, 'You know, there's a new name. It's unexplained aerial phenomenon, UAP; that's the latest nomenclature.' Joseph G. Buchman, who was a key organizer and moderator for the 2013 Citizen Hearing on Disclosure in Washington, D.C., added, 'Hillary has embraced this issue with an absolutely unprecedented level of interest in American politics.'" Podesta, in his foreword for the book, *UFOs: Generals, Pilots, and Government Officials Go on the Record,* written by investigative journalist Leslie Kean and released in 2010, adjoined, "The time to pull back the curtain on the topic is long overdue."[427]

And the threads tying such occult elite, sex perverts and wealthy families don't stop there. Ever heard of "the Séance that changed America"? It all started with a man named Andrija Puharich and is linked to Gene Roddenberry, CIA mind-control experiments, the assassination of John F. Kennedy, and a group of "aliens" that claimed to be the creators of humanity. As Derek Gilbert and Josh Peck explain:

> Let's back up to World War 2. During the war, Andrija Puharich, the son of immigrants from the Balkans, attended Northwestern University outside Chicago, where he earned a bachelor's degree in philosophy in 1942 and his M.D. in 1947. Through an invitation from a well-off family friend, who'd married into the Borden dairy family, Puharich found himself in Maine in early 1948, where he established a research institute to pursue his interest in parapsychology, the Round Table Foundation of Electrobiology, usually shortened to the Round Table.
>
> This book isn't big enough to hold a full account of what Puharich was up to for the U.S. Army in the 1950s, but the upshot is that he was apparently researching parapsychology and chemical substances that might stimulate the human mind to reach into realities beyond those we can normally perceive with our natural senses. And at one of his gatherings in Maine, on New Year's Eve in 1952, Puharich and his Round Table, working with a Hindu channeler named Dr. D. G. Vinod, conducted a seance that apparently made contact with something calling itself The Nine. Thus began a truly breathtaking chapter in America's mostly hidden programs that searched for ways to weaponize the occult.

Some months later, on June 27, 1953, the night of the full moon, Puharich gathered around him what was to be a core group of the Round Table Foundation for another session with Vinod. The membership of this group of nine members—á la The Nine—is illuminating. Henry Jackson, Georgia Jackson, Alice Bouverie, Marcella Du Pont, Carl Betz, Vonnie Beck, Arthur Young, Ruth Young, and Andrija Puharich. Dr. Vinod acted as the medium. Imagine the Fellowship of the Ring, with government funding and a security classification that was, well, "cosmic." This group included old money—very old money. The Du Pont name is obvious, but some of the others were no less prominent. Alice Bouverie was an Astor—a descendent of John Jacob Astor and the daughter of Col. John Jacob Astor IV, who built the Astoria Hotel and went down with the Titanic. Arthur Young was the designer of the Bell helicopter; his wife had been born Ruth Forbes. Yes, that Forbes. Ruth's previous marriage had been to another old-money family that traced its roots back to the early days of the American colonies, George Lyman Paine. Their son, Michael Paine, married a woman named Ruth Hyde, and in 1963, Michael and Ruth Paine became friends with a young couple newly arrived from Russia, Lee and Marina Oswald. Yes, that Lee Oswald. Lee Harvey. So. A Du Pont, an Astor, and a Forbes/Paine, in a psychic research group funded by the U.S. government, communicating with…what? And what was the monkey god doing there? Dr. Vinod sat on the floor, the nine members of the group in a circle around him, with a copper plate on his lap, prayer beads in his hands, and a small statue of "Hanoum," a Hindu god that the author believes to be Hanuman, the Monkey King [which president Obama kept / keeps in his pocket as a "charm"). If this is so, it is interesting in that Hanuman was a human being, a minister, before becoming divine due to his devotion and courage. The half-human, half-divine image is one that becomes more important and more obvious as this study progresses. Another important aspect of Hanuman is his depiction in much Indian art as holding an entire mountain in one hand (and a club in the other). When—in the Ramayana and during the battle of Rama and Ravana—Lakshmana was mortally wounded, Hanuman raced to a mountain covered with different healing herbs. Not knowing which one Lakshmana required, Hanuman simply brought the entire mountain. Hanuman—as well as his fellow monkey-men, the Vanaras of southern India—is often shown with his hand in front of his mouth, signifying "silence" as well as obedience, in much the same way western occultists depict Harpocrates. In this sense, replete with silence, obedience, a club, and a mountain of herbs, Hanuman might easily have been the patron saint of MK-ULTRA.

What an interesting, um, coincidence. Remember that Aleister Crowley believed The Book of the Law was dictated to him by Aiwass, the messenger of Hoor-Paar-Kraat—Harpocrates.

Anyway, The Nine disclosed that they wanted the Round Table to lead a spiritual renewal on Earth, and eventually revealed that they were extraterrestrials orbiting the planet in a giant, invisible spacecraft.

Riiiight.

Still, consider that the group assembled that night included highly intelligent, very successful people. Puharich later wrote, "We took every known precaution against fraud, and the staff and I became thoroughly convinced that we were dealing with some kind of an extraordinary extraterrestrial intelligence." In other words, if this was a hoax, it worked on some very smart people.

On the other hand, the decades-long career of Andrija Puharich suggests that it may also have been a case of "leading the witnesses," in a sense. He appears to have been a seeker who, like Fox Mulder in The X-Files, really wanted to believe.

But it was more than that. The Nine declared, "God is nobody else than we together, the Nine Principles of God."

So extraterrestrial and divine. Remember that while the Round Table was hearin from The Nine, Aleister Crowley's acolyte Kenneth Grant was developing his occult system based on an ET god from Sirius.

The Nine, Fifteen Years Later

Dr. Vinod returned to India a short time later, and contact with The Nine was interrupted for more than fifteen years. Then, in 1971, Puharich discovered Israeli psychic Uri Geller.

Geller, best known for his alleged power to bend silverware with his mind, became for a time the new link to The Nine. Through Geller, The Nine informed Puharich that his life's mission was "to alert the world to an imminent mass landing of spaceships that would bring representatives of The Nine."

Well, that didn't happen. And Geller decided to move on in 1973, so Puharich had to find someone else to bridge the gap between Earth and the giant, invisible craft allegedly orbiting the globe. He eventually connected with former race-car driver Sir John Whitmore and Florida psychic Phyllis Schlemmer. She became the authorized spokesperson for their contact within The Nine, an entity who identified himself as "Tom."

Puharich, Whitmore and Schlemmer then set up Lab Nine at Puharich's estate in Ossining, New York. The Nine's disciples included multi-millionaire businessmen (many hiding behind pseudonyms and including members of Canada's richest family, the Bronfmans), European nobility, scientists from the Stamford Research Institute and at least one prominent political figure who was a personal friend of President Gerald Ford.

A member of Lab Nine in 1974 and '75 was Star Trek creator Gene Roddenberry, who reportedly wrote a screenplay based on The Nine. Some suggest that concepts from the channeling sessions Roddenberry attended surfaced in the early Star Trek movies and in the series Star Trek: The Next Generation and Star Trek: Deep Space Nine.

Big surprise there, right?

Before Lab Nine folded in 1978, the identities of Tom and the Other Eight were finally revealed: Tom was Atum, he said, the creator of the Great Ennead, the Egyptian gods worshipped at Heliopolis, near modernday Cairo. Besides Atum, the Ennead included his children Shu and Tefnut; their children Geb and Nut; and their children Osiris, Isis, Set, Nephthys, and sometimes the son of Osiris and Isis, Horus [so we see this come full circle again to the U.S. capital city where the dome and obelisk center around the veneration of Osiris].

Connecting dots between Andrija Puharich, who was almost certainly a CIA asset during much of the time he conducted parapsychological research, and the volunteers of his Round Table and Lab Nine, we can link the United States government (and specifically the U.S. Army and CIA during the period of mind-control research projects like BLUEBIRD and MKULTRA), members of upper-class society from the East Coast and Canada, the creator of the most successful science fiction entertainment franchise in history, extraterrestrials, and gods. And not just any gods—the pantheon that included the chaos god, Set, who Crowleyite Kenneth Grant believed was the spirit of the age.

Oh, yes—and the Kennedy assassination.

How do we wrap our heads around this? Considering that Puharich was likely doing this research for the government and that he led the witnesses, suggesting to Geller and at least one of his successors while they were under hypnosis that they were being contacted by The Nine, it appears that this was a long PSYOP to stir up belief in the existence of ETIs and the return of the old gods.

To what end? For Puharich and his superiors, maybe it was an experiment into group dynamics, or maybe a test of how people would react to the imminent arrival of extraterrestrial visitors.[428]

Artwork Demons Love

Last but not least we can also add to the Podesta-Hillary-Parsons-Puharich alien-sex magick equations that, like John's brother Tony Podesta, Jeffrey Epstein had a disturbing corpus of occult and pedophilic artwork overtly similar to the highly suggestive and disconcerting collection belonging to Tony Podesta, which depicts numerous ritualist themes, including cannibalism, decapitation, mutilation, and what some consider child porn.

For example, among Tony Podesta's "art" is Louise Bourgeois' *The Arch of Hysteria*—an eight-foot-long sculpture of a decapitated naked man's contorted body (which hangs from the ceiling of the Podestas' stairwell) and pictures of naked children and paintings of near-naked, sad-looking children whose buttocks are red as if they have been punished.

Epstein also collected and displayed such "art" involving a nude female hanging from a chandelier, prosthetic eyeballs, and even an image of Bill Clinton dressed in a Monica Lewinsky-style blue dress with high heels, gesturing seductively to viewers.

On the decapitated sculpture in Tony Podesta's home, Harrison Koehli at SOTT.net (Signs of the Times) sees the art as more than the weird and disturbing attraction of deviant minds. He notes something important connecting sex rituals with human sacrifice: "Whether intentional or not, the sculpture bears a resemblance to one of serial killer Jeffrey Dahmer's victims." Koehli then points to a link where one of Dahmer's fatalities was photographed, which for all intents and purposes looks identical to Podesta's headless art piece. A caption on the photograph of Dahmer's subject reads: "Dahmer photographed his victims' bodies in various positions that he found sexually significant." Koehli adds, "I could find no indication that Bourgeois (the artist that made Podesta's figurine) intentionally modelled the sculpture on the Dahmer photograph [but] the similarities are striking, including the arched position, the slender frame, the prominent ribs, and the lack of a head."[429]

If readers want to know more about the unnerving art collections of these depraved minds, I suggest reading *Saboteurs*. Meanwhile, this curious excursion into the macabre world of deviants and sex fiends finally delivers us to Epstein's intersecting interests in having his "seed" used to create new versions of humanity, a desire drawn straight from the sexual activity instigated in the demonic, human-sacrificing days of Noah and repeated by Aleister Crowley, Jack Parsons, and L. Ron Hubbard.

Before Epstein's death, the *New York Times* and other news sources discovered that he had what they called "an unusual dream: He hoped to seed the human race with his DNA by impregnating women at his vast New Mexico ranch."

Like other things, this "dream" seems to have been connected with powerful and blasphemous ritualistic sex.

For example, at the ranch—which featured an eight-person party shower and underground strip club where teens "entertained" VIP pedophiles—a large crucified Jesus hung directly above the headboard of one of the beds, the purpose of which reminded me of what Dr. Judd Burton said earlier: "With the placement of a cross in the design, it occurs to me that this may be a location where adepts/participants could perform [sex] rites that opened a portal (or whatever appellation you choose), activated likely by the spoiling of innocence and/or bloodshed, in the attempt to communicate with/draw power from the realm of demons/Fallen angels."[430]

One of the bedrooms at Epstein's Zorro Ranch includes a sculpture of Jesus on a golden cross that covers nearly the entire wall and is positioned with chains so that the crucified Christ leans forward, looking down on the sexual activity.

Mr. Epstein over the years confided to scientists and others about his…longstanding fascination with what has become known as transhumanism: the science of improving the human population through technologies like genetic engineering and artificial intelligence.[431]

It is worth noting that, during this time, Epstein worked secretly with billionaire Microsoft founder Bill Gates to funnel millions of dollars to MIT for what most investigators believe were transhuman and/or population-control projects, monies that the research lab attempted to keep covered up.[432]

Many of you undoubtedly know that I've written extensively on the subject of transhumanism via several books and numerous published papers, and have even argued publicly in media and in conference presentations that this movement could provide fulfillment of end-times prophecy, including the words of Jesus in Matthew 24:37 that say the days just before His Second Coming will be "as the days of Noah were, so shall also the coming of the Son of man be." I was even recently featured in the peer-reviewed religion and science journal *Zygon* in a piece written by Professor S. Jonathon O'Donnell, from the Department of Religion and Philosophies at the University of London, titled, "Secularizing Demons: Fundamentalist Navigations in Religion and Secularity," in which the good professor determined that I am the face of the modern transhuman resistance. Throughout his heady thesis, O'Donnell repeatedly referred to me and my co-obstructionists as "Horn's Milieu" or "leaders of the transhuman resistance" (Defender Publishing produced an entire book on this last year titled *The Milieu: Welcome to the Resistance*).

In pursuing this field of study, I have found most people unaware of the magnitude of resources being poured into transhuman-related and ultimately posthuman revolutionary plans, including those allocations by the United States government through its National Institute of Health and Defense Department budgets.

This includes research reminiscent of the conduct of fallen angels from antiquity that mingled human and animal biology to create giants and other monstrosities.

In fact, as I'm writing this book, several Asian countries, including China and Japan, have announced plans to raise to full maturity part-human, part-animal chimeras for xenotransplantation and other experimental purposes.

As the director of the Future of Humanity Institute and a professor of philosophy at Oxford University, Nick Bostrom is a leading advocate of this approach to transhumanism who, as a young man, was heavily influenced by the works of Friedrich Nietzsche (from whom the phrase "God is dead" derives) and Goethe, the author of *Faust*. Nietzsche was the originator of the *Übermensch* or "Overman" that Adolf Hitler dreamed of engineering, and the "entity" that man—who is nothing more than a rope "tied between beast and Overman, a rope over an abyss"—according to Nietzsche, will eventually evolve into. Like the ancient Watchers before him (Watchers were fallen angels that mingled human DNA with animals and their seed to produce giants), Bostrom envisions giving life to Nietzsche's Overman (posthumans) by remanufacturing men with animals, plants, and other synthetic life forms through the use of modern sciences, including recombinant DNA technology, germline engineering, and transgenics (in which the genetic structure of one species is altered by the transfer of genes from another).

When describing the benefits of such man-with-beast combinations in his online thesis, "Transhumanist Values," Bostrom cites how animals have "sonar, magnetic orientation, or sensors for electricity and vibration," among other extrahuman abilities. He goes on to assert that the range of sensory modalities for transhumans would not be limited to those among animals, and that there is "no fundamental block to adding, say, a capacity to see infrared radiation or to perceive radio signals and perhaps to add some kind of telepathic sense by augmenting our brains,"[433] a position verified by the US National Science Foundation and Department of Commerce in the report, *Converging Technologies for Improving Human Performance.*

Bostrom and the US government are correct in that the animal kingdom has levels of perception beyond human. Some animals can "sense" earthquakes and "smell" tumors. Others, like dogs, can hear sounds as high as 40,000 Hz—and dolphins can hear even higher. It is also known that at least some animals see wavelengths beyond normal human capacity. This is where things start getting interesting, perhaps even supernatural, as Bostrom may understand and anticipate. According to the biblical story of Balaam's donkey, certain animals see into the *spirit world*. Contemporary and secular studies likewise indicate that animals may at times be reacting to intelligence beyond normal human perception. Will this have peculiar consequences for enhanced humans with animal DNA? Elsewhere I have described how opening supernatural gateways that exist within the mind can be achieved through altered mental states induced by psychoactive drugs such as DMT and absinthe. Do transhumanists and/or military scientists imagine a more stable pathway or connection with the beyond—the ability to see into other dimensions or the spirit world—as a result of brain enhancement through integrating men with beasts? Do they envision reopening the portions of the mind that some scholars believe were closed off following the Fall of man? Late philosopher and scientist Terrance McKenna, originator of "novelty theory," speculated that brain enhancement following technological singularity might accomplish this very thing—contact with otherdimensional beings. A few years back, at Arizona State University (ASU), where the Templeton Foundation has been funding a long series of protranshumanist lectures titled "Facing the Challenges of Transhumanism: Religion, Science, Technology,"[434] some of the instructors agreed that radical alteration of Homo sapiens could open a door to *unseen intelligence*. Consequently, in 2009, ASU launched another study, this time to explore discovery of—and communication with—"entities." Called the Sophia Project (after the Greek goddess), the express purpose of this university study was to verify communication "with deceased people, spirit guides, angels, otherworldly entities/extraterrestrials, and/or a Universal Intelligence/God"[435]—in other words, those same specters with whom Hillary Clinton, John Podesta, and Jack Parsons before them sought contact. Imagine what this could mean if government laboratories with unlimited budgets working beyond congressional review were to decode the gene functions that lead animals to have preternatural capabilities of sense, smell, and sight, and then blended them with Homo sapiens. Among other things, something that perhaps DARPA (Defense Advanced Research Projects Agency) has envisioned for years could be created for use against entire populations—genetically engineered "nephilim agents" that appear to be human but that hypothetically see and even interact with invisible forces. Overnight, the rules for spiritual warfare as well as regular warfare would take on an unprecedented (at least in modern times) dimension.

No matter how daring that sounds, the ramifications of using science to manipulate human DNA or to create entirely new species could lead to mysterious germline connections with the armies of Armageddon and the kingdom of Antichrist. This is because as interbreeding begins between transgenic animals, genetically modified humans, and species as God made them, the altered DNA will quickly migrate into the natural environment. When that happens (as is already occurring among genetically modified plants and animals), "alien" and/or animal characteristics will be introduced to the human gene pool and spread through intermarriage, altering the human genetic code and eventually eliminating humanity as we know it. According to many theologians, this is what happened before the Great Flood, allowing for nephilim incarnation and perhaps has been the whole idea for the end times as well—to create a generation of genetically altered "fit extensions" for the resurrection of underworld nephilim hordes in preparation of Armageddon.

Think that will never happen? I encourage you to read Derek and Sharon Gilbert's groundbreaking new masterpiece, *Veneration: Unveiling the Ancient Realms of Demonic Kings and Satan's Battle Plan for Armageddon* to learn just how deeply this concept is tied to Bible prophecy.

Regardless of how this all ultimately turns out, it appears that Jeffrey Epstein and his pedophilic friends certainly craved more from young people than just physical pleasure. They were—as many in the Deep State continue to be—allured by forbidden spirits through promises of immortality…even if that bargain with Mephistopheles requires their souls as payment.

This is something even Freemason Manly P. Hall, whom we have cited earlier, understood. Speaking of the misuse of science with dark magic, he acknowledged in *The Secret Teachings of All Ages*:

> By means of the secret processes of ceremonial magic it is possible to contact these invisible creatures and gain their help in some human undertaking… but the evil spirits serve only those who live to pervert and destroy…The most dangerous form of black magic is the scientific perversion of occult power for the gratification of personal desire… A man will barter his eternal soul for temporal power, and down through the ages a mysterious process has been evolved which actually enables him to make this exchange.[436]

chapter six

How Progressive "Christianity" Became Part of the Problem

In the previous chapter, we ended by noting how so many in the Deep State are allured by power procured through selling their souls to demonic spirits, something even Freemason Manly P. Hall understood. This typically unfolds through practical magic and the use of talismans and occult symbols and rituals employed during "the secret processes of ceremonial magic...to contact these invisible creatures and gain their help in some human undertaking...for the gratification of personal desire.... A man will barter his eternal soul for temporal power, and down through the ages a mysterious process has been evolved which actually enables him to make this exchange."[437]

Far more concerning is the role that people *inside* the Body of Christ have recently played through self-defilement of both its people and the buildings they gather in to worship.

Now, it might appear in the next few pages that I am devoting a great deal of attention to only one news story that, when compared to the rest of this book, seems a little unrelated. However, I believe I can better communicate the occult state of the Church today, as well as the influences of the occult on society in general (and, by extension, the Church's current failure in resisting it), by giving a well-presented example.

I will cover in detail only one story from the plethora of similar stories available showing how the Church is allowing and openly engaging in blasphemous and heretical activities, and then defending such acts on the weakest (and most New Age) theological concepts.

Worshipping Demons at the Church in New York

Only days ago at the time of this writing, United Presbyterian Church of Binghamton (UPCB), a PC (USA) assembly stationed in a two-centuries-old church in New York, proudly displayed a pagan idol where their communion table normally sits within the sanctuary. This took place during the Luma Festival—a light festival during which "projection mapping" technology is used to illuminate certain buildings or works of art to "create the illusion that enormous structures are transforming as if by magic. City hall turns into a gingerbread house. The courthouse becomes Stonehenge. The light overpowers the surface and the effect seems real."[438] The totem-style idol—modeled after the Slavic god Svetovid (this Luma Festival idol was given the alternative spelling "Sviatovid"), the deity of divination, war, fertility, abundance, the four seasons, and the four cardinal directions (north, south, east, west)—was sculpted in such a way that when the projectors are turned on and the lights "dance" upon its faceted angles, the idol appears to come to life.[439] Like his namesake, this totem-idol crafted by artist Bart Kresa conquers all four cardinal directions in certain portions of the light show like a giant, four-faced entity leering out to his audience while watching over and experiencing the world from every which way all at once.

As the light-show Svetovid sat on his pedestal in a place of honor, onlookers flocked to the church, ooohing, aahing, ogling, and gawking in appreciation of the majestic display. It received a tremendous amount of attention, and no doubt the image garnered much praise for its impressive demonstration of the Slavic god's supernatural abilities/powers.

Hmm…Strange that the only place in the state of New York that could set up a pagan idol for the purposes of praise and adoration would be in the house of the same God who prohibits such practice (see Exodus 20:3–6 as merely one example of numerous verses forbidding such a thing).

Think about what this church did: It literally evicted Jesus' sacred communion table and, in its place, erected the image of a pagan deity that, with its flashy presentation, evoked the same brand of awe and focus that should be given to our Lord upon that same holy ground.

Although the wording on the Luma Festival's website was later changed by Kresa to omit the word "altar" (Presbyterian churches do not involve altars),[440] the original feature page stated eerily that "*Sviatovid will materialize* [!!!] on the altar of Binghamton United Presbyterian Church."[441]

Well, whether lights were the only presence that "materialized" in that church as a result of celebrating a pagan god in the center of Christ's house is a worthy question. That society at large is oblivious as to why this display would be blasphemy of the worst kind is a given; I don't expect people off the street to know the Christian theological definition of idolatry or what the Word says about tolerating (let alone endorsing) idol worship *in the very house of God*. Nor do I blame the artist for the offense, as Kresa claims no accountability to religious affiliation for or behind the art he openly creates for such secular companies as "Universal Studios, Disney, ABC, HBO, Fox, General Motors, Warner Bros, The Grammy Awards, Playboy, Bulgari, and T-Mobile."[442] No, the leaders of the *church* are the parties responsible for sanctioning an exhibition that their very own doctrine proclaims as a great offense to God, and when that kind of spiritual crime is carried out knowingly and blatantly, there may be more than just lights invited into that sanctuary.

First, let's visit what the Word of God—the *one and the same* Word of God to which Presbyterians claim to universally adhere—says on the subject. Not only will this be pertinent to the Svetovid fiasco, it will apply to all the other occult practices implemented in Christian churches across the nation today, which we will consider later in the chapter. (Note that this isn't even close to an exhaustive list on the topic of idolatry and its the consequences; these are just a few of the most glaring prohibitions, effects, and outcomes of this transgression.)

- Leviticus 26:1: God's people aren't allowed to make or own a single sacred idol, pillar, or image of a pagan deity (the Kresa piece was factually all three: a pillar-like idol with dancing images). Not only are these objects not to even be created—and God forbid that they be anywhere inside the sacred temple—but also, according to this verse, they were not even allowed to be anywhere on the property—"on your land."

- Ezekiel 6:9: For allowing idols on their land, entertaining idol worship, or revering any likeness or graven image of any pagan deity whatsoever, God's people have been "adulterous" against Him; they have completely turned their backs on Him despite their deliverance from Egypt. In fact, their actions have actually "hurt" Him (ESV) or "broke [His heart]." (Western Christianity takes God so lightly that it's easy to forget He can even *be* hurt by the actions of mere people. Many treat Him only as if He's an impenetrable, universal, authoritative, omnipotent, and omniscient force; although He *is* all of those things, we tend to forget that He is also a Person with feelings and emotions [Psalm 2:4; 7:11; 11:5; 78:41; 135:14], but "hurt" and/or "broken" are precisely what His Word says results from of our idolatrous actions.) By engaging in idolatry, God's people make themselves "harlots," and they will regret their evils so much that they will come to "loathe themselves" for their actions, which this verse identifies as "abominations."

- Ezekiel 16:36–37: God's people chose to make "lovers" of idolatrous nations and people groups by tolerating and incorporating the foreign gods into their own worship. Because of this, God will make the current "lovers" ally with His people's enemies (nations like Ammon, Edom, and Moab, etc.) and join together to torment the Jews. In other words, by allowing an idolatrous sort of "new family" into their tribes—probably with the interest of bolstering their own numbers against enemy nations—the Jews ironically make themselves ten times more vulnerable to attack by the enemy nations *and* their own "new family" when God turns the "lovers" against Israel. The lesson: We cannot incorporate idolatrous people and their gods into the Church in the name of "loving" them; doing so establishes relationships without God's blessing and can end in disaster for everyone involved.

- Ezekiel 6:5, 13: Because images of pagan deities are scattered about their property, set atop their "high hills" and "mountain[tops]," and under their "green tree[s]," the Israelite men who die in these battles between themselves, their once-new family, and the enemy nations will be slain right in front of the idols. Thus, in an act of poetic justice and divine irony, the smell of their rotting corpses now rises where once the sweet incense was lit for the gods.

- Ezekiel 14:4: Regardless of whether God's people openly and outwardly worship physical idols made of wood, stone, gold, or silver, if any hint of an idolatrous thought or feeling enters the "heart" of God's people, they will answer to God and face punishment.

Speaking about what the Bible, itself, says about all this, it doesn't stop with recounting what horrors the ancients inflicted on themselves when they tolerated idols. For Christians who may assume that, because of the grace and redemption of Christ and the New Covenant that "made all that Old Testament stuff less important" (an attitude currently and haphazardly poisoning an enormous fraction of today's Body), the Word of God goes on to give timeless end-time warnings from the New Testament:

- Almost every apocalyptic devastation unfolds because of the tolerance of and participation in idolatry (Revelation 9:20; 13:14; 19:20; etc.). The smaller, "only a work of art" idols honoring pagan gods that we bring into God's house to applaud, admire, and celebrate (praise?) today are preparing mighty fine groundwork for tomorrow's Antichrist idol or "image of the beast." When we eventually reach that terrifying and tragic day when people face certain execution for refusing to worship this image/idol/monster (Revelation 13:15), some Christians may, while they wait in line for their death, reflect upon the Church's history and remember these early years when the so-called Body of Christ traded "resistance" for "acceptance," selling their souls for progressive religion.

• Because the church at Pergamos (also known as Pergamum) was home to the "seat of Satan" or "Satan's throne" (which "most plausibly relates to the throne-like altar of Zeus, itself a symbol of the idolatry that held sway in Pergamum,"[443] though some scholars suggest it refers to the locally worshiped throne of Roman Emperor Augustus), and because it tolerated the false teachings of "Balaam," the once-faithful church that had withstood the test of time was now coming under Satan's grip (Revelation 2:12–17). What was Balaam teaching? He held to the Nicolaitans' claim that the Mosaic Law could be tossed out in the interest of a permissive and progressive religion under the grace of Christ. This passage in the letters to the seven churches provides the eternally applicable guarantee that any church willing to toss out the Ten Commandments or the Law as it relates to worshiping any other god or person or the installation of any idol will face God's judgment if it does not repent. Scholar Michael Heiser's favorite commentator of Revelation, G. K. Beale, states: "The situation in the Asia Minor churches is generally relevant for *all churches until the return of Christ*.... The trans-historical nature of [Revelation] ch. 13 is a basis for universalizing the application of vv. 15–17 to all times."[444] Therefore, the "repentance" message of the church at Pergamos is as much for us today as any congregation of any other time (and a church that "unseats" Christ's communion table and "seats" a pagan idol in its place is, most definitely, in need of repenting, if we're going to call the kettle black here...).

- Scholars sometimes interpret that "The 'abomination [of desolation]' in Dan. 11:31 was fulfilled in the altar or pagan image of Zeus (Jupiter) erected by Antiochus IV in the Jerusalem temple in December, 167 B.C. (1 Macc. 1:47, 54, 59; 2 Macc. 6:4–5; Josephus *Antiquities* 12.5.4; cf. Dan. 8:13)."[445] In other words, this "abomination of desolation" (which the *Anchor Yale Bible Dictionary* says "we should translate…as 'appalling sacrilege'"[446]) was a literal and historical idol to a pagan god set up in God's house in Jerusalem. However, when Jesus spoke of the "abomination of desolation" during His Olivet Discourse in Matthew 24:15 and Mark 13:14, He spoke of the event in the *future* tense. Scholars suggest that Jesus' words might, then, have been pointing to one or both of the other two "abomination" references within Daniel (9:27; 12:11), since the 8:13 reference is associated to a past occurrence. To put it more simply, the "abomination of desolation" occurred in the past and will occur again in the future. (Biblical prophecies have frequently demonstrated what scholars refer to as "dual fulfillment," meaning that there is a short-term *and* a long-term fulfillment, the former serving [among other things] as a sort of example" for the latter, also called a "type" [look up "prophecy typology" on any search engine online for a more thorough treatment of this concept].) "Most scholars associate this NT [future] 'abomination of desolation' with (1) the destruction of the temple, (2) the eschatological antichrist, or (3) both. It could refer to…the eschatological Antichrist…mentioned in 2 Thess. 2:3–12."[447] Yikes. The greatest "appalling sacrilege" against God in human history is related to a pagan god, or the literal Antichrist (or an idol *of* the Antichrist, aka, the "image of the beast") being placed in God's house. So *if*, as these scholars believe, the installation of the "abomination of desolation" is the very slap-in-God's-face catalyst that relates to the apocalyptic judgments of the book of Revelation, then the following statement is fair: Idols representing pagan deities in God's churches/temples eventually can and will provoke judgment so harsh that it results in the destruction, and therefore the end, of the world.

In addition to the Scripture passages that directly and deafeningly rebuke and veto *even toying with the idea* of allowing idols in God's house or on His land, let's look at a few other areas of the Word on the topic of the sanctity of God's house and His presence.

In the Old Testament, the Holy of Holies was the sacred and extremely restricted area behind the veil within the Temple where God's presence appeared on the mercy seat of the Ark of the Covenant, which held the Ten Commandments. So consecrated was this space, because of God's choice to inhabit the room, that only the Jewish high priest from the tribe of Levi was allowed to enter, and even he could only enter one day per year (Yom Kipper/Day of Atonement). Similarly, God's presence was sacred even outside the Temple. When God appeared to Moses in the form of a burning bush, Moses was told he had to remove his sandals because he was standing upon "holy ground" (Exodus 3:5; Acts 7:33). God's presence in a place was taken very seriously. Then, Jesus' sacrifice upon the cross resulted in the tearing of the veil (Matthew 27:51), allowing for atonement of all sins without the high priest's mediation, and symbolizing that all people—*anyone*, from any background, including Jew and Gentile—now had access to the Holy of Holies, or the presence of God. Psalm 22:3 says that God is personally present in the place where His people gather to worship. He factually "inhabits the praises of His people," the verse says, and this blessed Scripture took on fresh meaning after the tearing of the veil, when the Holy of Holies came to mean literally *any* space, any place, any building dedicated to the worship of God and therefore inviting Him to be present with us.

Woe to us on the day we fill our own Holy of Holies spaces with pagan idols. The God who struck Nadab and Abihu dead for unlawfully entering the Holy of Holies (Leviticus 10:1–2) is the same God who joins us in a place dedicated to worshiping Him. How can we offer anything less to Him than to treat His space with the ultimate inviolability?

Follow this trail: 1) Pagan idols are demonic (1 Corinthians 10:20); 2) God refuses to share His glory or His praises with other gods (Isaiah 42:8); therefore, 3) Svetovid and God *cannot* occupy the same space. Any church that allows an idol of a little-*g* god has traded in its holy ground to become the church at Pergamos in Satan's grip. Such a congregation is in severe danger of being among those described in the terrifying Matthew 7:21–23 rejection:

> Not every one that saith unto me, Lord, Lord, shall enter into the kingdom of heaven; but he that doeth the will of my Father which is in heaven. Many will say to me in that day, Lord, Lord, have we not prophesied in thy name? and in thy name have cast out devils? and in thy name done many wonderful works? And then will I profess unto them, I never knew you: depart from me, ye that work iniquity.

Do all these verses sound like they're describing a God who would allow His house today—built and dedicated to the sole purpose of worshiping *Him*—to feature a pagan idol brought to life by lights and sounds revered and praised by His own people? Does this God of these Scriptures appear to be the kind who would want lost souls from the streets of New York to wander in and see a flashy, glitzy demonstration of Svetovid, and then think it might—*in any way, shape, or form*—represent what the God of the Bible is about in His own home? When would we ever be allowed to "decorate God's house" with other gods, which He vehemently opposes?

This makes as much sense as showing honor to US President Donald J. Trump by installing a shadowbox in his office containing the ashes of a burned American flag under a golden Swastika. It's the most radically offensive imagery one could ever bestow on a person of that position. In fact, it's not a stretch to imagine that Trump (or any other recent president) would interpret such a "gift" as such a sign of terrorism that the building would have to be evacuated and swept for bombs or other threats, and the symbolism would be such an affront to all America stands for that the entire administration would be obligated to launch an investigation pouring millions or billions of dollars into tracking down and apprehending the offender.

Think I'm being sensationalistic with this White House comparison?

The *New Dictionary of Biblical Theology* acknowledges: "In the Bible there is no more serious charge than that of idolatry. Idolatry called for the strictest punishment, elicited the most disdainful polemic, prompted the most extreme measures of avoidance, and was regarded as the chief identifying characteristic of those who were the very antithesis of the people of God…. Idolatry is the *ultimate expression of unfaithfulness to God.*"[448] Funny thing is, this source makes this statement casually, as if it's rudimentary information and the real "meat" will be addressed only after the "everybody-knows" basics are covered. Then it and about fifteen other reference books on this subject go on to explain that even though an idol crafted by human hands and therefore doesn't move, walk, talk, or interact like a god, the idol itself is an obvious invitation to the presence of real demons, like a portal of demonic energy that God's own people have opened (Deuteronomy 32:16–17; 1 Corinthians 10:20).

Anyone without much exposure to Christianity (especially those who think it is a cult religion of judgmental, legalistic elitists and snobs who believe Jesus came so we could all be wealthy, which is an impression recent decades have solidified for many) might not inherently know that Svetovid has nothing to do with our beliefs. In fact, without a basic theological foundation of Christianity, a passerby may even make the mistake of assuming that we are honoring one of our own "gods" or members of the Trinity we hold in our fundamental statements of faith.

But let's pretend for a moment that one of these sightseers actually asked a member of the UPCB staff which one of the Christian gods this was. What would be the answer? *Any* answer would be trouble: 1) Suggesting we adopt Svetovid into some crazy "Christian pantheon" idea breaks the very first two of our Ten Commandments and denies monotheism; 2) Admitting that Svetovid is not "one of our gods" suggests that "monotheistic" Christianity is inconsistently polytheistic in that it appreciates, tolerates, embraces, and features as a crowd-puller the little-*g* gods of any world religion; 3) Avoiding the question altogether and redirecting the trail of thought to some irreligious, "only a work of art" approach com-

municates that the Body of Christ is flaky enough to abandon our own
tenets of faith and everything we believe any time a light show or festival
comes to town, and that, worst of all, we disregard the biblically acknowledged risk that setting up an idol opens doorways for demonic activity
and entities in that very spot (which, in this case, happens to be where
the communion table of Jesus Christ is set up). I could offer several more
"excuses"—but again, not one justifies polluting a Christian place of worship by showcasing a pagan idol.

By now, you're probably wondering what official statement the staff of
this Presbyterian church gave for the controversial display?

In my opinion, this might be the biggest offense of all.

After Josiah Aden of the *Juicy Ecumenism* blog wrote his article, "New
York Presbyterian Church Hosts Pagan Deity,"[449] female pastor of UPCB,
Reverend Kimberly Chastain, posted a lengthy defense on the church's
Facebook profile, the overarching theme of which screams "straw-man
comeback" (one of the weakest I've ever seen), because: 1) She completely
avoids responding to the Scripture Aden quoted that indisputably prohibits UPCB's action during the Luma Festival; 2) Although Aden states that
UPCB refused to comment when he reached out (and Chastain admits in
her post that she was certainly given the opportunity), the article indirectly
challenges the leadership of UPCB to explain and justify their actions on
biblical grounds, and Chastain's Facebook response surprisingly doesn't
quote or even allude to a single Scripture verse in defense of that choice
(any true Christian knows that the Word of God is the first, continual,
and final word on what decisions we make, and when we choose to do
something that could mislead the "world of the lost" around us or mis-
represent Christ, we need to be ready to provide a *biblical* answer—one
involving verses from the *Bible*); 3) The decision to involve an idol in the
house of God was eventually supported by the idea that God, Himself,
would have gifted this work of art, which He sees as sacred (again, without a single quoted verse); 4) Chastain launches into miniature diatribes
about issues unrelated to Aden's article (such as artist Kresa's Polish background and the Westminster Catechism's statement about enjoying God),

and attempts to make Aden look foolish for covering certain details that *she* found irrelevant (such as the UPCB's dramatic decrease in attendance over the last several years—a "detail" that is far more pertinent to Aden's piece than most of Chastain's was on her straw-man rebuttal).

The rhythm of Chastain's kickback went like this:[450]

1. Question whether journalist Josiah Aden knows the congregation personally, or if he attended the presentation of the harmless idol (irrelevant)

2. Question Aden's choice to list attendance demographics, and then proceed to explain the hardships the church has been under in the last few years, with many deaths (irrelevant)

3. Address Svetovid's presence with the fallacy that the Westminster Catechism, Presbyterianism's historical confession, acknowledges that God's grace has made everything sacred, *or* that nothing could be considered sacred except through God's love (confusing, theologically empty statements that are not found anywhere in the larger or shorter Westminster Catechism at all; one commenter gently asked Chastain where this was found in the confession, and she chastised the commenter for attempting to trap and attack her, but not surprisingly, she never provided an answer to the legitimate question)

4. Explain that Christ's communion table (the one allegedly moved to make room for the idol) is nothing more than a simple table, and that if we assign any more holiness to it than that, then it is Christ's *table* that becomes the idol in the room (redirecting the thread about Svetovid's presence in Christ's place by suggesting Christ's place could be idolatry in itself was a clever, but once again frantically straw-man, tactic that only revealed Chastain's desperation)

5. Finally give the closest thing to a direct defense for the idol, which itemized: 1) if God's grace is *not* concerned with or covering

Svetovid, then it is of a material and nonspiritual matter…that it would be nothing more than a secular issue to host the pagan deity image in the spot where the congregation worships Christ; 2) if an idol of Svetovid *is* considered a sacred item, then it could only be God's grace and love that made it so, and therefore the idol doesn't represent a concern about idolatry but commemorates God's direct and personal bestowing of such a gift on that community (oh my goodness!!!)

6. Talk about the artist, his homeland and its folk myths, and expound upon the journey-through-the-cosmos backstory on Svetovid and his godlike, multiple faces and eyes, etc., all to give a (weak, but) positive slant on the concept of self-transformative voyaging around the known universe (yada yada)

7. Celebrate the copious number of opportunities that the UPCB staff had during the Luma Festival display to share their faith in Christ with outsiders (a sort of "conform to the world to reach the world" concept that is foundationally oppositional to New Testament teaching [see, for example, Romans 12:2; 1 John 2:15; Colossians 3:2; 1 Peter 1:14; and countless others])

8. Quote a Scripture (it's about time…), but keep it unrelated (whoopsie), using Micah 6:8b ("do justly, and to love mercy, and to walk humbly with thy God") as a mission statement of UPCB, and then give a long list of ways the church has involved itself in the community

9. Conclude with the most ironic, self-condemning, contradictory, and paradoxical zinger anyone in Chastain's position could have chosen: "Anyone with eyes to see, let them see" (a slight rewording of Mark 8:18; Matthew 13:15–16)

Believing that this whole idol affair might have caught UPCB off-guard (thereby producing a theologically void response like the one above), and trusting that I would find at least some semblance of foundational

Christian doctrine on this Christian church's official mission statement page, I took my browser to their site. I was amazed to see that there was not one Scripture verse on the "Our Beliefs"[451] page. Actually, there wasn't a single theological statement about what the church knows to be true about God, the Bible, Jesus, verses showing what a "Presbyterian" is as opposed to "Pentecostal," denominational dogmas, spiritual principles as adapted from the life of Christ, or anything of that nature. In the one location you would assume you'd get the mother lode of this church's theological creeds is a lackluster statement confirming only that they: a) believe in Jesus; b) welcome everyone from all races, ages, genders, and sexual orientations to attend their services; c) commit to community programs that benefit the world around them; d) generally love people; and e) want to glorify and honor the Lord by reaching and teaching people with church programs and ministries. Some of these are great things to have as *part of* a mission statement, but by itself, this list *cannot* be perceived as a statement of faith. New believers viewing this site wouldn't have the first clue as to what concepts about God would be poured into them if they visited this place of worship.

Yet…this church isn't anything we didn't see coming. Paul predicted two thousand years ago that churches like this would one day be all over the place (2 Timothy 4:3).

The Dangers of "Residual Energy"

To this point, it's only been mildly suggested that a space or object can be attached to a spirit or spiritual force. Apart from the fact that Paul identified handmade idols as a literal resting place for demons (1 Corinthians 10:20), there are far too many bizarre testimonies regarding paranormal activity around specific objects or places to dismiss them all as having originated from imagination or paranoia.

One phenomenon discussed among psychics, oracles, mediums, spiritists, clairvoyants, and others within the realm of parapsychology, and known since just about the beginning of mankind, is called "residual energy" (though the terminology has varied): the "clinging on" of an energy (some will admit "presence") to an item or location. The mercy seat within the Holy of Holies was, again, a literal example of an item that held the presence of a supernatural entity, though in this case it was the Almighty God (Exodus 25:22).

So sacred was this item, and so imbued with the power of God it was, that when Uzzah, an Israelite, steadied the Ark of the Covenant with his bare hands when an ox pulling the vessel stumbled, he was struck dead (2 Samuel 6:6–8). As a representation of God's provision and attendance amidst His people, the Ark was carried by the Israelites throughout their forty-year wilderness trek. The very waters of the Jordan River parted for the feet of the priests who bore its weight as they walked across on dry land (Joshua 3:13–17; 4:7). And when the Philistines later conquered Israel and captured the Ark, "the glory [was] departed from Israel; for the Ark of God [was] taken" (1 Samuel 4:22).

No doubt about it: This sacred item was saturated in the Spirit and presence of God. It says something about the power of an object when its removal from a nation causes that nation to lose its "glory." But the opposite was also true. The procurement of the Ark boded poorly for the pagans who served other gods.

Thinking they were going to show off by placing the Ark of God next to the idol of their pet god, Dagon, the Philistines woke to see Dagon prostrate before the Ark; when they reset the idol in its place, the following morning heralded not only a prostrate little-*g* god again, but a decapitated one with no hands (1 Samuel 5:1–4). Anyone with even a fundamental education in Christian theology knows that this was not a true battle between the wood/stone/gold idol of Dagon and the Ark of the Covenant, but between the dark spirit(s) attached to the idol of Dagon and the Almighty God whose presence bathed the Ark. This "clinging presence" of sorts is real, regardless of whether we wrap the phenomenon into pop-culture terms like "residual energy."

This phenomenon isn't limited to psychic paranormal practice or the Old Testament; countless Christian missionaries have witnessed this occurrence abroad. For instance, a friend told me years ago that as part of his collection of souvenirs from the mission field, he had acquired a drum from a curiosity shop. He thought it was pretty and would look cool in his office. Soon after he brought it home, he and his family began experiencing sickness with maladies that seemed to come from nowhere. One day, his friend, also a missionary, saw the drum and asked where he had gotten it. Once he heard the answer, he told him to get rid of it right away; the instrument had belonged to an infamous shaman and was possessed by active, evil supernaturalism. After my friend burned the drum and repented, his family regained their health.

We can claim from the rising to the setting of the sun that we're only honoring a work of art—or we can make the shoddier claim that we are harmlessly adjusting our ecclesiastical practices (translation: "conforming to the ways of this world") in order to draw lost souls into our churches—but the facts remain the same: Bringing paganism into the Church (both the buildings and the people) communicates to the Almighty that we're more interested in compromising the temple and "doing religion our way" than in keeping His house pure and holy. When we commit this blasphemy, we open the widest door spiritually possible for dark influences to enter and attach themselves to objects and locations. If or when God decides that any congregation has gone too far in its idolatry or occult practices, He may, as He did with Ephraim, "leave that assembly to join their idols" (cf. Hosea 4:17). The result of this is, at best, a New Age social club that's hijacked the name of Christ for its own vanity and, at worst, a demonic temple (1 Corinthians 10:21).

Vilest of all, this mischievous influence can and most certainly *will* appear to be pure, holy, and filled with light (2 Corinthians 11:14). We must remember that Paul warned us about these last days, when the "doctrines of devils" would infiltrate the Church (1 Timothy 4:1).

Infiltration of the Occult

Due to limited space, we can't cover examples of every current of occult infiltration into the Christian Church here. That's why I chose instead to begin with one story about the UPCB and build upon that for two reasons.

First, though many believers gasp at the mention of a pagan idol in a Christian place of worship, far fewer can articulate *why* and *how* that is such an affront to God in today's society (perhaps with the exception of being able to offer an insecure citation of a couple of the Ten Commandments). We've arrived at a time when, as my scholar friend Dr. Michael Heiser says, "Clear theological thinking is on life support in many congregations."[452] He goes on to say:

> What else can you conclude when…51 percent of American churchgoers do not know what the Great Commission is? [Or] that 41 percent of Millennials "do not know the Great Commission," while just 10 percent of the same demographic "have heard of and remember [the words to] the Great Commission."
>
> Contemporary theological illiteracy manifests in other ways as well. Many people who grow up in Christian contexts cannot see why there would be any tension between the Bible and New Age beliefs. A blend of the two worldviews is inconsequential to them.[453]

Reverend Chastain from UPCB is a good example of how even the very reverends of our flock are, in this cultural climate, underperforming in their responsibility to understand *and implement* even the most fundamental Christian theology.

My first goal in this breakdown was to illustrate how nonchalant the Body of Christ is toward the occult, how trivially we respond to outrageous insults to God, and how this undoubtedly originates from theological ignorance *within* the Church.

Second, after showing readers multiple angles and layers of why and how this particular UPCB case represents a far greater spiritual offense than a mere art exhibition, I can now explore, in a much more truncated manner, two other concerns we should all have regarding the occult infiltration of the Church, using this as an example of how one "inconsequential incident" can have devastating and eternal consequences.

Cartomancy Redressed

Cartomancy, the use of a card deck to predict the future or practice divination (for instance, tarot cards), has made its way into Christian churches via "destiny cards" or "prophecy cards." God's direct and unquestionable prohibition of divination (Leviticus 19:26) was made even clearer in His Word when He compared its wickedness to child sacrifice (Deuteronomy 18:9–12), and elsewhere when He said that it made His people just like the other nations that do not belong to Him (Jeremiah 10:2).

Ministries choosing to dabble in cartomancy under the redressed "destiny" or "prophecy" terminology are, with as many layers and from as many angles as our earlier UPCB example, blatantly bringing paganism into the house of God. There has also been an across-the-board tendency for the spokespeople behind such "Christ-centered" ministries to justify the use of their unscriptural ritualism from a completely secular, humanistic, moralistic (as opposed to biblical) platform. And that's not to mention that even the card-readers themselves sometimes don't understand the purpose or effects of their craft well enough to defend it with even basic rhetorical logic.

For instance, one "destiny cards" ministry says on its website that its cards "are more *predictive* and higher than other card readings"[454]—but when challenged to explain the apparent synonymity between its "predictive" readings and barefaced tarot-card fortune-telling, they firmly contradicted themselves: "They [the destiny cards] are all *non-predictive* [make up your mind!], but we call them destiny cards as we believe that giftings and callings given by God for people are certainly part of their destiny."[455]

Despite this declaration-then-denial inconsistency, this ministry makes the skin-crawling admission that its cards "carry a special presence."[456]

In light of the brief "clinging demonic residual energy" analysis covered earlier, that's an enlightening statement, indeed.

Spiritualism Redressed

Spiritualism is the practice of contacting the evolving dead, or hyperintelligent "spirit guides," through either a designated medium or divining oracle tool (like a "spirit board"). In addition to breaking every rule in the Book regarding God's watertight ban on communication with the dead (Leviticus 19:31; Deuteronomy 18:10–12; Isaiah 8:19; etc.), spiritualism is innately interwoven with necromancy, sorcery, black magic, and so on, widening the scriptural veto exponentially. Some of the Holy Bible's most chilling warnings are those that candidly identify a specific sin, followed by the unwavering statement that those who commit that sin "shall not inherit the kingdom of God." Spiritualism is one such atrocity, according to Galatians 5:19–21.

It's no secret that the foremost occult tool in the shed for spiritualism witchcraft is the "spirit board" or "talking board," more commonly called the Ouija board today, thanks to Parker Brothers' and Hasbro's beloved board game (if you can even call it a "game") of the same name. Even the *Encyclopedic Dictionary of Cults, Sects, and World Religions* acknowledges: "On a popular level, spiritualism has been touted by the Ouija board manufactured and sold by Parker Brothers."[457] Thankfully, Christians wouldn't allow themselves to be found guilty of gathering around a game board to conduct a séance...would they?

Tragically, the latest occult "redressing" on the Christian church scene is the "angel board." It is identical (in design, purpose, use, and result) to the spirit/talking/Ouija board in every way except one: The "angel board" contacts your "guardian angels" instead of the spirits of dead humans.

I know, I know... You readers are smart enough that you've probably already thought of the most obvious and relatable of all the Word's 31,102 verses: that Satan, himself, can appear as an "angel of light" (2 Corinthians 11:14). And since this is true, in addition to spiritualism being defiantly hostile against the Word of God, in every possible, *literal* way, an angel board is an open door inviting Satan, himself, to arrive and say hello. There is no reason (logically or theologically) to believe that God would step in and protect a person who's openly going against His command from inadvertently contacting Satan just because he or she *thought* the communication line was only extending to the "good, pretty, dance-on-purple-cloud angels" the box advertised.

Certain Satanists and ex-Satanists have admitted that their initial "involvement in the occult started with a Ouija board."[458] Even Parker Brothers recognized in its published pamphlet that the "game" is specifically marketed to and enjoyed by people "interested in the occult."[459] Anyone purchasing an angel board with the idea that it would only contact something with good intentions—and not a deceiving, fallen angel, like the biblical one who can appear or "feel" just like the "pretty" ones—is revealing a gullible streak at best. He or she is also likely unaware that *even experts on and within the occult* "have echoed Christian warnings, cautioning inexperienced persons away from [spirit boards]"[460] due to their serious and dangerous nature.

My heart goes out to one woman who gave her testimony via a review on an online webstore that sells angel boards. She tells of a frustrating episode when she initially established contact with her higher spirit guide merely through a Ouija board, and the communication link she made with the entity was tense and troublesome, as if there was a spiritual static keeping them from wholly connecting. After much difficulty, the planchette (wooden pointer that the spirit moves on Ouija boards) finally identified the first letter of the apparition's name, but the "conversation" died out. This made the woman doubt whether she was spiritually mature enough to operate these kinds of devices with any success, so she tried one last thing: She asked if the spirit guide wanted her to invest in an official angel board (remember, the angel board is *identical* to a Ouija board, except they often have a picture of an angel on the front between the numbers and letters), and the spirit offered his answer by moving the planchette to "yes." Shortly thereafter, when the woman had obtained her new tool, she again tried to establish an open communication line, and met immediate triumph, wherein the "angel" was now able to freely comfort her and reassure her. After this event, she concluded that doubting her own ability to operate a spirit-guide talking board was equal to doubting God, Himself, and His angels.

It pains me to know that the Body of Christ is becoming open-minded regarding the occult in the first place. But it grieves me deeply to see someone so misled by these practices that they would label their initial Ouija board reservations to a lack of faith in God. Not to mention, this woman's story has an innate theological flaw: Her spirit guide *did* speak with her on the "regular" board, but needed her to buy one with a picture on it in order for their line of communication to completely clear. But if God had sanctioned this method of interaction, His celestial messengers would be powerful enough to see past this detail. This logic is as faulty as saying we can't read a letter because it's written in pen instead of pencil.

Another reviewer wrote something equally haphazard: If you ask God's angels to protect you before the session, then no *other* entity will be able to get through to you or cause you harm. Here again, the logic (and theology) is grasping: You can't ask the Father's host of guardian spirits to protect you while you open a biblically forbidden door that creates spiritual vulnerability. It's as nonsensical as jumping off a cliff and asking your earthly father, whose grip and protection you've left back on safe ground above, to save you before you hit the ground.

Spiritual Disease Killing the Body from Within

I want to ask a very important question: How can Christians stand firm against the world when we conform to it? How can the army of God eradicate the enemy's threat of evil while we're exercising the very evils of the enemy within our ranks?

Today, we have many different "brands" or denominations in the

Church around the world. They are filled with and operated by different types of liturgy, orthodoxy, worship styles, and practices. What distinguishes the true Church of Jesus Christ from worldly organizations, civic clubs, or social groups is that the true Church is based solidly on the teachings of Jesus Christ, the only begotten Son of God.

The modern-day Church experiences freedom from a hierarchical body that functions like a "government" over each individual believer. The "priesthood of the believer" allows celebration of the differences between personal convictions (although we frequently fight interdenominational wars over such issues as speaking in tongues, women in ministry, or forms of baptism, etc.). However, there are times such freedom can present a challenge, because it leads to the formation of either subdenominations or practices within denominations that are, at best, bizarre, and at worst, heretical and blasphemous.

Consider this passage of Scripture:

This know also, that in the last days perilous times shall come. For men shall be lovers of their own selves, covetous, boasters, proud, blasphemers, disobedient to parents, unthankful, unholy, without natural affection, trucebreakers, false accusers, incontinent, fierce, despisers of those that are good, traitors, heady, high-minded, lovers of pleasures more than lovers of God; Having a form of godliness, but denying the power thereof: from such turn away. (2 Timothy 3:1–5)

When Paul wrote his second letter to the church of Corinth, he shared a major concern for their well-being (11:3–4). He said he feared that just as the enemy deceived Eve in the Garden of Eden by way of his shrewdness, the Church might also be led astray from their devotion to Christ. He warned of a day when "Christians" would proclaim another, *different* Jesus than the one taught in the Scriptures. He also said that the believers in Corinth might even accept a completely different gospel.

Elsewhere, in his letter to the church in Galatia, Paul "took it to a ten," as we say around SkyWatch, going as far as to say that anyone who preaches a gospel contrary to the one *he, Paul*, preached would be accursed. Then He said it *again* for emphasis: "As we said before, so say I now again, If any man preach any other gospel unto you than that ye have received, let him be accursed" (Galatians 1:6–9).

We're witnessing the very day when local "churches" have lost their moorings. Many are no longer—in appearance or practice—following the model of the hurch in the book of Acts, and have thus become a serious part of the wrong side of the culture war. Some have even taken down the cross, the symbol of Christ's victory over death, hell, and the grave, so as not to offend non-Christian neighbors within their communities.[461]

Worse, some, like the Binghamton congregation of New York, no longer fear or revere a God who commands: "You shall have no other gods before me" (Exodus 20:3).

Other offenses like these are equally blatant, and perhaps even more concerning in the long term (especially when the occult tools are implemented to communicate to the Christian God or His messengers), but because they fit our Western culture, they aren't recognized as a threat.

The Role of Deep-State Influences in Nurturing Occult-ianity

Elsewhere in this book, a guest chapter by my friend Carl Gallups details how America may have been victim to the greatest political scam in our nation's history and, should the world continue, historians will undoubtedly record how it was partly the messianic fervor surrounding the election of Barack Obama as president of the United States that reflected not only widespread disapproval for Bush-administration policies, but how, in the aftermath of September 11, 2001, the American psyche was primed to accept expansive alterations in society, including redefining moral absolutes, politics, and financial policies with an overarching scheme for salvation from chaos, and that by almost any expense. Among these historians, a few will undoubtedly also argue that, as National German Socialists did in the years following World War I, Barack Hussein Obama appealed to the increasingly disenfranchised voters among American society by playing on their understandable fears in order to posture himself as the essential agent of change. What most of these historians are not likely to record, however, is the involvement before and after the 2008 US presidential election by occult unseen shapers of the New World Order. If they did, vast numbers of people would not believe it anyway, the idea that behind the global chaos that gave rise to Obama's popularity was a secret network, a transnational hand directing the course of civilization. Yet no account of history, including recent times, is complete or even sincere without at least acknowledging the behind-the-scenes masters who manipulate international policy, banking and finance, securities and exchange, trade, commodities, energy resources, and yes, even religious ideas. Numerous works, including scholarly ones, have connected the dots between this ruling "superclass" and the integration of policy handed down to governing bodies of nation-states and supra-national organizations.

The Economist newspaper in the year of Obama's first election as president of the United States pointed to research by academic David Rothkopf, whose book, Superclass: The Global Power Elite and the World They Are Making, documented that only a few thousand people worldwide actually dictate the majority of policies operating at a global scale. The Economist described this comparatively small number of elites as being "groomed" in "world-spanning institutions...[who] meet at global events such as the World Economic Forum at Davos and the Trilateral Commission or...the Bilderberg meetings or the Bohemian Grove seminars that take place every July in California."[462] In a 2011 Swiss Federal Institute (SFI) study, less than 150 technocratic "Super Entities"—mainly banks and the families who own them—were shown to control 40 percent of the world's wealth. My good friend, long-time radio host, and author of Brotherhood of Darkness, the late Stanley Monteith, once said such persons are part of an "occult hierarchy" that rules the world and directs the course of human events. "The movement is led by powerful men who reject Christianity, embrace the 'dark side,' and are dedicated to the formation of a world government and a world religion," he wrote. "They control the government, the media…many corporations, and both [US] political parties."[463]

The objectives of these secret orders and the very real forces they serve are seldom perceived by citizens of democratic societies who choose to believe that national officials actually rule their countries and represent their interests. Yet, according to sacred texts, not only does an active collaboration exist between unregenerate social architects and fallen angels, but politicians in particular are vulnerable to "principalities and powers." As "fleshy gloves" of these unseen agents, presidents and politicians may be unaware of their role as chess pieces on a terrestrial gameboard, sliding in and out of position as they are moved by "the god of this world" toward a phantasmogoric end game (see 2 Corinthians 4:4). If researchers like Dr. Monteith are correct, and world governments are to this day influenced by dark angelic powers, the elite who head the current push to undermine Christianity in the West are directly connected to an endless stream of influencers working toward an Antichrist system, whether they know it or not.

Their influence—like the judges of the Old Testament—can definitely hold sway over public sentiment and philosophical ideas, which in turn affects the destiny of nations.

Recall how, in the lead-up to Obama's presidential election (so many, including this author, were astonished that Obama was reelected in 2012 instead of being assigned to the dustbin of a failed one-term presidency. Given his beyond-dismal record of governance [the worst in American history] and the horrific state of the economy under his leadership [also the worst in history], most businessmen and political conservatives were convinced he could never serve a second term. Obviously, we were wrong), he spent significant time distancing himself from conservative Christians, evangelicals, and especially the Religious Right (which had held prominent sway over Republicans since Ronald Reagan held office), countering that his faith was more universalist and unconvinced of Bible inerrancy. There is no doubt the turn away from American religious orthodoxy since is connected to Obama's efforts to reorient America away from traditional Christianity. In a five-minute video available on YouTube, a preelection speech by Obama was highly cynical of Bible authority and even derided specific Old and New Testament Scriptures. "Whatever we once were," Obama says on the video, "we're no longer a Christian nation."[464] He added, "Democracy demands that the religiously motivated translate their concerns into universal, rather than religion-specific values.... This is going to be difficult for some who believe in the inerrancy of the Bible, as many evangelicals do."[465] Consequently, the conscious effort by Obama to realign America away from conventional Christianity was widely embraced by people who identified with the man known to sport Masonic emblems, a ring that says "There Is No God Except Allah," and a tiny idol of the Hindu god Hanuman in his pocket—whose blessings he sought in the race to the White House—a deity about whom Rudyard Kipling wrote the short story, "The Mark of the Beast." For Obama, who grew up in a household where the Bible, the Koran, and the Bhagvat Gita sat on a shelf side by side (similar to the temple room at the House of the Temple, headquarters of Scottish Right Freemasonry in Washington, DC) organized religion was best defined as "closed-mindedness dressed in the garb of piety," but a useful political tool nonetheless. And so, he used it masterfully, and earned a cult following in doing so. By February 2009, Obama had replaced Jesus Christ as America's number-one hero according to a Harris poll, and dedication to his come-one, come-all mysticism has continued to spread in esoteric circles, with evangelists of the new religion calling for the "tired" faith of our fathers to be replaced with a global new one.

Although it is more difficult to understand the broad appeal of Obama's New Age philosophy to the many evangelical and Catholic voters who supported him, the phenomenon can be explained to some degree as the result of a changing culture. Over the past fifty years, and especially as Baby Boomers listened attentively to pastors telling them to focus on human potential and the "god within us all," Eastern philosophies of monism, pantheism, Hinduism, and self-realization grew, providing Americans with an alluring opportunity to throw off the "outdated ideas" of fundamental Christianity and to embrace "The Second Coming of the New Age," monistic worldview ("all is one"). Aimed at accomplishing what the builders of the Tower of Babel failed to do (unify the masses of the world under a single religious umbrella), God was viewed as pantheistic, and humans were finally understood to be divine members of the whole "that God is." Pagans argue that this principle of inner divinity is older than Christianity, which is true. The gospel according to such New Age concepts—a gospel of "becoming god"—is as old as the Fall of man. It began when the serpent said to the woman "ye shall be as gods" (Genesis 3:5), and it will zenith during the reign of the anti-Christian god-king.

chapter seven

Lessons from Where the Antelope Don't Play

Some have accused me of not being patriotic enough. My response to this has always been to explain that when you understand my values, you will see that I am a patriot of the most organic kind. I believe that our Constitution was formed in those earliest stages of our country by men who wanted to do more than just create a place where a person could dwell in liberty for his or her own lifetime; they were attempting to create a legislature wherein people had the necessary tools available for *protecting* that freedom, thus sustaining it for forthcoming descendants.

However, somewhere along the way, despite the creation of our great Constitution and other provisions set into place for the preservation of our way of life, those who would seek to take control of the masses for their deviant motives and self-serving gains began to find ways to manipulate the system for their own purposes. Often, one thinks that the governing rule is a representation of the majority's preference, but our political structures are perfectly capable of being manipulated by the puppeteering elite. Do you think this can't happen? I assure you that it occurs around us all the time, its symptoms hidden in plain sight. However, a less subtle example of such tactics played out in extremes can sometimes help the observer identify these elements within society. Such a set of circumstances became the subject of much interest in 2018, when Netflix released a docuseries entitled *Wild Wild Country*, which followed (and, I daresay, romanticized) the state of affairs that took place in Antelope, Oregon, in the 1980s, wherein a group of foreigners entered the US, invaded a rural setting, took over a nearby town, and demonstrated that our democracy can be used against us.

I pastored in Oregon at the time this all went down, and my wife, Nita, and I understand well how the lessons from this story are reflected in the dangers radiating today from the DC Swamp across the heartland.

The Newcomers

In 1981, a man named Bahgwan Shree Rajneesh (also known as "The Bhagwan," then later as "Osho") purchased a large plot of rural desert land just over twenty miles outside Antelope, Oregon. He did so with the help of his assistant and secretary, Ma Anand Sheela, who selected the lot, negotiated the purchase, and traveled there with other followers of Bhagwan to begin construction at the selected location. Once sufficient amenities had been erected, Rajneesh himself planned to join these people in Oregon to continue pursuit of a town they would take over.

Despite initial claims of intended farming use on the agriculturally zoned land (a front that, at first, the group made appearances at accommodating), the subsequently emergent motive became an open statement by all Rajneeshees (followers of the Bhagwan): to build what they called a peaceful, religious, utopian society, where all could live together in harmony and love. Who could have known that the ensuing fiasco would find Oregon's newest invaders at the center of a massive federal investigation, a nationwide pursuit, and international media coverage? Amongst the scandal were multiple assassination attempts; the "largest biological terrorism attack in U.S. history, poisoning at least 700 people [with salmonella];"[466] investigation into the biggest illegal wiretapping process ever discovered by authorities;[467] the largest immigration fraud case in the history of the United States;[468] the out-weaponizing of all of Oregon state's authorities east of the Cascade Mountains;[469] and attempts to tamper with elections via both a ruse involving biological warfare and a recruited influx of displaced homeless citizens from across the nation.

Bahgwan Shree Rajneesh had become well known throughout India and other regions as a guru and philosopher who presented a worldview that not only condoned any behavior an individual may desire, but asserted that without such hedonistic explorations of a person's appetites, he or she resided in bondage to the expectations of culture, intrusive religious indoctrination, and confining social limitations. Particularly, the undertone permeating his teachings was that through open and free sex, one is set free from the restraints set by societal confines, and that seeking such fulfillment through any means a person enjoyed would contribute greatly to his or her freedom as an individual. Rajneesh's teachings involved a method called "Dynamic Meditation,"[470] which became a great means of income for his ventures. This technique involves a sequence of phases that utilize a combination of laborious breathing in an effort to make and maintain contact with the spiritual forces in a person's core; a time of "release," wherein a person is instructed to cry, scream, or otherwise let go of inner pain; and a time of silence. Each segment of this meditation is referred to as a ritual.[471] (During these sessions, it is not unusual for those "releasing" negative emotion to become violent, to sexually assault or physically beat one another, or behave in otherwise depraved manners.)

Through Rajneesh's publications of his philosophies about life, and by recruiting many within the therapeutic fields to utilize and promote his procedures of meditation, his name swelled in fame, and thus in followers. His pamphlets funded his earliest endeavors, and before long, he had large sources of financial backing from professionals across the globe.[472] When his communal cities were built (the first being Poona, India, and the subsequent Rajneeshpuram near Antelope, Oregon), many followers (also sometimes called Sannyasins) who joined at those locations sold off all their possessions and contributed the sum of their fiscal gains to the Bhagwan's ever-growing empire, to which conservative estimates numbered at least $10 million per year.[473]

The Old Muddy Ranch

The purchased ranch consisted of an eighty-thousand-plus-acre plot of land in Oregon: sixty-four thousand acres purchased, and an additional eighteen thousand acres legally owned by the Oregon Bureau of Land Management and was leased in conjunction with the sale.[474] This property had previously been known as the Big Muddy Ranch, and, as mentioned earlier, was zoned by Oregon's Wasco County as agricultural land—a detail of vital importance, because it meant that any building on the property required an official permit, after the purpose and specifics of the structure were reviewed and approved by the county.[475] Attempting to fly under the radar with their true intentions for the newly acquired land, Sannysasins temporarily abandoned their typical Rajneeshee garments—tell-tale orange and red clothing worn with Bhagwan prayer beads—and attended initial planning meetings with Oregon's Wasco county officials in their plain clothes, simultaneously using their birth—not Rajneeshee—names.[476] They explained that this land was to be utilized for a "farming commune," and that the houses built were to be dwellings for the workers they brought in to join their agricultural endeavors. Initially, they stated that they intended to lodge up to 150 personnel and that these people weren't religiously affiliated.[477] Wasco county officials became suspicious when site inspections revealed that the group was actually putting up dorm-type quarters, with no kitchens or living rooms, discrediting the concept of individual, single-family dwellings. What they didn't learn until later was that during these official inspections, additional immigrants (and their mattresses) were hidden in a separate location on the property.[478]

Early on in their residency, this new populace was met with a tentative guardedness from citizens of the nearby town of Antelope, Oregon. This could have been partly due to suspicions that construction taking place on the land wasn't in accordance with the group's stated intended use of the land. There could have been concern that the water supply—a carefully managed resource in this dry, desert area—would be spread too thin by all the newcomers. Perhaps the caution was in response to circulating rumors stating that a "cult" had bought up the large plot of rural land. Maybe it was the influx of seemingly "hypnotized"[479] people donned in orange and red garb and wearing prayer beads. Regardless, it was as though these retirees *knew* things weren't right with their new neighbors, but for the moment, they were unable to put their finger on the underlying issue. After all, their sleepy, modest town boasted little more than a restaurant, a school, a post office, a grocery store, and a population of just over forty. These citizens were distrustful of the strange outsiders and were likewise unprepared for the sensational and scandalous adversity ahead. On the contrary, many residents had selected this rural area as a peaceful place to retire due to its quiet, economically feasible conditions.

However, by the time the new community members began receiving deliveries of amounts of construction materials equaling far more than what one "agricultural commune" could ever make use of, the Oregonians' initial wariness gave way to full-scale suspicion.

An agency called "1,000 Friends of Oregon" was made up of businessmen who were sticklers for making sure that Oregon land was used in precisely the way it was permitted/zoned. Likewise, the group closely scrutinized the newcomers' activity as construction progressed. The farther their activities varied from what appeared to be traditional agricultural efforts, the more closely the Friends watched the red-wearers. In 1981, Rajneesh's lawyers met with the Friends to explain that making a functional farm out of the rural, rocky, and barren land had become a larger undertaking than originally anticipated; and for this reason, they said, they needed to construct more housing and bring more people on board. Additionally, they began to state their "need" to make their compound its own, independent city. When 1,000 Friends of Oregon resisted this effort, Sheela, Rajneesh's secretary, offered the organization a bribe, which only made things worse.[480] Soon, a mud-flinging match was raging between the Rajneeshee commune and the 1,000 Friends, with the Friends attempting to barricade the efforts of Rajneeshpuram, and Bhagwan followers accusing the Friends of being "more interested in crushing a religion than protecting land,"[481] despite their previous claims of having a nonreligious mission within the new development.

Rajneeshpuram

The commune quickly met the necessary population requirements set by the state of Oregon to charter as its own, independent city, which they named Rashneeshpuram.[482] When the budding municipality began to close down the roads going through or around their property, guardedness on behalf of neighbors mounted into opposition. By now, it was obvious that the *guise* of a farming community was precisely that.

With Rajneeshpuram officially established, these people now had the right to issue their own building permits, assemble (and arm) their own law-enforcement agents, and appoint their own civic officials.[483] Additionally, each time they needed expertise in any particular field, they recruited from within their own followers, growing their like-minded community while supporting autonomy. Working in a cooperative manner, they managed to build their city, including such utilities as a septic/lagoon system, an electrical grid that could support ten thousand residents,[484] medical facilities "in which deadly substances of various kinds were stockpiled, and were in instances actually deployed,"[485] and even a crematorium.[486] Additionally, the town constructed banks, houses, restaurants, shopping centers, and meditation halls; implemented solar power systems; established a self-sufficient farm complete with irrigation system; and even built an airport and a dam that created a lake in the center of the otherwise dry, unfertile area.[487]

When Bhagwan Shree Rajneesh had arrived at the ranch in Oregon after coming to America on a tourist visa[488] he had obtained under the pretext of needing to visit America for medical treatment,[489] he was welcomed with music, rolled-out carpets, and, of course, hundreds of followers who bought into his desire for enlightenment, individual (and sexual) freedom, and the goal of creating a new, enlightened, awakened, universal man.[490] He also claimed to be equal to Jesus, stating: "When you call Jesus, really

you have called me. When you call me, really you have called Jesus."[491]
The guru even promised "instant enlightenment to anyone who…[died]
within a 24-mile radius of him."[492]

If residents of the quiet town of Antelope hadn't yet seen an interrup-
tion of their low-profile, post-retirement lives, they certainly did when a
local newspaper ran an article on behalf of the newcomers, recruiting any
who would like to join in the exploration of their sexuality or connect with
their spirituality.[493] Incoming letters from citizens living near the Bhagwan's previous locale in India began to arrive at the city offices of Antelope, warning of the allegedly illegal nature of Rajneeshee activities, based
on the group's conduct when they resided in India. Accusations included
(but were not limited to) tax fraud and illicit behavior. When Antelope
authorities made inquiries to Rajneeshpuram's city officials regarding the
letters, they were met with an aloof refusal to answer questions.

Just a few years earlier, in November of 1978, the world had been
shaken by what became known as the Jonestown Massacre, wherein cult
leader Jim Jones had caused more than nine hundred people to commit mass suicide (at gunpoint) by drinking a cyanide-laced beverage, after
having lured them to live at his compound in a remote part of Guyana.
The cult leader had originally promised the arrangement would be an
"agricultural commune," abundant with food, peaceful living conditions,
and a utopian social and religious climate.[494] For Antelope residents, these
events remained fresh in their psyche and, combined with the sensationalistic nature of the Rashneeshees' recruiting newspaper ads, rumors of
Rajneeshpuram being a cult, the influx of letters from citizens of India,
and the seeming condescending attitude of Bhagwan's followers toward
nearby local authorities' rules or inquiries, hostility between locals and the
newcomers in red continued to mount.

Ashram in Poona and the Disturbing Therapy

For residents near Rajneeshpuram, any remaining ambiguity about what
was taking place there became quickly dispelled when, in November 1981,

a man named Wolfgang Dobrowolny released an eighty-three-minute, unrated, documentary film called *Ashram in Poona*,[495] which revealed to the outside world the scandalous goings-on of the Rajneeshees. The movie featured some of the Bhagwan's "dynamic meditation therapy sessions" (displaying the phases of vigorous breathing, releasing, and silence described earlier in this chapter, and including all deplorable behavior that took place during such assemblies) in which violent sexual encounters and ferocious physical outbursts are captured, followed by subsequent interviews with some of the filmed gathering's attendees. (After the fact, former Sannyasins came forward, stating that during these sessions, some individuals became so unstable that they later had to be institutionalized, while others became so distraught that they attempted or committed suicide. Still others were inadvertently killed due to the violence of the outbursts. It was said that in such cases, the remains were burned in Rajneeshpuram's crematorium before an outside investigation could be conducted.[496]) Bhagwan's explanation for the method behind this therapy was that it facilitates the breaking down of the human psyche, which he claimed was necessary for personal growth: "I can help you only if I destroy you. If I destroy your past, your knowledge, your ideas, your conditionings, your personality, only by destroying you, I can give you a new birth."[497] Those who had previously suspected that the up-and-coming town was not all it presented itself to be were appalled when their fears were confirmed by the "scenes of graphic sexual sordidness and paganlike ritual [that] would be difficult for even the modern hedonist to sit through."[498] For residents of Antelope, their quiet lifestyle had been infiltrated by outsiders of strange, almost hypnotic demeanor who brought with them—under the guise of therapy and/or self-discovery—violence, sexual perversion, orgiastic rituals, unnatural and unnerving screaming and grunting, along with other outlandish, volatile eruptions.

The Invasion of Antelope

Alarmed, the townspeople began to assemble and strategize regarding their rights to keep the Rajneesh lifestyle out of their own culture. Quickly brought to the forefront of the discussion was their manner of land utilization, which had, since the beginning, failed to correlate with the legally zoned land-use parameters of the acreage the newcomers had purchased. By now, it was clear that the thriving city certainly was no mere farming commune. According to the law, each structure built on agriculturally zoned property in Oregon was required to serve a purpose *directly related to* farming. As Antelope residents leaned more heavily than ever on the intervention of 1,000 Friends of Oregon, the agency began to file legal action against the city of Rajneeshpuram, demanding that its buildings, built illegally under false pretenses (due to the fact that they were not agricultural), be torn down.

(Before the city of Rajneeshpuram was chartered, these red-wearers had requested to build or operate a printing press that would publish the Bhagwan's media, which was a vast source of their income. However, such an undertaking could never be considered an agricultural endeavor, and thus would never be deemed permissible on the ranch land they had purchased. This caused their attention to turn inward toward Antelope, where they began to show interest in buying or building a location where they could publish their works. Citing water-shortage issues as prohibiting such a large workforce from moving into their city [the printing plant would need to be approximately eighteen thousand square feet and have a workforce of at least 120 people],[499] the town of Antelope refused. Once the newcomers were able to officially charter Rajneeshpuram, they backed off of these requests, but the invasion of Antelope had already begun, and continued, possibly on the matter of principle.)

During this time, Bill Bowerman, cofounder of Nike, became a visible force behind the anti-Rajneesh campaign led by the 1,000 Friends. As friction between the small town and the rapidly growing city mounted, some residents of Antelope grew weary of the fight. A few placed their properties for sale, a move they may not have made had they suspected the outcome. Quickly, citizens of Rajneeshpuram purchased this real estate and made it a point to spend an adequate number of nights in the Antelope homes to meet the minimum requirements of residency in Antelope.

Some from Rajneeshpuram stated that it was necessary for the newcomers to buy dwellings in Antelope due to a housing shortage in their own community (undoubtedly a snarky retaliation to having been denied permission to build more structures earlier on).[500]

Soon, overflow from Rajneeshpuram's population roamed the streets of the Antelope, and not long after, the incoming crowd began to act as vocal members of the town. As Bhagwan followers began to outnumber the original citizens of Antelope, the majority status rotated, causing a change in the community. Property taxes in the city were raised, and funds collected did not go toward allocated purposes. For example, monies were collected for street maintenance, but such upkeep halted.[501] Resulting demoralization and tax increases caused others to place their homes on the market, which were likewise quickly purchased by the newcomers. As the population of the town shifted, local businesses closed and reopened to cater to Rajneesh clientele. Before long, the original, forty-member roster of Antelope was whittled significantly, and the town was teeming with Bhagwan followers. As this momentum continued, those who had nearly lost hope of enjoying the quiet retirement they had dreamed of found themselves selling their own property to those who came to their homes donned in red clothing and prayer beads—a transaction they took in the hopes that money from the sale would allow them a peaceful relocation elsewhere.

As friction between the two factions mounted, threats and vandalism began to take place throughout Antelope. The serene way of life that residents had previously known was now disrupted by the Rajneeshees' rampant nudity and openly audible sexual exploits. When confronted about their activities, the invaders claimed they were being treated hatefully. Citizens of Antelope claimed they were being harassed by the Rajneeshees, as they would employ such intimidation tactics as follow Antelope residents down the street, videotaping their every move, photographing their homes,[502] or shining bright lights into their windows late at night. In response, the townsfolk made threats to the newcomers, but those threats were met with more forceful and aggressive harassment..

Next, Rajneeshees made inquiries about vacancies on the Antelope school board, and this is where citizens drew the line.[503] The friction hit a boiling point when town members decided they would rather see their tiny municipality disband than have it continue in the direction that it was going. "Better dead than red"[504] became the theme for the movement toward officially unchartering Antelope, which, to townsfolk, became the sad but necessary step to bring about the end of what they saw as tyrannical intervention into their formerly serene lives. The disincorporation of the city of Antelope became the central focus of an election held on April 15, 1982.[505] By then, the situation had caught the attention of national media, and Americans watched closely to see what the ballots would reveal. The vote for dissolution failed because of the fifty-five Bhagwan followers who voted for the city to remain incorporated.[506] Adding insult to injury, the newcomers, now in the electoral majority over Antelope, soon thereafter renamed the town Rajneesh and assigned new, Rajneeshee-chosen names to each of the city's streets. Soon, speculation began to circulate as to whether the county, then the state, would be next to become overrun by these antagonistic newcomers.

Hostility Mounts

Sheela's inflammatory attitude toward local authorities did nothing to put such speculations at rest. Her vocal and antagonistic representation of the Bhagwan-following community caused all who took note to polarize between the pro- and anti-Rajneeshee movements. Soon, agencies such as the 1,000 Friends of Oregon and other environmental and sociopolitical groups were using the Rajneeshees—and Sheela's image—as their icon for gathering political, social, and even financial support.

Then, on July 29, 1983, a game-changing event occurred. At the Hotel Rajneesh in Portland, Oregon, at 1:22 a.m., a bomb was detonated. This was quickly followed by two additional and related blasts that went off within the following hour. Later, Stephen P. Paster, associated with a fundamental Methodist group, was convicted of the bombing and served time in the Oregon State Penitentiary for the attack.[507] Apparently, he had attended a therapy session at the ranch only days before under an alias. Authorities had no reason to connect him with those who had previously opposed Bhagwan's followers or otherwise affiliate him with any anti-Rajneesh movement other than religious fanaticism, but this didn't matter; the damage had been done. Rajneeshpuram's city authorities declared themselves to be under threat and openly announced that they had weaponized. Bhagwan followers who roamed the streets of Antelope bore arms as well, and its citizens endured stronger intimidation tactics than ever.

(Interesting to note is that the Rajneesh commune in Poona, India, had likewise been fire-bombed years before, when things there had been heating up between Rajneeshees and Indian government before the group relocated to America. Fire insurance had conveniently been purchased shortly before the incident, and the Sannyasins quickly pointed the finger at "religious bigots," despite subsequent rumors—*stated by Sannyasins*—that the explosion had been arranged by an insider.[508])

Sheela's previously incendiary verbal attacks on Oregon's government leaders became even more provocative, further fueling questions regarding how much these people would take over before they were satisfied. Sheela's public answers to such questions were disturbingly clear: "[Oregon's Wasco] county is so [expletive removed] bigoted it *deserves* to be taken over!"[509] Furthermore, Rajneeshpuram's arms increased, and friction continued to swell between Bhagwan followers and their surrounding neighbors. In fact, Sheela made it very clear that if any of their members were injured, there would be militant consequences, stating to the press: "If even one of us is harmed, I will have 15 of their [Oregonians'] heads, and I mean business!"[510] The transition from former Antelope into the new Bhagwan-controlled, recently renamed town of Rajneesh continued as the infiltrators eventually took over the city's council, electing a majority of officials from their own, red-wearing community. The city park was declared an area for nude sunbathing.[511] The (formerly Antelope) police force, now dominated by Rajneeshees, was renamed the "Peace Force," and it reminded citizens of its authority by conducting such antics as blaring sirens throughout the night and openly patrolling the streets with guns.[512] Those who attempted—even peaceably—to resist this tyranny were arrested under such charges as "menacing." (One man walked silently up and down the street holding a sign that read "better dead than red" and was apprehended under such charges.[513]) As a consequence of this conflict, gun sales in surrounding towns increased. International attention, however polarized, broadened the Bhagwan's fame, resulting in increased sales of published work and additional followers showing their political, social, and financial support. Correlating with this additional growth, new Rajneeshee communes began to pop up all over the world—Europe, Australia, Italy, Germany, Switzerland, and Portugal—with Rajneeshpuram in Oregon considered the headquarters.[514]

Oregon Attorney General Dave Frohnmayer began to challenge the city legally, explaining that the nature of the establishment violated the constitutional separation of church and state. He accused the Bhagwan of "religion exercising the power of a government,"[515] explaining that the two elements were so intertwined within the community that it was impossible to tell where the authority and influence of one ended and the other began.[516] He noted that the Rajneeshee symbolism was widespread throughout the school—a place he felt should be free of spiritual indoctrination—and expressed concerns that citizens were allowing their leadership to tell them how to vote. Particularly concerning to Frohnmayer was the weaponization of a potentially radical/fanatical group whose boundaries between religion and government were so cloudy, especially when considering the privileges extended to all city governments—now including Rajneeshpuram—such as the special weapons allowances endowed to law enforcement and access to national/federal criminal and security databases.[517]

The outcry from Rajneeshpuram was to accuse Frohnmayer of abusing America's Constitution to displace people of nonpreferred ethnicity or religious following from their homes and destroy their establishment. Tensions escalated as the now-armed (with guns and tear gas[518]) police force of Rajneeshpuram and Rajneesh (formerly Antelope) seemed to outsiders to be following the orders of two key individuals: Ma Anand Sheela and Bhagwan Shree Rajneesh. The volatile and insecure situation left surrounding non-Rajneeshee citizens uncertain of their safety.

The 1,000 Friends of Oregon joined forces with Frohnmayer and Oregon's then Governor Victor Atiyeh to come at Rajneeshpuram with three legislative orders that would force the city to disband on the grounds that its founders had deceived Oregon regarding their intents for the establishment's purpose. The goal was to repeal the official charter of Rajneeshpuram and restore Antelope to its former (pre-Rajneesh) condition. The newcomers in red—particularly Sheela—continued to maintain that the Sannyasins had only done what was necessary to preserve their way of life—actions necessitated by a bigoted outside world that continually forced these people to defend their position.

An Early Version of Sanctuary Cities, Open Borders, and Progressive Socialism

Then, Ma Anand Sheela began employing a different strategy. A new program was launched by the Rajneeshees called the Share-a-Home program.[519] Through this endeavor, Bhagwan followers traveled the nation recruiting homeless individuals to move to Oregon and join the compound. Large cities were targeted, where homeless populations were sizeable and often destitute. These people were brought, usually by bus, to Rajneeshpuram and given homes, jobs, food, a community that embraced them, and two beers a day.[520] *And,* many of incoming folks were told that if they were unhappy in their new dwelling, Bhagwan would buy them a bus ticket back to their hometown. Sounds like quite a deal, right? Just one small hitch in this grandiose giveaway: The men and women were encouraged—like illegal aliens for liberal Democrats are today—*to vote.*

Local pre-Bhagwan citizens, however, were uncomfortable with the influx of unsavory characters either being brought to their area by the multitudes or showing up in nearby towns on their own initiative looking for Rajneeshpuram. Furthermore, they mistrusted the Sannysasins' motives for the relocation of more than six thousand people from other cities. Immediately, these individuals believed that the underlying goal was to amass numbers for the upcoming election—which, consequently, had several candidates on the ballot who were specifically, openly anti-Rajneesh. Simultaneously, Bhagwan himself declared that he wanted to see three representatives and two county commissioner seats elected as Rajneeshees in Wasco County.[521] But rather than have these individuals campaign openly, his plan was for his followers to register to vote and flood the election with write-in candidates, who would then secure the offices for their faction.[522] One particular Sannyasin, whose birth name (more subtle than using her Rajneeshee name), Bonnie Barlow, who was to be penned in on the ballot, was disqualified from running when she was caught voting under both her birth name and her Rajneeshee name.[523]

Since this uprising community had become more open about their goal to take over Wasco County (and later, they stated their intentions were to take over the entire state of Oregon), non-Rajneeshees saw these maneuvers as an increasing threat to their way of life. The incursion of so many strangers through the Share-A-Home project just before the 1984 election was cause for extreme alarm. Oregonians accused newcomers of attempting to abuse voters' privileges, while Sheela intensely provoked the homeless recruits to demand their full, constitutional rights as citizens. In response, other anti-Rajneesh Oregonians currently residing in other counties threatened to drive to Wasco County and register to vote as well in an effort to counter the more than seven thousand potential voters that Rajneeshpuram now held.[524]

When busloads of the newly enlisted Rashneeshees arrived at a Wasco County official building to register to vote, County Clerk Sue A. Profit announced that she would not be accepting any new voters' registrations—beginning on October 10, 1984—until individual residency hearings were held.[525] Surely, this process would drag out until long after the November 6, 1894, election. This maneuver was said by Federal District Judge Edward Leavy to be the "narrowest and least burdensome way" to ensure that the election was carried out free of fraud or outside threat.[526]

Recent Rajneesh converts were furious at this, as a confrontational

Sheela continued to spurn their feelings of denial of what many began to call their "birthright."[527] Anger was the trending mood amongst the previously homeless citizens, and the setting became so volatile that population control within Bhagwan's community became a clear obstacle. When Rajneeshpuram's Peace Force had to sedate one individual to calm his violent temper, the decision was made to lace the recruits' beer—without their knowledge or consent, of course—with the powerful antipsychotic drug haloperidol.[528]

Salmonella Outbreak

Ten days before the 1984 election, it was rapidly becoming apparent that the Share-a-Home recruiting tactic had failed. Sheela made an announcement to the "Street Population" (the recent homeless recruits) of Rajneeshpuram: In the upcoming days, people would begin to receive orders to leave the Ranch. When this happened, people were to obey those orders peaceably, or they would be escorted off the premises by armed security. These were then bused out of Rajneeshpuram and dropped off in random places throughout the surrounding towns and communities. Desolate, used, and abandoned, many of these rejected individuals became violent toward locals within their new environments. Others turned to theft to survive. People in adjacent towns armed themselves and refused to leave their homes and property unattended, as they now faced the problem of thousands of overflow transients being dropped off—literally deserted—in their neighborhoods. Homeless shelters in surrounding counties filled up, and the trail of displaced vagrants extended beyond Portland. Many of the exiled individuals began to traverse the entire West Coast, often hitching rides up and down Highway 101, which spans the Pacific region from northern Washington to southern California. (At this time, I pastored in Crescent City, California, and I recall seeing an upsurge of drifters during this era, many of whom came to the door asking for food or other provisions. In researching and writing this segment of this book, I realized the high probability that the people my wife and I provided food and shelter for were very likely those who had been cast off by a previous "family" that had promised to welcome and care for them. One never knows—when a person has been placed in our lives, requesting a kind or caring act—what type of spiritual seed we have the opportunity to sow.)

Another strange anomaly began to manifest in the weeks before the vital 1984 election throughout Wasco County: Many people started experiencing flu-like symptoms. The outbreak was so profound, in fact, that more than 750 cases were presented to officials as townspeople became increasingly, violently ill. Authorities began to blame a strange type of food poisoning, but were unable to pinpoint the source of the trouble; no specific, common carrier of the germ could be isolated. While some tried to point fingers at their red-wearing adversaries, there was no *proof* that these people were behind the seemingly sporadic sickness. As elections drew nearer, the upsurge in ailment continued. Later, it was discovered that these outbreaks were the result of a bioterrorist attack on Wasco county. After many failed attempts at poisoning the masses via spreading bacteria at local grocery stores, community buildings, and political gatherings, Sheela had directed her subordinates to poison local restaurants' salad bars in an attempt to diminish voter turnout.[529]

However, the Wasco County election that year showed a record high voter turnout: 93 percent.[530] Since the newcomers were unable to register, Bhagwan's agenda was outnumbered and results maintained a non-Rajneeshee agenda. These infiltrators stated that this was due to the fact that Wasco County—with backing from the state of Oregon—had manipulated its laws to deny legal citizens their "birthrights."

Unusual occurrences continued to take place. There was a fire at the county's planning office, which was discovered to have been ransacked. Anonymous gifts—boxes of chocolates with courteous notes—were sent to key officials; the gifts were later discovered to be laced with poison— a fact uncovered when an office employee was nearly killed.[531] Authorities who, at one point, visited the commune Rajneeshpuram were served drinking water that was likewise tainted with toxic material, and one of them nearly died as well.[532] The threat felt by Oregonians, at this point, had become so palpable that a hotline was set up for callers to communicate Rajneeshee-related rumors so that officers could get the jump on possible hazards. The line was subsequently flooded with phone calls from concerned or fearful citizens, some stating that Sheela had threatened to bomb the Wasco County Courthouse.[533]

As US Attorney Charles Turner searched for charges that could be filed against Sheela and Bhagwan in an attempt to have them deported, immigration fraud was discovered. Bhagwan had ordered countless US residents within his commune—similar to what American liberals are doing today—to intermarry with foreigners to gain American citizenship.[534] This tactic was challenging at first for authorities to pinpoint, since Bhagwan would assign the residents to travel to major cities all over the country—Dallas, Texas; cities in Southern California; Seattle, Washington; Trenton, New Jersey; Philadelphia, Pennsylvania, etc.—to stage a life together with an American and exchange nuptials, which made a paper trail that was difficult to track. In response, Rajneeshpuram leadership deemed Turner an enemy and began to plot his assassination.[535]

In the meantime, interpersonal issues began to erode the solidity of Bhagwan's core personnel, and the organization began to crumble from the inside out. Claiming that it was for his own protection, Sheela had the Bhagwan's living quarters wiretapped. New, incoming Rajneeshee followers with prestige and vast monetary resources began to impact the unified direction of the commune's key people. When Sheela suspected that the Bhagwan had recruited his personal physician to help him commit suicide on Master's Day, July 6, 1985, she took matters into her own hands by selecting a small, core group of trusted insiders to murder his doctor before the plan of self-termination could be carried out. This plot was initiated by injecting the physician with poison in a crowded setting on Master's Day, but it was unsuccessful, leaving the core leadership of Rajneeshpuram irreconcilably divided.

Soon thereafter, Sheela and her trusted inner circle fled Rajneeshpuram. The Bhagwan saw his opportunity to deflect all investigations from local and state authorities onto Sheela so that his former secretary—

now his scapegoat—received blame for all pending suspicion. He claimed no knowledge (nor endorsement) of wrongdoing, including the murder and assassination attempts, theft, wiretapping, and threats to and harassment of civilians, not to mention "Sheela's" plot to crash a plane into Wasco County's Courthouse. He likewise stated that she had *even robbed him*, stealing $55 million from his compound before leaving.[536] Then, in an ultimate effort at feigning innocence in the eyes of Oregonians, the man invited local authorities *into Rajneeshpuram* to investigate Sheela's actions. Citing indignation regarding her actions, the Bhagwan even went so far as to state that he would conduct his own investigation if local and state powers did not. What he likely didn't count on was that these allegations not only presented the opportunity for state and local officials to investigate, but invited the FBI's scrutiny as well. Soon, investigators uncovered volumes of recordings that had been hidden in Sheela's house, evidence of what soon became known as the "largest wiretapping incident in the history of any nation."[537] US Navy divers searched the manmade lake at Rajneeshpuram for weapons or other evidence that could have possibly been thrown into the water, with a specific focus on finding arms purchased to assassinate officials such as attorneys David Frohnmayer or Charles Turner. (A subsequent draining of the lake revealed "a stockpile of rust-covered guns," allegedly acquired for the specific goal of ending Turner's life.[538] Because Turner served as a federal prosecutor, the assassination plot was eligible for trial on a federal level.) Additionally, the Bhagwan quickly pointed at Sheela for the upsurge in the instances of the "mystery illness" (impacting more than 750 people) that had struck just before the 1984 election, stating that her aim was to make numerous voters too ill to show up and cast their votes. When police were able to genetically match the salmonella strand found in a laboratory at Rajneeshpuram to that which had impacted so many during the outbreak, the link between bioterrorism and the community was confirmed.[539] Of course, for many, Bhagwan's willingness to throw Sheela under the bus indicated a certain element of desperation, which, in their opinion, implicated him as a coconspirator. His supporters maintained that, like themselves, he was unaware of Sheela's underhanded activities, but many viewed such protests as the naive assertions of loyal (and perhaps brainwashed) followers.

Soon thereafter, any public appearances made by Bhagwan or Sheela were merely for mud-flinging between the two, each using press coverage as an opportunity for blame-shifting. Caught in the crossfire were loyal supporters who had moved to Rajneeshpuram over the course of its existence; especially brokenhearted were those who had been a part of it since its origination, those who had worked to build the city or who had given all their monetary gains toward the vision of the commune. A great number weren't aware that friction between key leaders had come to such a boiling point, nor did most know that such grotesque illegal activity had taken place. Likewise, this collective was largely unaware that a great number had been eavesdropped upon via wiretapping and sedated by antipsychotics added to their beverages during their stay at Rajneeshpuram.[540] In light of the sudden gap left in city management by those who had abandoned their posts, Rajneesh appointed new officials. Simultaneously, Sheela's robes were burned publicly (a display affirming that the former secretary was excommunicated), and Bhagwan ordered the Rajneeshee religious books to be incinerated at the commune's crematorium; stating that the commune was not—and had never been—of religious constitution.

The seeming cooperation between Rajneeshpuram and outside authorities' investigations was halted when FBI agents—alongside federal, state, and local police—raided the city with search warrants. Bhagwan was furious and ordered his followers to stop cooperating with outside law enforcement. They were told not to report anything, reveal information, or otherwise surrender material to the officials. His statement became that the community would resist efforts of the American government to gain any additional evidence, and furthermore, that they would *not* leave the area. He stated that if Oregon wanted the Rajneeshee collective to leave their homes, it would have to be accomplished with force—an action he stated would expose democracy as being nonexistent in America.[541]

One of Bhagwan's once-trusted core leaders, Krishna Deva (previously the mayor of Rajneeshpuram), grew concerned about the consequences of the charges the US government was amassing. With Sheela having fled the country, Deva realized he could be next in line to be implicated n crimes. Taking a proactive approach, he struck a bargain with the federal government in the hopes of receiving a lighter sentence, an effort that proved beneficial for both sides. He was placed under the Federal Witness Protection Act while former comrades were indicted for such crimes as immigration fraud, murder, and "conspiracy to defraud the United States."[542] Impending arrests for Bhagwan Shree Rajneesh, Ma Anand Sheela, and several of their colleagues had to be coordinated carefully. On one hand, Sheela had been quietly located in West Germany, but authorities feared that the apprehension of Bhagwan would tip her off, possibly causing her to flee (again); thus, the "holy" man's seizure had to be carefully orchestrated due to the weaponry and open hostility at Rajneeshpuram. Officials estimated that, by this time, the red-wearers had stockpiled enough firepower to outgun "all police forces in Oregon combined."[543] They were known to have semiautomatic Uzi rifles, Russian AK47s, and over a million rounds of ammo for these firearms. Authorities and citizens outside Rajneeshpuram, frazzled from the mounting interpersonal conflict (and still recalling events like the Jonestown Massacre), wondered if an arrest attempt would turn violent, and if so, whether it would be on a small or large scale. Followers of Bhagwan stood unwavering that his orders not to cooperate with law enforcement would be followed. When their leader said any attempt to remove their commune would have to be carried out by force, many were uncertain as to whether they should expect officials to invade with violence. If so, they were ready to defend themselves. Asked how much firepower they had should the need arise, one Sannyasin answered resolutely, "Enough."[544] This stance confirmed authorities' suspicions that those arrested likely wouldn't go peaceably, so they prepared for a possibile weaponized confrontation, hopefully without casualties. The Oregon National Guard, Army National Guard, and Air National Guard were on standby should the situation escalate, and the National Guard stationed assistance throughout the wilderness-outskirts of Rajneeshpuram.[545]

Authorities determined that apprehensions in Rajneeshpuram and West Germany needed to occur simultaneously, which required law enforcement in both countries to collaborate. As details were being finalized, two Learjets within the compound suddenly took off, and an informant told police that their leader had been on one of them.

A nationwide chase ensued, with the Federal Aviation Administration (FAA) tracking the two planes across the country. Arrests at this point had to be pursued carefully, as authorities suspected the Bhagwan was headed for Bermuda, where it would be impossible to extradite him to the States. Refueling stops for the aircrafts were to take place in different cities: one in Salt Lake City, Utah, and one in Pueblo, Colorado, with a common, final refueling point in Charlotte, North Carolina.[546] The airport in Charlotte was staked out by agents who waited to arrest the passengers of both jets. When the planes landed, a pursuit throughout the airport landing zone took place until armed customs officials successfully surrounded and apprehended all passengers of both crafts. Interestingly, Bhagwan had taken with him his throne, expensive jewelry, weapons, and $55 thousand in cash—the very amount he had accused Sheela of taking when she fled.[547]

Quickly after the airborne fugitives were detained, German Secret Police closed in on Sheela and her comrades, making several arrests. Sheela was extradited to America, where she was indicted and pled guilty to charges including "attempted murder, assault, arson, electronic eavesdropping, immigration fraud and conspiracy."[548] She was sentenced to four and a half years in prison and was ordered to pay $469,000 in fines.[549] Additionally, when she finished serving her time, she was to leave the US for good. Bhagwan pled guilty to violations of immigration policy and was deported, relocating once again to Poona, India.[550]

As the infrastructure of Rajneeshpuram's management subsequently fell apart, those who remained learned that the compound was carrying unsurmountable debt, many speculated to the tune of $55 million.[551] Followers, eventually forced to leave the property, relocated throughout other regions, the Rajneesh Rolls-Royce collection was sold off, and an insurance company foreclosed on the property.[552] The town of Antelope rein-stated its former name, abandoning both the name "Rajneesh" and the Sannyasins' assigned street names. The property remained uninhabited until 1991, when a man named Dennis Washington purchased it, then donated it to friends of ours in a Colorado-based youth-outreach ministry called Young Life, which operates a yearly summer camp ministry on the site.[553]

Do the Tactics Look Familiar?

Considering the events that took place in Oregon, many would, on the surface, believe that simple religious people were just looking for a quiet place to carry out their unimposing way of life, until those from the out-side provoked them. Others believe this group came to Oregon looking for trouble: a search that rendered more than they bargained for. How-ever, key tactics were at play, and once we identify them, it becomes easy to see the current social, societal, and political setting in a new light. Let's review some of the devices that the Rajneesh leadership employed—both on its own people, and those in the surrounding communities—in an effort to bring new insight to our current political climate. Mind you, I'm not equating every aspect of our modern culture to those of a cult, but this provides solid, extreme examples of such devices that, once recognized, become more obvious to the onlooker who studies society as a whole.

Flying Under the Radar

Through the Rajneeshees' early attempts at keeping their true motives for the land purchase secret, their first tactic of deceit was avoidance. Recall that, initially, when they wanted to obtain permits for buildings that were not agricultural, they used their birth names, not their Rajneeshee names. Additionally, they dressed in regular clothes and didn't wear prayer beads to the meetings with county officials. They stated that proposed dwell-ings were for farming partners coming in to join in their endeavors, and they even hid immigrants (and their mattresses) during official visits.[554] Furthermore, they initially publicly denied having any religious affiliation. Looking around in society today, we see this tactic utilized everywhere within open-border policies and sanctuary cities that progressives celebrate despite clear and present dangers to legal citizens. Often (if not usually), the truth is much different beneath the surface than the picture that meets the public eye.

The Power of Us v. Them

Another shrewd strategy for manipulating the masses is provoking a common enemy. The psychology is very simple. Bhagwan himself stated that by inciting a mutual adversary, a group would unite more effectively. He even quoted Hitler's approach to hatred as both wisdom and as the backbone for bringing people together: "He [Hitler] writes…that people are not united because of love…love has no power. All power comes through hatred. Create hatred, and they will become united. And I [Bhagwan Rajneesh] can fully understand his insight."[555] One can certainly see how this approach worked for Rajneesh. Recall that, after Sheela had left the compound and arrests were impending, he commanded his followers not to cooperate with authorites, insinuating that arrests could be initiated with police brutality. This suggestion of impending violence prompted many Sannyasins who were otherwise peaceful to be ready to defend themselves and their compound with weaponry, should the need arise.

Furthermore, consider how the friction between factions began: While Antelope citizens at first resisted the red-wearers, the real catalyst of altercation was the release of the film *Ashram in Poona*, wherein the Oregonians learned what their new neighbors were *actually* up to. This provided the perfect opportunity for Rajneesh to cement the bond among his own followers by pointing all negative energy toward an outside force. Considering this, one has to wonder precisely *who* made that movie and *what* the *motivation* was for showing it to outsiders. Despite initial assertions that Bhagwan's followers rejected the motion picture, a little digging reveals that Wolfgang Dobrowolny (the creator of the film) was actually a follower of Bhagwan, not an outsider.[556] Furthermore, the film was made with the consent of participants, who even gave interviews regarding their altered states of mind during recorded therapy sessions.[557] With this in mind, it seems obvious that the film's release was to provoke animosity from the outside, to which Bhagwan could then "respond" by inciting an equally unified reaction from *within* his compound.

When the masses are watching a distant enemy, they're less wary of their own leadership. It makes one more curious about modern-stated government concerns such as global warming, the war on terrorism, or even homeland issues such as the split between conservatives and liberals. Uniting a people toward a common enemy releases and channels their hatred, and when that begins to grow, judgment is impaired and the direction of the masses can be easily controlled by a few key people.

Utilize the Media

News these days is polarized. More often than ever, complaints abound that media reports are one-sided, lack objectivity, or even come off as hostile to certain worldviews. One must wonder sometimes where this volatility comes from. After all, not everybody in society can agree on everything at all times, so why can't both sides on any issue merely present their arguments and allow the populace to reach a peaceable decision? The answer is simple: the passion—and sometimes adrenalin—incited by public debate stirs momentum that divides the onlookers. Consider Sheela's inflammatory provocation of Wasco County officials, engaged through confrontational press coverage: Her demeanor and hot-blooded attitude branded her as a public icon, until she stirred national—and international—attention, thus recruiting more supporters for the Rajneeshpuram position. Many times, *hype* in the media is precisely that: intentionally stirred up to drive the public apart. Often, continued observation reveals an underlying motivation for this manufactured strife.

Upheaval of Personal Identity

When Rajneeshees arrived in Oregon, they visibly stood out with their red and orange attire and their Bhagwan prayer beads.[558] Moreover, the Sannyasins were given new names when they joined the community, to which prefixes were added: "Ma" for women and "Swami" for men. Besides the fact that many of the members had given all their wealth to the community upon joining, it wasn't unusual for them to sever ties to their families.[559]

One of the first tactics that cults use to implement mind control of incomers is to detach them from their sense of identity. They commonly separate a person from his or her past, personhood, and family through the strategies Rajneesh used and even via other, more intrusive means. However, there are subtler ways to accomplish similar effects. When an authority figure causes a person or group of people to change according to the assembly's overall identity, it renders them personally vulnerable and insecure to the point that they incur a deep psychological dependence on the leader.[560] When an individual has been broken down over a period of time and new layers of personhood have been added to replace those stripped away, the introduction of a common enemy is more intense, because the personal investment in the collective is more profound. Maneuvers toward the outside adversary take on the theme of being "for the greater good" or "to protect our way of life." In separating people from their families, Bhagwan's own words are revealing: "I teach the commune, not the family. The family is the unit of the nations, of the state, of the church; of all that is ugly."[561] When we look at modern society and the erosion of personal identity, we have to wonder if seeds of confusion are intentionally sown in the hopes that those lost in the search for individuality will be recruited into causes that serve the nefarious few.

When we understand this tactic, great concern should be raised over the bitter fruit being sown by Soros-Obama-Alinsky types and the memes they widely disseminate.

Sedate, Surveil, or Overwork the Population

During the construction of Rajneeshpuram, residents often worked six days a week for up to twenty hours a day in the heat.[562] Many who balked at doing this were told that their other option was to leave the compound.[563] Recall how, as a method of crowd control—particularly toward the end of the Share-A-Home program—the population was surveilled or sedated without their knowledge or consent. When the leadership deemed it necessary, permissible, or appropriate, people's rooms were wire-tapped, and, as the anger of the crowd swelled in response to being denied the right to vote, the management's solution was to lace their beer with powerful antipsychotic drugs.

While these tactics manifest under a more effective shroud at present, many individuals will agree that exhausting work hours, along with unknown/nonconsensual surveillance are present in modern society. Some even venture so far as to speculate about elements such as chemtrails and city drinking water; holding ingredients suspect and presuming their role in a larger, more underhanded scheme. While the former elements are often suspect only to the most conspiratorial minds, there is truth to the assertion that, increasingly, we are watched and eavesdropped upon. Between smart televisions, smartphones, smart technology in our cars, thermostat and climate-control systems with the capability of surveillance, and countless other means of digital communication, few can deny that, anymore, we're almost never alone. And saying the wrong thing—even when we think we're alone—can be captured by these thousands of smart devices surrounding us today, followed by our being shadow-banned in social media and elsewhere if our commentary doesn't meet the approved dialectic of the state (see chapter 1 and Oceania's "doublethink" and "newspeak").

Squeeze the "Little Guy" Out of His Place

There are many ways to squeeze, intimidate, or flat-out bully a less-powerful individual from his or her place if one is really determined to do so.

We see this in the Rajneeshee encounter in more than one way. First, as immorality began to sweep through Antelope, those who felt threatened by the influx of depravity or who were otherwise resistant to the invasion were met with hostility and the pressure to accept what they didn't agree with. Recall the street intimidation by the Sannyasin's "Peace Force" and the nude sunbathing in the city park—not to mention the disconcerting public sexual encounters which, if not *seen* by neighbors at all hours of the day and night, could be *heard* by them. When this activity didn't push those who held a different standard of morality out of their way, the effort to displace citizens became more overt. During the Antelope overthrow, as mentioned previously, property taxes were raised while city mainte- nance saw a decline,[564] causing further diminishment of property values, followed by offers made by those in red to buy out these desperate people. For those still holding their ground, the Share-A-Home invasion was a no-holds-barred attempt to simply outnumber them.[565] Looking around at modern society, perhaps we're seeing a similar tactic play out through intimidation, accusations of hate speech, exorbitant tax rates, the decline of public services such as education, and the influx of refugees.

Fearmongering and Accusations of Bigotry

When the few Antelope residents who remained refused to give up the fight for their city, the newcomers, who had claimed to be a peaceable populace, intensified their approach through the use of vandalism, street harassment with cameras, and antics such as police sirens blaring late at night or flashlights shining in windows of citizens trying to sleep.[566] Even armed police on the streets became visible icons of this controversy, while quiet protestors (such as the Antelope man who carried a sign saying "bet- ter dead than red") ran the risk of being arrested for "menacing." As ten- sions mounted, those who didn't assimilate into the Sannyasin way of life were called "religious bigots" or were accused of spewing hate speech. The fearmongering that took place here is similar to what's going on in society today. It is likely an undertone anytime an individual speaks out regarding what he or she believes is moral and is subsequently silenced.

Think About This

It may seem like a stretch to compare a 1980s cult led by a foreigner to modern society. However, consider this: If this had been a political party or social movement carried out by US citizens, what would have happened? If these methods had been more understated, the lifestyle more subtly invasive rather than shockingly intrusive, and if this takeover of a small town had stretched over the time span of three decades rather than three years, would they have succeeded? As it stands, what enabled Oregon to get rid of Rajneesh was deportation and immigration fraud. Had he been an American citizen, it would have been much more difficult to halt the hostile seizure of American territory. Moreso, what if this had been a political party rather than a cult? Surely, at the incrimination of one leader, another would simply rise to take his or her place and the push would continue. All crimes could potentially be tagged onto one scapegoat or merely swept under the rug, and the momentum would have remained steady. Perhaps they would have succeeded in commandeering Wasco County, followed by Oregon, and then, who knows? Possibly the country…

No earthly governmental is flawless, and any leadership, when manipulated by the right people, can be used against its own citizens. However, God can use anything as a force for good. His redeeming power never fails, when people surrender to His will and allow Him to have control of their lives, their churches, and their country. The facilities of Rajneeshpuram, as stated previously, were purchased by Dennis Washington in 1991, and now are used annually for summer camp facilities by Colorado-based Young Life Ministries.[567]

chapter eight

Where Are We Going?
Visions for America's Future

Like most of you, I enter the new year realizing the presidential election—while very important to the future of the United States—is but one of numerous challenges facing conservatives and Christians at a time when nearly everything we once held sacred is under attack.

This was on my mind recently when reviewing a sermon I had preached more than twenty years ago titled, "Where is America Going?" That message was a blistering analysis of critical trends and social decay that appeared to me then, and moreso today, symptomatic of something far more alarming than political and social cycles.

Across the US, well-respected minds agree with that sentiment and offer disturbing forecasts for the future of this country. Social academics and cultural scientists are increasingly concerned that, for the past fifty years, America has systematically divorced higher moral authority from public policy, which in turn has delivered a nation at a breaking point in the stability of definitive Western culture. Even our language is contaminated by political correctness to the point we are incapable of recognizing and defining the most basic ethical certainties and scientific realities, including civil liberties based on natural law, the ultimate source of US constitutional protections. What citizens once called "promiscuity" has become "sexually active," cold-blooded murderers are now "victims of rage," and so on.

These facts—coupled with the latest statistics on crime, suicide, drug and alcohol abuse and other facts indicative of social decay—reveal what should be obvious to anyone paying attention: Without an urgently needed moral and spiritual awakening, America is racing toward calamity reminiscent of the fall of Rome and the decline of other past great civilizations.

I include the language of "spiritual awakening" above, because deteriorating social values and growing political incivility are but warning signs of a profounder malady. America's founders, though in many cases deists and Freemasons, knew this and proffered the stability of great and lasting government as best guided by ultimate moral supremacy, or "God." Men like George Washington and John Adams were students of history and perceived correctly from the time of the Great Flood to the fall of Egypt, Assyria, Babylon, and Rome, that the Holy Scriptures, religious faith, and the family unit as described in the Bible were unsurpassable ingredients in formulating civilian allegiance and lasting national strength.

"Religion and morality are the essential pillars of civil society," Washington once wrote.[568] He later affirmed, "Of all the dispositions and habits which lead to political prosperity, religion and morality are indispensable supports. In vain would that man claim the tribute of patriotism, who should labor to subvert these great pillars of human happiness, these firmest props of the duties of men and citizens."[569]

When we understand this part of our nation's spiritual heritage and survey the polarization surrounding us today, we are forced to conclude America has lost sight of our Great Sovereign. Like a ship adrift in the ocean and needing direction to find land, we stand "lost at sea," blinded by humanist aspirations and intellectual achievements while facing certain societal downing. For the last five decades, we've allowed progressive extremists to redefine values, to saturate culture with explicit sex education for children and to propagate anti-Christian curricula through television moguls and Hollywood elites denigrating Judeo-Christian faith while mocking virtues of purity through the illusion of "entertainment." The highest courts in the land (especially under the Obama regime) ruled with imperious decree against God, prayer, evangelism, and other expressions of biblical religion. The net result of this and other unrelenting confrontations is that the United States has quickly become one of the most profane and spiritually dangerous places in the industrialized world. We sowed to the wind and now are reaping the whirlwind (Hosea 8:7).

The question is; Will it get better before it gets worse?

Let's consider several illustrations where spiritual and political polarization is dividing Americans today, and whether such vast and growing differences between liberals and conservatives will play a defining role in the destiny of One Nation Under God, including the possibility of civil war, which a growing number of Americans believe is coming.

The Rotten Fruits of Progressive Occultism:
Example 1 – *Roe v Wade*

The Nation Watches the Supreme Court

On January 22, 1973, the Supreme Court ruled that under the 14th amendment to the Constitution, a woman had the right to end her pregnancy by abortion.[570] Since then, the number of legally obtained termination procedures has increased dramatically, with new statistics showing that one in four women in the US have had it done before they reach the age of forty-five.[571]

The Supreme Court is—for all practical purposes—the final authority regarding legislation in this country. Certainly, many other agencies and elements are involved in creating laws, but the Supreme Court ultimately has the last word on whether these boundaries stand.[572] This entity holds the power to overrule maneuvers made by the president, Congress, or individual states, should it deem that such regulation has stepped outside what is allowable in the American Constitution. This is why there is such attention—and *tension*—as the American population watches to see what will be done with *Roe v. Wade*—one of the most controversial laws passed in the history of this nation. As the representation between conservative and liberal shifts within the Supreme Court, the upcoming election, and the rapidly changing distinct state statute, the fate of the 1973 ruling stands in the balance.

Will Roe v. Wade *Remain, Out of Respect for Precedent?*

Since the president retains those he sees fit to occupy vacancies within the Supreme Court, who vote into the White House plays a large role in the entire slant of American law. Furthermore, since these positions are held indefinitely, the sway created by a particular presidential term (and the appointees made during this period) can be long-lasting. Since the Supreme Court is made up of nine selected justices, for many years, the abortion issue was held at pro-choice position, often gridlocked with four votes against five. However, when Trump delegated conservative justices Neil Gorsuch and Brett Kavanaugh to take the seats of the late Justice Antonin Scalia and Retired Justice Anthony Kennedy, it fortified the pro-life stance of the Supreme Court. This does not mean, however, that conservatives can presume that a *Roe v. Wade* overturn is certain; many speculate that even conservative Supreme Court justices will allow the law to remain in place out of respect for precedent.[573] When addressing a previous (unrelated to *Roe v. Wade*) case where the Supreme Court felt it faced the decision of whether to adhere to standard, Chief Justice Roberts stated: "Fidelity to precedent…is vital to the proper exercise of the judicial function…and contributes to the actual and perceived integrity of the judicial process."[574] These words could cause the reader to lose hope in the possibility that the situation with *Roe v. Wade* could be changed, making it seem as though we may be permanently compelled to adhere to the law simply because—once upon a time in 1973—it was initiated into federal legislature. However, further commentary penned by Roberts seems to include room for adjustments within the law *when there is call to make such a maneuver.* "At the same time… [precedent] is neither an 'inexorable command'…nor a 'mechanical formula of adherence to the latest decision'…we must balance the importance of having constitutional questions *decided* against the importance of having them *decided right.*"[575] Many speculate that any shift the Supreme Court makes on this issue will be made slowly. *Washington Post* writer Robert Barnes elaborates: "The Court in general—and Chief Justice John G. Roberts Jr. in particular—prefers a step-by-step process when shifting the court's jurisprudence rather than disposing of an iconic, landmark ruling in one grand gesture."[576]

For *Roe v. Wade* to be overturned, the Supreme Court will need to see a judicially sound reason to deviate from established standard and opt for a new interpretation of law. For pro-lifers, this is simple: The right to terminate a pregnancy on demand should come second to an unborn's right to life. For those in the pro-choice camp, the fetus is viewed as mere tissue and the woman's authority over her own body should receive priority. As the country watches to see what the Supreme Court's forthcoming actions on the issue will reveal, states scramble to position legislation in anticipation of a possible overturn *of Roe v. Wade.*

Will the Supreme Court Directly Tackle Roe v. Wade?

Some believe that Trump has used the vacancies in the Supreme Court to gain favor with the populace on this very subject, thus increasing his odds for reelection in 2020, by "consistently appointing judges to the federal courts that he believes are committed to the goal of overturning Roe… [thereby] reshaping the supreme court…the court of appeals…and the district courts"[577] according to Bill Clinton's selection, former US District Judge Shira Scheindlin. Furthermore, the Supreme Court will be handling state cases regarding limitations on abortions, and for some of these cases, Supreme Court rulings will be made in the thick of the 2020 election season.[578] Some, however, believe the Supreme Court will take the most indirect approach possible by tackling the mildest available cases rather than directly overruling *Roe v. Wade*, at least until *after the election.* Others believe the Supreme Court will have no problem tackling *Roe v. Wade* head-on; these point to the recent overturn of previous precedent within the Supreme Court as evidence of willingness to take such action within this jurisdiction. The 1979 case *Franchise Tax Board of California v. Hyatt*—tackling whether a private court in one state can file suit against another state—was recently unraveled by the Court, "not because…any relevant facts had changed but because a bare majority of the Court would have ruled differently had they heard the case in the first place."[579] Furthermore, many believe that *Roe v. Wade's* days are numbered if the 2020 election brings in a Republican president who has the opportunity to replace either or both Justices Stephen Breyer and Ruth Bader Ginsburg.[580]

If *Roe v. Wade* were to be overturned as some speculate, then legislation surrounding the issue would likely be given over to individual states to decide, leaving a dual polarization of abortion availability between red and blue states. Throughout the Supreme Court's recent transition, eyes across the nation watched in suspense to see which side of the dispute would prevail. Pro-choicers cringed and pro-lifers cheered when Kavanaugh confirmed his stance by "[writing] an opinion to shrink abortion rights."[581]

Pro-choice Arguments for Legalized Abortion

While the debate seems fraught with arguments about a woman's right to terminate her pregnancy in cases of rape, incest, and endangerment to the mother's life, research shows that such instances are extremely rare. In fact, only 1 percent take place because of rape and 0.5 (half of one) percent are due to incest.[582] These cases are so rare that people such as Florida State College of Law Professor Mary Ziegler readily admits that allowances for rape- and incest-related concessions are "much more 'symbolic than they are relevant.'"[583]

The percentage of pregnancies terminated for the sake of the mother's safety are ambiguous, since doctors classify this criteria in different ways, and many who cite medical reasons to perform the procedure—such as in the case of ectopic, or "tubal," gestation—do not consider it a "procured abortion."[584] For many physicians who support a woman's right to choose, elements covered under the header of "mother's well-being" are vague and could mean anything from an additional child causing elevated anxiety to that of an immediate medical risk, while other doctors assert that to treat a pregnant woman is caring for *two* patients, both of whom deserve the best life-saving intervention available under modern medical technology.

Surprising in this debate is the number of abortions that take place that are not for any of the three most common reasons for guarding these rights—rape, incest, and endangerment to the mother. While these causes are asserted as noble reasons to protect pro-choice rights, they diminish greatly when statistics are revealed showing why women are actually opting for the procedure: 59 percent were already mothers of at least one child (and likely do not want to take on more children), and 51 percent claim to have been on some type of contraceptive when they became pregnant (thus they did not want the pregnancy to begin with).[585] Additionally, the Guttmacher Institute reported high numbers of gestation termination taking place for reasons of personal preference: 74 percent of women polled stated that opting for delivery would drastically alter the course of her life,[586] while 73 percent felt they could not take on the financial obligation of a child.[587] Nearly half of women who opted to terminate their pregnancies named relationship issues or single-parent status as a large contributing factor to their decision, and almost 40 percent stated that they were finished with their child-raising years.[588]

In 2017, 18 percent of pregnancies in the US ended via abortion—approximately a total of 862,320 unborn killed in that year alone.[589] Encouragingly, this number was down from 2016, when statistics showed closer to one-fourth of pregnancies being ended, for a casualty count of just over 926,000.[590]

States Scramble to Generate Preemptive Legislation

While some states are quickly placing trigger laws in anticipation of what they deem to be an impending overturn of *Roe v. Wade*, others are more skeptical that such a drastic overhaul will take place. According to the Guttmacher Institute, "21…restrictions were enacted…in the first three months of 2019, with the largest trend being the fetal heartbeat bill."[591] Certainly, even as these conservative territories fight to illegalize such procedures, others are relaxing the parameters under which an abortion is legally available to send a message of pro-choice support to the federal government.

Is the population so certain that the Supreme Court will reverse rights previously granted? Not completely, but motions currently being approved are closely scrutinized, since the outcomes may give clues to the overall fate of *Roe v. Wade*.

For example, in the near future, the Supreme Court is set to hear the case of *June Medical Services v. Gee*, wherein Louisiana law will be challenged for its legislation regarding facility and personnel regulations for abortion providers.[592] Many pro-choice individuals find laws such as these particularly frustrating, because rather than to place an outright ban, they strictly standardize the caregivers credentials or facility's amenities, claiming that these "[make] access…more difficult by design…without the public trigger of saying that they're overruling *Roe v. Wade*."[593]

On the other hand, many pro-lifers claim these stipulations apply to *all* medical facilities and that those who assert that these providers are being singled out or picked on in any way are merely crying "wolf." Pro-choicers respond by citing many regulations as *TRAP laws* (Targeted Regulation of Abortion Providers)—protocols on providers and facilities that they claim are made with the primary intention of making it difficult for such clinics to remain open.[594] While, in all fairness, it is possible for more conservative states to take a monitoring approach to minimizing the availability of such procedures, it is still true that they are keeping the service available to those who are willing and able to jump through hoops. This strategy, in such cases, is possibly preferred for conservative states that wish to operate within the legislation provided by the Constitution rather than pass a trigger law that could subsequently be blocked or overturned, but who still want to see the application diminished.

There again, medical facilities of any kind are increasingly subject to heightened scrutiny and guidelines pertaining to sanitation, sterilization, technique, storage and disposal of various materials, procedures, recordkeeping, and credentials of personnel. As Robert Field, JD, MPH, PhD, chairman of the Department of Health Policy, Public Health, and professor of Health Policy at University of the Sciences in Philadelphia, Pennsylvania, stated: "The path to practicing medicine is paved with an array of regulatory hurdles implemented by an assortment of bureaucracies."[595] Bearing this in mind—especially when considering the emphasis made by pro-choicers on the need for abortion services to be kept *safe*—it is understandable that the need for overregulation would exist. Yet, it is simultaneously believable that many facilities offering procedures would see protocols made on their facility as an attack, although these may be considered par for the course at another type of clinic.

However, in the case of *June Medical Services v. Gee*, the outcome may be very telling regarding the Supreme Court's attitude toward the future status of *Roe v. Wade*. *Services v. Gee*, which has been placed on hold until the Supreme Court hears the case, essentially challenges Louisiana's Act 620, which mandates that "abortion providers in the state…have 'admitting privileges' at a licensed hospital within 30 miles of the clinic."[596] Since such privileges are difficult for providers to obtain, the ordinance is being challenged under the argument that it places "undue burden"[597] on those seeking such services (this has become the ambiguous term under which pro-choice activists can find a margin of defense, since it is not legally permissible to place "undue burden" on a woman seeking the procedure. Justice Roberts has never—once—found just cause to grant protection under the heading in his tenure.[598]) Those in support of Act 620 state that the regulations in question are necessary and reasonable, while those who are pro-choice see this as an under-the-radar means of limiting—or nearly eliminating—abortion services in Louisiana. The Supreme Court will begin hearing this case in the forthcoming months, and many onlookers will be watching intently in anticipation of their ruling, hoping that the outcome will provide an impression of *Roe v. Wade's* fate.

Is Roe v. Wade *Likely to be Overturned?*

For *Roe v. Wade* to be overturned, the majority vote at the Supreme Court would have to return in favor of the upheaval. At this point, states and citizens across the nation are more verbal than ever on this issue, attempting to send a message to the Supreme Court stating where they stand. On that note, here are a few overall statistics of the general US populace at this time: More than 60 percent of American adults surveyed by the Pew Research Center in 2019 stated they believe abortion "should be legal in all or most cases"[599] while nearly 40 percent believe it "should be illegal all or most of the time."[600] The religion gap contributes greatly to this debate; more than 80 percent of those claiming no religious affiliation believe that it should be legal, while nearly 80 percent of white, evangelical Protestants believe the opposite.[601] In 2017, a Pew Research survey showed that nearly 50 percent of Americans felt that it was ethically wrong to terminate pregnancy, while 20 percent felt that it was not.[602] The remaining 30 percent asserted that this was not a question of morality.[603] As for the matter's impact on the presidential elections, 45 percent of voters in 2016 stated that this topic influenced their votes.[604]

Significance of Trigger Laws

Recently, in anticipation of action from the Supreme Court, individual states have begun to create their own legislation surrounding the matter. As stated previously, some states have placed bans on abortion, while others have loosened its limitations. The movements have brought polarized reactions from citizens across the country, yet these laws aren't in effect at the moment. Why not? Because these are what are known as "trigger laws,"[605] meaning that they remain dormant until such occasion should present itself for the law to take effect. For example, many states have laws regarding various ethical issues—such as cloning—in place, despite the fact that the technology isn't yet available on a mainstream platform. Creating such anticipatory laws allows the states to deliberate their legal position *in advance* so that, if and when such circumstances present themselves, the laws can immediately become effective. Taking such legal steps ahead of time keeps a matter of ethics—such as cloning—from getting out of hand while the court system juggles with the red tape of illegalizing such practices.

So, what do "trigger laws" mean regarding *Roe v. Wade*? Essentially, the existence of so many new laws—created at the state level—banning abortion, despite its protection under the blanket of *Roe v. Wade*, is acknowledgement across the nation that people believe the Supreme court *may* overturn it. These serve as each state's message to the federal government, acting as billboards for conservative or liberal states' attitudes toward the issue.

As the country remains aware that the Supreme Court has seen a shift from Democratic to Republican (and likewise from liberal to conservative), the possibility of *Roe v. Wade* being overturned is more real than ever—which would make conservative trigger laws *immediately* effective. In fact, many believe that the overturn of *Roe v. Wade* is imminent. Furthermore, under many of these laws, abortion could be classified as a felony offense, meaning that those who perform the procedure can be charged with murder and even go to prison;[606] a surefire way for these territories to be nearly instantly rid of the participating providers and their facilities. If *Roe v. Wade* is overturned, the Guttmacher Institute states that just the obstacle of increased travel distances alone would prevent 93,500–143,500 women from obtaining the procedure each year.[607] States on the reverse side of this issue have responded by updating their own laws. For example, New York recently passed a law removing abortion from the state's criminal code, even for those performed after twenty-four weeks of pregnancy.[608] According to Florida State University

College of Law Professor Mary Ziegler, the quickly polarizing state roster of public opinion on this dispute "sees a post-Roe future that exacerbates differences across state lines."[609]

In the meantime, ACLU (American Civil Liberties Union) representatives have been vocal about their intention to fight such laws to keep them from ever taking effect in the US. On May 14, 2019, in response to the new ban instituted in their state, the ACLU of Alabama tweeted that it would join forces with the national organization, assuring that they would "sue in court to make sure none of those laws ever go into effect."[610] At times, there is confusion as to which prohibitions will take effect immediately or in subsequent months and which will remain dormant until the Supreme Court overturns *Roe v. Wade* (if it happens). In such a complex political and legal issue, there is much ambiguity about what is intended to be used as a state-mandated law and what are considered "trigger laws." However, one truth remains: As long as *Roe v. Wade* is upheld by the Supreme Court, these laws will be impeded, challenged, and likely blockaded. Perhaps this is why many states opt to limit access through regulation of facilities and providers rather than taking the direct-banning approach, which they believe could be overthrown by higher courts. The polarization between red and blue states continues to increase.

Pro-Life States

As noted, because of the current focus on the Supreme Court's position on *Roe v. Wade*, many states are establishing their own legislation on abortion. Conservative regions attempt to limit access, while the pro-choice areas loosen regulations. As a result, there is much confusion about where such services are and are not legal. After all, a "ban" announced in one state that still has open clinics seems contradictory. The element of confusion often lies in the fact that many of the laws being passed will not take effect until more information is released from higher courts. For example, a recent law in Alabama (more on this in just a bit) was immediately blockaded by pro-choicers who claimed that it was unconstitutional under the Supreme

Court's 1973 ruling about *Roe v. Wade*. With this in mind, many states currently labor over laws they know will be blocked as long as *Roe v. Wade* stands, but will take effect the moment it is overturned. In the upcoming pages, I will discuss some of the laws the states are trying to set into motion, but it is necessary to understand that *many of these laws have been obstructed at this time.*

On May 14, 2019, a flood of emotion swept across the state of Alabama as Gov. Kay Ivey signed into law a bill banning abortion except in the case of the mother's life being in danger. This includes cases of rape and incest.[611] Many cheered, seeing this as a victory for the pro-life crew, while others protested vehemently, stating that one of the most basic American rights granted a female—the right over *her own body*—had been stripped away.

In April, 2019, Ohio passed a "heartbeat bill," which—as the name suggests—prohibits termination once a heartbeat can be detected in the fetus.[612] The only exception listed in this bill regards the safety of the mother's health, but it does not provide for rape or incest.[613] Under this bill, physicians performing the procedure could face felony charges, prison time, and monetary penalties. Pro-choice advocates protest this law, explaining that it could limit abortion to the first five to six weeks of gestation, before the mother is aware she is pregnant.[614] Similar to its response in Alabama, the ACLU and Planned Parenthood agencies of Ohio quickly promised to sue in court to blockade the institution of this law, citing it as unconstitutional under the provision of *Roe v. Wade*.[615] In addition, in 2018, Ohio passed a law banning post-twenty-week terminations and the "dilation and evacuation" practice.[616] Furthermore, legislation is in the works in that state that would require the "burial or cremation of fetal remains."[617] (The significance of stipulating the disposal of fetal remains will be discussed in upcoming pages.) Early in 2018, Mississippi Gov. Phil Bryant signed a law similar to that of Ohio's, forbidding abortion after fifteen weeks of pregnancy except for the sake of the mother's safety or in case of serious abnormality (allowances for rape or incest were not included).[618]

Georgia likewise passed a bill making abortion illegal after six weeks of gestation. Georgia's law differs from the aforementioned states in the sense that it *does* include exceptions, but it requires a police report when there are accusations of sexual crimes.[619] The Missouri Senate passed a bill outlawing termination after the eight-week mark,[620] and later instituted a "reason ban," wherein certain factors were prohibited under discrimination laws.[621] South Carolina's House passed a heartbeat bill that forbids termination—with no concessions for rape or incest—once the pregnancy has manifested a heartbeat.[622]

Kentucky Gov. Matt Bevin—self-proclaimed to be the "most pro-life governor in America"[623]—passed a six-week heartbeat bill with discrimination bans for the fetus; this law also requires that a woman obtaining a medical abortion be advised that the initial steps of the course are reversible, should she change her mind during the process. This state has also illegalized the dilation and evacuation procedure and abortions after twenty weeks, and it even attempted to create a law wherein providers are required to perform and show an ultrasound to a mother considering a termination.[624] Indiana had attempted to prohibit a woman's right to choose based on discriminatory laws (similar to those initiated in other states) and likewise placed strict restrictions on the treatment of fetal remains. This case went all the way to the Supreme Court, which upheld the limitations on remains, but overturned those on opting for the service based on race, gender, or fetal anomaly.[625] This particular case was scrutinized by the public because it was the first *Roe*-related case heard by the Supreme Court since the newest justices were appointed. The country will continue to watch closely as the laws attempted by Louisiana (regarding the previously discussed *June Medical Services v. Gee*) and Alabama (the near-total ban mentioned in previous pages) will likely be quickly approaching on their docket.[626]

South Dakota has gone so far as to create a law requiring that women receive counseling at least seventy-two hours before termination, and has a legality in place that would prohibit abortion completely if *Roe v. Wade* is overturned. Furthermore, post-twenty-week abortion is currently outlawed there.[627]

Pro-Choice States

On the other side of this subject, many pro-choice states are loosening the reins to show the Supreme Court their support for *Roe v. Wade*. The motivation is to secure such rights for women by having legislation in place should the Supreme Court overturn *Roe v. Wade*, thus returning authority to state-level governments. In January 2019, the state of New York signed a bill entitled the Reproductive Health Act (RHA), which "allows [some] medical professionals [such as widwives, nurse practitioners, or physician assistants[628]] who are not doctors to perform abortions"[629] and "takes abortion out of the criminal code [by removing felonious penalties for performing them], making it a public health issue."[630] The law also makes it legal for the procedure to be performed after twenty-four weeks under conditions of "absence of foetal viability,"[631] or in circumstances wherein the mother's well-being is threatened.[632] One specific contention in the dispute regarding this bill is the concern that by removing it from the criminal code, victims of domestic violence who miscarry as a result of assault would legally have no recourse with which to prosecute for the rights of their unborn children—having had such unborns redefined legally as having no individual rights to life.[633] Others who debate the validity of this law explain that the well-being, health, or safety of a mother uses language that is too vague to quantify when it is legitimate to allow a post-twenty-four-week abortion. Terminology such as this could easily be manipulated to mean any number of things: It could represent the mother's *actual, physical safety in direct connection to remaining pregnant*, or it could mean something as vague as an additional (or first) child causing the mother anxiety, depression, economic struggle, or duress due to career impediment. Many who oppose this law feel that this blanket language leaves no *real* limitations on late-term procedures, so long as the physician carefully categorizes concerns. New York State Assemblywoman Nicole Malliotakis criticized the bill for its allowance of nonphysician staff members to perform them and for the fact that "if a fetus died as the result of an assault on a woman there would be no prosecution."[634] Furthermore,

Malliotakis stated that this bill was merely a means of expanding legalized termination through the end of pregnancy.[635] This law is regarded as "'the most aggressive' abortion law in the country."[636]

In June of 2019, Rhode Island passed the Reproductive Privacy Act, which essentially bans an individual or agency from interfering in any way with a woman's right to choose to terminate. The core purpose of this law is to substantiate the current conditions of *Roe v. Wade* should the Supreme Court overturn it. As such, the state is prohibited from restricting contraceptives or abortion procedures before fetal viability (the unborn's ability to live outside the womb); from informing a husband of his wife's decision (even in cases of partial-birth techniques); and releases medical personnel from threat of felony charges in conjunction with the practice.[637] President and CEO of Planned Parenthood Votes! of Rhode Island celebrated the law by saying: "Abortion is health care…and health care is a human right."[638] In similar fashion, Vermont has a bill in the works that would reinforce the precedent set by *Roe v. Wade*, although, due to the state's liberal allowances, the new legislation would not change things at this time, practically speaking. However, with concerns regarding the fate of *Roe v. Wade*, officials in Vermont feel that a symbolic gesture reaffirming these rights needs to be sent to the federal government as "a resonant message to the nation about Vermont's views."[639] Likewise, the officials seek to set permanent safeguards into place by "amending the [Vermont] State Constitution to protect abortion rights."[640]

Illinois recently made a strong statement for the pro-choice team, signing a bill shielding such rights and repealing previous regulation that criminalized some procedures, alongside undoing Illinois' Partial-birth Abortion Ban Act. The new directive states: "a fertilized egg, embryo, or fetus does not have independent rights under the law [of Illinois]."[641] Furthermore, Governor Pritzker openly invited women in restrictive states to seek services in Illinois.[642]

As legislation changes throughout these states, the availability of abortion services reflects the local climates on the issue, and polarization between the red and blue states becomes more evident. Between 2014 and

2017, the number of facilities offering abortions grew by 20 percent in the US Northwest and West regions, while declining 15 percent throughout the Midwest and the South.[643]

A recent study released by the Guttmacher Institute revealed that "as of September 1, 2019, 29 states were considered hostile toward abortion rights, 14 states were considered supportive and seven states were somewhere in between."[644] As for population disbursement, the same article stated that 58 percent of women of fertile age live in states that are unreceptive to such rights.[645]

The People Caught Up in This Issue

For many, the pro-life/pro-choice issue is a cut-and-dried debate between conservative and liberal, Democrat and Republican, red state and blue state, or even Christian and non-Christian. However, sometimes taking a look at individuals involved in the controversy reveals unexpected players on each roster. Surprisingly, the division between factions doesn't always manifest in the personnel that many would predict. This can be disconcerting to someone seeking guidance; for a vulnerable woman standing in the valley of decision, the question is not readily presented as "good guys" vs. "bad guys." In fact, on each side of this dispute are people who claim their cause is noble, who appear to be compassionate, and who make compelling arguments. This can cause a woman who is struggling with the decision to be unsure of where to turn for direction.

For example, a video featuring a Mississippi clinic fighting to stay open was shown on television during facility crackdowns made by the state that had individuals on all sides who were passionately involved in the bout.[646] Outside, conservative protestors holding pro-life signs were villainized on camera for calling out to providers and patients, asking them to change their activities and choices. Those inside remained determined to provide abortion services for as long as they could keep their clinic open. Clinic owner Diane Derzis was cast in a compassionate light, with claims that her actions were moral, and she even stated that she has "made peace with

God"[647] about advocating for and facilitating abortions.[648] After much difficulty finding a doctor willing to serve the conservative area where her Mississippi clinic was located, Derzis finally enlisted the assistance of an obstetrician/gynecologist, Dr. Willie Parker, who lived in Chicago but traveled to Derzis' facility to perform services on designated days. Parker is likewise cast in a benevolent light; he claims to be an evangelical Christian moved by "compassion" to provide such services.[649] Over just one two-day visit to the Mississippi clinic, he would perform up to thirty terminations and advise up to fifty women.[650] He justifies his actions by stating that his mission is to ensure that "every pregnancy is a planned pregnancy, and every child is a wanted child."[651] These individuals (Dervis, Parker, and many others like them) claim that, with this goal in mind, their work is justified.

For those who are pro-abortion, heartbreaking scenarios are brought to the forefront of the pro-choice argument. For example, Dina Zirlott was only seventeen years old when she was raped, a crime against her that resulted in pregnancy. She wanted to terminate, but was told that she was too far along to obtain a legal abortion. To make matters worse, she then learned that her baby had a congenital brain defect. The infant girl was born "blind, deaf, intellectually stunted, and living in incredible pain"[652] and lived a short, medically thwarted life wherein she suffered seizures and endured a slow, painful death at the age of one year.[653] Many people believe that victims such as these should have the right to opt out of delivery, and that legally forcing the young woman to suffer these events in addition to the violation of her body was a cruel injustice. Surely, this story is tragic. One can only imagine the pain and devastation faced by this teen mother, but, as stated previously, cases like this account for 1 percent or less of the currently occurring abortions, and even many pro-lifers are willing to concede for exceptions in such cases.

In the meantime, spokespersons attempting to trace the problem to a dark spiritual origin suffer persecution. Take, for example, Fox News host Todd Starnes, who was recently fired after insinuating that Democrats may be worshiping the ancient god Moloch—who was appeased by child sacrifice—by fighting for such rights.[654] While such a comment may seem offensive to many within the pro-choice stadium, it is still true (or should be) that our constitutional right to free speech protects our ability to make religious correlations between modern political and cultural behaviors. It is apparent from such occurrences that this subject—and other current, hot-topic political issues—become "sacred cows" in the public view, and one who speaks out could run the risk of losing employment in the public arena.

The Virginia-based organization *Democrats for Life of America* is a pro-life organization that endorses preserving life regardless of which phase it is in.[655] Kristen Day, the organization's leader, represents a group of people who primarily share their party's values, yet believe that life is sacred from conception on, a balance that makes the unique (and seemingly oxymoronic) condition of such pro-life Democrats. This narrow category of individuals seems meet adversity from their liberal coparty members, who say their beliefs are contradictory and that citizens who hold such values should simply reclassify themselves as Republican. Day's response to this assertion is pragmatic: "[They are]…trying to make the party smaller… if you get rid of the pro-life Democrats, what happens usually is they're replaced with Republicans."[656] Day went on to explain that, should friction within their party heighten, they would "have to…say that we are not going to continue to support a party that doesn't want us."[657]

In addition, some pro-lifers are willing to concede to exceptions for rape and incest on legislation, regardless that they would personally like to see *all* abortions banished. They view the diminished numbers of terminations for these reasons as paling in comparison to those made because of personal preference. On the matter of agreeing to make allowances for rape and incest, president of pro-life group Students for Life of America, Kristan Hawkins, summed this stance up well by saying: "I personally have lobbied on behalf of regulation which includes exceptions because if we can work with people on the other side to ban 98% of abortions we'll take it."[658]

In the meantime, there are those who attempt to make pro-life/pro-choice an issue of race, claiming that regardless of laws limiting access, those who have ample wealth will always be able to obtain a safe, sterile procedure. Thus, many say that all prohibitions do is limit the availability of safe abortions to specific races and income brackets. To elaborate, 75 percent of women terminating their pregnancies claim income below the federal poverty level,[659] and statistics for 2014 show the ethnic distribution: 39 percent were white, 28 percent were African American, 25 percent were Hispanic, and other combined ethnicities were 9 percent.[660]

Contradictory Legislation

Some injunctions prevent the abortions from being legal if the mother has chosen to terminate the pregnancy based on race/ethnicity/gender of the child,[661] or in cases of "fetal genetic anomaly"—a condition that could result in Down Syndrome or other birth defects.[662] While initially these may seem fairly simple, the ironies are perplexing. For instance, the laws banning abortion based on race seem to be related to the concept that a woman of color would be coerced into aborting as a means of contributing to the genocide of her own race. Regardless of which side of the abortion debate a person is on, this logic seems racially slanted. After all, where does one come up with the idea that an individual would subject themselves to such a notion, and why would we assume that one race is more susceptible to this kind of thinking than another? The Guttmacher Institute explains how this stereotyping, while attempting to protect the unborn from racial discrimination, places *precisely that* on the mother: "These bans stigmatize pregnant people of color who seek abortions by questioning the motivation behind their…decision."[663] Furthermore, the Institute elaborates on how such demeaning laws "send the message that women, especially of color, cannot be trusted to make their own medical decisions."[664] It seems that such a train of thought insults the intelligence of these women.

Additionally, the prohibition in cases of fetal anomaly seems to contradict arguments in previous decades for *preserving* a woman's right to choose. After all, it has been regularly asserted that the possibility of a child being born with a defect is actually a reason to consider *terminating* a pregnancy. While I personally celebrate every opportunity to make a stand for the safety of the unborn, I find the nature of such laws convoluted—they're a breeding ground for dispute over terminology, exceptions, and conditions. Meanwhile, countless numbers of unborn babies die, as long as they are properly classified within the red tape of allowance.

Such bans on abortion protect the life of a fetus who is disabled or racially discriminated against. In order to enforce these limitations, one first must realize that the unborn are *living people* who have legal *rights*. This seems to contradict other legislation: either fetuses have rights and deserve to be legally sheltered or they don't. The subjective nature of these laws results in inconsistency, depending on one's location or the mother's frame of mind. For example, it's ironic that a woman has a right to *choose* not to deliver a child based on her career goals, financial situation, or relationship status, but a fetal anomaly (a potential developmental disability) alters this. If the pro-choice argument for a woman's right to abort for her own mental health, career ambitions, or well-being is actually a provision that is adhered to, then the delivery of a challenged child would seemingly reinforce this motivation. On the other hand, in some places, when such a condition presents, her rights are reversed, and she is legally obligated to carry out the pregnancy. Even on the liberal/pro-choice side, the laws are convoluted and contradictory.

One would think that this logic would be more acceptable in reverse. For example, if a woman is not allowed to abort, it would seem that this condition would loosen if she learns that her child is *likely* to be born with a genetic anomaly. But instead, even from the liberal, pro-choice standpoint, the laws of protection for the unborn often seem to refute themselves, and words such as "discrimination" apply at certain times and not at others. In the meantime, it appears that representatives from both pro-life and pro-choice camps have a heyday with such anomalies as they take turns spinning words against each other, but they never really get anywhere.

Furthermore, recent stories continue to show that mothers who have endangered their unborn are subject to charges such as manslaughter. For example, a woman in Indiana was charged with feticide for the death of her stillborn son after she took methamphetamines during her pregnancy.[665] Also, consider the 2014 case of Kansas' Scott Bollig, who laced his unsuspecting girlfriend's pancake with mifepristone, causing her to miscarry. He later was charged with first-degree murder and aggravated battery.[666] Even as recently as October 4, 2019, headlines were filled with reports of Samuel Turner of Lexington, Kentucky, who was involved in a head-on collision in 2018. His passenger, pregnant Kayla McCoy, passed away as a result of injuries she sustained in the crash. The slew of charges the man faced at the time of this writing included "second-degree manslaughter, third-degree homicide, first-degree wanton endangerment, possession of methamphetamine, DUI and persistent felony offender"[667]—offenses declared on behalf of both mother and unborn.

For the pro-life crowd, it is rare for one to balk when charges like these are filed. After all, *anytime* the public stands up for the rights of the unborn, they are supportive. Simultaneously, the pro-choice camp will likely affirm the pursuit of justice when one person's actions take the life of another, such as driving under the influence of illegal substances—or worse—administering an abortion-causing drug a woman without her consent. However, the issue of *intent* becomes so important in this matter of law that we land at a double standard. The question of *precisely when* a fetus has rights and when it does not has become so cloudy that it literally becomes subjective to a woman's will: If the mother wants to carry the gestation to full term and deliver the baby, then the fetus often has rights that are covered by the law. If a woman does not want to keep her pregnancy, but her reasons pertain to gender, ethnicity, or potential disability, then her rights could be overrun and the unborn could be protected under the heading of antidiscrimination laws. If a woman does not want to deliver, and her reasons don't fall inside the bracket of prejudice, then she is free to pursue abortion. In the end, the laws that align to fortify or remove a fetus' rights often depend on the mother's state of mind. Such confusing and conflicting lines of legality are the result of attempting to legislate an issue of morality in a society where individuals are free to choose their own convictions.

The Game-Changer of Medication Abortions

Before medication abortions were widely used, women had many obstacles to contend with in obtaining a pregnancy termination. In many states, the location of clinics offering such services requires hours of travel, and often, more than one appointment is necessary. In addition, many facilities aren't fully staffed with surgical-abortion providers every day of the week. Even after juggling all of the travel and scheduling logistics, women still face an expensive surgery. However, the industry has seen the arrival of a new day. Recently introduced drugs such as mifepristone— commonly known as the abortion pill—have changed all that. The way they work is as follows: Mifepristone is administered orally in pill form, which causes the placenta to detach from the womb, makes the cervix pliable, and allows contractions to begin. Then, some time later (how long depends on the physician), another drug, misoprostal, is administered, which increases contractions to induce a miscarriage.[668] These medications have become mainstream: In 2017, the number of medication abortions increased to 39 percent of all those performed from 2014's 29 percent,[669] and it appears this pattern will continue. For pro-lifers, this convenient, "clean" way of terminating a pregnancy is a blow; many deterrents that would have caused a woman in years past to rethink her decision have been removed, and taking a life has become detached and oversimplified. Additionally, clinics previously limited in their ability to provide surgical abortions (by the inadequate availability of qualified staff) can now dispense these pills any day of the week. Furthermore, even if a woman can't get the drugs from a clinic, she can easily (albeit illegally) purchase them online or by traveling to a nearby country such as Mexico, where they are available at pharmacies as an over-the-counter drug.

Defunding Planned Parenthood

In February of 2019, the Trump administration announced that it would prohibit "federally funded health care providers from making referrals to or even informing patients about abortion providers."[670] While many have claimed that this equates to the defunding of Planned Parenthood, this isn't entirely true. Instead, Title X, a federally subsidized program that provides terminations under the heading of "family planning," will still be active, but patients will be required to obtain the service at a separate facility—a move that requires organizations to keep separate financial ledgers for such services. Likewise, they will now operate without referrals.[671] While the impact of this move was not exclusive to Planned Parenthood, the organization is responsible for "about 40 percent of the 4,000 Title X clinics in the country."[672] This change in regulation will make more pro-life facilities eligible for funding because clinics will be allowed to omit abortion while advising a woman about her options. Likewise, this will yield added funds for "teen pregnancy prevention programs...that emphasize sexual abstinence over contraception."[673] Pro-lifers celebrated this as a victory, while agencies such as Planned Parenthood stated that it would withdraw from Title X (and its funding) before it would comply with the "gag rule"[674]—the prohibition of making referrals for the procedure or discussing it as an option. Planned Parenthood literally put its money where its mouth was in August of 2019, announcing that it would withdraw from Title X after lawsuits filed attempting to impede Trump's legislation were upheld by the 9th Circuit Court of Appeals.[675]

The Sinister Underbelly of the Issue

In March of 2017, undercover journalists David Daleiden and Sandra Merritt of the Center for Medical Progress were charged with fifteen counts of felony for making and releasing videos of Planned Pregnancy executives being unwittingly interviewed at the 2014 and 2015 National Abortion Federation's annual meetings[676] about the option of selling fetal remains; discussing prices and negotiating types of specimens to procure; and discussing procedures that would make different types of tissue available.[677] (Consequently, these videos have been deemed by the US Court of Appeals for the Fifth Circuit as "undoctored."[678]) Up to this point, many people weren't aware that the fetus had a destination beyond its abortive termination. Charges against the two agents—who used aliases Robert Sarkis and Susan Tennenbaum—included felony invasion of privacy and penalty for posing as purchasers of fetal matter for a fake company called Biomax.[679]

"Doe 7" was unknowingly videotaped during this endeavor, and testified in court that she had no idea when she was at the National Abortion Federation's annual meeting—since everyone signs a confidentiality agreement upon entry—that she was in a place where it might have been unsafe to speak openly about the industry and its practices.[680] Heightened security at such an event and additional policies regarding anonymity (such as not leaving your conference badge in the hotel room) increase the privacy of such an event.[681] Those who dislike what Daleiden and Merritt did state that this breach of confidentiality is punishable by law. However, the lawyers for pro-life activists Daleiden and Merritt state that if the method of an abortion was altered to procure a more intact specimen, or if the fetal tissue was sold without the mother's consent, then the action would legally qualify as medical battery against the mother. Under this qualification, the recordings *could* be redefined as the collection of evidence in a potential criminal case rather than the nonconsensual, felony invasion of privacy they're now classified under. Recategorizing these videos in such a way could result in dismissal of the charges against Daleiden and Merritt.

Since the release of these videos, agencies such as StemExpress and Planned Parenthood Northern California have come under investigation for sale of fetal tissue/organs by the FBI and US Department of Justice.[682] StemExpress is a small, five-year-old biomedical company that has since severed ties with Planned Parenthood as a result of the video's release, saying that they "only facilitated the donation of fetal tissue for medical research with a patient's consent,"[683] but that due to the negative publicity and association with Planned Parenthood in the eyes of abortion opponents, the small company needed to "focus…[its] limited resources on resolving [related] inquiries."[684]

When Daleiden and Merritt released these videos, Dr. Forrest Smith, former abortionist who performed more than fifty thousand terminations, was originally angry at Daleiden, calling him a fraud.[685] However, after watching all the videos that Daleiden had made, the doctor changed his tune, stating that these undercover journalists had exposed a horrible truth about the underworld of abortion. Likewise, he indicated that they *barely skimmed the surface of the evils being carried out in the industry.*[686] Dr. Smith became the expert witness for the defense in the case against Daleiden and Merritt and, in September of 2019, he stated under oath that he had no doubt that babies were born alive during abortion procedures for the purpose of harvesting organs.[687]

Let's take a minute to process that thought. Dr. Forrest Smith—former abortionist—stated under oath in a court of law that he had no doubt that infants were purposely being delivered alive during gestational termination *for the purpose of harvesting their organs.* What has this world become? Yet, I digress…

How can this be? Wouldn't the mother be aware that the newborn is alive? Wouldn't the baby cry? Smith explained that the drug misoprostol *should* be administered over four days for second-trimester abortions, but in cases when it's administered in large doses in a single day instead, the process happens more quickly—placing the mother at increased risk but resulting in a live birth.[688] The purpose of this, he said, is to "obtain fresher, more intact organs."[689] Furthermore, the drug digoxin is typically used to stop the fetal heart—resulting in stillbirth—but in some cases, the drug is not administered, allowing the birth of a live baby.[690] The mother is unaware her child is born alive, because the drugs remove visible signs of movement or breath, yet there is still be a fetal heartbeat.[691]

In stunning testimony given in a preliminary hearing, a former director at Planned Parenthood, known as "Doe 10," confirmed that "the abortion business had no ban on altering abortion procedures in order to better harvest infant body parts that would later be sold, allegedly for a profit."[692] In fact, when these videos came out, Planned Parenthood had to carefully craft the lingo to ensure that they were not accused of operating outside the law. Since it is illegal to change the *method* of procedure to procure a fetus of a certain quality, semantics demanded that they introduce the term "technique" to the conversation, explaining that while *techniques* had been deviated from, *methods* had not been. Additionally, to harvest a more complete or intact specimen, the fetus is often rotated and the mother's cervix dilated to a larger extent, which places the mother at risk since it can damage the cervix and make it more difficult to carry future pregnancies to term.[693]

While people on both sides of the abortion issue are disgusted by the films, many ask the multimillion-dollar question: What on earth is postabortive fetal tissue used *for*—and furthermore, *shouldn't selling it be illegal?*

In 1999, Congress made it illegal to purchase or sell these specimens,[694] so the legal loophole used then became to make or collect a donation to compensate for the expense of harvesting, storing, and distributing the subjects. Medical professionals collecting the tissue assert that the material is greatly helpful in many types of stem-cell research, stating that it may help uncover cures for diseases such as Parkinson's, Alzheimer's, HIV, spinal-cord conditions, or type-1 Diabetes, explaining that "cells from embryos and very early fetuses have properties [particularly in embryonic and fetal stem cells] that fully developed cells do not."[695] Ironically, when results of two controlled trials returned in 2001 and 2003 showing the outcome of transplantation of aborted fetal cerebral substance into the brains of Parkinson's patients—yes, this *actually happened, and it was federally funded*—the verdict was that not only was this an unsuccessful trial; the patients' conditions actually *worsened.*[696] And yet, the research continued, amounting to big business: In fiscal year 2018 alone, the NIH (National Institute of Health) "spent $115 million on grants involving human fetal tissue research and is estimated to spend $120 million in FY [fiscal year] 2019."[697] A project that has genetically modified mice to hold a human immune property in conjunction with HIV research uses aborted fetal liver, bone marrow, intestinal matter, and thymus, and to date has held a total contract of $13,799,501.[698] (The process involves grinding fetal liver and injecting its extracted properties into the livers of newborn mice, creating what researchers call a "humanized mouse."[699])

Some within the medical research industry claim that this material is used to advance science and no equivalent substitute is available. However, other agencies state that this is a common and unsupportable myth. In fact, these organizations assert that *many* other options are available for varying types of research (to name a few: "peripheral blood, cord blood, bone marrow, and neonatal thymus,"[700]) and that halting fetal tissue-related research would not stop *even one* life-saving treatment from being researched, pursued, and administered.[701] The issue, these entities claim, is that the ease and availability of fetal matter make it a preferred method of research. And, of course, so do millions of those little things that make the world turn: *dollars.*

Trump Administration Tightens Regulations on Fetal Tissue Market

In June of 2019, the federal government announced that it would be placing new restraints on the use of fetal substances in research, stating that "the NIH…will no longer conduct research with human fetal tissue obtained from elective abortions, after using up any material they have on hand,"[702] and that it had furthermore halted federal funding to research facilities in California that used such matter in creating humanized mice. Other facilities operating under grants are allowed to continue their projects until the grants expired, at which time hearings would decide the future of such research based on forthcoming new ethics standards.[703] While many pro-lifers consider this a huge victory, it should be noted that *fetal tissue* is legally differentiated from *embryonic tissue,* a substance for which the battle may still be ahead.[704]

For some, the argument becomes, "If these babies are already going to die, why not put their remains to good use?" But this is backward thinking. One has to see a correlation between the aggressive drive for abortion rights and the multimillion-dollar industry that thrives on the tissue collected from the procedures. Furthermore, one *certainly* wonders why former Planned Parenthood employees such as Abby Johnson insist that—despite the organization's denial of holding quotas for quantities performed in their offices—Planned Parenthood indeed has such a quota.[705] Additionally, a quick study reveals that these agencies never personify the unborn by using words such as "baby" or even "fetus." These organizations refer to them with the term "POC" (for "product of conception") or "pregnancy tissue." It makes one wonder: Is the fetal remnant market a driving force behind the desire to keep abortion legal?

For a frightened woman facing an unplanned pregnancy, the concept of a mere "tissue removal" to undo the problem is a much softer sell than "killing the fetus/unborn baby." Thus, the procedure is marketed as a simple "POC removal," the remains and organs are harvested in trade for "donations," and the shadow industry that operates beneath that of abortion continues to thrive while unaware bystanders act under the notion that the fight is about women's reproductive rights.

Considering the magnitude of the disturbance brought to mind when we're made aware of issues such as fetal tissue marketing or organ harvesting, we may be tempted to find a strange solace in the procedures involving such drugs as mifepristone. After all, often these abortions manifest through induced miscarriages that take place hours after a woman's visit to the clinic, often in the privacy of her home. Advice from the physician is to flush the fetus in the toilet, which at least means we can be certain that the flesh and organs are not harvested and sold for profit or traded for "donations." Yet, even as I write this, I find myself thinking: *What am I saying?! The very idea that this would be an up side in such matters is deplorable!* How do the machinations of the mind of mankind arrive at such wicked and demonic innovations?

It is possible that some of the persecution Trump has dealt with is connected to his unwillingness to turn a blind eye to the fetal remnant/organ market. It is worth noting that conservative states looking to ban abortions often mandate cremation, burial, or other definite disposal of fetal matter. It seems plausible that this maneuver is intended to block the ability to sell or otherwise repurpose the substance in order to remove the incentive for quotas within clinics. Obviously, one industry feeds the other, so in order to combat the legality of termination, demand for such specimens has to be likewise diminished. As the 2020 election approaches, it will be interesting to see which candidates assert that they will reverse legislation pertaining to the tissue market and abortion in general. Surely, those who stand to profit from the sales of this matter have a reason for supporting the pro-choice agenda. As such, one can be assured that these two issues will likely go hand in hand in upcoming years.

The Heart of the Matter

At the crux of this topic is the fact that many in the United States view ending a pregnancy as a fundamental right, because ultimately we want to be free to choose what we do with our bodies. After all, *consent* as it pertains to anything that takes place with our bodies is ultimately a passionate, and usually justified, concept. However, the reason this dispute remains so polarized within politics is that many voters believe it embodies a person's general moral construct, and is thereby quickly judged as a one-symptom token of where a person—or even a presidential candidate—stands on other matters.

From a religious standpoint, those who believe that all life deserves to be preserved often see pregnancy as a consequence of actions or choices. While some see the ability to terminate as enabling people to be less regulatory about their own sexual conduct, others maintain that the best way to prevent the pregnancy is to more carefully standardize the ethics of one's sex life.

The issue then takes on a third, more deeply rooted angle of spirituality: *Who* makes the decision that life is worth preserving? For most people, this question is deeply connected to whether we as humans surrender to a higher power. Some people believe that only God should decide who lives and who does not (while some pro-lifers concede to a higher power other than the biblical Jehovah). For a human being to supersede his or her role and presume the authority to make such a call is close to ascending to God's level. When this concept is blended with the element that a pregnancy could be a result of sexual immorality, it appears to many as though those seeking abortions expect to live free of consequences of their actions by doing what they want to do, when they want to do it, and with whom they choose to do it. And, should nullifying the pregnancy mean taking a life, this is even worse. This is where the impassioned division between factions manifests.

However, as stated previously, statistics show that 59 percent of those obtaining the procedure are already mothers, while 49 percent live below the poverty line.[706] Could this be where, for the church, the battle is fought with honey, rather than with more bees? What if the church provided more resources for single or low-income parents? Perhaps if the church offered more help to some of these people, economics wouldn't play such a large role in the decision process of pregnant women.

For some people, there is frustration when individuals feel that pro-lifers are interested in protecting the unborn, but later, once the woman has given birth, she and her child are forgotten. When a woman chooses to attempt to raise a child (often by herself) and approaches parenthood with trepidation, she is increasingly likely to be overwhelmed by the ensuing demands and responsibilities. This is especially true if she has a low level of education or is without vital resources such as economic means, employment, familial or social support, and even mental health resources. For the pro-choice person, termination of a pregnancy becomes the way to delay childbirth until a couple has everything carefully arranged before adding a child to their lifestyle.[707] If we are to effectively combat this way of thinking, it must be done with resources for parents, and not just with words.

Other couples (or individuals) who feel unprepared for parenthood but are compelled to choose life could be encouraged to give the baby up for adoption. Some cite their own painful childhood memories as cause for abortion or adoption, stating they don't want to raise a child in a setting similar to the one that they grew up in.[708] This is one of many ways that the crumbling of the family unit in recent years has inflicted perpetual pain upon society.

In response to the notion that parents opt to terminate because they are haunted by recollections of their own youth, we need to change the popular commentary that says people have to be perfect to qualify for parenthood. We need to shut down the narrative that states a single mother can't offer enough to a child, or that people who have little money have nothing to give.[709] While there is value in understanding the timing of parenthood and trying to be prepared, each mother who is willing to carry a pregnancy to full term has *something* to give: *life*. Furthermore, each father who takes a stand and becomes involved with his children—even if he isn't married to or in a relationship with the mother—has many gifts to give, such as his influence, his companionship, and his involvement. Many people have a flawed understanding of what makes a person qualified for parenthood. They base qualifications on such accomplishments as a college degree, an established career, ownership of a home, financial success, and a tranquil and stable lifestyle. But these concepts are usually unrealistic. In fact, many successful generations have gone without any or all of the above. Many have been underprivileged children in families that struggled economically (or otherwise), with parents who have had little to offer other than a willingness to give their all to their children. Thus, allow me to make a bold statement: The best thing any parent can offer a child is precisely that: *his or her best*. We need to support those parents who take a brave stand for life not just by supporting them throughout pregnancy; but throughout all subsequent hardships.

The Rotten Fruits of Progressive Occultism:
Example 2—A Borderless Nation

Chaos Magic, Open Borders, and the Death of Old Glory

Imagine there's no countries
It isn't hard to do
Nothing to kill or die for
And no religion, too
Imagine all the people
Living life in peace
You may say that I'm a dreamer
But I'm not the only one
I hope someday you'll join us
And the world will be as one
—John Lennon, *Imagine*

Human imagination is a powerful thing. It is far more than just reverie or thought; it is a great force. As God's imagers on earth, humanity has the ability to imagine a project and make it happen. We can create good, and we can create evil—creating harmony or disharmony, order or chaos.

If you doubt this statement, consider the Lord's words in Genesis:

And the LORD said, Behold, the people is one, and they have all one language; and this they begin to do: and now **nothing will be restrained from them, which they have imagined to do.** (Genesis 11:6, emphasis added)

Zamam, the Hebrew word translated "imagined to do" here, implies a decision to create; to conceive and consider; to purpose a thing; to fix one's thought upon an outcome. Chaos magic—as described earlier in this book as being deployed by Deep-State provocateurs and energized by egregores—twists this God-given aspect to our minds and imagination just as Nimrod did during the construction of the Tower of Babel. Because all of mankind spoke a single language, they could use those thoughts to join their minds together for a single purpose: to bring forth the Watchers from beneath the Abyss. Derek and Sharon Gilbert put this into perspective in their new book, *Veneration*:

> Babel was not about God taking down people who'd gotten too big for their britches. The clue to the sin of Babel is in the name—and its location. Remember, the Hebrew prophets loved to play with language. We often find words in the Bible that sound like the original but make a statement—for example, Beelzebub ("lord of the flies") instead of Beelzebul ("Ba'al the prince"). Likewise, the original Akkadian words *bāb ilu*, which means "gate of god" or "gate of the gods," is replaced in the Bible with Babel, which is based on the Hebrew word meaning "confusion."… For one moment in human history, Enki [Lord of the Earth] induced a human dupe—Nimrod, the Sumerian king Enmerkar—to build what he hoped would **be a new abode of the gods,** the *bāb ilu*, to **rival Yahweh's mount of assembly.**[710] (Emphasis added)

Influenced by an unseen hand (Enki—read that as "Satan"), Nimrod imagined a place that would rival God's holy mountain. He influenced others to join him in his "imagined work" in order to construct this blasphemous, artificial mount. That is precisely what is happening today. We are being manipulated by the Shadowland bosses to overthrow the current order, to destroy borders and nations and tongues and laws—to create chaos so that a new order might take its place. The world of Antichrist will ascend to the top of this rival assembly and try to overthrow God Himself. And it all begins with a thought.

Thought forms and imagination are central to the concept of "chaos magic,"[711] where all actions and all matter derive from our will. According to this theory, the world we see exists only because we say it does; therefore, mankind's mind and imagination hold the keys to our future.

Austin Osman Spare, the father of "chaos magic" and a man whose writings influenced Aleister Crowley, saw human *belief* as a psychic force. It is another version of the law of attraction, which states that "like attracts like." If you choose happiness, then you will find happiness. If you choose to believe in a world of peace, then the world will be peaceful.

If then, this "law" defines the world according to "belief," then it is no different than chaos magic. We can imagine a new world and reshape it to fit our personal paradigm.

What does this have to do with immigration and the loss of borders? Everything. You and I are being duped by sleight-of-hand magicians who are directing our gaze at *geopolitics* when we should be looking at *theopolitics,* to those hidden hands upon the strings of mankind—the true spirits behind this modern Babel event. One might even say that, thanks to the common language of the Internet, we are all participating in a massive spell intended to bring about this new age, the *ordo ab chao* moment, when the current system of thrones and dominions yields to the single throne of Antichrist.

To achieve this, the old order must be torn asunder; the building blocks of earth's governments must be rearranged into the New World Order. And it is happening before our very eyes. When this spell finishes, all the countries of the world will lose their identities, including ours.

The Beginning of the End

When the World Trade Center towers fell in 2001, something changed. An atmospheric shift took place in the spirit realm, and though we sensed it, the true face of this shift remained hidden. In a "Morning Intelligence Brief" dated September 12, 2007, Stratfor made this startling statement:

> In thinking about 9/11, one thought keeps coming to mind: **a loss of control**. On that date, **everything went out of control** and in a very real sense, it has not yet come back into control.[712] (Emphasis added)

That "loss of control" is the very essence of chaos, but another type of chaos intends to replace it by the calling forth of "the old gods" in the form of *egregores* or thought forms. Chaos magic is used by men like Kenneth Grant, founder of the *Typhonian Ordo Templi Orientis* and Osman Spare, Grant's teacher. At its root, chaos magic teaches "imagination" and "belief" as creative powers within the human mind. That belief equals existence. With this in mind, the media (news, television, books, and film) and the Internet (social sites, chat rooms, and video-sharing platforms) become major ingredients in a modern magical working. We are being rearranged and deranged into a "primordial soup" matrix intended to give birth to a new "golden age." Removing borders, governments, and traditional values is only the first step in this diabolical plan.

While it's comforting to blame our current illegal immigration problem on a failure to police our borders, it goes much deeper than that; it's more insidious than that, far more evil. The prince of this world is the ultimate shadow within the Shadowlands. The Apostle Paul explained it to the Ephesians this way:

> And you were dead in the trespasses and sins in which you once walked, **following the course of this world, following the prince of the power of the air, the spirit that is now at work in the sons of disobedience**—among whom we all once lived in the passions of our flesh, carrying out the desires of the body and the mind, and **were by nature children of wrath, like the rest of mankind.** (Ephesians 2:1–3, ESV, emphasis added)

The Ephesians had once been enthralled with the *archon* (prince or ruler) of the governmental region of the air. This is an extraordinary statement! Paul is saying that Satan not only rules the atmosphere of earth, but he also presides as ruler of anything within it. That includes the so-called chaos magic and the Internet. He and his minions amongst the Watcher rebels (whom the Greeks called *egregore,* by the way, which connects chaos magic to the works of the Watchers) are using gullible humans to call them forth from the Abyss! It's Babel 2.0.

To do this, we must be stirred together like a human soup, rearranged to allow easier infiltration and the destruction of country loyalties and governmental laws. Order out of chaos. Think about that for a minute.

How is this being done? Former President Obama's DREAM Act opened the gates to a flood of illegal immigrants, but the real *dreamer* behind that act is the ancient puppet master whose aim is to redistribute humanity so that borders vanish and chaos reigns. *Ordo ab chao* is the mandate. It's like a mantra, being repeated again and again as a magical working to reset the world to zero. By reordering people groups, you leave humans without historical and cultural reference. You isolate them into new, weaker tribes, each speaking his own language, practicing his own laws. The mass migration and integration of these disparate tribes and cultures within an already weakened society brings changes in language, hygiene, disease, and crime, and most importantly, they bring new spirits and beliefs.

The Language of Chaos

Yes, I said "new spirits." We'll get to that near the end of this segment, but let's begin with language. What happened in Babel is a biblical event that nearly everyone knows. During a time when all men spoke the same language, a leader named Nimrod convinced everyone living within his jurisdiction to build him a massive, artificial mountain known as the Tower of Babel. The name "Babel" means "god gate," which most likely reflects the purpose of the structure. Not only was this a man-made recreation of God's sacred assembly, the *har moed*, but, according to scholars, it was actually built atop the E-Abzu of Enki in ancient Sumer. Derek Gilbert explained it well in his groundbreaking book, *The Great Inception*:

> For one moment in human history, Enki induced a human dupe—Nimrod, the Sumerian king Enmerkar—to build what he

hoped would be a new abode of the gods, the *bāb ilu*, to rival Yah-weh's mount of assembly. **It was to be the heart of a one-world totalitarian government.**

Yahweh put a stop to it. But as George Santayana wrote, "Those who cannot remember the past are condemned to repeat it." **The sin of Nimrod is being repeated today by the global-ist movement, slowly but surely leading us back to Babylon.**[713] (emphasis added)

A unified language gave early civilization *one mind*, which allowed them to do something so magical that YHWE had to come down and put a stop to it. How does this apply to our concerns about immigration and the movement of people groups? First, tear civilization apart by removing the language barriers God put into place, and then, once the dust settles, unify them with a single mind and a single purpose. More on this later, when we discuss the "world brain" idea.

Hygiene and Disease

Those of us living in first-world nations think of daily hygiene practices as a given. We wash our hands regularly, cover our mouths when we sneeze, and generally shower and clean our clothing on a routine basis. These habits help reduce the spread of pathogens and parasites. However, not all people practice with our first-world diligence. But even if they did, the fact remains that human immune systems require exposure to a pathogen in order to learn to recognize it. By training our "first responder" cells of our immune system to more rapidly counter an invasion of measles or chicken pox, the resulting symptomatic disease process can be curtailed or even stopped.

However, if humans are exposed to diseases for the first time ever as they come across the borders (in other words, they have no inherited or trained immunity), then infection and disease can and generally will occur. The common cold is an example. Many of us "catch" colds each year because the virus comes in so many shapes and sizes that our immune system can't keep up with the variations. Influenza is similar. Each year, we're exposed to multiple strains of viruses, and even vaccinations can be ineffective. Colds and flu are annoying and contribute to loss of labor force and productivity, but imagine an invading pathogen like smallpox or some other highly pathogenic organism, then exposure would have devastating results in a population.

Cholera, Ebola, MERS, SARS, polio, typhus, and even leprosy can mingle amongst an influx of migrants—be they legal or not. However, a massive onslaught at our borders on the order of magnitude that the Dream Act encourages opens the floodgates to whatever pathogens ride within the bloodstreams and in the gastrointestinal tracts of these dreamers. Sadly, our border facilities and personnel are strained to near breaking point, and at the time of this writing, there is no quarantine or medical testing done to screen for lethal pathogens. With asylum-seekers arriving from Congo, Angola, and Cameroon,[714] it's imperative that someone begins to screen for antibodies to Ebola, since survivors of the disease have been shown to pass the virus through sexual contact for up to two years after infection.[715] Remember, everyone develops immunity or tolerance for endemic diseases (those that occur naturally in one's 'backyard'), but when exposed to something from another country, we can fall prey to a contagion of these exotic pathogens.

Vaccination campaigns are all too familiar to those now reading this, and anti-vaxxers are branded heretics and conspiracy theorists. If vaccination programs are so important, then why aren't illegals automatically vaccinated upon arrival? Legal immigrants are required to submit proof of vaccination. Conservative journalist Michele Malkin makes this case:

> Legal immigrants and refugees must provide mandatory proof of vaccination for measles, mumps, rubella, polio, tetanus, diphtheria, pertussis, hepatitis A and B, rotavirus, meningococcus, chicken pox, pneumonia and seasonal flu. Moreover, the Centers for Disease Control, not Fox News or the Trump White House

or any other evil conservatives, reports that "most experts agree that testing for TB, hepatitis B, and HIV should be performed for most new arrivals to the United States. Clinicians should also make a habit of ensuring that this screening has been done for every new non-US-born patient they see, regardless of time since the person's arrival."[716]

Why then isn't this screening being conducted? The answer is likely that funding and manpower are inadequate to the task, but it is also a direct result of the overwhelming numbers now coming through our borders. One might assume that Mexican authorities would work with the US to stop the caravans, or that the journey would prove so difficult that the notion would deter most from the attempt. However, as Malkin reveals in her new book, *Open Borders, Inc.*, charities and NGOs (nongovernmental organizations) alike are finding it very profitable to "minister" to migrants as they pass through Mexico:

From longstanding Catholic shelters to Doctors without Borders clinics, to binational immigration lawyers embedded on both sides of the adjudication process, to travel guides peddling navigational apps, to smugglers, drug cartels, and document fakers, to MS_13 and other alien gangs, to foster-care providers and other social welfare contractors, to foreign government and nongovernment officials, multinational banks, money-transfer organizations, tech startups, and the Federal Reserve, this much is clear: The open-borders conspiracy enabling unrelenting waves of migrant outlaws is a colossal profit-seeking venture cloaked in humanitarian virtue.[717]

To my shock, Malkin reveals that migrants received cell phones and GPS location apps that helped them locate help stations along the route! If it's beginning to sound like something more than an organic, grassroots movement of people groups seeking shelter in a first-world nation, then you're on the right track. Mass migration is all about restructuring the world. We're watching it take place before our very eyes as chaos magic "'thought forms" (read that as "demonic spirits") press the reset button on civilization.

According to the Global Health Security (GHS) Index compiled by scientists from Johns Hopkins University Center for Health Security and the Nuclear Threat Initiative (NSI), a deadly pandemic influenza could kill eighty million people worldwide. Dubbed "Disease X," this theoretical pathogen could be passing through porous borders or flying on an airplane. No one knows when or where the next pandemic will arise, but if we're to believe the Book of Revelation, then a worldwide disease IS coming our way:

> And I looked, and behold a pale horse: and his name that sat on him was Death, and Hell followed with him. And power was given unto them **over the fourth part of the earth**, to kill with sword, and with hunger, and with death, and **with the beasts of the earth**. (Revelation 6:8)

It's possible that the *therion* ("little beasts") of the earth refer to actual beasts, but it is a diminutive of beast, implying that these creatures might be small—perhaps smaller than our human eyes can perceive unaided. Rider number four, called Thanatos or Death, will assuredly ride upon this earth and slay one-quarter of all living. A couple of years ago, Sharon Gilbert wrote a series called "Pale Rider" for our *SkyWatchTV Magazine*, and she had this to say regarding Thanatos (Death) and his weaponry:

> In Revelation 6:8, we see a list of the weapons given to Thanatos: sword, hunger, death, and beasts. The original Greek for this final word is *therion*. The precise meaning is multi-level and rich. Literally, *therion* is a diminutive of *thera* (beast) and therefore means "little beasts." Plato saw a connection to "bees," which indicates an ability to move rapidly, fly upon the wind, inflict injury and pain, but also to "think" as a unit. Homer imagined *therion* as a wilder, less sophisticated animal. The term is also used of the Man of Sin (the Beast of Rev. 13), implying brutality and savagery. However, in the context of Thanatos's arsenal, it may

be **more accurately portrayed as infectious diseases**—perhaps, a legion of plagues that act as one unit to infect entire populations and eventually slay one-fourth of mankind. (Emphasis added)

Satan and his minions will use our own rules and laws against us, allowing DACA, the so-called Dream Act, to lead to a world of nightmares. Am I blaming the individuals who seek a better life or safer shores? Not at all. I'm blaming the policies and allied organizations that lure them into boarding dangerous migrant caravans; into paying exorbitant fees to "coyotes" (the name for those who bring immigrants to the US);and into risking their own health if not their lives to "live the dream." While some within these caravans are infiltrators and terrorists, most probably just want to find a better life for themselves and their children. As Christians, we should pray for them, for Christ died for all.

Follow the Drugs and the Money

Crime is another aspect of the movement of people groups. It is an inevitable consequence of sin and freewill that the strong will prey upon the weak. Therefore, when people from developing nations enter our gates, they automatically bring their victims and their perpetrators along with them. MS-13 (MS stands for *Mara Salvatrucha*) is one of the most nefarious of the predator "wolf" gangs now lurking amongst the "sheep" of our cities. According to a report issued by American University and found online at the US Justice Department website:

> [MS-13] is not about generating revenue as much as it is about **creating a collective identity** that is constructed and reinforced by shared, often criminal experiences, especially **acts of violence and expressions of social control.**[718]

Notice that statement. This imported gang isn't concerned with becoming wealthy, but with sowing the seeds of violence and anarchy.

MS-13 has an estimated seventy thousand members distributed throughout the Americas and as far afield as Spain and Italy. The structure of this huge gang isn't centralized, nor does it have a single leader. Their *raison d'etre* is violence and mayhem, and it's likely their true leaders are fallen spirits. Our president had this to say about MS-13:

> "They kidnap, they extort, they rape and they rob," Trump said of the gang. "They prey on children. They shouldn't be here. They stomp on their victims, they beat them with clubs, they slash them with machetes, and they stab them with knives. They have transformed peaceful parks and beautiful quiet neighborhoods into bloodstained killing fields. They're animals."[719]

As I write this subsection, it's almost Halloween, a time when many different pagan religions observe veneration of the dead. And, to make the point, a raid last week on a drug cartel in Mexico City uncovered forty-two human skulls, thirty-one long bones, and a human fetus suspended in a jar. These gruesome objects were part of a veneration ceremony derived from a mixture of African, Caribbean, and Mexican traditions. This syncretistic religion is called *Palo Mayombe*, and requires that sacrifices be made to obtain the protection of the gods, presumably for the gang's influential leader, *El Lunares* (which means the "mole"). Such pagan beliefs and practices travel along with immigrants, redistributing not only the humans, but their personal gods as well. A follow-up to this story implies a connection between the drug cartel and the local police and even the military,[720] further demonstrating the political and social aspects to so-called gangs.

This is all about anarchism, the removal of government structure. (*An archos:* Greek for "without leader" or an "archon.") Ironically, when the current order is demolished through chaos magic, the "new world order" will most certainly be headed by an archon, the prince of this world. Drug-running is big money, but it also fuels the underlying hunger of secularist society for an infilling of something more—something spiritual.

And there are hundreds, if not millions, of fallen entities ready to indwell those empty souls.

The Spirits Behind it All

So, let's take a look at the real movers and shakers behind this remix of mankind. It's a sure bet that the "infernal council" (as Sharon K. Gilbert calls the fallen realm's rebel version of the "divine council" in her series, *The Redwing Saga*) is working hard to prepare for the return of Christ. The infernal council's members know Scripture far better than any preacher, but they lack the true understanding offered by the Holy Spirit. These *archons*, *exousia*, and *kosmokrators* seek to destroy us by whatever means at their disposal. They hate humankind and prey upon our weaknesses. They'll distract us from their activities by forcing our gaze upon distractions. Meme ideas like "It's all Trump's fault," "It's the Russians," and "It's Ukraine" permeate the posts on social media and the headlines of mainstream media.

…It's because of failed foreign policy.

…It's due to a weak military.

…It's budgetary constraints.

…It's an unwilling and lax border patrol.

…If only we had more money. More guns. A stronger, better, more high-tech wall. If only we had observation towers.

…If only we had drones deployed along the border.

We want something or someone to blame. The truth is that none of these solutions will stop the problem, nor can the situation be blamed on any one president or policy. The world doesn't want to admit it, but the problem is SIN.

Yes, SIN. But not just the sin of others. It's our sin, dear friends. You and I, and all who call upon the name of Christ, must shoulder the blame, for we've failed as a church to preach the gospel to all mankind, and we've failed to follow Christ's two commandments. We've not loved Him with all our hearts, souls, and minds, and we've failed to love others as we love ourselves. If we had, then our world would be a very different place. Instead, we've become distracted by the world. Our salt has lost its savor and our light flickers, threatening to go out.

But it is not too late. The shadows of the fallen realm may be using chaos magic to remix mankind into a new cauldron of hopelessness, but we can still add our precious, Christ-given salt to that mix! We can shine His light into those shadows!

How? By returning to our first love.

And by suiting up.

By STANDING.

Let me end this reasoning with the church of Ephesus. The Apostle Paul knew very well the troubles the Ephesians faced. He knew that they served and worked in a city rife with pagan beliefs and practices, in the place where Diana's temple stood. They were exposed to a constant influx of pagan beliefs and even false Christianity that invaded their homes and prayer circles with false apostles and the much-hated Nicolaitans. In the Book of Revelation, Jesus reminds the Ephesians that HE holds the stars (angels) in His hand. He controls the outcome and all Creation. The Ephesians remained faithful for the most part, but they began to bicker amongst themselves and lost some of their effectiveness due to an over-zealous desire to root out evil from within their midst. This is laudable, but they took the mission a little too far—so far, in fact, that they "lost their first love." Perhaps pride entered in. Perhaps they began to see them-selves, rather than Christ, as holding and controlling those stars.

We live in a world similar to that of Ephesus. Our country is being remixed with pagan worship and altered, adulterated forms of Christianity.

Migration and the chaotic redistribution of peoples threatens to erode far more than the current political structure of our country; it threatens the Church. As we seek to root out evil spirits from our pulpits and our pews, we must never forget that it is Christ who holds the stars in His hand.

That's what the fallen realm has forgotten. Paul's words to the Ephe-sians should be studied and memorized. He brings us the answer to chaos magic and thought forms. The answer to the enemy's plans:

Finally, be strong in the Lord and in the strength of his might. Put on the whole armor of God, that you may be able to **stand against the schemes of the devil**. For **we do not wrestle against flesh and blood**, but against the **rulers [archons]** against the **authorities [exousia]**, against the **cosmic powers [kosmokrators]** over this present darkness, against the **spiritual forces of evil [pneumotikos poneria]** in the heavenly places. Therefore take up the whole armor of God, **that you may be able to withstand in the evil day**, and having done all, to stand firm. Stand therefore, having fastened on the belt of truth, and having put on the breastplate of righteousness, and, as shoes for your feet, having put on the readiness given by the gospel of peace. In all circumstances take up the shield of faith, with which you can extinguish all the flaming darts of the evil one; and take the helmet of salvation, and the sword of the Spirit, which is the word of God, praying at all times in the Spirit, with all prayer and supplication. To that end keep alert with all perseverance, making supplication for all the saints, and also for me, that words may be given to me in opening my mouth boldly to proclaim the mystery of the gospel, for which I am an ambassador in chains, that I may declare it boldly, as I ought to speak. (Ephesians 6:12–20, ESV, emphasis added)

Are you ready to stand against the shadows? To expose the darkness by shining Christ's light into those shadowy corners? Are you willing to accept His leading as you put on the armor of His service? Rather than cower in a corner and bewail the political climate through social media memes, let us rush out into the streets, lifting up His cross and showing His love to all the world.

It's not too late to stop the shadowy chaos magic from resetting civilization. Witches and warlocks and cult leaders who are enthralled to their Shadowland masters might even stop to listen if you show them compassion and love. It's a radical idea, but then we who are covered by Christ's redemptive blood are a peculiar and radical people, aren't we?

I opened this segment with lyrics from John Lennon's song *Imagine*. These lyrics expose the subtle plan of the shadows. We're to imagine a world without country, nothing to live or die for, and no religion. That, my friends, is the essence of chaos magic. Imagine. Use your mind to conjure up reality; for nothing is real if we do not think it is real.

That is a lie from the pit of hell.

Like an impending birth, judgment is coming to this world, no matter what people choose to believe, and many within the Church are sleeping through its birth pangs. Rather than sleep, let's arise and hit our knees and pray for guidance. Let's bring down the power of the Holy Spirit and a great awakening to shock the world! Let's declare the message of Christ crucified, risen, and coming again to all the nations!

The shadows don't want us to do it. They're relying on us to remain complicit and complacent and asleep. They want us focused on political ads, congressional debate, gender issues, illegal migration, crumbling educational ideals, and so much more that is wrong with the world. The shadows want you to ignore their hidden hands and look only at the dazzling images of light that play across our computer, television, and phone screens.

They want us all to dream.

Remember, all ten virgins fell asleep. Let us awake, dear friends, and fill our lamps! Shine into the darkened corners and confront the shadows. It's time to suit up and stand up.

Christ is coming soon, and He must find us ready.

The Rotten Fruits of Progressive Occultism: Example 3—Socialism

Babel, Bradford, and Beveled-Rim Bowls: Socialism's Failure from Nimrod to Now

One of the most surprising developments of the recent political turmoil in the United States is a growing pile of survey data that reveals the desire of young Americans to give up their freedom for a few bowls of gruel. One recent poll found that more than 70 percent of Americans between the ages of twenty-three and thirty-eight were at least somewhat likely to vote for a socialist in the presidential election in 2020.[721]

That so many voting Americans are ready and willing to give socialism the old college try just one generation after the collapse of the Soviet Union, the most successful communist state in history, must be a shock to seniors who lived through the Cold War and the defeat of Hitler's Germany (because, although liberals never admit it, Nazis are just another flavor of socialist). This is a classic example of George Santayana's observation that "those who cannot remember the past are condemned to repeat it."[722]

This lesson should have been learned by now. While the Soviet Union is the biggest example of socialism's failure in recent memory, there are others. Venezuela, for instance, which has been spectacularly transformed from the wealthiest nation in South America into an economic wreck in less than forty years.

Socialism is only part of the problem that destroys centrally planned economies, but it's the part that makes the root cause worse—the way squirting gasoline on a smoldering fire accelerates the exothermic chemical process. In this example, the desired result is putting *out* the fire rather than burning down the village, which in our simple model represents the society that our elders fought and bled to build and keep.

Yet here we are, in the middle of a campaign season in which one of America's two main political parties is dominated by presidential candidates who seem to be competing to present the most unaffordable, unsustainable, and frankly unrealistic policy proposals. We've been promised free healthcare (even for people in the country illegally), free childcare (and free abortions for those who don't want to be burdened with caring for children), debt-free college education, guaranteed jobs, guaranteed income (perhaps even for those who don't want to work),[723] affordable housing, and reparations for a variety of groups with politically correct grievances.

If nothing else, this election proves that twentieth-century journalist

H. L. Mencken really understood human nature as expressed through politics:

> The state—or, to make the matter more concrete, the government—consists of a gang of men exactly like you and me. They have, taking one with another, no special talent for the business of government; they have only a talent for getting and holding office. Their principal device to that end is to search out groups who pant and pine for something they can't get, and to promise to give it to them. Nine times out of ten that promise is worth nothing. The tenth time it is made good by looting A to satisfy B. In other words, government is a broker in pillage, and every election is a sort of advance auction sale of stolen goods.[724]

That's where socialism fails. Specific proposals put forward by Democrats in the 2020 election cycle, such as the pie-in-the-sky Green New Deal, are so ludicrous that even liberal pundits admitted they'd put their presidential candidates "in an uncomfortable position."[725] Financing for these schemes has never been adequately explained, aside from vague suggestions that making rich people pay their fair share will bring in enough money to make everything free for regular folks like us.

Like socialism in general, "soaking the rich" ignores basic human nature. Rich people have at least one thing in common with us commoners: They hate paying taxes. Where they're different is that they're affluent enough to do something about it. When taxes become a real burden, the wealthy move themselves and/or their money out of the jurisdiction that's trying to tax them or they simply pass the losses forward by raising costs on durable goods and services, which in turn is paid by the middle class. In other words, unfair taxes on the rich is unfair taxes on the poor.

France learned this the hard way in 2014. The socialist government of Francois Hollande was forced to drop its 75 percent "supertax" on earnings over one million euros (about $1.12 million) per year because it failed to bring in the expected revenue. Why? The richest man in France moved to Belgium, famous actor Gerard Depardieux obtained Russian citizenship, and high-paying soccer players threatened to go on strike while team executives warned they'd no longer be able to attract world-class players.[726]

You see, wealthy people are just as selfish as the rest of us, but their money buys them more options. They avoid paying taxes when it's cheaper to hire experts who can help them do so.

Some of the highest-profile initiatives put forward by leading Democrats since 2016 are so vague that pinning down specifics is like trying to nail Jell-O to a wall. Sen. Ed Markey (D-MA), who cosponsored the Green New Deal with Rep. Alexandria Ocasio-Cortez (D-NY), defended the deal's lack of specifics thusly: "There's no individual prescriptions in the resolution, which is why we think we will be able to get a broad base of support, and then we'll let the debates begin on the individual solutions."[727]

That's an echo of House Speaker Nancy Pelosi's infamous 2010 comment on the Affordable Care Act, better known as Obamacare: "We have to pass the bill so that you can find out what is in it." Considering that one estimate put the cost of the Green New Deal between $51 and $93 trillion, which includes $36 trillion for universal health care and up to $44.6 trillion for guaranteed jobs,[728] vague proposals with this kind of price tag attached don't generate warm fuzzies in the hearts of those who'll have to pick up the check. (Bear in mind that the annual gross domestic product of the US is only about $19 trillion, and GDP includes government spending.)

You'd think liberals would have learned. This kind of nonspecific proposal registers as both devious and condescending. "Don't worry your pretty little head about it. Leave the thinking to us professionals." That patronizing attitude, and the failure of mainstream Republicans to truly oppose that kind of government overreach, is exactly why Donald Trump was elected president in 2016. He understood the visceral anger of voters in flyover country at smug Beltway elites like former President Obama, who dismissed working-class Americans in old industrial towns as "cling[ing] to guns or religion or antipathy to people who aren't like them,"[729] and characterized accepting tax increases and raising the federal debt ceiling as "eating our peas."

Nobody likes being lectured, especially when the lecture is followed by being told that we have to pay the bill.

Socialism's fatal flaw is that it depends on people acting contrary to human behavior. At no time in recorded history have entire cultures willingly volunteered the fruits of their labor to central governments for redistribution. This is even supported by evidence collected by archaeologists from the years before the invention of writing.

In fact, socialism has been failing as an economic system since before cuneiform symbols were first pressed into wet clay. The first socialist state emerged long before the Bolshevik Revolution and God Himself put a stop to it. He intervened for reasons beyond mere economics, of course, but control of the distribution of wealth was an important factor in the administration of this early empire.

This would-be socialist paradise was the ancient kingdom of Uruk. You've read about its rise in chapter 10 of the Book of Genesis.

First, a word about the king of this nation: Nimrod gets a bad rap. He was no angel, to be sure; you have to transgress pretty badly for God to personally come to earth and stage an intervention. But Nimrod is incorrectly blamed for the occult system of Babylon, which the Apostle John used as the symbol for the end-times church of the Antichrist. Nimrod died more than a thousand years before the city of Babylon was founded, and it was centuries more before Hammurabi the Great transformed Babylon into a world power.

No, Nimrod was not responsible for the occult wickedness of Babylon, although his sin was similarly progressive. You see, Nimrod, builder of the Tower of Babel, was the father of socialism.

Let's clear up the confusion between Babel and Babylon. Contrary to what you've heard, Babel was not in Babylon.

It's an easy mistake to make. The names sound alike, and Babylon is easily the most famous city of the ancient world. The original Akkadian *bāb ilu*, which means "gate of god" or "gate of the gods," is replaced in the Bible with "Babel," from the Hebrew word meaning "confusion." But Babylon didn't exist when the tower was built. It didn't even become a city until about a thousand years after the tower incident, and even then it was an unimportant village for another five hundred years or so.

Traditions and sources outside the Bible identify the builder of the tower as Nimrod. Our best guess is that he lived sometime between 3800 and 3100 BC, a period of history called the Uruk Expansion. This tracks with what little the Bible tells us about Nimrod. In Genesis 10:10, we read "the beginning of his kingdom was Babel, Erech, Accad, and Calneh, in the land of Shinar."

The land of Shinar is Sumer. Erech is the ancient city of Uruk, which was so important to human history that Nimrod's homeland is *still* called Uruk, five thousand years later. We just spell it differently—Iraq.

Accad was the capital city of the Akkadians, which still hasn't been found but is probably buried under modern Baghdad.[730] Babylon itself was northwest of Uruk, roughly three hundred miles from the Persian Gulf in what is today central Iraq. It wasn't founded until around 2300 BC, probably more than seven hundred years after Nimrod died, and it wasn't really Babylon as we think about it until the time of Hammurabi in the eighteenth century BC, the days of Abraham and Isaac.

That being the case, where should we look for the Tower of Babel?

The oldest and largest ziggurat in Mesopotamia was at Eridu, the first city built in Mesopotamia. In recent years, scholars have learned that the name "Babylon" was interchangeable with other city names, including "Eridu."[731] So, "Babylon" didn't always mean the city of Babylon in ancient texts.

Even though Eridu never dominated the political situation in Sumer, it was so important to Mesopotamian culture that more than three thousand years after its founding, Hammurabi, the greatest king of the old Babylonian empire, claimed in his famous law code to have "reestablished Eridu," which appears to have been abandoned when the last Sumerian dynasty to rule Mesopotamia collapsed around 2000 BC.

But the point of this chapter is not what happened at the Tower of Babel. We're interested in how Nimrod administered his kingdom.

Archaeological evidence of the Uruk Expansion, which covers the period from about 3800 BC to about 3100 BC,[732] shows that Nimrod extended his kingdom from Uruk in southeastern Iraq to northwestern Iran and southeastern Turkey. Pottery from Uruk has been found more than five hundred miles from the city. To put it into context, Uruk at its peak controlled more territory than Iraq under Saddam Hussein.

This was not always peaceful. An ancient city called Hamoukar, located in what is now northeastern Syria, was destroyed and burned by an army from Uruk sometime around 3500 BC.[733] Scholars identified the origin of the army by the style of pottery they left behind. In a day when Styrofoam, paper, and plastic didn't exist, soldiers and workmen often carried and prepared their meals in dishware made of clay.

Hamoukar was overwhelmed and burned by attackers who used clay bullets fired from slings to defeat the city's defenders. That was how the kingdom of Nimrod obtained raw materials like metals, timber, precious stones, wine, and other things that were scarce in the plains of Sumer.

Of course, there is no way to absolutely prove that Nimrod was responsible for the Uruk Expansion, which is a polite way of describing the process of conquering everybody within a two-month march from home. Artifacts from Uruk are everywhere in the Near East, especially a particular type of crude pottery. And this brings us to the theme of our subsection because it offers a fascinating glimpse into the way Uruk society was organized.

According to archaeologists, the dominant civilization in Mesopotamia just before the Uruk period, the Ubaid culture (c. 6500–3800 BC), became more stratified as people moved from rural settlements to cities. With improvements in agriculture came the freedom for some to devote all of their time to tasks other than working in the fields. This allowed the Ubaid civilization to produce high-quality pottery, which is identified by black geometric designs on buff or green-colored ceramic. Then, around 3800 BC, the emerging Uruk culture developed the world's first mass-produced product, a primitive type of pottery called the beveled-rim bowl.

The beveled-rim bowl is very rough compared to the pottery from the

Ubaid culture, a step backward in terms of technique and quality. Beveled-rim bowls are described as "the simplest and least attractive of all Near Eastern pots…among the crudest vessels in the history of Mesopotamia pottery."[734] This is odd, because other aspects of the Uruk culture, including large temples, complex administrative systems, and sophisticated art show that these were not simple, uneducated people by any means. Yet, the most common artifacts from the Uruk period by far are these crudely made mass-produced bowls. Archaeologists have found a *lot* of them. About three-quarters of all ceramics at Uruk sites are beveled-rim bowls. One of the fastest ways to confirm that an archaeological dig belongs to the Uruk period is digging up lots and lots of beveled-rim bowls.

Scholars agree that these simple, undecorated bowls were made on molds rather than wheels, probably in cone-shaped depressions in the ground. Most important for this topic, these bowls were probably used to dole out barley and oil for workers' rations.[735]

The way the bowls were produced left the hardened clay too porous for liquids like water or beer. The bowls were cheap and easy to make, so much so that they were apparently disposable. At some sites, large numbers of used, unbroken bowls have been found in big piles. Basically, these cheap bowls appear to have been the Sumerian equivalent of fast-food containers. In fact, the Sumerian picture sign for "bread," *NINDA*, looks just like a beveled-rim bowl, and the sign for "to eat" is a human head with a beveled-rim bowl at its mouth.[736]

The concept of rationed food implies an employer or controlling central authority responsible for doling out grain and oil to laborers. It's not a coincidence that the development of these crude bowls happened alongside Uruk's emergence as the first empire in history. After Noah's Flood, which may have marked the end of the Ubaid civilization that preceded the rise of Uruk, people in Mesopotamia gravitated to cities where they apparently exchanged their freedom for government rations. The recent polls we mentioned earlier suggest that younger Americans are in favor of a similar idea.

Maybe we're reading more into the evidence than is truly there. It could be that the beveled-rim bowl was nothing more than an easy way for people to carry lunch to work. Will future archaeologists conclude that Americans were paid in fast food because of the billions of Styrofoam containers and plastic straws in our landfills?

Still, given the unprecedented growth of the Uruk empire between about 3800 BC and 3100 BC, it's not going too far to speculate that those cheap, mass-produced ration bowls were a symptom of Nimrod's socialist utopia—until God put an end to it.

Even then, there was more wrong with Nimrod's kingdom than its dictatorial, centrally planned economy. Archaeologists have turned up evidence that hints at dark spirits behind Nimrod's ambition for world empire.

Nimrod, son of Cush, was born to the second generation after the Flood. Likewise, the Sumerian King List records that the second king of Uruk after the Flood was Enmerkar, son of Mesh-ki-ang-gasher, who in turn was called the son of the sun-god, Utu. The evidence suggests that Nimrod was probably this Enmerkar. In a Sumerian poem called *Enmerkar and the Lord of Aratta*, the king of Uruk put the squeeze on a neighboring kingdom, possibly the land of Urartu (Ararat) in modern Armenia, for building materials that were in short supply in the plains of Shinar. This is reflected in the archaeological record by Uruk's colonies and trading posts in northern Mesopotamia.[737]

Apparently, the conflict was a dispute between Enmerkar and the king of Aratta over who was the favorite of the goddess Inanna, the Sumerian goddess of sex and war. One of Enmerkar's pet building projects was a magnificent temple for Inanna, the *E-ana* ("House of Heaven"). He wanted Aratta to supply the raw materials, not just because there isn't much in the way of timber, jewels, or precious metal in the marshy plains of Sumer, but because Enmerkar wanted the lord of Aratta to submit and acknowledge that he was Inanna's chosen one.

To be honest, some of the messages exchanged by the kings of Uruk and Aratta were the kind of locker room talk that got Donald Trump into trouble during the 2016 presidential campaign. This isn't a surprise, considering Inanna's role in human history. The goddess has been known by many names: Inanna in Sumer, Ishtar in Babylon, Astarte in Canaan, Aphrodite in Greece, and Venus across the Roman world. And what you were taught about Aphrodite in high-school mythology class was way off. Without getting too far off track, let's just say Inanna wasn't a girl you'd bring home to meet your mother.

In fact, she wasn't always a *girl*. Inanna was androgynous, sometimes depicted with masculine features like a beard. Her cult followers included eunuchs and transvestites, and some of the hymns sung in her honor praise her ability to change the gender of her devotees:

> She [changes] the right side (male) into the left side (female),
> She [changes] the left side into the right side,
> She [turns] a man into a woman,
> She [turns] a woman into a man
> She ador[ns] a man as a woman,
> She ador[ns] a woman as a man.[738]

It's wonderfully ironic. The twenty-first-century progressive ideal of gender fluidity and socialism was personified more than five thousand years ago by the Sumerian goddess Inanna, a woman who craved sex and fighting as much (or more) than men, taking on all comers in love and war, and better than men at both. Her personality is celebrated by modern scholars as complex and courageous, transcending traditional gender roles, turning Inanna into an icon of independent man/woman/otherhood. In short, Inanna may have been the first "woke" entity on earth. And this is who Enmerkar/Nimrod wanted to make the patron deity of his capital city, Uruk.

But the transgression of Nimrod that provoked God to scatter his people was much more serious. Besides building a fabulous temple for the goddess of prostitutes, Nimrod also wanted to expand and upgrade the temple of the god of the *abzu*, which is the Sumerian word from which we get "abyss." This was the Tower of Babel episode from Genesis 11, and it's recorded in *Enmerkar and the Lord of Aratta*.

Let the people of Aratta bring down for me the mountain stones from their mountain, **build the great shrine for me, erect the great abode for me, make the great abode, the abode of the gods,** famous for me, make my me prosper in Kulaba, make the *abzu* grow for me like a holy mountain, **make Eridug** (Eridu) **gleam for me like the mountain range, cause the *abzu* shrine to shine forth for me like the silver in the lode.** When in the *abzu* I utter praise, when I bring the me from Eridug, when, in lordship, I am adorned with the crown like a purified shrine, when I place on my head the holy crown in Unug Kulaba, then may the ...... of the great shrine bring me into the *jipar*, and may the ...... of the *jipar* bring me into the great shrine. May the people marvel admiringly, and may Utu (the sun god) witness it in joy.[739] (Emphasis added.)

That was the issue right there. The tower project wasn't simply about pride or oversized ambition; Enmerkar/Nimrod wanted to build "the abode of the gods" *right on top of the abyss.*

If the *abzu* is the same place Peter called Tartarus, where the angels who sinned are kept in "chains of gloomy darkness...until the judgment,"[740] then it's possible that Nimrod's actual goal was to spring the Watchers of Genesis 6 from their supernatural prison.

Could he have succeeded? Who knows? The only thing certain about Babel is that God found it necessary to personally intervene and put a stop to construction of Nimrod's tower, the ziggurat of the god Enki at Eridu.

Interestingly, *Enmerkar and the Lord of Aratta* even records the confusion of speech mentioned in Genesis 11:7.

Another Sumerian myth, *Enki and Inanna*, tells the story of how the divine gifts of civilization, the *mes* (pronounced "mezz"), were stolen from the god of wisdom Enki by Inanna and transferred from Eridu to Uruk. While this tale may have been created as a bit of religious propaganda to justify the transfer of political authority from the holy city of Eridu to the military state controlled by Uruk, the same spirit is behind the veneration of the state at the core of today's socialist worldview.

Likewise, the modern drive to herd humanity into cities, transfer liberty from individuals to the collective, and from sovereign nation-states to a global authority is less a political ambition than a spiritual quest to undo God's original plan for humanity. We were designed to live in liberty, exercising free will to choose to love Him or not (being fully aware of the consequences), taking dominion over the earth as God's "imagers," His moral agents, to enjoy the fruits of our labors, and living according to two basic rules: loving our neighbors as ourselves, and loving Him with all of our hearts, souls, and minds.

Socialism turns that on its head, requiring individuals to give up free will to the dictates of the state, working for the collective rather than ourselves, and receiving what the state decides is fair in return. This philosophy is captured by the slogan "from each according to his ability, to each according to his needs," which was popularized by Karl Marx in a paper published after his death in 1883.

On the surface, it sounds like the basis for a fair and sustainable society, and it would be—if humans were fundamentally selfless. But we're not. At heart, we're just the opposite—selfish, jealous, and willing to take advantage of the misfortune of others for our own gain. And this is just as true of most Christians as for the rest of the world.

This is so self-evident as to make examples unnecessary. But to drive the point home, we refer you to the example of the Massachusetts Bay Colony, the Christian community established by the Pilgrims who landed at Plymouth Rock in 1620. The first governor, William Bradford, found that the concept of communal ownership sounded better in theory than it worked in practice.

> For the young men, that were most able and fit for labor and service, did repine that they should spend their time and strength to work for other men's wives and children without any recompense. The strong, or man of parts, had no more in division of victuals and clothes than he that was weak and not able to do a quarter the other could; this was thought injustice. The aged and graver

men to be ranked and equalized in labors and victuals, clothes etc., with the meaner and younger sort, thought it some indignity and disrespect unto them. And for men's wives to be commanded to do service for other men, as dressing their meat, washing their clothes, etc., they deemed it a kind of slavery, neither could many husbands well brook it.[741]

The solution was to abandon the communal approach to farming and allow each family private ownership of their land. The resulting increase in productivity saved the colony from collapse.

At length, after much debate of things, the Governor (with the advice of the chiefest amongst them) gave way that they should set corn every man for his own particular, and in that regard trust to themselves; in all other thing to go on in the general way as before. And so assigned to every family a parcel of land, according to the proportion of their number, for that end, only for present use (but made no division for inheritance) and ranged all boys and youth under some family. This had very good success, for it made all hands very industrious, so as much more corn was planted than otherwise would have been by any means the Governor or any other could use, and saved him a great deal of trouble, and gave far better content. The women now went willingly into the field, and took their little ones with them to set corn; which before would allege weakness and inability; whom to have compelled would have been thought great tyranny and oppression.[742]

Bradford, writing in his journal, rejected the notion that the "confusion and discontent" of communal ownership was due to a character flaw among the people of the Plymouth colony, arguing that things would have been even worse if they hadn't been "godly and sober" people.

This is human nature, plain and simple. It's been observed and well documented throughout the course of history. As Bradford noted, "seeing all men have this corruption in them, God in His wisdom saw another course fitter for them."[743] In other words, we're most productive when we get to keep what we work for, and when we don't, we work as little as we can get away with. Setting up their colony on principles that depended on people acting against their basic nature nearly led to starvation.

Military veterans know this basic truth: Any plan that depends on perfect execution is a bad plan. Humans are imperfect; planning on human perfection is planning for failure. In the case of the Plymouth colony, success depended on people *behaving* perfectly. That never happens, which is why socialism has never worked and never will.

Four hundred years later, a large segment of America has forgotten the lesson of those early days. Or, quite possibly, they've been taught by an education system sympathetic to socialist ideals that America's early European settlers were racist oppressors from whom nothing of value can be learned.

Further, some progressives blame human exceptionalism, the view that humans are unique among God's creation, and Christians who believe in end-times prophecy for a lack of concern about anthropogenic climate change,[744] because, as you've undoubtedly heard, the science is settled and we Christians are responsible because we're exploiting the earth instead of venerating it.

To be sure, there are many examples of abuse, both of the earth and our fellow humans, by European Christians who've settled in America over the last four hundred years. Still, we agree with William Bradford: It "would have been worse if they had been men of another condition."[745]

As noted earlier, socialism is not the root cause of the collapse of the civilizations that have tried it. The true culprit is the human heart—sin. Capitalism rewards hard work and penalizes indolence, which tends to make capitalist systems productive and prosperous. Contrary to what you may have heard, this is not inconsistent with biblical teaching. Paul warned the church at Thessalonica to "keep away from any brother who is walking in idleness.... If anyone is not willing to work, let him not eat."[746] Christians, while commanded to care for widows and orphans, are nowhere told in Scripture to commandeer the power of the state for the redistribution of wealth.

The danger of socialism is that it exploits our natural tendencies toward laziness and coveting what belongs to our neighbors, promising to right those perceived wrongs by building a utopian society where we can have everything we want without hard work. In a post-Christian America, where God's promise of a just, sustainable world to come is no longer believed, the allure of creating heaven on earth is understandable. The fact that no socialist society in history has delivered on that promise is dismissed. It's a new day; we have science, the Internet, robots, artificial intelligence, and green technologies just around the corner that will provide everything for everybody who bows the knee to the New World Order— and its prophesied leader, who will emerge just before the end of the age.

The road leading back to Babel ends not at an earthly paradise, but at a garbage dump filled with crudely made, disposable, ration containers. Thankfully, having read the end of The Book, we know that the world won't have to endure the socialist New Babel for very long.

Meanwhile, it's our job to educate those around us. Human civilization is like the aptly-named RMS *Titanic*: It's doomed, but there is still time to escape its fate. Our mission is to get as many on the lifeboats as we can before the end.

Summation: Where Is America Going?

The illustrations we've considered in this chapter—abortion, open borders, and socialism—are but three examples of contentious issues increasingly dividing Americans. According to US Attorney General William Barr, these polarizing issues are not random but "organized destruction" by "secularists and their allies [who] have marshaled all the forces of mass communication, popular culture, the entertainment industry, and academia in an unremitting assault on religion and traditional values."

Barr is not overstating this caution against tyranny. As the seventeenth-century founder of the English North American colony, the Province of

Pennsylvania, William Penn once wrote, "If we will not be governed by God, we must be governed by tyrants." Timothy Dwight, president of Yale University, likewise warned in 1798, "Where there is no religion, there is no morality.… With the loss of religion…the security of life, liberty and property are buried in ruins."

That in mind, we return to the question first posed in this chapter: Where is America going and what can conservatives and Christians do to reverse the path of destruction and set America back on track to moral and spiritual recovery? I believe, if righteous people respond appropriately, there is still time to overcome the efforts of *Shadowland* creatures and to experience a (final?) great awakening and national spiritual deliverance. As outlined in 2 Chronicles 7:14: "If my people, which are called by my name, shall humble themselves, and pray, and seek my face, and turn from their wicked ways; then will I hear from heaven, and will forgive their sin, and will heal their land."

Therefore, I submit ten things the Church must do if this generation is to have hope of healing.

1. We must be willing to see and accept the truth about where we are as a nation. We must humble ourselves and restore the message of repentance, integrity, and accountability to our churches and pulpits.

2. We must be hungry and willing for revival to begin in the house of the Lord through repentant saints refreshed with a new anointing.

3. We must pray—not just hold seminars on the mechanics of intercession, but implement its sacred activity within our closets and sanctuaries. S. D. Gordon once accurately said, "The greatest thing anyone can do for God and man is pray. It is not the only thing, but it is the chief thing. The great people of the earth are the people who pray. I do not mean those who talk about prayer; nor those who say they believe in prayer; nor yet those who can explain about prayer; but I mean those people who take time to pray."[747]

4. In addition to prayer, we must seek the Father through fasting and thereby refocus ourselves upon the supreme objective of the believers' adoration—the Godhead. In this we will find ultimate direction, authority, and power.

5. We must commit ourselves to spiritual warfare. "Pray without ceasing" was the message Paul sent to the troubled saints in Thessalonica (1 Thessalonians 5:17). To the Romans he wrote, "And the God of peace shall bruise Satan under your feet shortly" (Romans 16:20). To young Timothy he admonished, "Endure hardness, as a good soldier of Jesus Christ. No man that warreth entangleth himself with the affairs of this life: that he may please him who hath chosen him to be a soldier" (2 Timothy 2:3–4). And in Ephesians 6:10–13, he defined our battle, writing, "Finally, my brethren, be strong in the Lord, and in the power of his might. Put on the whole armour of God, that ye may be able to stand against the wiles of the devil. For we wrestle not against flesh and blood, but against principalities, against powers, against the rulers of the darkness of this world, against spiritual wickedness in high places. Wherefore take unto you the whole armour of God, that ye may be able to withstand in the evil day, and having done all, to stand."

6. The Church must wholly commit itself to the vocal community declaration of the gospel of Jesus Christ. It is the preaching of the gospel of Christ that embodies "the power of God unto salvation, both to the Jews and the Gentiles" (Romans 1:16).

7. We must include intercession specifically for political leaders. 1 Timothy 2:1–2 says, "I exhort therefore, that, first of all, supplications, prayers, intercessions, and giving of thanks, be made for all men; For kings, and for all that are in authority; that we may lead a quiet and peaceable life in all godliness and honesty." According to this text, praying for our leaders is one of the most effective opportunities we have, as it helps create "peaceful" conditions conducive to spreading the gospel, as opposed to government restrictions on religious expression.

8. Representatives in Congress should hear from conservatives. A single call or letter to your representatives is considered by most legislators to reflect the opinion of many thousands of others. Remember the axiom: The only thing necessary for evil to prevail is for good people to do nothing.

9. We should participate in the political process, but I'm not talking about dominionism, in which some preachers believe it is our Christian duty to take over government for the purposes of mandating biblical morality, without which Jesus Christ cannot return. That's heresy and an Antichrist-summoning theocratic scam. Jesus said His kingdom is not of this world (John 18:36) and, in fact, 2 Corinthians 4:4 makes it clear that Satan is the god of this world. Such dominionist aspirations aside, Christians nevertheless have a moral duty (1 Timothy 2:1–2) and Americans a patriotic privilege to vote for moral good. Besides voting, we can be salt and light by doing such things as talking to the public-school teacher to explain why our children will no longer attend explicit sex-education classes. We can call the local broadcasting channel and explain why we will no longer support PBS if they air programs vilifying our religious faith. We can attend campaign rallies and town hall meetings to express our feelings on issues regarding religious liberty. We can form citizen groups of four or five people, educate ourselves on issues of importance, and meet privately with representatives and senators when they are in town. Many congressmen report that this is the best way to get legislation made law.

10. At the forefront of each of our activities, let's remember the biblical admonition in 2 Chronicles 7:14. Revival and awakening is the primary key to overcome any nations' decay and to change destinies of civilizations by turning "the world upside down" (Acts 17:6). As Trump says, we *can* Make America Great Again (and by the way, items 1–7 listed above in particular may transpire suddenly and globally if my predictions in *The Wormwood Prophecy* (see ad at the end of this chapter) unfold as I believe they are going

to. Once the world understands the ramifications of asteroid Apophis impacting earth in just nine years from now, every knee is going to bow in desperation and every tongue is going to confess in great fear their need of salvation from chaos).

So where is America going? It depends on who our guide is. If we continue down the path we currently are on, we are in big trouble. But, if we sincerely look for guidance from the God who originally blessed, multiplied, enriched, and strengthened the United States (for our love of Israel and commitment to missiology), then there is reason for great hope concerning our nation's future. May God grant believers a holy resolve not to allow this moment to slip away. Instead, if the Lord tarry, may historians look back at this as a time of great spiritual awakening and national recovery.

Repentance, righteousness, prayer, fasting, a commitment to spiritual warfare, and evangelism are the weapons of our warfare mighty through God to pull down strongholds and to liberate a nation under demonic siege. Perhaps that is what Reverend Patrick Conroy—the House of Representatives chaplain in Washington, DC—was thinking when he cast demons out of the Capitol building in July, 2019, raising both hands to God and in a dramatic moment saying, "In Your most holy name, I cast out all spirits of darkness from this chamber."[748]

I Believe

In conclusion, I believe America really can be great again. A sovereign outpouring of God's merciful Spirit could sweep across America until the glory of God flows from sea to shining sea.

That's the way it could be. I also believe America is at a very dangerous crossroad and increasingly under control of Shadowland's *egregores* (Watchers), those immaterial entities discussed earlier in this book. Satan's forces have no original claim to the earth or its inhabitants. Everything they hold, they do so with adverse possession. But a time could come when the children of God grow tired of this propagation of deception, of perversion, of degradation—a time when dissatisfaction with materialism gives way to a revival of spiritual hunger. With holy resolve, God's children could respond with weapons against which our enemy has no recourse; no option to regroup or reseize captives. Rather, with astounding victory, today's Jesus People could sound the shofar and resound, "Let us go up and possess the land, for we are well able to overcome them" (Numbers 13:30).

I hope that time is now. I pray that time has come.

Other Important Works from Dr. Thomas R. Horn

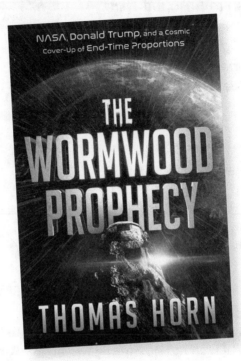

The Wormwood Prophecy: NASA, Donald Trump, and a Cosmic Cover-up of End-Time Proportions

Is the Wormwood star from Revelation 8 already headed toward earth? Are NASA and high-level government officials aware of an asteroid that is on a collision course with our planet? Is that why President Trump sanctioned a colossal increase to planetary defense? Do the prophecies from ancient cultures and religions across the globe all point to a catastrophic planetary event that has scientists and politicians taking extreme preventative measures under the public radar? Earth is not currently prepared for the scope of impact that may be just around the corner, and people in high places know it...

Available at: https://www.skywatchtvstore.com/

The Rabbis, Donald Trump, and the Top-Secret Plan to Build the Third Temple: Unveiling the Incendiary Scheme by Religious Authorities, Government Agents, and Jewish Rabbis to Invoke Messiah

For thousands of years, the world has heard warning that there is a coming a day when the man of sin, the Antichrist, will arise to pilot the greatest deception in human history. Whereas almost anyone alive today can discuss the dictatorial global economics, societal horrors, and eventual apocalypse that follows his arrival, few appear to comprehend that there are negotiations in the workings at this precise moment to build the very location where the abomination of desolation will stand in the holy place. This, as the Book of Daniel prophesied, will be the catalyst event to usher in the end of days.

Available at: https://www.skywatchtvstore.com/

Saboteurs: How Secret, Deep State Occultists Are Manipulating American Society Through a Washington-Based Shadow Government in Quest of the Final World Order

Saboteurs is the most critical and groundbreaking work to date by prolific investigative author Thomas Horn. From his earliest opus on secret societies and the occult to this new unnerving chronicle, Dr. Horn returns to Washington, DC, to expose a harrowing plot by Deep-State Alister Crowley and Masonic devotees that hold an almost unbelievable secret they do not want you to understand: American society is being manipulated through a Washington-based Shadow Government in quest of that Final World Order prophesied in the books of Daniel, Revelation, and on the Great Seal of the United States! *Saboteurs* goes beyond the superficial chaos currently playing out in the public square and in media against the Trump administration to unveil a far more sinister resistance made up of sorcerous elites, their secret societies, and world power brokers who plot the insidious rise of a messianic strongman figure they call The Grey Champion.

Available at: https://www.skywatchtvstore.com/

Blood on the Altar: The Coming War Between Christian vs. Christian

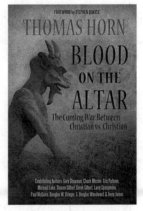

As the world races toward its momentous end-times encounter between good and evil (known in the Bible as Armageddon), a deepening antagonism is developing worldwide against conservative Christians. According to a 2014 Pew Research Center report, this hostility now includes the United States, which elevated from the lowest category of government restrictions on Christian expressions as of mid-2009 to an advanced category in only the last three years. This trend may point to one of the most overlooked aspects of Bible prophecy a war that ultimately pits born-again believers against religious Christians.

Available at: https://www.skywatchtvstore.com/

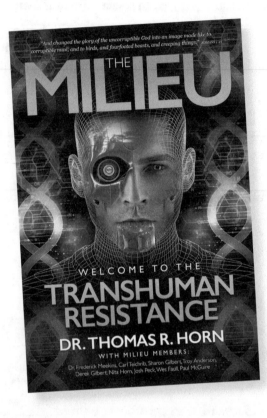

The Milieu: Welcome to the Transhuman Resistance

Utopia or dystopia? Shangri-La or purgatory? Paradise or perdition? What future truly awaits mankind on the other side of widespread human enhancement? With breakthrough advances in transhumanistic science and technology at an all-time high, it appears that people of all ages, backgrounds, and world cultures are lining up to embrace the alteration and augmentation of the human race. Remaining as the mere *Homo sapiens* God designed is no longer satisfactory as we rush toward the human-animal chimeric and human-machine hybrid era a point of no return.

Available at: https://www.skywatchtvstore.com/

Notes

1. Thomas Horn, *Saboteurs* (Crane, MO: Defender Publishing, 2018), 7.
2. https://www.whitehouse.gov/briefings-statements/the-inaugural-address/.
3. http://www.breitbart.com/radio/2017/03/03/robert-barnes-obama-chose-dangerous-precarious-path-encouraging-de-facto-coup-attempt-elements-deep-state/.
4. https://www.thegatewaypundit.com/2019/08/exclusive-ig-report-on-comey-provides-evidence-barack-obama-was-involved-with-deep-state-obstruction-trap-of-president-elect-trump/.
5. https://townhall.com/tipsheet/katiepavlich/2019/08/14/judicial-watch-finds-documents-showing-fusion-gps-working-directly-with-doj-to-frame-trump-with-ties-to-russia-n2551685.
6. https://www.nationalreview.com/2019/08/ball-of-collusion-book-excerpt-hillary-clinton-ruins-the-plan/.
7. https://www.dailymail.co.uk/news/article-7614563/Donald-Trump-accuses-Barack-Obama-TREASON-2016-campaign-spying.html.
8. Society of Professional Journalists. n.d. *Society of Professional Journalists.* Accessed October 19, 2019. https://www.spj.org/ethicsweek-whoarejournalists.asp.
9. Clinton, Hillary. 2011. "U.S. Department of State." *Freedom of Information Act.* U.S. Department of State. September 12. Accessed October 19, 2019. https://foia.state.gov/searchapp/DOCUMENTS/HRCEmail_NovWeb/273/DOC_0C05794192/C05794192.pdf.

10. Gowdy, Trey. 2016. "Chairman of the Select Committee on Benghazi." *U.S. House of Representatives.* Select Committee on Benghazi. June 28. Accessed October 19, 2019. https://archives-benghazi-republicans-oversight.house. gov/sites/republicans.benghazi.house.gov/files/documents/TG%20letter%20 to%20Speaker%20Ryan%206.28.16.pdf.

11. Select Committee on Benghazi. 2016. *The Select Committee on Benghazi.* July 8. Accessed October 19, 2019. https://archives-benghazi-republicans-oversight.house.gov/NewInfo.

12. Ibid.

13. Accountability Review Board. 2012. *Accountability Review Board (ARB) Report.* Washington, D.C.: U.S. Department of State, 1.

14. Select Committee on Benghazi. 2016. Appendix K: Analysis of Accountability Review Board, House Armed Services Committee and House Permanent Select Intelligence Committee Reports. Washington, D.C.: U.S. House of Representatives, 22–25.

15. Select Committee on Benghazi. 2016. Report of the Select Committee on the Events Surrounding the 2012 Terrorist Attack in Benghazi. IV Compliance with Congressional Investigations. Washington, D.C.: U.S. House of Representatives, 47–49.

16. Committee on Foreign Relations. 2013. "Benghazi: The Attacks and the Lessons Learned." *Hearing before the Committee on Foreign Relation.* Washington, D.C.: U.S. Government Printing Office. 28.

17. Select Committee on Benghazi. 2016. *Report of the Select Committee…* 352.

18. U.S. Congress. 2016. "Freedom of Information Act Statute." January 4. Accessed October 19, 2019. https://www.foia.gov/foia-statute.html.

19. Powell, Colin. "Re: Question." Email, 2016. Accessed October 2019. https://foia.state.gov/Search/Results.aspx?collection=Powell_9-23-2016.

20. Reid, Donald. "FW: URGENT: Meeting with Cheryl Mills Tuesday." Email, 2009. Accessed October 2019. https://www.judicialwatch.org/wp-content/uploads/2016/03/JW-v-State-Hillary-BB-NSA-IAD-00646-pg-4.pdf

21. "Hillary Clinton on Her Personal Electronic Mail Account," *C-SPAN,* MARCH 10, 2015, Video, 20:53, https://www.c-span.org/video/?324777-1/hillary-clinton-news-conference.

22. Select Committee on Benghazi. *Report of the Select Committee…* 609–615.

23. Ibid., 395, 604.

24. "Hillary Clinton Testimony at House Select Committee on Benghazi, Part 1," *C-SPAN*, October 22, 2015, Video, 03:19:05, https://www.c-span.org/video/?328699-1/hillary-clinton-testimony-house-select-committee-benghazi-part-1.

25. Select Committee on Benghazi. *Report of the Select Committee…* 602.

26. Ibid., 604.

27. Ibid., 607–609.

28. "Hillary Clinton on Her Personal…"

29. Hillary Clinton, interview by John Dickerson, "Face the Nation," *CBS Interactive Inc.*, May 8, 2016. Accessed October 2019. https://www.cbsnews.com/news/face-the-nation-transcripts-may-8-2016-clinton/.

30. Hillary Clinton, interview by David Muir, "World News Tonight," *ABC News*, Sep 9, 2015. Accessed October 2019. https://abcnews.go.com/Politics/full-transcript-abcs-david-muir-interviews-hillary-clinton/story?id=33607656.

31. Comey, James. "Statement by FBI Director James B. Comey on the Investigation of Secretary Hillary Clinton's Use of a Personal E-Mail System," *FBI National Press Office*, July 5, 2016, Accessed October 2019. https://www.fbi.gov/news/pressrel/press-releases/statement-by-fbi-director-james-b-comey-on-the-investigation-of-secretary-hillary-clinton2019s-use-of-a-personal-e-mail-system.

32. "Hearing Before the Select Committee on Intelligence." *Intelligence Committee*, June 8, 2017. https://www.intelligence.senate.gov/hearings/open-hearing-former-fbi-director-james-comey#.

33. Quinn, Richard P. "Flag." Email, 2016. Accessed October 2019. https://www.judicialwatch.org/wp-content/uploads/2017/10/JW-v-DOJ-Clinton-Lynch-meeting-production-2-00421-pg-99-and-pg-151.pdf.

34. Comey, James. "Director Comey Letter to Congress Dated October 28, 2016." *Federal Bureau of Investigation*. Accessed October 21, 2019. https://vault.fbi.gov/director-comey-letter-to-congress-dated-october-28-2016/Director Comey Letter to Congress Dated October 28, 2016 Part 01 of 01/view.

35. Office of the Inspector General. 2018. "A Review of Various Actions by the Federal Bureau of Investigation and Department of Justice in Advance of the 2016 Election." *Department of Justice*. Accessed October 20, 2019. https://www.justice.gov/file/1071991/download.

36. Comey, James. "Director Comey Letter…Dated October 28, 2016…".

37. Comey, James. "Director Comey Letter to Congress Dated November 6, 2016." *Federal Bureau of Investigation*. Accessed October 21, 2019. https://valut.fbi.gov/director-comey-letter-to-congress-dated-november-6th-2016/director-comey-letter-to-congress-dated-november-6th-2016/view.

38. Office of the Inspector General. 2018. "A Review of Various Actions by the Federal Bureau of Investigation and Department of Justice in Advance of the 2016 Election." *Department of Justice*. Accessed October 20, 2019. https://www.justice.gov/file/1071991/download.

39. Senate Finance Committee. 2018. "Investigation of the DOJ's and FBI's Handling of the Clinton Investigation." August 14, 2019. *United States Senate*. Last accessed October 21, 2019. https://www.grassley.senate.gov/sites/default/files/documents/2019-08-14%20Staff%20memo%20to%20CEG%20RHJ%20-%20ICIG%20Interview%20Summary%20RE%20Clinton%20Server.pdf

40. Ibid.

41. Ibid.

42. "Hillary R. Clinton Part 03 of 36." FBI Records Vault. *Federal Bureau of Investigation*. March 3, 2017. https://vault.fbi.gov/hillary-r.-clinton/Hillary R. Clinton Part 03 of 36/view.

43. James, Comey, "VIA ELECTRONIC TRANSMISSION," September 28, 2016, *United States Senate*, last accessed October 21, 2019, https://www.judiciary.senate.gov/imo/media/doc/2016-09-28 CEG to FBI (Combetta).pdf.

44. Senate Finance Committee. 2018. Investigation of the DOJ's and FBI's Handling of the Clinton Investigation. August 14, 2019. *United States Senate*. Last accessed October 21, 2019. https://www.grassley.senate.gov/sites/default/files/documents/2019-08-14%20Staff%20memo%20to%20CEG%20RHJ%20-%20ICIG%20Interview%20Summary%20RE%20Clinton%20Server.pdf.

45. Committee on the Judiciary, October 19, 2018. https://dougcollins.house.gov/sites/dougcollins.house.gov/files/10.19.18 Nellie Ohr Interview.pdf.

46. Steele, Christopher. "Steele Dossier." 2016. *BuzzFeed News*. Last accessed October 21, 2019. https://www.documentcloud.org/documents/3259984-Trump-Intelligence-Allegations.html.

47. Bensinger, Ken, Miriam Elder, and Mark Schoofs. "These Reports Allege Trump Has Deep Ties To Russia." *BuzzFeed News*. January 11, 2017. https://www.buzzfeednews.com/article/kenbensinger/these-reports-allege-trump-has-deep-ties-to-russia.

48. Trump, Donald. "Clinton campaign & DNC paid for research that led to the anti-Trump fake news dossier. The victim here is the president." *Twitter.com*. Last accessed October 21, 2019. https://twitter.com/realDonaldTrump/status/923147501418446849?ref_src=twsrc%5Etfw%7Ctwcamp%5Etweetembed%7Ctwterm%5E923147501418446849&ref_url=https%3A%2F%2Ftalkingpointsmemo.com%2Flivewire%2Ftrump-steele-dossier-sad-commentary-politics.

49. Steele, Christopher. "Steele Dossier."

50. Ibid.

51. State of the Union: Kellyanne Conway Interview. *CNN.com*, September 25, 2015. http://transcripts.cnn.com/TRANSCRIPTS/1609/25/sotu.01.html.

52. Nakashima, Ellen, Devlin Barrett, and Adam Entous. "FBI Obtained FISA Warrant to Monitor Former Trump Adviser Carter Page." *The Washington Post*. April 11, 2017. https://www.washingtonpost.com/world/national-security/fbi-obtained-fisa-warrant-to-monitor-former-trump-adviser-carter-page/2017/04/11/620192ea-1e0e-11e7-ad74-3a742a6e93a7_story.html.

53. Special Counsel Robert S. Mueller, III. "Report on the Investigation into Russian Interference in the 2016 Presidential Election." March, 2019, *U.S. Department of Justice*. Last accessed October 21, 2019, https://www.justice.gov/storage/report.pdf.

54. Grassley, Charles. "Committee on the Judiciary: Charles Grassley Letter to Wray." United State Senate, January 25, 2018. https://www.judiciary.senate.gov/imo/media/doc/2018-01-25 CEG to FBI (Strzok Page Texts - Clinton Conflict, Special Counsel, Records Alienation).pdf.

55. Grassley, Charles. "Committee on the Judiciary Letter to Rosenstein and Wray." United States Senate, May 11, 2018. https://www.judiciary.senate.gov/imo/media/doc/2018-05-11 CEG to DOJ FBI (Flynn Transcript).pdf.

56. United States v. Michael T. Flynn, Case 1:17-cr-00232-RC, last accessed October 21, 2019, https://www.justice.gov/file/1015121/download

57. Ibid.

58. Carter, Sara, and Jennie Taer. "Former FBI SSA Robyn Gritz's Letter to Judge Sullivan in Support Of Flynn." Sara A. Carter, December 29, 2018. https://saraacarter.com/former-fbi-sac-robyn-gritzs-letter-to-judge-sullivan-in-support-of-flynn/.

59. Johnson, Carrie, and Evie Stone. "Former FBI Agent Speaks Out: 'I Was Not Protected.'" *NPR*. April 15, 2015. https://www.npr.org/2015/04/15/399853577/former-fbi-agent-speaks-out-i-was-not-protected.

60. "Lieutenant General Michael Flynn Delivers Remarks at Republican National Convention." *C-SPAN*, October 21, 2019, 26:33, https://www.c-span.org/video/?c4611729/lieutenant-general-michael-flynn-delivers-remarks-republican-national-convention.

61. Grassley, Charles. "Committee on the Judiciary: Charles Grassley Letter to Wray"…January 25, 2018.

62. "Remarks by President Trump Before Marine One Departure." *The White House*. The United States Government, July 24, 2019. https://www.whitehouse.gov/briefings-statements/remarks-president-trump-marine-one-departure-54/.

63. Barr, William P. "AG March 24 2019 Letter to House and Senate Judiciary Committees." *Scribd*. March 24, 2019. https://www.scribd.com/document/402973652/AG-March-24-2019-Letter-to-House-and-Senate-Judiciary-Committees#fullscreen&from_embed.

64. https://www.foxnews.com/politics/graham-alleges-massive-criminal-conspiracy-in-fbis-russia-probe-in-blistering-hearing-statement.

65. https://townhall.com/columnists/derrickwilburn/2019/11/29/the-real-reason-the-dems-want-trump-gone-n2557211.

66. http://www.newsmax.com/Newsfront/war-liberals-resist-Big-Agenda/2017/03/07/id/777516/.

67. https://www.newsmax.com/newsmax-tv/david-horowitz-racism-the-hunt-liberal/2019/08/08/id/927939/.

68. https://www.thedailybeast.com/to-take-down-trump-take-to-the-streets-7.

69. https://thefederalist.com/2019/08/12/msnbc-panelist-white-people-destroy/.

70. https://pjmedia.com/trending/fliers-reading-death-camps-for-trump-supporters-now-in-ny-were-the-work-of-a-shock-theater-group/.

71. https://www.foxnews.com/politics/lindsey-graham-slams-dem-colleagues-for-brazen-warning-to-supreme-court.

72. http://nymag.com/intelligencer/2019/10/americans-say-u-s-is-two-thirds-of-the-way-to-civil-war.html.

73. https://townhall.com/columnists/walterewilliams/2019/10/23/us-in-moral-decline-n2555108.

74. https://www.justice.gov/opa/speech/attorney-general-william-p-barr-delivers-19th-annual-barbara-k-olson-memorial-lecture.

75. https://www.projectveritas.com/2019/08/14/google-machine-learning-fairness-whistleblower-goes-public-says-burden-lifted-off-of-my-soul/.

76. Ibid.

77. http://freebeacon.com/national-security/fired-nsc-aide-reveals-political-warfare-operation-targeting-trump/.

78. https://en.wikipedia.org/wiki/Irregular_warfare.

79. http://dailycaller.com/2017/05/07/obamas-non-profit-on-same-dubious-path-first-blazed-by-clinton-foundation/.

80. https://archive.org/stream/RulesForRadicals/RulesForRadicals_djvu.txt.

81. https://en.wikipedia.org/wiki/Saul_Alinsky.

82. https://www.washingtonpost.com/news/the-fix/wp/2016/07/20/hillary-clinton-saul-alinsky-and-lucifer-explained/?utm_term=.85ec7ced65cc.

83. http://nypost.com/2017/02/11/how-obama-is-scheming-to-sabotage-trumps-presidency/.

84. http://www.washingtontimes.com/news/2017/feb/15/shadow-presidency-against-trump-has-news-media-obs/.

85. https://pjmedia.com/parenting/church-hosts-summer-camp-to-train-grade-school-kids-to-be-antifa-activists/.

86. https://thefederalist.com/2019/06/18/last-minute-move-southern-baptist-convention-supports-anti-christian-racial-identity-politics/.

87. https://en.wikipedia.org/wiki/Doublethink.

88. Zemeckis, Robert, dir. *Forrest Gump* (United States: Paramount Pictures, 1994). DVD, 2h 22min.

89. ColdFusion. "Deepfakes—Real Consequences." April 28, 2018. YouTube Video, 13:12. Accessed September 6, 2019. https://www.youtube.com/watch?v=dMF2i3A9Lzw.

90. Stephan, Karl. "Seeing May Not Be Believing: AI Deepfakes and Trust in Media." *Mercatornet.* October 15, 2018. Accessed

September 6, 2019. https://www.mercatornet.com/connecting/view/seeing-may-not-be-believing-ai-deepfakes-and-trust-in-media/21827.

91. Kiely, Kathy. "Facebook Refusal to Curb Fake Nancy Pelosi Drunk Video Highlights Need for Responsibility." *USA Today*. May 28, 2019. Accessed September 10, 2019. https://www.usatoday.com/story/opinion/2019/05/28/facebook-fake-video-nancy-pelosi-drunk-responsibility-column/1249830001/.

92. Harwell, Drew. "Faked Pelosi Videos, Slowed to Make Her Appear Drunk, Spread across Social Media." May 24, 2019. Accessed September 10, 2019. https://www.washingtonpost.com/technology/2019/05/23/faked-pelosi-videos-slowed-make-her-appear-drunk-spread-across-social-media/.

93. "Why It's Getting Harder to Spot a Deepfake Video." *CNN Online* Accessed September 7, 2019. https://www.cnn.com/videos/business/2019/06/11/deepfake-videos-2020-election.cnn.

94. Derpfakes. "Nicholas Cage: Mega Mix Two." February 2, 2019. YouTube: 2:05. Accessed September 10, 2019. https://www.youtube.com/watch?v=_Kuf1DLcXeo.

95. Usersub. "Nick Cage DeepFakes Movie Compilation." January 31, 2018. YouTube: 2:17. Accessed September 10, 2019. https://www.youtube.com/watch?v=BU9YAHigNx8.

96. "What Is a Deepfake?" *The Economist*. August 7, 2019. Accessed September 6, 2019. https://www.economist.com/the-economist-explains/2019/08/07/what-is-a-deepfake.

97. Ibid.

98. ColdFusion. "Deepfakes-Real Consequences." April 28, 2018. YouTube Video, 13:12. Accessed September 6, 2019. https://www.youtube.com/watch?v=dMF2i3A9Lzw.

99. Ibid.

100. Ibid.

101. Ibid.

102. Ibid.

103. Ibid.

104. Ibid.

105. Ibid.

106. Ibid.

107. Usersub. "Nick Cage DeepFakes Movie Compilation." January 31, 2018. YouTube Video: 2:17. Accessed September 10, 2019. https://www.youtube.com/watch?v=BU9YAHigNx8&t=33s.

108. TheFakening. "Keanu Reeves as Forest Gump Deepfake – It's Breathtaking!" July 24, 2019. YouTube: 3:12. Accessed September 10, 2019. https://www.youtube.com/watch?v=cVljNVV5VPw&t=72s.

109. The Fakening. "President Donald Trump on Alec Baldwin Deepfake." February 19, 2019. YouTube: 0:42. Accessed September 10, 2019. https://www.youtube.com/watch?v=XdBDouKV828.

110. "What Is a Deepfake?" *The Economist*. August 7, 2019. Accessed September 6, 2019. https://www.economist.com/the-economist-explains/2019/08/07/what-is-a-deepfake.

111. Ibid.

112. Ibid.

113. *New York Times*. "Deepfakes: Is This Video Even Real? NYT Opinion." August 14, 2019. YouTube Video: 3:38. Accessed September 10, 2019. https://www.youtube.com/watch?v=1OqFY_2JE1c.

114. LaFia, John. "Intersections in Real Time." Babylon 5: Season 4, Episode 18. 1997; (Burbank, CA: Warner Brothers, 1997). DVD.

115. "What Is a Deepfake?" *The Economist*. August 7, 2019. Accessed September 6, 2019. https://www.economist.com/the-economist-explains/2019/08/07/what-is-a-deepfake.

116. Ibid.

117. Ibid.

118. https://www.dailystar.co.uk/news/world-news/deepfake-videos-will-cause-worldwide-20574174.

119. Ibid.

120. Stephan, Karl. "Seeing May Not Be Believing: AI Deepfakes and Trust in Media." October 15, 2018. Accessed September 10, 2019. https://www.mercatornet.com/mobile/view/seeing-may-not-be-believing-ai-deepfakes-and-trust-in-media/21827.

121. Ibid.

122. Ibid.

123. Porup, J.M. "How and Why Deepfake Videos Work—And What Is at Risk." *CSO US Online*. April 10, 2019. Accessed September 10, 2019.

https://www.csoonline.com/article/3293002/deepfake-videos-how-and-why-they-work.html.

124. Stephan, Karl. "Seeing May Not Be Believing: AI Deepfakes and Trust in Media." October 15, 2018. Accessed September 10, 2019. https://www.mercatornet.com/mobile/view/seeing-may-not-be-believing-ai-deepfakes-and-trust-in-media/21827.

125. Porup, J.M. "How and Why Deepfake Videos Work—And What Is at Risk." *CSO US Online.* April 10, 2019. Accessed September 10, 2019. https://www.csoonline.com/article/3293002/deepfake-videos-how-and-why-they-work.html.

126. Ibid.

127. Tangermann, Victor. "Congress Is Officially Freaking Out about Deepfakes." *Futurism Online.* June 13, 2019. Accessed September 10, 2019. https://futurism.com/congress-deepfakes-threat.

128. Ibid.

129. Corrigan, Jack. "DARPA Is Taking On the Deepfake Problem." *Nextgov.* August 6, 2019. Accessed September 10, 2019. https://www.nextgov.com/emerging-tech/2019/08/darpa-taking-deepfake-problem/158980/.

130. CNN Business. "Why It's Getting Harder to Spot Deepfake Videos." June 12, 2019. YouTube: 2:45. Accessed September 10, 2019. https://www.youtube.com/watch?v=wCZSMIwOG-o.

131. Ibid.

132. Corrigan, Jack. "DARPA Is Taking On the Deepfake Problem." *Nextgov.* August 6, 2019. Accessed September 10, 2019. https://www.nextgov.com/emerging-tech/2019/08/darpa-taking-deepfake-problem/158980/.

133. Ibid.

134. Ibid.

135. Ibid.

136. Sarkis, Stephanie. "11 Warning Signs of Gaslighting." *Psychology Today.* January 22, 2017. Accessed September 10, 2019. https://www.psychologytoday.com/us/blog/here-there-and-everywhere/201701/11-warning-signs-gaslighting.

137. "Dr. Claire Wardle: Co-Founder and Leader of First Draft." *Cyber Harvard.* September 25, 2018. Accessed September 10, 2019. https://cyber.harvard.edu/people/dr-claire-wardle.

138. *New York Times*. "Deepfakes: Is This Video Even Real? NYT Opinion."
     August 14, 2019. YouTube Video: 3:38. Accessed September 10, 2019.
     https://www.youtube.com/watch?v=1OqFY_2JE1c.

139. Powers, Benjamin. "'Deep Fake' Video Can Ruin Reputations. Can
     Life Logs Prevent That?" *Public Security Today Online*. November 28,
     2018. Accessed September 10, 2019. https://publicsecurity.today/
     deep-fake-video-can-ruin-reputations-can-life-logs-prevent-that/.

140. Ibid.

141. Ibid.

142. Ibid.

143. Ibid.

144. Ibid.

145. *New York Times*. "Deepfakes: Is This Video Even Real? NYT Opinion."
     August 14, 2019. YouTube Video: 3:38. Accessed September 10, 2019.
     https://www.youtube.com/watch?v=1OqFY_2JE1c.

146. Ibid.

147. https://en.wikipedia.org/wiki/Year_Zero_(political_notion).

148. https://www.good.is/articles/george-washington-racist-mural.

149. https://www.foxnews.com/us/
     which-confederate-statues-were-removed-a-running-list.

150. Gary Lachman, *Politics and the Occult: The Left, the Right, and the Radically
     Unseen*, (Quest Books; 1st Quest Ed edition, November 1, 2008), 97–98.

151. https://www.christianheadlines.com/contributors/mikaela-matthews/california-
     lawmakers-want-to-control-what-pastors-preach-about-lgbt-beliefs.html.

152. Office of the Press Secretary, "Weekly Address: President Obama
     Challenges Politicians Benefiting from Citizens United Ruling to
     Defend Corporate Influence in Our Elections," 8-21-2010. "https://
     obamawhitehouse.archives.gov/the-press-office/2010/08/21/
     weekly-address-president-obama-challenges-politicians-benefiting-citizen.

153. Pfeiffer, Dan. "President Obama's Long Form Birth Certificate," Accessed
     6-24-19. https://obamawhitehouse.archives.gov/blog/2011/04/27/
     president-obamas-long-form-birth-certificate.

154. A seven-minute synopsis video of the visual evidence of how the Obama
     certificate was digitally forged is available here: https://www.youtube.com/
     watch?v=8frqVINnQjc.

See the full one-hour third and final MCSO Press Conference here: "WOW: Sheriff Joe Arpaio Releases New Information on President Obama's Birth Certificate (FNN)," Fox 10 Phoenix, YouTube, posted 12-15-16, https://www.youtube.com/watch?v=jk3KRxTfkLM.

155. Hananoki, Eric. "Dobbs Repeatedly Makes Obama Birth Certificate Claims His CNN Colleagues Call "Total Bull," Media Matters, 7-17-09, https://www.mediamatters.org/research/2009/07/17/dobbs-repeatedly-makes-obama-birth-certificate/152170.

156. Lou Dobbs was eventually terminated at CNN. In large part, his termination was due to his engaging in the dreaded "birther movement." Dobbs is just one example of how the mainstream media eventually shut down all reporting on the Obama birth narrative and birth certificate fakery. Folkenflik, David. "What's Behind Lou Dobbs' Leaving CNN?" (The Birther Issue), NPR, 11-12-09. https://www.npr.org/templates/story/story.php?storyId=120351492.

157. Ashley Parker and Steve Eder. "Inside the Six Weeks Donald Trump Was a Nonstop 'Birther'," New York Times, 7-2-16. https://www.nytimes.com/2016/07/03/us/politics/donald-trump-birther-obama.html.

158. Prokop, Andrew. "Trump Fanned a Conspiracy about Obama's Birthplace for Years. Now He Pretends Clinton Started It." VOX, 9-16-16, https://www.vox.com/2016/9/16/12938066/donald-trump-obama-birth-certificate-birther.

159. **Deep State:** "The term was originally coined in a somewhat pejorative sense to refer to similar relatively invisible state apparatus in Turkey.... With respect to the United States, the concept has been discussed in numerous published works.... Allegedly, per George Friedman, the Deep State has been in place since 1871 and continues beneath the federal government, controlling and frequently reshaping policies." See: "Deep State in the United States," Wikipedia, https://en.wikipedia.org/wiki/Deep_state_in_the_United_States.

160. Murse, Tom. "President Obama's First Executive Order. Did the President Really Seal His Own Personal Records?" Updated 5-25-19, https://www.thoughtco.com/president-obamas-first-executive-order-3322189.

161. **The Big Lie:** This is a propaganda technique and logical trick (fallacy). The expression was coined by Adolf Hitler, when he dictated his 1925

book, *Mein Kampf,* about the use of a lie so "colossal" that no one would believe that someone "could have the impudence to distort the truth so infamously." The source of the *big lie* technique is in a particular passage, taken from chapter 10 of James Murphy's translation of *Mein Kampf.* (Adolf Hitler, *Mein Kampf,* vol. I, ch. X).

See: Big Lie: https://en.wikipedia.org/wiki/Big_lie.

162. Gardner, Daniel. "How Real Is 'Fake News,' and Who Coined the Phrase? Not Who You Think." Clarion Ledger, 7-31-18, https://www.clarionledger.com/story/opinion/columnists/2018/07/31/who-first-used-fake-news-phrase-not-donald-trump/864396002.

163. Darrah, Nichole. "Who Is Joe Arpaio? A Look at the Arizona Ex-sheriff," Fox News, 1-10-18, https://www.foxnews.com/politics/who-is-joe-arpaio-a-look-at-the-arizona-ex-sheriff.

164. **Sheriff Arpaio's first Obama Birth Certificate Press Conference** (March 2012) can be viewed here: https://www.youtube.com/watch?v=XWmWO18GTc8.

    Sheriff Arpaio's Second Obama Birth Certificate Press Conference (July 2012) can be viewed here: https://www.youtube.com/watch?v=alVzyfptF80.

165. See the entire one-hour, official, December 2016 press conference here: "WOW: Sheriff Joe Arpaio Releases New Information on President Obama's Birth Certificate (FNN)," Fox 10 Phoenix, YouTube, posted 12-15-16, https://www.youtube.com/watch?v=jk3KRxTfkLM.

    This video was filmed by local Phoenix, Arizona, Fox News affiliate. However, the national Fox News network not only never showed it; they never even mentioned it. When you watch it in full, you'll know why.

    A seven-minute synopsis video of the visual evidence of how the Obama certificate was digitally forged is available here: https://www.youtube.com/watch?v=8frqVINnQjc.

166. Cassidy, Megan. "Sheriff Joe Arpaio Renews Birther Claims about Obama's Birth Certificate," USA Today, 12-15-16, https://www.usatoday.com/story/news/nation-now/2016/12/15/sheriff-joe-arpaio-probe-proves-obama-birth-certificate-fake/95500958.

167. To witness the effect that this jaw-dropping presentation had on a certain Fox affiliate media reporter, as the conference unfolded live before her eyes,

watch this seven-minute video. You will be shocked by the reporter's analysis
of what she was witnessing.

"FOX NEWS REPORTER Gets Obama Birth Certificate FRAUD
Correct!" PNN News and Ministry Network, posted 1-28-17, https://www.
youtube.com/watch?v=RbWdm5n3PsA.

168. Greenburg, John. "Did Hillary Clinton Start the Obama
Birther Movement?" Politifact, 9-23-15, https://www.politifact.
com/truth-o-meter/statements/2015/sep/23/donald-trump/
hillary-clinton-obama-birther-fact-check.

169. Jake Tapper, Casey Capachi, and Jeremy Harlan. "Hillary Clinton Was Not
a Birther," CNN, 5-6-16, https://www.cnn.com/2016/05/06/politics/fact-
check-donald-trump-claims-that-hillary-clinton-started-birther-movement/
index.html.

From the article: "On March 19, 2007, then-Clinton adviser Mark Penn
wrote a strategy memo to Clinton about Obama. It did not raise the issue of
Obama's citizenship. But it did identify Obama's 'lack of American roots' as
something that 'could hold him back.'

What we see in 2008 from Clinton is a subtle stoking of questions about
Obama's identity.… Bottom line: Clinton stoked questions about Obama's
identity. But Clinton herself never questioned Obama's birth certificate."

Author's Note: Of course there never was a question about Hillary
questioning the actual birth certificate. The clear admission of CNN's
Tapper here is that Hillary herself was involved in "stoking questions about
Obama's identity." This goes directly to the entire birther movement. A
stunning admission on the part of CNN, ironically done while vehemently
attempting to "exonerate" her.

170. Xuan Thai and Ted Barrett. "Biden's Description of Obama Draws
Scrutiny," CNN, 2-9-07, http://www.cnn.com/2007/POLITICS/01/31/
biden.obama.

171. Pollack, Joel. "The Vetting—Exclusive—Obama's Literary Agent in 1991
Booklet: 'Born in Kenya and raised in Indonesia and Hawaii'," Breitbart
News, 5-17-12, https://www.breitbart.com/politics/2012/05/17/the-vetting-
barack-obama-literary-agent-1991-born-in-kenya-raised-indonesia-hawaii.

Author's Note: I have often made the point that this publicist's bio
statement does not "prove" Obama was born in Kenya. But, being an author

of numerous best-selling books myself, I know for a fact that an author's bio must be reviewed and approved and sometimes even written by the author himself before it goes to print. The fact that Obama's bio stated he was born in Kenya, in his "official" bio, and existed in those words for seventeen years, tells me that either he was in fact born in Kenya or for seventeen years he allowed the known incorrect information to proliferate solely for his benefit. Neither of these scenarios bode well for Obama's character. However, this document does *prove* that Obama himself was the very first birther.

172. Ibid. Pollack, Joel. "The Vetting—Exclusive—Obama's Literary Agent in 1991 Booklet: 'Born in Kenya and raised in Indonesia and Hawaii.'"

173. Pinter, Jason. "Obama's Literary Agency Error: A Clarification and Rebuttal," *Huffington Post*, 5/22/2012 Updated Dec 06, 2017, https://www.huffpost.com/entry/obama-birthplace_b_1530399.

174. Green, Joshua. "Penn Strategy Memo, March 19, 2007," *The Atlantic*, 8-11-08, Accessed June 24, 2019, https://www.theatlantic.com/politics/archive/2008/08/penn-strategy-memo-march-19-2008/37952.

175. Hemingway, Mark. "Someone Isn't Telling the Truth about Sidney Blumenthal and the Clinton Campaign," Weekly Standard, 9-20-16, https://www.weeklystandard.com/mark-hemingway/someone-isnt-telling-the-truth-about-sidney-blumenthal-and-the-clinton-campaign.

176. Jake Tapper, Casey Capachi, and Jeremy Harlan. "Hillary Clinton Was Not a Birther," CNN, 5-6-16, https://www.cnn.com/2016/05/06/politics/fact-check-donald-trump-claims-that-hillary-clinton-started-birther-movement/index.html.

177. Ibid. Green, Joshua. "Penn Strategy Memo, March 19, 2007."

178. "The McClatchy Company…operates 29 daily newspapers in fourteen states and has an average weekday circulation of 1.6 million and Sunday circulation of 2.4 million. In 2006, it purchased Knight Ridder, which at the time was the second-largest newspaper company in the United States (Gannett was and remains the largest). In addition to its daily newspapers, McClatchy also operates several websites and community papers, as well as a news agency, McClatchyDC, focused on political news from Washington, D.C." See: https://en.wikipedia.org/wiki/McClatchy. See: https://mediabiasfactcheck.com/mcclatchydc.

179. James Asher is an award-winning investigative journalist and

winner of the 2017 Pulitzer Prize in journalism for explanatory reporting. Four other investigations he directed were Pulitzer finalists. See: https://www.ap.org/ap-in-the-news/2017/ap-names-asher-to-news-editor-position-in-washington.

180. Ibid. Hemingway, Mark. "Someone Isn't Telling the Truth about Sidney Blumenthal and the Clinton Campaign."

181. MSNBC, "Hardball with Chris Matthews—for Dec. 18," updated 12/19/2007 11:14:09 AM ET, http://www.nbcnews.com/id/22326842/ns/msnbc-hardball_with_chris_matthews/t/hardball-chris-matthews-dec/#.XQ6jGehKjIW.
Author's Note: The transcript is lengthy. To find this particular quote, one will have to go almost to the end of the article. I suggest simply doing a webpage word search at the link above, by putting the first words of the quote in the search engine (CTRL-F). I have archived a screenshot of the page at its original URL, and the Matthews' comment, in case the pag, or the quote happens to disappear.

182. Video File—*MrFortheloveoftrut*h. "Hillary Clinton—Gives Birth to the Birthers in 2007 as per Morning Joe Scarborough," YouTube video of the actual MSNBC broadcast—posted 9-16-2016, accessed June 24, 2019, https://www.youtube.com/watch?v=-lnOqecl-wc.
Author's note: In this video portion of Morning Joe on MSNBC, Scarborough, Brzezinski, and Heilemann several times are emphatic that the "whole thing" (birther movement) "started with Hillary Clinton."
Audio file of the same show: http://adam.curry.com/enc/1474227883.158_morningjoeandmikaremindeveryonewhoactuallybeganbirtherism-may2016.mp3. Accessed June 24, 2019.

183. Riddell, Kelly. "Classic Clinton Doublespeak," *Washington Times*, 5-26-16, https://www.washingtontimes.com/news/2016/may/26/kelly-riddell-classic-clinton-doublespeak.

184. Boehlert, Eric. "Hillary Clinton, 60 Minutes, and the Muslim Question," Media Matters, 3-11-08, https://www.mediamatters.org/research/2008/03/11/hillary-clinton-60-minutes-and-the-muslim-quest/142844.

185. "Media Matters for America," accessed 6-24-19, https://www.conservapedia.com/Media_Matters_for_America#cite_ref-4.

186. PND. "Media Matters Receives $1 Million from George Soros,"
      Philanthropy News Digest, 10-22-10, https://www.philanthropynewsdigest.
      org/news/media-matters-receives-1-million-from-george-soros.

187. Eileen McGuire-Mahony. "Governor Abercrombie's Inability to Release
      Obama's Birth Certificate Causes Hawaiian Legislators to Step In,"
      Ballotpedia, 1-28-11, https://ballotpedia.org/Governor_Abercrombie%27s_
      inability_to_release_Obama%27s_birth_certificate_causes_Hawaiian_
      legislators_to_step_in.

188. Hot Air. "New Hawaii Governor: We're Going to Put a Stop to This Birther
      Crap Once and for All," 12-27-10, https://hotair.com/archives/2010/12/27/
      new-hawaii-governor-were-going-to-put-a-stop-to-this-birther-crap-once-
      and-for-all.

189. Meghan Ashford-Grooms, Ciara O'Rourke. "State Rep. Leo
      Berman Says Hawaii Governor Can't Find Anything That Says
      Obama Was Born in Hawaii," Politifact, 2-27-11, https://
      www.politifact.com/texas/statements/2011/feb/27/leo-berman/
      state-rep-leo-berman-says-hawaii-governor-cant-fin.

190. Ibid.

191. Ibid.

192. Mike Evans' original claim about Abercrombie: Bigone5555J "Abercrombie
      Admits There Are No Obama Birth Records in Hawaii," YouTube video,
      posted 1-24-11, https://www.youtube.com/watch?v=hvrb7YqdvxE.
      Mike Evans walks his entire story back: Bigone5555J "Mike Evans Back
      Tracks on Birth Certificate Story," YouTube video, posted 1-24-11, https://
      www.youtube.com/watch?v=4lkYK_QcqHY.
      Author's note: I have both of these original interviews in my archives.

193. PBS News Hour. "Trump Defends Years of Obama 'Birther'
      Rumors," YouTube video, 9-26-16, https://www.youtube.com/
      watch?v=KjU6wZgyLh8&t=34s.

194. Cheney, Kyle. "No, Clinton Didn't Start the Birther Thing. This Guy
      Did," Politico, Sept. 16, 2019, https://www.politico.com/story/2016/09/
      birther-movement-founder-trump-clinton-228304.

195. McAskill, Ewen. "Clinton Aides Claim Obama Photo Wasn't Intended as a
      Smear," *The Guardian*, 2-25-08, https://www.theguardian.com/world/2008/
      feb/25/barackobama.hillaryclinton.

196. Ibid. Cheney, Kyle. "No, Clinton Didn't Start the Birther Thing. This Guy Did."

197. Hemingway, Mark. "Someone Isn't Telling the Truth about Sidney Blumenthal and the Clinton Campaign," *Weekly Standard*, 9-20-16, https://www.weeklystandard.com/mark-hemingway/someone-isnt-telling-the-truth-about-sidney-blumenthal-and-the-clinton-campaign.

198. Jake Tapper, Casey Capachi, and Jeremy Harlan. "Hillary Clinton Was Not a Birther," CNN, 5-6-16, https://www.cnn.com/2016/05/06/politics/fact-check-donald-trump-claims-that-hillary-clinton-started-birther-movement/index.html.

199. Rondeau, Sharon. "Maj. Gen. Paul E. Vallely: We Need to Demand Resignations of Obama, His Cabinet, and Members of Congress," Post & Email, 6-16-10, https://www.thepostemail.com/2010/06/16/maj-gen-paul-e-vallely-we-need-to-demand-resignations-of-obama-his-cabinet-and-members-of-congress.

200. Linkins, Jason. "Fox News Military Analyst Comes Out As Birther," Huffington Post, 9-1-10, https://www.huffpost.com/entry/fox-news-military-analyst_n_702516.

201. Kenber, Billy. "More than Bradley Manning's Fate Lies with Judge Denise Lind…" *Washington Post*, 7-24-13, accessed 7-5-19, https://www.washingtonpost.com/world/national-security/more-than-bradley-mannings-fate-lies-with-judge-denise-lind-in-case-about-leaking-info/2013/07/24/fb546d14-f496-11e2-aa2e-4088616498b4_story.html?utm_term=.8036e9ea1841.

202. Wikipedia. "Court-martial of Terry Lakin," Accessed July 5, 2019, https://en.wikipedia.org/wiki/Court-martial_of_Terry_Lakin.

203. WND, "From A to Z: What's Wrong with Obama's Birth Certificate?" 5-13-11, https://www.wnd.com/2011/05/296881.
See also: Birther Report YouTube video audio interview with General Paul Vallely, "Major General Vallely: CIA Agents Say Obama Birth Certificate Fraudulent" Posted 6/13/11, https://www.youtube.com/watch?v=jTMv2XAUHP4.

204. Abbott, Matt C. "Professor Charles Rice on Obama's 'Eligibility' by Dr. Charles E. Rice," Renew America, 2-27-11, http://www.renewamerica.com/columns/abbott/110227.

205. Bowden, John. "Arpaio Says He Will Resume Challenging Obama's Birth Certificate if Elected," The Hill, 3-27-18, https://thehill.com/homenews/campaign/380533-arpaio-says-he-will-resume-attacking-obamas-birth-certificate-if-elected.

206. Azcentral. "Sheriff Joe Arpaio: I'm Still Investigating President Barack Obama's Birth Certificate," 9-20-16, https://www.azcentral.com/story/news/politics/arizona/2016/09/21/arizona-joe-arpaio-still-investigating-obamas-birth-certificate/90743412.

207. Cassidy, Megan. "Sheriff Joe Arpaio Renews Birther Claims about Obama's Birth Certificate," USA Today, 12-15-16, https://www.usatoday.com/story/news/nation-now/2016/12/15/sheriff-joe-arpaio-probe-proves-obama-birth-certificate-fake/95500958/.

208. CNN. "Arpaio: Obama's Birth Certificate a Phony," YouTube video, posted 1-10-18, accessed 6-29-19, https://www.youtube.com/watch?v=PFfY6_hcfxk.

209. Farley, Robert. "Obama's Birth Certificate: Final Chapter. This Time We Mean It!," Politifact, 7-1-2009, https://www.politifact.com/truth-o-meter/article/2009/jul/01/obamas-birth-certificate-final-chapter-time-we-mea.

210. Rondeau, Sharon. "Attention Bill O'Reilly: The Rest of the Story," Post & Email, 4-4-11, https://www.thepostemail.com/2011/04/04/attention-bill-oreilly-the-rest-of-the-story.

211. Ibid. Rondeau, Sharon. "Attention Bill O'Reilly: The Rest of the Story."

212. Treason. Dictionary.com, Accessed July 3, 2019, https://www.dictionary.com/browse/treason.

213. Stucky, Philip. "Biden: 'Not One Single Whisper of Scandal' During Obama Administration," Daily Caller, 4-26-19, https://dailycaller.com/2019/04/26/biden-no-scandal-obama-administration.

214. Office of the Press Secretary, "Weekly Address: President Obama Challenges Politicians Benefiting from Citizens United Ruling to Defend Corporate Influence in Our Elections," 8-21-2010, https://obamawhitehouse.archives.gov/the-press-office/2010/08/21/weekly-address-president-obama-challenges-politicians-benefiting-citizen.

215. Martin. Nick R. "Joe Arpaio's Birther Obsession Just Keeps Getting Stranger," Talking Points Memo, 7-19-12, https://talkingpointsmemo.com/muckraker/joe-arpaio-s-birther-obsession-just-keeps-getting-stranger.

216. Murse, Tom. "President Obama's First Executive Order: Did the President Really Seal His Own Personal Records?" Updated 5-25-19, https://www.thoughtco.com/president-obamas-first-executive-order-3322189.

217. Executive Order 13489—https://www.govinfo.gov/content/pkg/FR-2009-01-26/pdf/E9-1712.pdf.

218. Ibid. Murse, Tom. "President Obama's First Executive Order: Did the President Really Seal His Own Personal Records?"

219. CBS News, "Obama Admin Spent $36M on Lawsuits to Keep Info Secret," Updated 3-14-17, https://www.cbsnews.com/news/obama-administration-spent-36m-on-records-lawsuits-last-year.

220. NARA website. "Unauthorized Disposition of Federal Records," accessed 6-29-19, https://www.archives.gov/records-mgmt/resources/unauthorizeddispositionoffederalrecords.

221. Lipscomb, Thomas. "Crisis at the National Archives," Real Clear Politics, June 6, 2018, https://www.realclearpolitics.com/articles/2018/06/10/crisis_at_the_national_archives_137241.html.

222. Rondeau, Sharon. "Zullo Recaps Missing Records from National Archives the Week of Obama's "Birth"," The Post & Email, 6-17-18, https://www.thepostemail.com/2018/06/17/zullo-recaps-missing-records-from-national-archives-the-week-of-obamas-birth.

223. Birther Report YouTube video audio interview with Major General Paul Vallely, "Major General Vallely: CIA Agents Say Obama Birth Certificate Fraudulent" Posted 6/13/11, https://www.youtube.com/watch?v=jTMv2XAUHP4.

224. Pfeiffer, Dan. "President Obama's Long Form Birth Certificate," Accessed 6-24-19, https://obamawhitehouse.archives.gov/blog/2011/04/27/president-obamas-long-form-birth-certificate.

225. Azcentral. "Sheriff Joe Arpaio: I'm Still Investigating President Barack Obama's Birth Certificate," 9-20-16, https://www.azcentral.com/story/news/politics/arizona/2016/09/21/arizona-joe-arpaio-still-investigating-obamas-birth-certificate/90743412.

226. Ibid. Cassidy, Megan. "Sheriff Joe Arpaio Renews Birther Claims about Obama's Birth Certificate."

227. Ibid. Murse, Tom. "President Obama's First Executive Order: Did the President Really Seal His Own Personal Records?"

228. Ibid. Rondeau, Sharon. "Mike Zullo Describes 'Collusion with Media Executives.'"

229. Philip Rucker and Ellen Nakashima. "Trump asked Sessions about Closing Case against Arpaio, an Ally Since 'Birtherism,'" *Chicago Tribune*, 8-26-17, https://www.chicagotribune.com/nation-world/ct-trump-sessions-arpaio-case-20170826-story.html.

230. Cassidy, Megan. "Maricopa County Sheriff Joe Arpaio Officially Charged with Criminal Contempt," AZ Central, 10-25-16, https://www.azcentral.com/story/news/local/phoenix/2016/10/25/maricopa-county-sheriff-joe-arpaio-officially-charged-criminal-contempt/92472998.

231. Attested to at the 1:24:50 mark in this interview. "[1330 AM | 99.1 FM] Freedom Friday 6-29-19 | BREAKING NEWS! Mike Zullo (whole show) New Intrigue surrounding CIA informant Dennis Montgomery," internationally live-broadcast radio show. Podcast posted 6-29-19, https://carlgallups.blogspot.com/2019/06/1330-am-991-fm-freedom-friday-6-29-19.html.

232. Kevin Liptak, Daniella Diaz and Sophie Tatum. "Trump Pardons Former Sheriff Joe Arpaio," CNN, 8-27-17, https://www.cnn.com/2017/08/25/politics/sheriff-joe-arpaio-donald-trump-pardon/index.html.

233. Beamon, Todd. "WashPost: Trump Asked AG Jeff Sessions to Drop Joe Arpaio Case," Newsmax.com, 8-26-17, https://www.newsmax.com/newsfront/joe-arpaio-jeff-sessions-trump-sessions/2017/08/26/id/809989.

234. Lauter, David. "One Last Look at the Polls: Hillary Clinton's Lead Is Holding Steady," *Los Angeles Times*, 11-8-16, https://www.latimes.com/nation/politics/trailguide/la-na-election-day-2016-a-last-look-at-the-polls-clinton-lead-1478618744-htmlstory.html.

235. Ortiz, Erik. "Trump Kept 'Birther' Beliefs Going Long After Obama's Birth Certificate Was Released," NBC News, 9-16-16, https://www.nbcnews.com/politics/2016-election/trump-kept-birther-beliefs-going-long-after-obama-s-birth-n649346.
    Note: The birth certificate was eventually posted in April 2011. Donald Trump had been prodding Obama in the matter at least since late 2010.

236. Hawaii News Now, "Trump, Abercrombie Spar over 'Birther' Issue," April 19, 2011 at 11:16 PM HST, Updated June

23, https://www.hawaiinewsnow.com/story/14479029/
trump-abercrombie-spar-over-birther-issue.

237. O'Conner, Claire. "Donald Trump Tells Forbes Why He's Offering $5
      Million for Obama's Records," *Forbes*, 10-24-12, https://www.forbes.com/
      sites/clareoconnor/2012/10/24/trump-tells-forbes-why-hes-offered-5-
      million-for-obamas-records/#14f74d493e9a.

238.   Daniel Chaitin. "Trey Gowdy Blasts Peter Strzok's 'Source'
      behind the 'Insurance Policy,'" *The Washington Examiner*,
      3-14-19, https://www.washingtonexaminer.com/news/
      trey-gowdy-blasts-peter-strzoks-source-behind-the-insurance-policy.

239. Actually, we now know that the Comey FBI had already launched a Russia
      probe investigation into Trump and his campaign as early as July 2016, four
      full months before the actual presidential election. Could the now infamous
      FBI Peter Strzok's "insurance policy" have been put into motion at about
      that time?
      Matishak, Martin. "Comey: FBI launched Trump-Russia probe in
      July," Politico, 3-20-17, https://www.politico.com/story/2017/03/
      fbi-trump-russia-probe-timeline-236258.

240. Schwab, Nikki. "Trump Says Biggest Regret Was Appointing Jeff
      Sessions," *New York Post*, 6-23-19, https://nypost.com/2019/06/23/
      trump-says-biggest-regret-was-appointing-jeff-sessions.

241. Solomon, John. "The Case for Russia Collusion…against the Democrats,"
      The Hill, 2-10-19, https://thehill.com/opinion/white-house/429292-the-
      case-for-russia-collusion-against-the-democrats.
      See Also:
      L. Brent Bozell III and Tim Graham, "How The Media Covered Up the
      Real Collusion, Between Russians and the Hillary Campaign," Daily Caller,
      6-4-19, https://dailycaller.com/2019/06/04/how-the-media-covered-up-the-
      real-collusion-between-russians-and-the-hillary-campaign.

242. Davis, Sean. "The Only 2016 Campaign That Deliberately
      Colluded with Russians Was Hillary Clinton's," The
      Federalist, 3-28-19, https://thefederalist.com/2019/03/28/
      campaign-colluded-russians-2016-hillary-clintons.

243. Hains, Tim. "Trump: Mueller Probe Was Strzok and Page's 'Insurance
      Policy,' Comey Should 'Come Clean.'" Real Clear Politics, 5-30-19, https://

www.realclearpolitics.com/video/2019/05/30/trump_mueller_probe_was_
strzok_and_pages_insurance_policy_comey_should_come_clean.html.

244. Solomon, John. "Lisa Page Bombshell: FBI Couldn't Prove Trump-Russia
Collusion Before Mueller Appointment," The Hill, 9-16-18, https://thehill.
com/hilltv/rising/406881-lisa-page-bombshell-fbi-couldnt-prove-trump-
russia-collusion-before-mueller.

245. Ibid. Daniel Chaitin. "Trey Gowdy Blasts Peter Strzok's 'Source' behind the
'Insurance Policy.'"

246. The Editors of Encyclopaedia Britannica. "Robert Mueller, American Law
Enforcement Official," Encyclopaedia Britannica, Accessed June 24, 2019,
https://www.britannica.com/biography/Robert-Mueller.

247. Solomon, John. "FISA Shocker: DOJ Official Warned Steele Dossier Was
Connected to Clinton, Might Be Biased," The Hill, 1-16-19, https://thehill.
com/opinion/white-house/425739-fisa-shocker-doj-official-warned-steele-
dossier-was-connected-to-clinton.

248. Reid, Paula. "James Comey Calls Trump 'Morally Unfit,'"
CBS News, 4-16-19, https://www.cbsnews.com/video/
james-comey-says-trump-is-morally-unfit-to-be-president.

249. YouTube video of CNN Broadcast. "7-22-18 Clapper Says Obama Was
behind the Whole Thing," posted 7-22-18, accessed 6-25-19. https://www.
youtube.com/watch?time_continue=1&v=DpwUr_JFXYY.

250. Schwartz, Ian. "Clapper: Obama Ordered the Intelligence Assessment That
Resulted in Mueller Investigation," Real Clear Politics, 7-24-18, https://
www.realclearpolitics.com/video/2018/07/24/clapper_obama_ordered_the_
intelligence_assessment_that_resulted_in_mueller_investigation.html.

251. Truax, Chris. "Trump-Mueller Showdown Will Be a Historic Test of
America's Institutions and Rule of Law," USA Today, 12-10-18, https://
www.usatoday.com/story/opinion/2018/12/10/sentencing-memo-flynn-
cohen-manafort-mueller-donald-trump-russia-column/2257509002.

252. Glasser, Susan B. "This Is Not a Normal Time": Trump and the
Rapidly Expanding 'Witch Hunt,'" The New Yorker, 12-14-28,
https://www.newyorker.com/news/letter-from-trumps-washington/
this-is-not-a-normal-time-trump-and-the-rapidly-expanding-witch-hunt.

253. Ian Prasad Philbrick. "The Articles of Impeachment Against Donald J.
Trump: A Draft," New York Times, 6-5-19, https://www.nytimes.com/

interactive/2019/06/05/opinion/impeachment-trump-democrats-nixon-clinton.html.

254. Bart Jansen and Kevin Johnson. "Robert Mueller, in First Public Remarks, Says Charging Trump Was 'Not an Option We Could Consider,'" *USA Today*, 5-29-19, https://www.usatoday.com/story/news/politics/2019/05/29/robert-mueller-speak-russia-investigation-and-2016-election/1269060001.

255. Sperry, Paul. "Who Were the Mueller Report's Hired Guns?", Real Clear Politics, 5-11-19, https://www.realclearpolitics.com/articles/2019/05/11/who_were_the_mueller_reports_hired_guns_140289.html. **Also See**: Scarborough, Rowan. "How Much Did the FBI Rely on a Discredited Trump-Russia Dossier?" *Washington Times*, 6-2-19, https://www.washingtontimes.com/news/2019/jun/2/william-barr-seeks-dossiers-influence-fbis-trump-r/.

256. Solomon, John. "FISA Shocker: DOJ Official Warned Steele Dossier Was Connected to Clinton, Might Be Biased," The Hill, 1-16-19, https://thehill.com/opinion/white-house/425739-fisa-shocker-doj-official-warned-steele-dossier-was-connected-to-clinton.

257. Rondeau, Sharon. "Government Spying: How High Does It Go?" Post & Email, 3-2-17. https://www.thepostemail.com/2017/03/02/government-spying-high-go/.

258. See the entire one-hour official December 2016 press conference here: "WOW: Sheriff Joe Arpaio Releases New Information on President Obama's Birth Certificate (FNN)," Fox 10 Phoenix, YouTube, posted 12-15-16, https://www.youtube.com/watch?v=jk3KRxTfkLM.

259. A seven-minute synopsis video of the visual evidence of how the Obama certificate was digitally forged is available here: https://www.youtube.com/watch?v=8frqVINnQjc.

260. The two examination companies involved were: 1. *FORLAB Multimedia Forensics Laboratory* in Prato, Italy. https://www.forlab.org/en. 2. *Reed Hayes Handwriting and Document Examiner,* Honolulu, Hawaii. http://www.reedwrite.com.

261. Hayes, Reed. "Decision to Examine the Obama Certificate of Live Birth," Reed Hayes Handwriting and Document Examiner, 8-3-16, accessed June 25, 2019, http://www.reedwrite.com/index.php/2016/08/03/obama-birth-certificate.

262. The originally posted Obama PDF purporting to be a copy of his genuine birth certificate on file at the Hawaii Department of Health. Accessed June 26, 2019, https://obamawhitehouse.archives.gov/sites/default/files/rss_viewer/birth-certificate.pdf.

263. **Perkins Coie** is counsel of record for the Democratic National Committee, Democratic Leadership Council, the Democratic Senatorial Campaign Committee, and the Democratic Congressional Campaign Committee. Other political clients include nearly all Democratic members of the United States Congress. It has also represented several presidential campaigns, including those of John Kerry, Barack Obama, and Hillary Clinton. See: https://en.wikipedia.org/wiki/Perkins_Coie.

     While I am not accusing Perkins Coie Law Firm of any legal wrongdoing whatsoever, it is a matter of record that this law firm was directly involved in the delivery of the Obama "birth certificate" to the White House, as well as the legal handling of the Steele dossier. See below references for verification of these facts.

     See: *Washington Post*, "Clinton Campaign, DNC Paid for Research That Led to Russia Dossier," 10-24-17, https://www.washingtonpost.com/world/national-security/clinton-campaign-dnc-paid-for-research-that-led-to-russia-dossier/2017/10/24/226fabf0-b8e4-11e7-a908-a3470754bbb9_story.html?utm_term=.b60822b6ca91.

     See: *Legal Times*. "Perkins Coie Got Obama's Birth Certificate," 4-27-11, https://legaltimes.typepad.com/blt/2011/04/perkins-coie-judith-corley-got-obamas-birth-certificate.html.

     See: Canada Free Press, "President Trump and Perkins Coie," 10-27-17, https://canadafreepress.com/article/president-trump-and-perkins-coie.

264. *The Blog of Legal Times*, "Perkins Coie Got Obama's Birth Certificate," 4-27-2011, accessed June 25, 2019, https://legaltimes.typepad.com/blt/2011/04/perkins-coie-judith-corley-got-obamas-birth-certificate.html.

265. Admittedly, there were a few national "print media" outlets that covered the story, like the one by *USA Today* (see link below). However, that same piece, while talking *about* the "9 points of fraud" video, never showed that video or examined the actual demonstrated points of fraud. In that regard, the *USA Today* piece actually turns out to be a non-report.

     See: Cassidy, Megan. "Sheriff Joe Arpaio Renews Birther Claims about Obama's Birth Certificate," *USA Today*, 12-15-16, https://www.usatoday.com/story/news/nation-now/2016/12/15/sheriff-joe-arpaio-probe-proves-obama-birth-certificate-fake/95500958.

266. Hawaii News Now. "Hawaii Health Director Killed after Plane Crash Had Infant Life Vest," May 5, 2016, https://www.hawaiinewsnow.com/story/31899587/ntsb-no-safety-briefing-given-prior-to-2013-molokai-plane-crash-that-killed-hawaii-health-director.

267. Kissner, Jason. "Barack Hussein Soebarkah?" *American Thinker*, 1-22-14, https://www.americanthinker.com/articles/2014/01/barack_hussein_soebarkah.html.

268. Charles Creitz. "NY State Dem Chair: Trump 'Dirt' Comments 'Whole Different Scenario' than Clinton Campaign Using Steele Dossier," Fox News, June 13, 2019, https://www.foxnews.com/politics/trump-dirt-clinton-comments-different-tucker-carlson.

269. McCarthy, Andrew. "The Steele Dossier and the 'Verified Application' That Wasn't," The National Review, 5-18-19, https://www.nationalreview.com/2019/05/the-steele-dossier-and-the-verified-application-that-wasnt.

270. Solomon, John. "Collusion Bombshell: DNC Lawyers Met with FBI on Russia Allegations before Surveillance Warrant," The Hill, 10-3-2018, https://thehill.com/hilltv/rising/409817-russia-collusion-bombshell-dnc-lawyers-met-with-fbi-on-dossier-before.

271. Rondeau, Sharon. "Zullo on Obama Birth Certificate Retraction, 'Phony' Documents, Life Narrative," Post & Email, 12-24-17, https://www.thepostemail.com/2017/12/24/zullo-obama-birth-certificate-retraction-phony-documents-life-narrative.

272. Hutzler, Alexandra. "Republicans Claim John Brennan Was the 'Evil Force' behind the Intel's Use of Steele Dossier': They Tried to Bring Down a Sitting President." *Newsweek*, March 28, 2019, https://www.newsweek.com/rand-paul-steele-dossier-john-brennan-1378437.

273. Hanson, Victor Davis. "Victor Davis Hanson: Fear of a Deep State Coup Is Not Just Right-Wing Paranoia," Fox News, 11-21-19, https://www.foxnews.com/opinion/victor-davis-hanson-coup-concerns.

274. Ibid.

275. Albert Barnes, *Barnes Notes on the New Testament* (Grand Rapids, MI: Baker Book House, 1979), Corinthians, Introduction, IV, v.

276. https://en.wikipedia.org/wiki/The_Clinton_Chronicles.

277. Ibid.

278. https://en.wikipedia.org/wiki/Barry_Seal.

279. George Archibald, *Journalism Is War* (Crane, MO: Defender Publishing / HighWay, August 1, 2009), 189–192.

280. Ibid., 193.

281. https://www.aim.org/aim-column/something-stinks-the-fishy-vince-foster-case./

282. Archibald, *Journalism Is War*, 195–196.

283. https://www.politifact.com/texas/statements/2017/jul/05/pete-olson/pete-olson-said-bill-clinton-basically-told-lorett/.

284. https://www.washingtonpost.com/politics/trump-escalates-attack-on-bill-clinton/2016/05/23/ed109acc-2100-11e6-8690-f14ca9de2972_story.html.

285. https://www.businessinsider.com/laura-ingraham-lifezette-hillary-clinton-bill-2016-10.

286. Ibid.

287. https://dcdirtylaundry.com/ann-coulter-move-epstein-to-a-super-max-prison-before-he-is-suicided/.

288. https://en.wikipedia.org/wiki/William_E._Dannemeyer#Post-Congressional_activities.

289. https://www.wnd.com/2016/08/clinton-death-list-33-most-intriguing-cases/.

290. Ibid.

291. https://news.yahoo.com/exclusive-the-true-origins-of-the-seth-rich-conspiracy-a-yahoo-news-investigation-100000831.html.

292. https://washingtonmonthly.com/2019/07/09/did-russia-launch-the-seth-rich-conspiracy-theory/.

293. https://www.washingtonpost.com/news/powerpost/wp/2017/05/21/gingrich-spreads-conspiracy-theory-about-slain-dnc-staffer/.

294. https://www.coreysdigs.com/law-order/rudy-rico-and-clinton-inc-racketeering/.

295. https://www.wnd.com/2016/08/clinton-death-list-33-most-intriguing-cases/.

296. https://www.baltimoresun.com/news/bs-xpm-1998-03-09-1998068020-story.html.

297. https://dcdirtylaundry.com/media-blackout-detective-who-led-epstein-investigation-died-after-brief-illness-at-50/.

298. https://www.wnd.com/2016/08/clinton-death-list-33-most-intriguing-cases/.

299. https://www.thegatewaypundit.com/2019/09/second-kevin-spacey-accuser-dies-in-midst-of-assault-lawsuit-against-actor/.

300. https://dcdirtylaundry.com/meet-jessica-collins-self-described-epstein-victim-who-claims-she-was-forced-to-have-sex-with-joe-biden-and-john-mccain/.

301. https://en.wikipedia.org/wiki/Jeffrey_Epstein.

302. https://en.wikipedia.org/wiki/Jeffrey_Epstein#Investigation.

303. https://www.thenation.com/article/epstein-science-sex-abuse-eugenics/.

304. https://freebeacon.com/politics/waters-epstein-was-trumps-best-friend/.

305. https://www.nytimes.com/2019/07/09/us/politics/trump-epstein.html.

306. https://www.businessinsider.com/trump-epstein-had-falling-out-havent-spoken-in-15-years-2019-7.

307. https://www.motherjones.com/politics/2019/08/lynne-patton-hillary-bill-clinton-jeffrey-epstein-conspiracy-theory/.

308. https://twitter.com/Harlan/status/1160179279860129792?ref_src=twsrc%5Etfw%7Ctwcamp%5Etweetembed%7Ctwterm%5E116017927 9860129792&ref_url=https%3A%2F%2Fwww.washingtonexaminer. com%2Fnews%2Fthis-smells-very-fishy-skepticism-ensues-after-shocking-epstein-suicide-death.

309. https://twitter.com/RepAlGreen/status/1160230987621703681?ref_src =twsrc%5Etfw%7Ctwcamp%5Etweetembed%7Ctwterm%5E116 0230987621703681&ref_url=https%3A%2F%2Fwww.nbcnews. com%2Fpolitics%2Fpolitics-news%2Focasio-cortez-demands-answers-after-epstein-found-dead-apparent-suicide-n1041101.

310. https://www.yahoo.com/news/jeffrey-epstein-death-conspiracy-theories-163046929.html.

311. https://twitter.com/clairecmc/status/1160198456671162368.

312. http://www.rasmussenreports.com/public_content/politics/general_politics/august_2019/americans_say_murder_more_likely_than_suicide_in_epstein_case.

313. https://www.cnn.com/2019/08/16/us/jeffrey-epstein-autopsy/index.html.

314. https://talkingpointsmemo.com/news/epstein-lawyers-we-are-not-satisfied-with-the-conclusions-of-the-medical-examiner.

315. https://www.foxnews.com/media/jeffrey-epstein-suicide-homicide-suspicious.

316. https://www.usatoday.com/story/news/health/2019/08/15/mystery-surrounds-hyoid-break-epstein-death-suicide-murder/2017579001/.

317. Ibid.

318. https://www.thegatewaypundit.com/2019/08/boom-dr-mark-siegel-jeffrey-epstein-suffered-hemorrhaging-in-the-throat-a-sign-of-homicide-video/.

319. https://www.wnd.com/2019/08/chief-of-doctors-group-doubts-epstein-autopsy/.

320. https://nypost.com/2019/10/30/famed-pathologist-michael-baden-says-jeffrey-epsteins-death-was-homicide/.

321. https://thehill.com/blogs/blog-briefing-room/news/468445-de-blasio-questions-details-surrounding-jeffrey-epsteins-death.

322. https://www.dailymail.co.uk/news/article-7784529/Virginia-Roberts-claims-FBI-warned-credible-death-threat-against-her.html.

323. https://www.dailymail.co.uk/news/article-7779829/Virginia-Roberts-posts-chilling-Twitter-message-claiming-Im-not-suicidal.html.

324. https://nypost.com/2019/08/20/jail-guards-threatening-former-epstein-cell-mate-nicholas-tartaglione-lawyer/.

325. https://thehill.com/homenews/news/458922-video-from-camera-outside-epstein-jail-cell-unusable-report.

326. https://www.thegatewaypundit.com/2019/08/here-it-is-complete-list-of-inconsistencies-in-prison-policy-surrounding-jeffrey-epsteins-death/.

327. https://consortiumnews.com/2019/08/12/how-holmes-would-work-the-epstein-case/.

328. https://www.salon.com/2019/08/18/qanon-is-the-conspiracy-theory-that-wont-die-heres-what-they-believe-and-why-theyre-wrong/.

329. https://www.thedailybeast.com/jeffrey-epstein-unsealed-documents-name-powerful-men-in-sex-ring.

330. https://www.collective-evolution.com/2019/09/19/another-alleged-epstein-prince-andrew-victim-comes-forward-implicating-joe-biden-many-others/.

331. http://nymag.com/intelligencer/2019/07/does-the-jeffrey-epstein-indictment-qanon.html.

332. https://www.washingtonpost.com/news/morning-mix/wp/2018/08/01/
we-are-q-a-deranged-conspiracy-cult-leaps-from-the-internet-to-the-crowd-
at-trumps-maga-tour/.

333. https://www.nytimes.com/2018/08/01/us/politics/what-is-qanon.html.

334. https://www.yahoo.com/news/federal-records-hastert-released-prison-
minnesota-125049060.html.

335. http://www.npr.org/sections/thetwo-way/2017/03/26/521545788/
conspiracy-theorist-alex-jones-apologizes-for-promoting-pizzagate.

336. https://www.theepochtimes.com/top-fbi-official-made-crimes-against-
children-note-in-connection-to-weiners-devices_2568226.html.

337. https://www.lifesitenews.com/opinion/drag-queens-
who-want-access-to-your-children-linked-to-
satanism-occult-practices?utm_source=LifeSiteNews.
com&utm_campaign=43182cc1e8-Daily%2520Headlines%2520-
%2520U.S._COPY_619&utm_medium=email&utm_
term=0_12387f0e3e-43.

338. https://dcdirtylaundry.com/investigative-journalist-jen-moore-found-dead-
1-week-after-interview-of-bill-clinton-rape-victim-reporting-to-fbi-doj/.

339. https://bigleaguepolitics.com/revealed-fbi-documents-suggest-link-between-
satanic-finders-cult-and-cia-investigation-cover-up/.

340. https://www.naturalnews.com/2019-11-13-federal-intelligence-agencies-
covered-up-child-sex-cult.html.

341. https://en.wikipedia.org/wiki/
Deborah_Jeane_Palfrey#Speculation_surrounding_her_death.

342. https://www.washingtonpost.com/video/politics/trump-promises-to-
solve-human-trafficking-epidemic-in-white-house-meeting/2017/02/23/
e6baf42e-fa08-11e6-aa1e-5f735ee31334_video.html.

343. http://thefreethoughtproject.com/
fmr-congresswoman-child-trafficking-trump-top/.

344. https://www.yahoo.com/news/blogs/upshot/pentagon-declined-investigate-
hundreds-purchases-child-pornography.html.

345. https://thehill.com/policy/cybersecurity/451383-house-bill-aims-to-stop-
use-of-pentagon-networks-for-sharing-child.

346. https://thedcpatriot.com/were-two-former-gop-senators-investigating-child-
trafficking-when-murdered/.

347. Ibid.
348. https://www.globalresearch.ca/heres-what-happened-when-journalist-exposed-pedo-sex-ring-mexico/5684900.
349. Ibid.
350. https://thefreethoughtproject.com/cps-worker-defies-gag-order-exposes-horrifying-violent-child-sex-ring-in-foster-system/.
351. https://www.coreysdigs.com/learn-how-to/dissecting-criminal-nests-webs/.
352. https://en.wikipedia.org/wiki/America%27s_Next_Top_Model.
353. https://www.dailymail.co.uk/news/article-7371693/Jean-Luc-Brunel-gave-Jeffrey-Epstein-three-poor-12-year-old-triplets-France-birthday-present.html.
354. https://www.youtube.com/watch?v=PUSAg66nwEw.
355. https://www.usatoday.com/story/opinion/nation-now/2018/01/30/sex-trafficking-column/1073459001/.
356. https://www.newsweek.com/eyes-wide-shut-missing-footage-epstein-kubrick-death-1449108.
357. https://www.mintpressnews.com/blackmail-jeffrey-epstein-trump-mentor-reagan-era/260760/.
358. https://www.mintpressnews.com/blackmail-jeffrey-epstein-trump-mentor-reagan-era/260760/.
359. https://bigleaguepolitics.com/crime-boss-closing-arguments-in-nxivm-trial-satanism-mexico-child-trafficking-hillary-schumer-and-gillibrand-ties/.
360. Foster Bailey, *The Spirit of Freemasonry* (New York: Lucis Press, 1957).
361. Pike, 89–90.
362. https://www.insider.com/jeffrey-epstein-private-island-temple-2019-7
363. https://vigilantcitizen.com/latestnews/burying-tunnels-epstein-delivered-100000-of-cement-delivered-to-his-island-before-his-arrest/.
364. https://vigilantcitizen.com/latestnews/jeffrey-epstein-the-true-ugly-face-of-the-occult-elite/.
365. Ibid.
366. http://www.masonicdictionary.com/ketstone.html.
367. Euripides, *The Bacchantes*, Dramatis Personare (Messenger to Pentheus concerning the Bacchantes), 410 BC.
368. Thomas Horn, *Zenith 2016*, (Crane, MO: Defender Publishing, 2013), 182–186

369. https://www.theosociety.org/pasadena/edge-uml/edge-uml.htm.

370. https://en.wikipedia.org/wiki/Watchtower_(magic).

371. Manly P. Hall, *Secret Destiny of America* (Penguin Group, 2008), chapter 18.

372. See: http://en.wikipedia.org/wiki/Hermetic_Order_of_the_Golden_Dawn.

373. See: http://en.wikipedia.org/wiki/Ars_Goetia#Ars_Goetia.

374. See: *http://www.redmoonrising.com/Giza/DomDec6.htm.*

375. Manly P Hall, *The Secret Teachings of All Ages*, 623–633.

376. http://john80202.tripod.com/FMASONRY/SACRIFIC.HTM.

377. http://www.sacred-texts.com/oto/aba/chap12.htm.

378. http://john80202.tripod.com/FMASONRY/SACRIFIC.HTM.

379. https://books.google.com/books?id=xMBb2hyRCUAC&pg=PA31
9&lpg=PA319&dq=In+the+East,+they+are+known+as+the+%E2
%80%98Brothers+of+the+Shadow,%E2%80%99&source=bl&ots
=yT__aXDYSa&sig=ACfU3U0H-3rLF-#v=onepage&q&f=false.

380. https://www.bioedge.org/bioethics/
the-bizarre-transhumanist-fantasies-of-jeffrey-epstein/13158.

381. Email exchange between Dr. Judd Burton and Thomas Horn, August 27,
2019.

382 Orkneyjar, *The Odin Stone.*

383. They were built between 5,400 and 4,500 years ago; http://www.historic-
scotland.gov.uk/propertyresults/propertydetail.htm?PropID=PL_280.

384. "The 9,000-Year-Old Underground Megalithic Settlement of Atlit Yam,"
Ancient Origins, http://www.ancient-origins.net/ancient-places-asia/9000-
year-old-underground-megalithic-settlement-atlit-yam-001579.

385. Yuval Ne'eman, "Astronomy in Israel: From Og's Circle to the Wise
Observatory," *Cataclysmic Variables and Related Objects, Astrophysics and
Space Science Library,* Volume 101, 1983, 323–329.

386. Michael Heiser, "The Nephilim," http://sitchiniswrong.com/nephilim/
nephilim.htm (accessed December 31, 2014).

387. Howard Schwartz, *Tree of Souls: The Mythology of Judaism* (Oxford: Oxford
University, 2004) 461. google books link here.

388. "Solving the Mystery of a Megalithic Monument in the Land of
Giants," http://popular-archaeology.com/issue/september-2011/article/
solving-the-mystery-of-a-megalithic-monument-in-the-land-of-giants.

389. Barry Chamish, "Did Biblical Giants Build the Circle of the Refaim?" http://www.ccg.org/Creation%20Articles/Circle%20of%20the%20Refaim.htm (accessed February 28, 2015).

390. Barry Chamish, "Did Biblical Giants Build the Circle of the Refaim?" http://www.ccg.org/Creation%20Articles/Circle%20of%20the%20Refaim.htm (accessed February 28, 2015).

391. David Rapp, "In the Wildcat's Pile of Stones: Rujm al-Hiri in the Golan Heights is not a burial ground around which a monumental site was erected, but rather a monumental site in which there is a burial ground," *Haaretz*, May 2, 2003, http://www.haaretz.com/life/arts-leisure/in-the-wildcat-s-pile-of-stones-1.11251 (accessed September 29, 2014 and February 19, 2015).

392. Ibid.

393. Wolfgang Rölling in "Eine neue phoenizische Inschrift aus Byblos" (Neue Ephemeris für Semitische Epigraphik, vol 2, 1–15 and plate 1) 1974, http://archiv.ub.uni-heidelberg.de/propylaeumdok/1101/.

394. 7496 rapha in *New American Standard Hebrew-Aramaic and Greek Dictionaries,* ed. Robert L. Thomas, (Anaheim: Foundation Publications, 1998).

395. "Necromancy" in *Encyclopedia of Occultism and Parapsychology*, 5th edition, editor J Gordon Melton (Detroit: Gale Group, 2001) 1096.

396. Francis Barrett, *The Magus or Celestial Intelligencer Book II, Part II, The Cabala; or The Secret Mysteries of Ceremonial Magic* (London: Lackington, Alley, and Co: 1801) 69. http://www.sacred-texts.com/grim/magus/ma231.htm.

397. Judd Burton, *Interview With the Giant*, http://www.lulu.com/us/en/shop/judd-burton/interview-with-the-giant/paperback/product-5943477.html, 80.

398. https://www.history.com/news/aztec-human-sacrifice-religion.

399. https://en.wikipedia.org/wiki/Aztec_sun_stone.

400. William Henry and Mark Gray, *Freedom's Gate: Lost Symbols in the U.S.* (Hendersonville, TN: Scala Dei, 2009), 3.

401. Ibid., 4.

402. Thomas Horn, *Apollyon Rising*, (Crane, MO: Defender Publishing, 2009), 289–290.

403 http://en.wikipedia.org/wiki/Sacrifice_in_Maya_culture.

404. http://discoverplaces.travel/journal/
the-mysterious-christ-in-the-labyrinth-of-alatri/.

405. https://en.wikipedia.org/wiki/Sacrificial_victims_of_Minotaur.

406. https://www.breitbart.com/crime/2019/09/02/modeling-agent-alleged-to-
have-dirt-on-jeffrey-epstein-vanishes-like-a-ghost/.

407. https://nypost.com/2019/08/10/
meet-jeffrey-epsteins-gang-of-accused-slave-recruiters/.

408. http://archive.is/k28Cy.

409. https://news.yahoo.com/jeffrey-epstein-accuser-blames-
victorias-200447195.html.

410. https://nypost.com/2019/10/16/ghislaine-maxwell-hiding-out-in-brazil-
with-jeffrey-epsteins-modeling-scout-report/.

411. https://www.thetimes.co.uk/article/ghislaine-maxwell-facing-charges-as-net-
closes-in-on-jeffrey-epsteins-friends-sx62wvjx8.

412. John Greer, *The New Encyclopedia of the Occult*, 9781567183368.

413. Hugh B. Urban, *Magia Sexualis: Sex, Magic, and Liberation in Modern
Western Esotericism* (Berkeley, CA: University of California Press, 2006)
135–37.

414. George Pendle, *Strange Angel: The Otherworldly Life of Rocket Scientist John
Whiteside Parsons*, 266.

415. Hillary Rodham Clinton (October 26, 1947), a potential 2016 presidential
candidate, https://www.readyforhillary.com/splash/hillary.

416. http://www.sacred-texts.com/oto/lib49.htm.

417. https://en.wikipedia.org/wiki/Hilary_(name).

418. https://www.nytimes.com/2016/05/11/us/politics/hillary-clinton-aliens.
html.

419. https://wikileaks.org/podesta-emails/emailid/1802.

420. https://en.wikipedia.org/wiki/Xenu.

421. Thomas Horn, *Saboteurs*, (Crane, MO, Defender Publishing, 2018),
143–147.

422. https://thepoliticalinsider.com/steve-bannon-hillary-clinton-is-going-to-run-
again-in-2020/?source=WayneDupree.

423. https://www.frontpagemag.com/fpm/274525/
marianne-williamson-reveals-democrats-are-cult-daniel-greenfield.

424. https://www.youtube.com/watch?v=SS7uSmG-R34.

425. https://www.frontpagemag.com/fpm/274525/
marianne-williamson-reveals-democrats-are-cult-daniel-greenfield.

426. https://dcdirtylaundry.com/
hillary-clinton-could-a-satan-worshipper-really-become-president/.

427. Derek Gilbert, Josh Peck, *The Day the Earth Stands Still*, (Crane, MO:
Defender Publishing, January 2018), 93–95.

428. Ibid., 81–86.

429. https://www.sott.net/article/334002-Progressive-liberal-values-Tony-
Podestas-creepy-taste-in-art-the-creepy-people-he-hangs-out-with-and-
Pizzagate.

430. Email exchange between Dr. Judd Burton and Thomas Horn, August 27,
2019.

431. https://www.nytimes.com/2019/07/31/business/jeffrey-epstein-eugenics.
html.

432. https://dcdirtylaundry.com/
bill-gates-worked-with-jeffrey-epstein-to-funnel-2-million-to-mit/.

433. Nick Bostrom, "Transhumanist Values," www.nickbostrom.com.

434. "Facing the Challenges of Transhumanism: Religion, Science, Technology,"
Arizona State University, http://transhumanism.asu.edu/.

435. http://lach.web.arizona.edu/Sophia/.

436. https://www.sacred-texts.com/eso/sta/sta24.htm.

437. https://www.sacred-texts.com/eso/sta/sta24.htm.

438. "About," *Luma Festival*, last accessed October 4, 2019, https://lumafestival.
com/about/.

439. "Bart Kresa Mapping 5-Metre Tall Projection Sculpture, Sviatovid," a
YouTube video, uploaded by blooloop on July 3, 2019, last accessed
October 4, 2019, https://www.youtube.com/watch?v=_z0SoNC7kKs.

440. See Kresa's personal apology to the head pastor of the church in the
conversation they had in the comments section under the Facebook
rebuttal, posted by Reverend Kimberly Chastain on September 13, at 3:39
in the afternoon, on the "United Presbyterian Church of Binghamton"
account, last accessed October 4, 2019, https://www.facebook.com/
UPCBinghamton/posts/1387642211411481.

441. Tyler O'Neil, "Liberal Pro-LGBT Church Hosts Pagan Idol in Art Exhibit,"
September 13, 2019, *PJ [Political Justice] Media*, last accessed October 4,

2019, https://pjmedia.com/faith/liberal-pro-lgbt-church-hosts-pagan-idol-in-art-exhibit/; emphasis added.

442. "About BKS," *Bart Kresa*, last accessed October 7, 2019, https://www.bartkresa.com/.

443. Beasley-Murray, G. R. 1994. Revelation. In D. A. Carson, R. T. France, J. A. Motyer, & G. J. Wenham (Eds.), *New Bible commentary: 21st century edition* (4th ed., p. 1429). Leicester, England; Downers Grove, IL: Inter-Varsity Press.

444. Beale, G. K., & Campbell, D. H, *Revelation: A Shorter Commentary,* (Grand Rapids, MI; Cambridge, U.K.: William B. Eerdmans Publishing Company, 2015), 282; emphasis added.

445. Miller, S. R. "Abomination, Abomination of Desolation," in C. Brand, C. Draper, A. England, S. Bond, E. R. Clendenen, & T. C. Butler (Eds.), *Holman Illustrated Bible Dictionary* (Nashville, TN: Holman Bible Publishers, 2003), 10.

446. Wenham, D. "Abomination of Desolation." In D. N. Freedman (Ed.), *The Anchor Yale Bible Dictionary.* (New York: Doubleday, 1992), vol. 1, p. 29).

447. Miller, S. R. *Holman Illustrated.*

448. Rosner, B. S. 2000. "Idolatry," in T. D. Alexander & B. S. Rosner (Eds.), *New Dictionary of Biblical Theology* (electronic ed., p. 570). (Downers Grove, IL: InterVarsity Press) emphasis added.

449. Aden, Josiah, "New York Presbyterian Church Hosts Pagan Deity," September 12, 2019, *Juicy Ecumenism,* last accessed October 10, 2019, https://juicyecumenism.com/2019/09/12/binghamton-presbyterian-sviatovid/.

450. Kimberly Chastain, in an untitled, public response to Josiah Aden's article over the United Presbyterian Church of Binghamton Facebook account on September 13, 2019, at 5:38 in the evening. Last accessed October 10, 2019, https://www.facebook.com/UPCBinghamton/posts/1387642211411481.

451. "Our Beliefs," United Presbyterian Church of Binghamton home site, last accessed October 10, 2019, http://upcbgm.org/get-to-know-us/our-beliefs.

452. Dr. Michael Heiser, in the foreword to: Josh Peck and Steven Bancarz, *The Second Coming of the New Age: The Hidden Dangers of Alternative Spirituality*

in Contemporary America and its Churches (Crane, MO: Defender Publishing, 2018), x.

453. Ibid.

454. "Our Cards Lead the Way…" *ChristAlignment*, last accessed October 16, 2019, https://www.christalignment.org/destinyreadingcards; emphasis added.

455. In a letter of defense written by Jenny Hodge of Christ Alignment to Bethel Church in Redding, CA; as quoted by: Anugrah Kumar, "Bethel Church Responds to 'Christian Tarot Cards' Controversy," January 06, 2018, *Christian Post*, last accessed October 16, 2019, https://www.christianpost.com/news/bethel-church-responds-christian-tarot-cards-controversy.html.

456. "Our Cards Lead the Way…" *ChristAlignment*, last accessed October 16, 2019, https://www.christalignment.org/destinyreadingcards.

457. Nichols, L. A., Mather, G. A., & Schmidt, A. J., *Encyclopedic Dictionary of Cults, Sects, and World Religions* (Grand Rapids, MI: Zondervan; 2006), 283.

458. Ibid, 256.

459. Ibid.

460. Bill Ellis, *Raising the Devil: Satanism, New Religions, and the Media* (University Press of Kentucky, 2000), 65.

461. By typing "churches taking down crosses" or some equivalent into any online search engine, readers will see hundreds of stories on this topic, however, as merely one example, see: Robert Spencer, "Canada: Church Takes Cross Off Wall to Avoid Offending Muslims," December 26, 2018, *Jihad Watch*, last accessed September 26, 2019, https://www.jihadwatch.org/2018/12/canada-church-takes-cross-off-wall-to-avoid-offending-muslims.

462. "The Global Ruling Class," *The Economist* (April 24, 2008) (http://www.economist.com/books/displaystory.cfm?story_id=11081878).

463. Stanley Monteith, "The Occult Hierarchy: Part 1" *Radio Liberty* (May 2005) (http://www.radioliberty.com/nlmay05.html).

464. https://www.youtube.com/watch?v=tmC3IevZiik.

465. See (http://uk.youtube.com/watch?v=LXcvbnzNIjg&feature=related).

466. Zaitz, Les. "25 years after Rajneeshee Commune Collapsed, Truth Spills Out—Part 1 of 5." *OregonLive*. Accessed August 27, 2019. https://www.oregonlive.com/rajneesh/2011/04/part_one_it_was_worse_than_we.html.

467. Ibid.

468. Ibid.

469. Smithsonian Channel. "How the Rajneesh Cult Overran This Oregon Town." April 6, 2018. YouTube Video, 1:28. Accessed August 27, 2019. https://www.youtube.com/watch?v=u6KX-d03SHA.

470. Way, Maclain & Way, Chapman. *Wild, Wild Country, Episode 1.* United States: Duplass Brothers Productions, 2018. Accessed through www.netflix.com by membership. 64 Minutes.

471. Ibid.

472. Knudsen, Fredrik, "Rashneeshpuram: Down the Rabbit Hole." January 23, 2018. YouTube Video, 39:15. Accessed August 28, 2019. https://www.youtube.com/watch?v=Gwx9nqknu-c.

473. Herzog, Kenny. "Every Question That *Wild Wild Country* Didn't Answer." *Vulture.* Accessed August 27, 2019. https://www.vulture.com/2018/03/wild-wild-country-bhagwan-rajneesh-questions.html.

474. Sarasohn, David. "Antelope's Last Stand." *The New Republic.* April 12, 2018. Accessed August 27, 2019. https://newrepublic.com/article/147876/antelopes-last-stand.

475. Knudsen, Fredrik, "Rashneeshpuram: Down the Rabbit Hole." January 23, 2018. YouTube Video, 39:15. Accessed August 28, 2019. https://www.youtube.com/watch?v=Gwx9nqknu-c.

476. Zaitz, Les. "25 Years after Rajneeshee Commune Collapsed, Truth Spills Out—Part 1 of 5." *OregonLive.* Accessed August 27, 2019. https://www.oregonlive.com/rajneesh/2011/04/part_one_it_was_worse_than_we.html.

477. Ibid.

478. Little W***e Records. "Rajneesh Cult Exposed A.K.A. the Disco Sex Guru (Weird rituals) PT 3/4." April 16, 2016. YouTube Video: 14:59. Accessed August 30, 2019. https://www.youtube.com/watch?v=vLUen-1zyQE.

479. Way, Maclain & Way, Chapman. *Wild, Wild Country, Episode 2.* United States: Duplass Brothers Productions, 2018. Accessed through www.netflix.com by membership. 64 Minutes.

480. Zaitz, Les. "25 Years after Rajneeshee Commune Collapsed, truth Spills Out—Part 1 of 5." *OregonLive.* Accessed August 27, 2019. https://www.oregonlive.com/rajneesh/2011/04/part_one_it_was_worse_than_we.html.

481. Ibid.

482. Way, Maclain & Way, Chapman. *Wild, Wild Country, Episode 2.* United States: Duplass Brothers Productions, 2018. Accessed through www.netflix.com by membership. 64 Minutes.

483. Ibid.

484. Ibid.

485. McCormack, Win. "Outside the Limits of the Human Imagination: What the new documentary 'Wild, Wild Country' doesn't capture about the magnetism and evil of the Rajneesh cult." *The New Republic.* March 27, 2018. Accessed August 27, 2019. https://newrepublic.com/article/147657/outside-limits-human-imagination.

486. Ibid.

487. Way, Maclain & Way, Chapman. *Wild, Wild Country, Episode 2.* United States: Duplass Brothers Productions, 2018. Accessed through www.netflix.com by membership. 64 Minutes.

488. Pace, Eric. "Baghwan Shree Rajneesh, Indian Guru, Dies at 58." *The New York Times.* January 20, 1990. Accessed August 29, 2019. https://www.nytimes.com/1990/01/20/obituaries/baghwan-shree-rajneesh-indian-guru-dies-at-58.html.

489. Knudsen, Fredrik, "Rashneeshpuram: Down the Rabbit Hole." January 23, 2018. YouTube Video, 39:15. Accessed August 28, 2019. https://www.youtube.com/watch?v=Gwx9nqknu-c.

490. Way, Maclain & Way, Chapman. *Wild, Wild Country, Episode 1.* United States: Duplass Brothers Productions, 2018. Accessed through www.netflix.com by membership. 64 Minutes.

491. Little W***e Records. "Rajneesh Cult exposed A.K.A. the Disco Sex Guru (Weird rituals) PT 1/4." April 16, 2016. YouTube Video: 14:54. Accessed August 30, 2019. https://www.youtube.com/watch?v=mWh2brWKA-I.

492. Little W***e Records. "Rajneesh Cult exposed A.K.A. the Disco Sex Guru (Weird rituals) PT 4/4." April 16, 2016. YouTube Video: 14:53. Accessed August 30, 2019. https://www.youtube.com/watch?v=mWh2brWKA-I.

493. Way, Maclain & Way, Chapman. *Wild, Wild Country, Episode 2.* United States: Duplass Brothers Productions, 2018. Accessed through www.netflix.com by membership. 64 Minutes.

494. Kennedy, Lesley. "Inside Jonestown: How Jim Jones Trapped Followers and Forced 'Suicides.'" *History.com.* November 13,

2018. Accessed August 27, 2019. https://www.history.com/news/jonestown-jim-jones-mass-murder-suicide.

495.   Maslin, Janet. "Film: Life at an Ashram, Search for Inner Peace." *The New York Times* (New York, NY), November 13, 1981, Section C, Page 9. As accessed at https://www.nytimes.com/1981/11/13/movies/life-at-an-ashram-search-for-inner-peace.html. Accessed August 27, 2019.

496.   Little W***e Records. "Rajneesh Cult exposed A.K.A. the Disco Sex Guru (Weird rituals) PT 1/4." April 16, 2016. YouTube Video: 14:54. Accessed August 30, 2019. https://www.youtube.com/watch?v=mWh2brWKA-I.

497.   Ibid.

498.   Herzog, Kenny. "Every Question That *Wild Wild Country* Didn't Answer." *Vulture*. Accessed August 27, 2019. https://www.vulture.com/2018/03/wild-wild-country-bhagwan-rajneesh-questions.html.

499.   Sarasohn, David. "Antelope's Last Stand." *The New Republic*. April 12, 2018. Accessed August 27, 2019. https://newrepublic.com/article/147876/antelopes-last-stand.

500.   Ibid.

501.   Little W***e Records. "Rajneesh Cult exposed A.K.A. the Disco Sex Guru (Weird rituals) PT 4/4." April 16, 2016. YouTube Video: 14:53. Accessed August 30, 2019. https://www.youtube.com/watch?v=mWh2brWKA-I.

502.   Sarasohn, David. "Antelope's Last Stand." *The New Republic*. April 12, 2018. Accessed August 27, 2019. https://newrepublic.com/article/147876/antelopes-last-stand.

503.   Ibid.

504.   Way, Maclain & Way, Chapman. *Wild, Wild Country, Episode 2.* United States: Duplass Brothers Productions, 2018. Accessed through www.netflix.com by membership. 64 Minutes.

505.   "Town May Abolish Itself to Bar Sect's Takeover." *New York Times*. March 12, 1982. As accessed at https://www.nytimes.com/1982/03/12/us/town-may-abolish-itself-to-bar-sect-s-takeover.html. Accessed august 27, 2019.

506.   Sarasohn, David. "Antelope's Last Stand." *New Republic*. April 12, 2018. Accessed August 27, 2019. https://newrepublic.com/article/147876/antelopes-last-stand.

507.   Perry, Douglas. "Rajneeshees Embraced Portland, Opening Wild Nightclub, Hotel That Became Bomber's Target." *Oregon Live Online*. March 28,

2018. Accessed August 28, 2019. https://expo.oregonlive.com/erry-2018/03/3356fec09a/rajneeshees_embraced_portland.html.

508. Little W***e Records. "Rajneesh Cult exposed A.K.A. the Disco Sex Guru (Weird rituals) PT 2/4." April 16, 2016. YouTube Video: 14:54. Accessed August 30, 2019. https://www.youtube.com/watch?v=mWh2brWKA-I.

509. Peters, Andrea. "'Wild Wild Country' Review." *The Boar*. June 21, 2018. Accessed August 28, 2019. https://theboar.org/2018/06/wild-wild-country-review/.

510. Bains, Grace. "12 Quotes by Ma Anand Sheela That Prove She Puts the 'Wild' In Wild Wild Country." *India Times Online*. April 5, 2018. Accessed August 28, 2019. https://www.indiatimes.com/lifestyle/12-quotes-by-ma-anand-sheela-that-prove-she-puts-the-wild-in-wild-wild-country-342883.html.

511. Way, Maclain & Way, Chapman. *Wild, Wild Country, Episode 3*. United States: Duplass Brothers Productions, 2018. Accessed through www.netflix.com by membership. 64 Minutes.

512. Ibid.

513. Ibid.

514. Ibid.

515. Ibid.

516. Ibid.

517. Ibid.

518. Ibid.

519. Ibid.

520. Ibid.

521. Ibid.

522. "Limit on Voters by Oregon County Is Upheld." *New York Times*. October 23, 1984. Accessed August 28, 2019. https://www.nytimes.com/1984/10/23/us/limit-on-voters-by-oregon-county-is-upheld.html.

523. Knudsen, Fredrik, "Rashneeshpuram: Down the Rabbit Hole." January 23, 2018. YouTube Video, 39:15. Accessed August 28, 2019. https://www.youtube.com/watch?v=Gwx9nqknu-c.

524. "Limit on Voters bby Oregon County Is Upheld." *New York Times*. October 23, 1984. Accessed August 28, 2019. https://www.nytimes.com/1984/10/23/us/limit-on-voters-by-oregon-county-is-upheld.html.

525. Ibid.

526. Ibid.

527. Way, Maclain & Way, Chapman. *Wild, Wild Country, Episode 3.* United States: Duplass Brothers Productions, 2018. Accessed through www.netflix.com by membership. 64 Minutes.

528. Knudsen, Fredrik, "Rashneeshpuram: Down the Rabbit Hole." January 23, 2018. YouTube Video, 39:15. Accessed August 28, 2019. https://www.youtube.com/watch?v=Gwx9nqknu-c.

529. Zaitz, Les. "25 Years after Rajneeshee Commune Collapsed, Truth Spills Out—Part 1 of 5." *OregonLive.* Accessed August 27, 2019. https://www.oregonlive.com/rajneesh/2011/04/part_one_it_was_worse_than_we.html.

530. Way, Maclain & Way, Chapman. *Wild, Wild Country, Episode 4.* United States: Duplass Brothers Productions, 2018. Accessed through www.netflix.com by membership. 64 Minutes.

531. Ibid.

532. Ibid.

533. Ibid.

534. Ibid.

535. Ibid.

536. Ibid.

537. Way, Maclain & Way, Chapman. *Wild, Wild Country, Episode 5.* United States: Duplass Brothers Productions, 2018. Accessed through www.netflix.com by membership. 64 Minutes.

538. "2 From Oregon Commune Convicted in Murder Plot." *LA Times.* July 29, 1995. Accessed August 29, 2019. https://www.latimes.com/archives/la-xpm-1995-07-29-mn-29091-story.html.

539. Way, Maclain & Way, Chapman. *Wild, Wild Country, Episode 5.* United States: Duplass Brothers Productions, 2018. Accessed through www.netflix.com by membership. 64 Minutes.

540. Ibid.

541. Ibid.

542. Ibid.

543. Ibid.

544. Ibid.

545. Ibid.

546. Ibid.

547. Ibid.

548. Pace, Eric. "Baghwan Shree Rajneesh, Indian Guru, Dies at 58." *The New York Times*. January 20, 1990. Accessed August 29, 2019. https://www.nytimes.com/1990/01/20/obituaries/baghwan-shree-rajneesh-indian-guru-dies-at-58.html.

549. Way, Maclain & Way, Chapman. *Wild, Wild Country, Episode 5*. United States: Duplass Brothers Productions, 2018. Accessed through www.netflix.com by membership. 64 Minutes.

550. Pace, Eric. "Baghwan Shree Rajneesh, Indian Guru, Dies at 58." *The New York Times*. January 20, 1990. Accessed August 29, 2019. https://www.nytimes.com/1990/01/20/obituaries/baghwan-shree-rajneesh-indian-guru-dies-at-58.html.

551. FitzGerald, France. "II-Rajneeshpuram." *The Chicago Tribune*. September 21, 1986. Accessed August 29, 2019. https://www.newyorker.com/magazine/1986/09/29/ii-rajneeshpuram.

552. Pace, Eric. "Baghwan Shree Rajneesh, Indian Guru, Dies at 58." *The New York Times*. January 20, 1990. Accessed August 29, 2019. https://www.nytimes.com/1990/01/20/obituaries/baghwan-shree-rajneesh-indian-guru-dies-at-58.html.

553. Gajanan, Mahita. "The Rajneeshpuram Commune from Netflix's *Wild Wild Country* Is Now a Young Life Christian Youth Camp." April 6, 2018. Accessed August 29, 2019. https://time.com/5230714/wild-wild-country-netflix-commune-camp/.

554. Little W***e Records. "Rajneesh Cult Exposed A.K.A. the Disco Sex Guru (Weird rituals) PT 3/4." April 16, 2016. YouTube Video: 14:59. Accessed August 30, 2019. https://www.youtube.com/watch?v=vLUen-1zyQE.

555. Little W***e Records. "Rajneesh Cult exposed A.K.A. the Disco Sex Guru (Weird rituals) PT 4/4." April 16, 2016. YouTube Video: 14:53. Accessed August 30, 2019. https://www.youtube.com/watch?v=mWh2brWKA-I.

556. Maslin, Janet. "Film: Life at an Ashram, Search for Inner Peace." *The New York Times* (New York, NY), November 13, 1981, Section C, Page 9. As accessed at https://www.nytimes.com/1981/11/13/movies/life-at-an-ashram-search-for-inner-peace.html. Accessed August 27, 2019.

557. Ibid.

558. Little W***e Records. "Rajneesh Cult Exposed A.K.A. the Disco Sex Guru (Weird rituals) PT 2/4." April 16, 2016. YouTube Video: 14:54. Accessed August 30, 2019. https://www.youtube.com/watch?v=mWh2brWKA-I.

559. Little W***e Records. "Rajneesh Cult exposed A.K.A. the Disco Sex Guru (Weird rituals) PT 1/4." April 16, 2016. YouTube Video: 14:54. Accessed August 30, 2019. https://www.youtube.com/watch?v=mWh2brWKA-I.

560. Ibid.

561. Little W***e Records. "Rajneesh Cult exposed A.K.A. the Disco Sex Guru (Weird rituals) PT 2/4." April 16, 2016. YouTube Video: 14:54. Accessed August 30, 2019. https://www.youtube.com/watch?v=mWh2brWKA-I.

562. Little W***e Records. "Rajneesh Cult exposed A.K.A. the Disco Sex Guru (Weird rituals) PT 3/4." April 16, 2016. YouTube Video: 14:59. Accessed August 30, 2019. https://www.youtube.com/watch?v=vLUen-1zyQE.

563. Little W***e Records. "Rajneesh Cult exposed A.K.A. the Disco Sex Guru (Weird rituals) PT 2/4." April 16, 2016. YouTube Video: 14:54. Accessed August 30, 2019. https://www.youtube.com/watch?v=mWh2brWKA-I.

564. Herzog, Kenny. "Every Question That Wild Wild Country Didn't Answer." Vulture. Accessed August 27, 2019. https://www.vulture.com/2018/03/wild-wild-country-bhagwan-rajneesh-questions.html.

565. Little W***e Records. "Rajneesh Cult exposed A.K.A. the Disco Sex Guru (Weird rituals) PT 4/4." April 16, 2016. YouTube Video: 14:53. Accessed August 30, 2019. https://www.youtube.com/watch?v=mWh2brWKA-I.

566. Little W***e Records. "Rajneesh Cult exposed A.K.A. the Disco Sex Guru (Weird rituals) PT 2/4." April 16, 2016. YouTube Video: 14:54. Accessed August 30, 2019. https://www.youtube.com/watch?v=mWh2brWKA-I.

567. Gajanan, Mahita. "The Rajneeshpuram Commune from Netflix's Wild Wild Country Is Now a Young Life Christian Youth Camp." April 6, 2018. Accessed August 29, 2019. https://time.com/5230714/wild-wild-country-netflix-commune-camp/.

568. https://www.azquotes.com/quote/579378.

569. https://en.wikipedia.org/wiki/George_Washington%27s_Farewell_Address.

570. "Roe v. Wade." History Online. November 13, 2009. Accessed October 1, 2019. https://www.history.com/this-day-in-history/roe-v-wade.

571. "Induced Abortion in the United States." Guttmacher Institute Online.

2019. Accessed October 2, 2019. https://www.guttmacher.org/fact-sheet/induced-abortion-united-states.

572. "The Role of the Supreme Court, Adapted from The Presidency, Congress, and the Supreme Court, Scholastic, Inc." 1989, *Scholastic Inc. Online*, last accessed March 22, 2017, https://www.scholastic.com/teachers/articles/teaching-content/role-supreme-court/.

573. Bach, Natasha. "Can Roe v. Wade Be Overturned?" *Fortune Online*. May 20, 2019. Accessed October 3, 2019. https://fortune.com/2019/05/20/can-roe-v-wade-be-overturned/.

574. Roberts, C. J. "Supreme Court of the United States: Citizens United, Appellant v. Federal: Election Commission (No. 08-205)." January 21, 2010. Obtained from *Law.Cornell.Edu.* Accessed October 3, 2019. https://www.law.cornell.edu/supct/html/08-205.ZC.html.

575. Ibid.

576. Barnes, Roberts. "States Racing to Overturn Roe v. Wade Look to a Supreme Court That Prefers Gradual Change." *Washington Post Online*. May 15, 2019. Accessed October 3, 2019. https://www.washingtonpost.com/politics/courts_law/a-race-to-overturn-roe-v-wade-looks-to-a-supreme-court-that-prefers-gradual-change/2019/05/15/7296749e-7713-11e9-b7ae-390de4259661_story.html.

577. Scheindlin, Shira. "If Roe v Wade Is Overturned, We Should Worry about the Rule of Law." *The Guardian Online*. May 21, 2019. Accessed October 3, 2019. https://www.theguardian.com/commentisfree/2019/may/21/trump-abortion-roe-v-wade-supreme-court-judges.

578. Barnes, Roberts. "States Racing to Overturn Roe v. Wade Look to a Supreme Court That Prefers Gradual Change." *Washington Post Online*. May 15, 2019. Accessed October 3, 2019. https://www.washingtonpost.com/politics/courts_law/a-race-to-overturn-roe-v-wade-looks-to-a-supreme-court-that-prefers-gradual-change/2019/05/15/7296749e-7713-11e9-b7ae-390de4259661_story.html.

579. Lemieux, Scott. "Yes, Roe Really Is in Trouble." *Vox Online*. May 15, 2019. Accessed October 3, 2019. https://www.vox.com/2019/5/15/18623073/roe-wade-abortion-georgia-alabama-supreme-court.

580. Ibid.

581. Millhiser, Ian. "The Fight to End Roe v. Wade Enters Its
      Endgame Next Week." September 27, 2019. Accessed October
      2, 2019. https://www.vox.com/2019/9/26/20873873/
      supreme-court-gut-roe-v-wade-next-week-abortion.

582. Dastaigir, Alia. "Rape and Incest Account for Hardly any Abortions. So why
      are they now a focus?" *USA Today Online.* May 24, 2019. Accessed October
      2, 2019. https://www.usatoday.com/story/news/nation/2019/05/24/
      rape-and-incest-account-few-abortions-so-why-all-attention/1211175001/.

583. Ibid.

584. "Abortion Exceptions." *American Life League.* Accessed October
      2, 2019. https://www.all.org/learn/abortion/abortion-exceptions/
      common-abortion-exceptions-the-mothers-life/.

585. "Induced Abortion in the United States." *Guttmacher Institute Online.*
      2019. Accessed October 2, 2019. https://www.guttmacher.org/fact-sheet/
      induced-abortion-united-states.

586. Dastaigir, Alia. "Rape and Incest Cccount for Hardly any Abortions. So why
      are they now a focus?" *USA Today Online.* May 24, 2019. Accessed October
      2, 2019. https://www.usatoday.com/story/news/nation/2019/05/24/
      rape-and-incest-account-few-abortions-so-why-all-attention/1211175001/.

587. Ibid.

588. Ibid.

589. "Induced Abortion in the United States." *Guttmacher Institute Online.*
      2019. Accessed October 2, 2019. https://www.guttmacher.org/fact-sheet/
      induced-abortion-united-states.

590. Ibid.

591. Boghani, Priyanka. "How States Are Preparing for A Potential
      Roe v. Wade Challenge." *PBS Online.* April 23, 2019. Accessed
      October 3, 2019. https://www.pbs.org/wgbh/frontline/article/
      how-states-are-preparing-for-a-potential-roe-v-wade-challenge/.

592. Bach, Natasha. "Can Roe v Wade Be Overturned?" *Fortune Online.* May
      20, 2019. Accessed October 3, 2019. https://fortune.com/2019/05/20/
      can-roe-v-wade-be-overturned/.

593. Ibid.

594. "Targeted Regulations of Abortion Providers." *Center for Reproductive*

Rights. Accessed October 4, 2019. https://reproductiverights.org/document/targeted-regulation-abortion-providers-trap.

595. Field, Robert. "Why Is Health Care So Complex?" *NCBI Online*. October, 2008. Accessed October 3, 2019. https://www.ncbi.nlm.nih.gov/pmc/articles/PMC2730786/.

596. Epps, Garrett. "A Temporary Win for Abortion Rights." *The Atlantic Online*. Feb 10, 2019. Accessed October 3, 2019. https://www.theatlantic.com/ideas/archive/2019/02/june-medical-services-v-gee-abortion-rights-win/582463/.

597. Ibid.

598. Barnes, Roberts. "States Racing to Overturn Roe v. Wade look to a Supreme Court That Prefers Gradual Change." *Washington Post Online*. May 15, 2019. Accessed October 3, 2019. https://www.washingtonpost.com/politics/courts_law/a-race-to-overturn-roe-v-wade-looks-to-a-supreme-court-that-prefers-gradual-change/2019/05/15/7296749e-7713-11e9-b7ae-390de4259661_story.html.

599. Lipka, Michael and Gramlich, John. "5 Facts about the Abortion Debate in America." *Pew Research Center*. August 30, 2019. Accessed September 25, 2019. https://www.pewresearch.org/fact-tank/2019/08/30/facts-about-abortion-debate-in-america/.

600. Ibid.

601. Ibid.

602. Ibid.

603. Ibid.

604. "Top Voting Issues in 2016 Election." *Pew Research Center*. July 7, 2016. Accessed September 25, 2019. https://www.people-press.org/2016/07/07/4-top-voting-issues-in-2016-election/.

605. CBS News. "States Moving to Enact Abortion 'Trigger' Laws." March 19, 2019. YouTube Video, 2:52. Accessed September 30, 2019. https://www.youtube.com/watch?v=m8uezY2LMP8.

606. Ibid.

607. "Induced Abortion in the United States." *Guttmacher Institute Online*. 2019. Accessed October 2, 2019. https://www.guttmacher.org/fact-sheet/induced-abortion-united-states.

608. Boghani, Priyanka. "How States Are Preparing for a Potential Roe v. Wade Challenge." *PBS Online*. April 23, 2019. Accessed October 3, 2019. https://www.pbs.org/wgbh/frontline/article/how-states-are-preparing-for-a-potential-roe-v-wade-challenge/.

609. Ibid.

610. ACLU Alabama: Twitter. May 14, 2019. Accessed October 4, 2019. https://twitter.com/aclualabama/status/1128477817623187457?lang=en.

611. ABC News. "Pro and Anti-Abortion Rights Activists on Future of Alabama Abortion Bill." May 16, 2019. YouTube Video, 9:14. https://www.youtube.com/watch?v=6ssJD4mfYBU.

612. Rosenburg, Gabe. "A Bill Banning Most Abortions Becomes Law in Ohio." *NPR Online*. April 11, 2019. Accessed October 4, 2019. https://www.npr.org/2019/04/11/712455980/a-bill-banning-most-abortions-becomes-law-in-ohio.

613. Ibid.

614. Ibid.

615. Ibid.

616. Ibid.

617. Ibid.

618. Gathright, Jenny. "Mississippi Governor Signs Nation's Toughtest Abortion Ban into Law." *NPR.Org*. March 19, 2018. Accessed October 4, 2019. https://www.npr.org/sections/thetwo-way/2018/03/19/595045249/mississippi-governor-signs-nations-toughest-abortion-ban-into-law.

619. Dastaigir, Alia. "Rape and Incest Account for Hardly any Abortions. So why are they now a focus?" *USA Today Online*. May 24, 2019. Accessed October 2, 2019. https://www.usatoday.com/story/news/nation/2019/05/24/rape-and-incest-account-few-abortions-so-why-all-attention/1211175001/.

620. Bach, Natasha. "Can Roe v Wade Be Overturned?" *Fortune Online*. May 20, 2019. Accessed October 3, 2019. https://fortune.com/2019/05/20/can-roe-v-wade-be-overturned/.

621. Smith, Kate. "Missouri's 8-week Abortion Ban Was Blocked, but These New Restrictions Are Still Going into Effect." August 28, 2019. Accessed October 4, 2019. https://www.cbsnews.com/news/missouri-abortion-law-missouri-abortion-ban-was-blocked-down-syndrome-ban-goes-into-effect-today-2019-08-28-live/.

622. Wilks, Avery. "Abortion Ban That Gives no Exceptions for Birth Defects Blasted by SC Moms, Doctors." *The State Online*. September 10, 2019. Accessed October 2, 2019. https://www.thestate.com/news/politics-government/article234920577.html.

623. Gillespie, Lisa. "Here's a Rundown of Kentucky's New Anti-Abortion Laws—And What's Next." *WFPL Online*. April 1, 2019. Accessed October 4, 2019. https://wfpl.org/heres-a-rundown-of-kentuckys-new-anti-abortion-laws-and-whats-next/.

624. Ibid.

625. Barnes, Robert. "Supreme Court Compromise on Indiana Abortion Law Keeps Issue Off Its Docket." *Washington Post Online*. May 28, 2019. Accessed October 4, 2019. https://www.washingtonpost.com/politics/courts_law/supreme-court-compromise-on-indiana-abortion-law-keeps-issue-off-its-docket/2019/05/28/18636792-814b-11e9-933d-7501070ee669_story.html.

626. Ibid.

627. "State Facts about Abortion: South Dakota." *Guttmacher Institute Online*. Accessed October 4, 2019. https://www.guttmacher.org/fact-sheet/state-facts-about-abortion-south-dakota.

628. WQAD Digital Team. "How New York's Abortion Law Has Changed." *WQAD Online*. January 25, 2019. Accessed October 8, 2019. https://wqad.com/2019/01/25/how-new-yorks-abortion-law-has-changed/.

629. Ibid.

630. Pierpoint, George. "New York Abortion Law: Why Are So Many People Talking about It?" *BBC Online*. January 28, 2019. Accessed October 8, 2019. https://www.bbc.com/news/world-us-canada-46994583.

631. Ibid.

632. Ibid.

633. Ibid.

634. WQAD Digital Team. "How New York's Abortion Law Has Changed." *WQAD Online*. January 25, 2019. Accessed October 8, 2019. https://wqad.com/2019/01/25/how-new-yorks-abortion-law-has-changed/.

635. Ibid.

636. Ibid.

637. Kelly, Caroline. "Rhode Island Governor Signs Abortion Protection Bill."

CNN Politics Online. June 20, 2019. Accessed October 8, 2019. https://
www.cnn.com/2019/06/20/politics/rhode-island-governor-signs-abortion-
protection-bill/index.html.

638. Ibid.

639. Taylor, Kate and Turkewitz, Julie. "Vermont Moves to Protect Abortion
Rights as Other States Impose Bans." *The New York Times Online.* May 21,
2019. Accessed October 8, 2019. https://www.nytimes.com/2019/05/21/
us/vermont-abortion-bill-h57.html.

640. Ibid.

641. Kelly, Caroline. "Illinois Governor Signs Sweeping Abortion Protection Bill
into Law." *CNN Politics Online.* June 12, 2019. Accessed October 8, 2019.
https://www.cnn.com/2019/06/12/politics/illinois-governor-signs-abortion-
protection-law/index.html.

642. Ibid.

643. "Induced Abortion in the United States." *Guttmacher Institute Online.*
2019. Accessed October 2, 2019. https://www.guttmacher.org/fact-sheet/
induced-abortion-united-states.

644. Ibid.

645. Ibid.

646. ABC News. "Inside Mississippi's Lone Abortion Clinic." August 1, 2013.
YouTube Video, 15:40. Accessed October 8, 2019. https://www.youtube.
com/watch?v=KP4FYkVKrGU.

647. Ibid.

648. Ibid.

649. Ibid.

650. Ibid.

651. Ibid.

652. ABC News. "Pro and Anti-Abortion Rights Activists on Future of Alabama
Abortion Bill." May 16, 2019. YouTube Video, 9:14. https://www.youtube.
com/watch?v=6ssJD4mfYBU.

653. Ibid.

654. Ellefson, Lindsey. "Fox News Host Todd Starnes Out after Suggesting
Democrats Worship Pagan God Moloch." *The Wrap Online.* October
2, 2019. Accessed October 9, 2019. https://www.thewrap.com/
exclusive-host-todd-starnes-out-at-fox-news/.

655. HBO. "The Democrats Who Want to Overturn Roe v. Wade." May 22, 2019. YouTube Video, 5:32. Accessed October 14, 2019. https://www.youtube.com/watch?v=bI59-XUrnKE.

656. Ibid.

657. Ibid.

658. Dastaigir, Alia. "Rape and Incest Account for Hardly Any Abortions. So why are they now a focus?" *USA Today Online.* May 24, 2019. Accessed October 2, 2019. https://www.usatoday.com/story/news/nation/2019/05/24/rape-and-incest-account-few-abortions-so-why-all-attention/1211175001/.

659. "Induced Abortion in the United States." *Guttmacher Institute Online.* 2019. Accessed October 2, 2019. https://www.guttmacher.org/fact-sheet/induced-abortion-united-states.

660. Ibid.

661. Barnes, Roberts. "States Racing to Overturn Roe v Wade Look to a Supreme Court That Prefers Gradual Change." *Washington Post Online.* May 15, 2019. Accessed October 3, 2019. https://www.washingtonpost.com/politics/courts_law/a-race-to-overturn-roe-v-wade-looks-to-a-supreme-court-that-prefers-gradual-change/2019/05/15/7296749e-7713-11e9-b7ae-390de4259661_story.html.

662. "Medical Genetics: Ypes of Genetic Changes." *Stanford Childran's Health Online.* Accessed October 4, 2019. https://www.stanfordchildrens.org/en/topic/default?id=types-of-genetic-diseases-90-P02505.

663. "Banning Abortions in Cases of Race or Sex Selection or Fetal Anomaly." *Guttmacher Institute Online.* Accessed October 14, 2019. https://www.guttmacher.org/evidence-you-can-use/banning-abortions-cases-race-or-sex-selection-or-fetal-anomaly.

664. Ibid.

665. "Woman Charged with Baby's Death after Police Say She Admitted to Drug Use During Pregnancy." *The Indy Channel.* February 15, 2018. Accessed October 4, 2019. https://www.theindychannel.com/news/local-news/madison-county/woman-charged-with-babys-death-after-police-say-she-admitted-to-drug-use-during-pregnancy.

666. "Man Accused of Killing Fetus with 'Abortion Pancake.'" *BCS News Online.* July 14, 2014. Accessed October 4, 2019. https://www.cbsnews.com/news/man-accused-of-killing-fetus-with-abortion-pancake/.

667. "Richmond Man Indicted on Manslaughter, Fetal Homicide Charges in Deadly Lexington Crash." *WKYT: Lexington KY News Online.* October 3, 2019. Accessed October 3, 2019. https://www.wkyt.com/content/news/Richmond-man-indicted-with-manslaughter-fetal-homicide-in-deadly-Lexington-crash-562067931.html.

668. "Mifepristone and Misoprostol for Abortion." *American College of Cardiology.*August 31, 2012. Accessed October 8, 2019. https://www.cardiosmart.org/healthwise/tw12/91/tw1291.

669. "Induced Abortion in the United States." *Guttmacher Institute Online.* 2019. Accessed October 2, 2019. https://www.guttmacher.org/fact-sheet/induced-abortion-united-states.

670. Chen, Michelle. "Trump's Title X rule Defunding Planned Parenthood Yet Another Blow to Low-Income Women." *Think Online.* August 23, 2019. Accessed October 8, 2019. https://www.nbcnews.com/think/opinion/trump-s-title-x-rule-defunding-planned-parenthood-yet-another-ncna1045471.

671. Belluck, Pam. "Trump Administration Blocks Funds for Planned Parenthood and Others over Abortion Referrals." *The New York Times Online.* February 22, 2019. Accessed October 8, 2019. https://www.nytimes.com/2019/02/22/health/trump-defunds-planned-parenthood.html.

672. Khazan, Olga. "The Biggest Consequence of Trump's New Abortion Rule Won't Be for Abortion." *Atlantic Online.* March 5, 2019. Accessed October 8, 2019. https://www.theatlantic.com/health/archive/2019/03/trumps-title-x-rule-change-planned-parenthood/584005/.

673. Belluck, Pam. "Trump Administration Blocks Funds for Planned Parenthood and Others over Abortion Referrals." *New York Times Online.* February 22, 2019. Accessed October 8, 2019. https://www.nytimes.com/2019/02/22/health/trump-defunds-planned-parenthood.html.

674. Chen, Michelle. "Trump's Title X Rule Defunding Planned Parenthood Yet Another Blow to Low-Income Women." *Think Online.* August 23, 2019. Accessed October 8, 2019. https://www.nbcnews.com/think/opinion/trump-s-title-x-rule-defunding-planned-parenthood-yet-another-ncna1045471.

675. Gonzalez-Ramirez, Andrea. "It's Official: Planned Parenthood Blocked from Millions in Federal Funds." *The Refinery Online.* August

15, 2019. https://www.refinery29.com/en-us/2019/06/236042/ abortion-appeals-court-ruling-title-x-domestic-gag-rule-trump.

676. Dinzeo, Maria. "Criminal Hearing BeginsoOver Undercover Video by Abortion Foes." *Courthouse News Online*. September 3, 2019. Accessed October 9, 2019. https://www.courthousenews.com/ criminal-privacy-hearing-on-undercover-video-by-abortion-foes-begins/.

677. Prestigiacomo, Amanda. "Planned Parenthood Exec Makes Major Admission about Baby Body Part Harvesting." *The Daily Wire Online*. September 13, 2019. Accessed October 9, 2019. https://www.dailywire.com/news/ planned-parenthood-exec-makes-major-admission-amanda-prestigiacomo.

678. Ibid.

679. Dinzeo, Maria. "Criminal Hearing Begins over Undercover Video by Abortion Foes." *Courthouse News Online*. September 3, 2019. Accessed October 9, 2019. https://www.courthousenews.com/ criminal-privacy-hearing-on-undercover-video-by-abortion-foes-begins/.

680. Ibid.

681. Ibid.

682. Prestigiacomo, Amanda. "Planned Parenthood Exec Makes Major Admission about Baby Body Part Harvesting." *The Daily Wire Online*. September 13, 2019. Accessed October 9, 2019. https://www.dailywire.com/news/ planned-parenthood-exec-makes-major-admission-amanda-prestigiacomo.

683. Haberkorn, Jennifer. "Human Tissue Firm Cuts Ties with Planned Parenthood." *Politico Online*. August 14, 2015. Accessed October 9, 2019. https://www.politico.com/story/2015/08/ planned-parenthood-fetal-tissue-company-cuts-ties-videos-121371.

684. Ibid.

685. Prestigiacomo, Amanda. "Abortionist Testifies: 'No Question' Babies Being Born Alive to Harvest Organs." *The Daily Wire Online*. September 26th, 2019. Accessed October 8, 2019. https://www.dailywire.com/news/ abortionist-testifies-no-question-babies-being-born-alive-to-harvest-organs.

686. Ibid.

687. Ibid.

688. Ibid.

689. Ibid.

690. Ibid.

691. Ibid.

692. Prestigiacomo, Amanda. "Planned Parenthood Exec Makes Major Admission about Baby Body Part Harvesting." *The Daily Wire Online*. September 13, 2019. Accessed October 9, 2019. https://www.dailywire.com/news/ planned-parenthood-exec-makes-major-admission-amanda-prestigiacomo.

693. Ibid.

694. Fox, Maggie. "Planned Parenthood Video: Why Use Tissue from Aborted Fetuses?" *NBC News Online*. July 17, 2015. Accessed October 9, 2019. https://www.nbcnews.com/health/health-news/ planned-parenthood-video-raises-question-why-use-tissue-fetuses-n393431.

695. Ibid.

696. "Use of Aborted Fetal Tissue: Questions and Answers." *Charlotte Lozier Institute*. June 5, 2019. Accessed October 9, 2019. https://lozierinstitute.org/ use-of-aborted-fetal-tissue-questions-answers/.

697. Ibid.

698. Ibid.

699. Wadman, Meredeth. "The Truth about Fetal Tissue Research." *Nature Online*. December 7, 2015. Accessed October 9, 2019. https://www.nature. com/news/the-truth-about-fetal-tissue-research-1.18960.

700. "Use of Aborted Fetal Tissue: Questions and Answers." *Charlotte Lozier Institute*. June 5, 2019. Accessed October 9, 2019. https://lozierinstitute.org/ use-of-aborted-fetal-tissue-questions-answers/.

701. Ibid.

702. Andrews, Michelle. "FAQ: How Does New Trump Fetal Tissue Policy Impact Medical Research?" *Kaiser Health News Online*. June 7, 2019. Accessed October 9, 2019. https://khn.org/news/ faq-how-does-new-trump-fetal-tissue-policy-impact-medical-research/.

703. Ibid.

704. Ibid.

705. "Planned Parenthood Abortion Quotas Exposed." *World Net Daily Online*. November 4, 2009, Accessed October 9, 2019. https://www.wnd. com/2009/11/115000/.

706. ABC News. "Pro and Anti-Abortion Rights Activists on Future of Alabama Abortion Bill." May 16, 2019. YouTube Video, 9:14. https://www.youtube.com/watch?v=6ssJD4mfYBU.

707. Obenhaus, Mark, and Leiter, Elizabeth. Producers. *The Abortion Divide.* United States: Frontline of WGBH/Boston. 2019. Last accessed September 30, 2019. https://www.pbs.org/wgbh/frontline/film/the-abortion-divide/.

708. Ibid.

709. Ibid.

710. Gilbert, Sharon K. and Derek P., *Veneration: Unveiling the Ancient Realms of Demonic Kings and Satan's Battle Plan for Armageddon,* (Crane, MO: Defender Publishing, November 15, 2019), 186, 196.

711. Wikipedia entry for "Chaos Magic," https://en.wikipedia.org/wiki/Chaos_magic, accessed November 4, 2019).

712. Wikileaks document, Stratfor email, https://wikileaks.org/gifiles/docs/36/361263_fw-i-like-this-one-almost-pensive-again-it-is-ol-w-that.html (accessed on October 29, 2019).

713. Derek Gilbert, *The Great Inception,* (Crane, MO: Defender Publishing, 2017), 70.

714. Rivera, Madeleine, Immigration Officials See Drastic Rise in African Migrants Arriving at US-Mexico Border, FoxNews.com, https://www.foxnews.com/us/africa-san-antonio-mexico-border-illegal-immigration (accessed October 29, 2019).

715. Surani, et al, *Ebola Virus: An emerging sexually transmissible infection pathogen,* originally published in the Indian Journal of Sexually Transmitted Diseases, 2018, found online at https://www.ncbi.nlm.nih.gov/pmc/articles/PMC6111642/ (Accessed November 4, 2019).

716. Malkin, Michele, "Unvetted Illegals Threaten Public Health," November 4, 2018, TribLive, https://archive.triblive.com/opinion/editorials/14249404-74/michelle-malkin-unvetted-illegals-threaten-public-health (accessed October 29, 2019).

717. Malkin, Michele, *Open Borders, Inc.,* (Regnery Publishing, September 2019), Kindle version, location 1162.

718. Insight Crime Report, *MS-13 in the Americas,* American University publication, found online at https://www.justice.gov/eoir/page/file/1043576/download - accessed October 30, 2019.

719. Quote from speech at Long Island by President Donald Trump, July 28, 2017 as reported by CBS News and Associated Press.

720. "120 Police Officers Investigated for Collusion with Mexico City Drug Cartel," Mexico News Daily, October 24, 2019, available online via https://mexiconewsdaily.com/news/officers-investigated-for-collusion-with-drug-cartel/ (accessed October 30, 2019).

721. Megan Henney, "Most Millennials Would Vote for a Socialist over a Capitalist, Poll Finds." *Fox Business* (October 29, 2019), https://www.foxbusiness.com/money/millennials-socialist-vote-capitalist-poll, retrieved 11/2/19.

722. George Santayana, *The Life of Reason* (New York: Charles Scribner's Sons, 1920), 284.

723. This was in the FAQs (Frequently Asked Questions) released with the Green New Deal proposed by Rep. Alexandria Ocasio-Cortez and Sen. Ed Markey, although the staff of Rep. Ocasio-Cortez responded to criticism by variously claiming that an early draft had been released or that their website had been hacked.

724. H. L. Mencken, "Sham Battle," *Baltimore Evening Sun* (Oct. 26, 1936). In *On Politics: A Carnival of Buncombe*, Malcolm Moos ed. (Baltimore: Johns Hopkins Press, 1956), 331.

725. Tara Golshan and Ella Nilsen, "Alexandria Ocasio-Cortez's Rocky Rollout of the Green New Deal, explained." *Vox* (February 11, 2019), https://www.vox.com/policy-and-politics/2019/2/11/18220163/alexandria-ocasio-cortez-green-new-deal-faq-tucker-carlson, retrieved 12/30/19.

726. Anne Penketh, "France Frced to Drop 75% Supertax after Meagre Returns." *The Guardian* (December 31, 2014), https://www.theguardian.com/world/2014/dec/31/france-drops-75percent-supertax, retrieved 10/30/19.

727. Ibid.

728. Douglas Holtz-Eakin, Dan Bosch, Ben Gitis, Dan Goldbeck, Philip Rossetti, "The Green New Deal: Scope, Scale, and Implications." *American Action Forum* (Febuary 25, 2019), https://www.americanactionforum.org/research/the-green-new-deal-scope-scale-and-implications/, retrieved 11/2/19.

729. Ed Pilkington, "Obama Angers Midwest Voters with Guns and Religion

Remark." *The Guardian* (April 14, 2008), https://www.theguardian.com/world/2008/apr/14/barackobama.uselections2008, retrieved 10/30/19.

730. Christophe Wall-Romana, "An Areal Location of Agade." Journal of Near Eastern Studies Vol. 49, No. 3 (1990), 205–245.

731. Stephanie Daley, "Babylon as a Name for Other Cities Including Nineveh." *Proceedings of the 51st Rencontre Assyriologique Internationale* (Chicago: The University of Chicago, 2008), 25.

732. Kjetil Sundsdal, "The Uruk Expansion: Culture Contact, Ideology, and Middlemen." *Norwegian Archaeological Review* 44:2, 164–185.

733. William Harms, "Evidence of Battle at Hamoukar Points to Early Urban Development." *The University of Chicago Chronicle* Vol. 26, No. 8 (Jan. 18, 2007), http://chronicle.uchicago.edu/070118/hamoukar.shtml, retrieved 11/2/19.

734. A. R. Millard, "The Bevelled-Rim Bowls: Their Purpose and Significance." *Iraq*, Vol. 50 (1988), 49–50.

735. Ibid., 50.

736. Ibid.

737. Guillermo Alglaze, "The Uruk Expansion: Cross-cultural Exchange in Early Mesopotamian Civilization." *Current Anthropology* 30, No. 5 (Dec. 1989), 571.

738. A. W. Sjoberg, "In-nin Sa-gur-ra: A Hymn to the Goddess Inanna," *Zeitschrift fur Assyriologie* 65, no. 2 (1976), 225.

739. Black, J.A., Cunningham, G., Fluckiger-Hawker, E, Robson, E., and Zólyomi, G. "Enmerkar and the Lord of Aratta," The Electronic Text Corpus of Sumerian Literature (http://etcsl.orinst.ox.ac.uk/cgi-bin/etcsl.cgi?text=t.1.8.2.3#), retrieved 11/1/19.

740. 2 Peter 2:4.

741. William Bradford, *History of Plymouth Plantation.* https://sourcebooks.fordham.edu/mod/1650bradford.asp#Private%20and%20communal%20farming, retrieved 11/2/19.

742. Ibid.

743. Ibid.

744. Bernard Daley Zaleha and Andrew Szasz, "Why Conservative Christians Don't Believe in Climate Change." *Bulletin of the Atomic Scientists* 71, No. 5 (2015), 19–30.

745. Bradford, op. cit.

746. 2 Thessalonians 3:6, 10 (ESV).

747. https://www.goodreads.com/
    quotes/124496-the-greatest-thing-anyone-can-do-for-god-and-man.

748. https://townhall.com/tipsheet/timothymeads/2019/07/18/house-chaplain-
    casts-out-demons-during-morning-prayer-in-capitol-building-n2550303.